HISTORY AND TRUTH IN HEGEL'S
Phenomenology

HISTORY AND TRUTH
IN HEGEL'S
Phenomenology

MEROLD WESTPHAL
Department of Philosophy
Hope College

NEW JERSEY: HUMANITIES PRESS
SUSSEX: HARVESTER PRESS

First published in the United States of America
in 1979 by Humanities Press Inc.
Atlantic Highlands, NJ 07716

Copyright © 1978 by Humanities Press Inc.

Reprinted in 1982 by Humanities Press Inc.
and in England by Harvester Press by
arrangement with the author.

 (U.S.A.)   0 391 00557 X
(England)   0 7108 0374 5

MANUFACTURED IN THE UNITED STATES OF AMERICA

With appreciation to
Arthur F. Holmes
and
John E. Smith
mentors, scholars, friends

GUIDE TO FOOTNOTES

A typical reference to the *Phenomenology* will be: PhG, x/y/z.

x   = pagination of the first edition, also available in the Ullstein edition and to be included in the new critical edition in GW (see below).

y   = pagination in Hoffmeister's 1952 edition, the handiest German text.

z   = pagination in the Baillie translation.

Where other references are divided with a '/' the German is given first, then the corresponding English translation, as given below.

HTJ   = *Hegels Theologische Jugendschriften,* ed. Nohl. English translation, where given from *On Christianity: Early Theological Writings,* tr. and ed. Knox and Kroner.

            Volksreligion = Volksreligion und Christentum

            PCR I = *The Positivity of the Christian Religion* (1795-96)

            PCR II = *The Positivity of the Christian Religion* (1800)

            SC = *The Spirit of Christianity and its Fate*

            Fragment = one of the fragmentary drafts appended to HTJ.

GW   = *Gesammelte Werke* (Deutsche Forschungsgemeinschaft Ausgabe)

            Differenz = Differenz des Fichte'chen und Schelling'schen Systems der Philosophie

            Skepticismus = Verhältniss des Skepticismus zur Philosophie

            Glauben = Glauben und Wissen

            Naturrecht = Über die wissenschaftlichen Behandlungsarten des Naturrechts

Werke   = Werke in zwanzig Bänden (Theorie Werkausgabe, Suhrkamp)

            The German Constitution is cited from this German text and in English translation from Pelczynski *Hegel's Political Writings.*

Sittlichkeit   = *System der Sittlichkeit,* ed. Lasson.

Realphilosophie = *Jenaer Realphilosophie* (see Ch. 3, n. 37).

SL = *Wissenschaft der Logik,* ed. Lasson. English translation, *Science of Logic* by A. V. Miller.

SW = *Sämtliche Werke,* ed. Glockner

HP = *Vorlesungen über die Geschichte der Philosophie.* English translation, *Hegel's Lectures on the History of Philosophy* by Haldane and Simson.

LL = *Encyklopädie der philosophischen Wissenchaften im Grundrisse.* Part I, the Logic is known as the Lesser Logic. English translation, *The Logic of Hegel* by Wallace.

CONTENTS

INTRODUCTION

This essay represents my attempt to write the book I looked for in vain during my own first encounter with the *Phenomenology of Spirit*. I felt the need for something more detailed and comprehensive than the chapter or two which so many good books on Hegel devote to this aspect of his work and less overwhelming both in size and complexity than the two great French commentaries of Hyppolite and Kojève. More specifically I desired help in discovering what Hegel's overall strategy was and how the widely varied parts of the text contributed to carrying out his plan.

My goal, consequently, has been an ambitious one — to show that a single argument runs through the text from start to finish. For those coming to the *Phenomenology* as newcomers, whatever success I have had will make it easier not to lose sight of the forest while wandering through the 750 pages of trees and heavy underbrush. For Hegel scholars, I hope to have put to rest discussions about the unity of the text, not by further analysis of its *Entstehungsgeschichte,* but by showing that unity in the text. My thesis is that the key to that unity is Hegel's radical discovery that transcendental subjectivity has a social history and that absolute knowledge is both an historically conditioned and essentially collective or social event.

The following summary of the argument correlates the chapters of this essay with the chapters of the *Phenomenology* discussed in each. While I have treated every part of Hegel's text, no attempt has been made to comment on all of them in equal detail. The degree of attention given to any particular section has been dictated by its importance for tracing Hegel's unifying argument. This accounts for the relatively brief treatment of Hegel's Chapter Five, for in my view it reiterates and anticipates but does little to advance the argument. An abbreviated table of contents for the *Phenomenology* would look like this:

Preface
Introduction
Chapter One   *Sense Certainty*
Chapter Two   *Perception*
Chapter Three *Understanding*
Chapter Four *The Truth of Self-Certainty*
Chapter Five *Reason*
Chapter Six   *Spirit*
Chapter Seven *Religion*
Chapter Eight *Absolute Knowledge*

Chapters One and Two (dealing with Hegel's Introduction and aspects of his Preface). The Introduction presents the task of the *Phenomenology* in exclusively noetic terms. Its target is the prevailing scepticism, Kantian and otherwise, which denies to philosophical reason the capacity to know the Absolute, which other traditions refer to as the Unconditioned, God, Truth, or Being Itself. By contrast the Preface directs our attention to the present standpoint of Spirit, the historical-cultural crisis of a European civilization which in 1807 had lost the substantial life and immediate unity with the divine it once possessed.

It is easy to relate the early, abstractly epistemological chapters of the *Phenomenology* to the former account of Hegel's project, the later socio-historical analyses to the latter. Such learned students of Hegel as Haering, Hoffmeister, and Pöggeler have concluded that the text is schizophrenic, with Hegel's philosophy of Spirit rather arbitrarily appended to an introduction to his *Science of Logic,* an introduction essentially completed midway through the text we now possess. The issue was raised first and most dramatically by Rudolf Haym when he rhetorically asked what possible relation could exist between the madness of Diderot's musician or the fanaticism of Marat and Robespierre as portrayed in Chapter Six and the earlier analyses of sense perception.

But this was not Hegel's view. Not only in the *Science of Logic* did he affirm the entire published *Phenomenology* to be the systematic presupposition of a truly philosophical logic; in the Preface of 1807, written after the rest of the text was completed, he affirmed the fundamental unity of the anti-Kantian and history-of-Spirit dimensions of his work. In doing so he provided important preliminary guidance for finding one's way through his labyrinthine text.

Chapters Three and Four (dealing with Hegel's first three chapters, collectively entitled Consciousness). Hegel begins like a true epistemologist, with the analysis of sense perception and natural scientific knowledge. This is not because he is primarily interested in the career of the sciences. His concern is always with philosophical knowledge, knowledge of the Absolute. He must begin where he does because of the tendency of the natural sciences to preempt the claim of philosophy to be scientific knowledge, a tendency to which various forms of philosophy, so-called, have increasingly contributed. These critical philosophies, which had set out to determine "the nature and limits of human understanding," had all too regularly concluded that human knowledge was by nature suited only to grasp the finite objects of sense perception and scientific theory and could never transcend the limits of what Kant called the conditioned. To show that and how knowledge of the Absolute is possible Hegel must undercut these various scepticisms. So as not to assert this possibility dogmatically over against equally dogmatic sceptical denials, Hegel must develop what he considers to be truly philosophical knowledge out of the very sort of reflection on sense perception and natural science which, when cut short too quickly, generates a scepticism which might be called critical finitism. The first step along this path is Hegel's reiteration of Kant's discovery that knowledge does not so much conform to its object as the object conforms to our knowledge of it. One can therefore speak of a subjectivity or selfhood which contributes essentially to the object as present in our knowledge of it, thereby shaping or constituting the world in which we live. Kant uses the term transcendental to designate that subjectivity, and his usage will be adopted in the chapters which follow.

Chapter Five (dealing with Hegel's fourth chapter and the latter two sections of his fifth). The crucial move beyond Kant does not come in a critique of the thing in itself, though the ending of his third chapter can be read as such a critique. It comes rather in Hegel's fourth chapter with the discovery that transcendental subjectivity as Kant presented it, within the limits of the purely theoretical, is a highly rarefied abstraction. Where Kant finds the conditions for the possibility of experience in transcendental subjectivity, Hegel asks what the conditions for the possibility of transcendental subjectivity may be. It is in answer to this question that he introduces the central notion of Spirit. As the practical-social condition for the possibility of transcendental subjectivity Spirit forms the bridge from the epistemological framework to the historical-cultural framework. Haym's question shows that he has not understood the central concept in Hegel's book.

Chapter Six (dealing with Hegel's sixth chapter). It is by this deepening of critical reflection that the question of knowledge becomes the question of the historical career of Spirit. There follows a socio-political interpretation of European history from classical Greece to the post-revolutionary world of Hegel's present. This culminates in the bold claim that Spirit, man's historical self-development, has become absolute, and that in the process the wisdom which previous philosophy merely loved or longed for has become actual as Absolute Knowledge.

Chapter Seven (dealing with Hegel's seventh chapter). Since Hegel finds it necessary to describe this result in theological language, its full clarification requires a retelling of the same story as the history of religion. While his sixth chapter interprets history as the apotheosis of the social, his seventh narrates the historical socializing of the divine. In this way the two accounts reinforce one another and render transparent the jointly theological and political nature of Hegel's conclusion, thereby incorporating into his systematic thought the central concerns of his so-called "early theological writings."

Chapter Eight (dealing with Hegel's eighth and final chapter). Hegel recapitulates this result in order 1) to refute (clairvoyantly) Marx's misinterpretation of the *Phenomenology* as a Stoic-idealist withdrawal from the actual, 2) to mediate his historicist account of Absolute Knowledge with the ideal of philosophy as eternal truth, and 3) to indicate briefly the tasks remaining to philosophical science once the historical conditions of its possibility have been presented.

In the chapters which follow I have *tried* to present this long and complex argument without speaking Hegelese myself. At the same time I have quoted him extensively. In other words, I have *tried* to present the argument in two different languages, Hegel's and ours. There are two reasons for this. There is first of all the usual matter of documentation, providing the reader with the texts upon which my interpretation primarily rests. More important, however, is my view of Hegelese. It is a dead language and should remain so. No one should learn to speak or write it. But it is obviously necessary to learn to read it if one is to study Hegel for oneself. I *hope* the alternation between our language and Hegelese will provide something of an entrance into that language for those to whom it is somewhat new as well as some clues on graceful exiting for those who fear or have already fallen prey to its seductive charms. The italicized words in this paragraph are my confession that my goal has exceeded my grasp. I can only take comfort from the poet's assurance that that's the way it ought to be, or what's a heaven for?

Finally I would like to express my appreciation to John Smith for his guidance and encouragement in my first serious encounters with Hegel and to David Carr and Ed Casey for their helpful comments on early drafts of my manuscript. I am also grateful to Yale University for the Morse Fellowship which permitted me to do some of my research in Heidelberg among some of Germany's most distinguished Hegel scholars.

Merold Westphal
Hope College
Holland, Michigan

CHAPTER ONE: The Task of the *Phenomenology:*

A) The Introduction

In his first critique of Kant Hegel defines the task of true philosophy as the absolute overcoming of all oppositions. This is accomplished only in knowing the Absolute. The Kantian philosophy, however, takes as its task not the knowing of the Absolute, but the critique of our knowing capacity. Thus it remains in the realm of opposition and in the strictest sense cannot be called philosophy. In fact it mistakes the death of philosophy for its highest fulfillment.[1] We can therefore expect Hegel's philosophy to take the form of a continuous debate with the critical philosophy; and we should not be too surprised when he defines philosophy as the refutation of Kant.[2]

It is in these terms that the *Phenomenology* presents itself in its Introduction. This is our starting point, if we read the book as it was written, for the longer and more famous Preface was written several months after the rest of the book was completed. The advantage of hindsight was greater than usual in this case, for the project grew considerably in the course of writing. Originally the plan was that the *Phenomenology* would not be an entity in itself, but only an introduction to the Logic, which would appear with it in the first volume of Hegel's System of Science. In light of this fact and the marked differences between the Preface and Introduction, it is natural to ask whether the latter remains an accurate statement of the *Phenomenology's* task, and even whether there is any single project which unifies the enormous whole of the text.

It is the thesis of this essay that we can meaningfully speak of *the* task of the *Phenomenology;* that there is a single coherent argument running through its entirety; and that when properly understood, the Preface can be seen not only as complementary to the Introduction but as growing directly out of it. This chapter and the next are concerned with a comprehensive view of the task of the *Phenomenology* as set forth in the Introduction and Preface. It will then fall to the remaining chapters to trace the argument from Sense Certainty to Absolute Knowledge.[3]

1

1A. Critical Philosophy as the Fear of Error and the Fear of Truth.

The Introduction defines phenomenology in terms of its opposition to all critical philosophy *as previously practiced*. Criticism is portrayed as a fear of error leading to the belief that knowledge must be examined before philosophy can get on with its job of knowing the Absolute, here defined as "what truly is" and "what is in itself." It argues that "since knowing is a faculty of a determinate kind and scope, without the more precise determination of its nature and limits we might take hold on clouds of error instead of the heaven of truth."[4]

It is clear from this description as well as from other writings of the Jena period[5] that Hegel's target is not just the transcendental critical philosophy of Kant and Fichte, but also the work of Locke and Hume and even of such lesser contemporaries as Jacobi, Schulze, and Krug. In fact Hegel is declaring his independence from the whole epistemological project as modern philosophy inherited it from Descartes.[6] "Now no more useful inquiry can be proposed than that which seeks to determine the nature and the scope of human knowledge . . . This investigation should be undertaken once at least in his life by anyone who has the slightest regard for truth, since in pursuing it the true instruments of knowledge and the whole method of inquiry come to light. But nothing seems more futile than the conduct of those who boldly dispute about the secrets of nature . . . without yet having ever asked whether human reason is adequate to the solution of these problems."[7]

It is Locke's formulation of this project which Hegel quotes in the Kant critique mentioned above as being definitive of the prevailing philosophical enterprise, with the comment that one can read the same thing in Kant. "For I thought that the first step towards satisfying several inquiries the mind of man was very apt to run into, was, to take a survey of our understandings, examine our own powers, and see to what things they were adapted . . . Thus men, extending their inquiries beyond their capacities, and letting their thoughts wander into those depths where they can find no sure footing, it is no wonder that they raise questions and multiply disputes, which, never coming to any clear resolution, are proper only to continue and increase their doubts, and to confirm them at last in perfect scepticism. Whereas, were the capacities of our understandings well considered, the extent of our knowledge once discovered, and the horizon found which sets the bounds between the enlightened and dark parts of things; between what is and what is not comprehensible by us, men would perhaps with less scruple acquiesce in the avowed ignorance of the one, and employ their thoughts and discourse with more advantage and satisfaction in the other."[8]

This is the background for Hegel's opening sentence: "It is natural to suppose that, before philosophy enters upon its subject proper—namely the actual knowledge of what truly is—it is necessary to come first to an understanding concerning knowledge ..." It sounds as if he is introducing his favorite joke about the poor fellow who wouldn't enter the water before he had learned to swim. But the passage continues, "which is looked upon as the instrument by which to take possession of the Absolute, or as the means through which to get sight of it."[9] It is to this metaphorical account of knowledge as an instrument or means to which our attention is directed, not the difficulties of a philosophy which assumes we can know knowledge but questions whether we can know anything else.

Hegel is particularly hostile to the first of these metaphors. In his essay of 1802 on "The Relation of Scepticism to Philosophy," he reproaches Schulze for treating concepts and principles as instruments which philosophy uses to ferret out hidden objects, as if it were seeking a rock under snow. "It is impossible to conceive of what is rational and of speculation in a cruder manner ... What happens here is not what the Devil demanded of Christ, to change stone to bread; rather the living bread of reason is eternally changed into stone."[10]

A similar scorn is directed against Kant in the *Lectures on the History of Philosophy.* "Knowledge is thereby represented as an instrument, as a method and means whereby we endeavour to possess ourselves of the truth. Thus before men can make their way to the truth itself they must know the nature and function of their instrument ... This would appear as though men could set forth upon the search for truth with spears and staves."[11]

Hegel's lack of charity towards the instrument metaphor is not arbitrary. It represents his disenchantment with the assumption that knowledge is power and that method is the means to this end. It is well known that Kant called the *Critique of Pure Reason* a treatise on method.[12] But it is less frequently noticed that he prefaced the second edition, in which this statement appears, with a quotation from Bacon. Fichte in turn included part of the same quotation in his *First Introduction to the Science of Knowledge,* including the sentence, " . . . I am laboring to lay the foundation, not of any sect or doctrine, but of human utility and power." To which Hegel replied, when lecturing on Bacon, "Even now our countrymen like to adorn their works with sententious sayings culled from him."[13] Descartes' conception of method, like Bacon's, is linked to this idea of knowledge as an instrument of power, as not only the *Discourse on Method* indicates, but even the brief quotation given above from the rules; and his influence on subsequent developments was not limited to providing the adornment of sententious sayings. The same could be said of Locke. Hegel can rightly claim that the instrument metaphor pervades the epistemological tradition he is seeking to transcend.

His deepest objections to the view of knowledge as method and power, as "controlling knowledge" (Scheler, Tillich) or "the logic of domination" (Marcuse), are moral. He agrees with Schiller that "utility is the great idol of the times,"[14] and he gives his own critique of this Enlightenment idol in Chapter Six of the *Phenomenology.* But in the Introduction he limits himself to epistemic matters. Knowledge conceived as an instrument is a means to the end of power. The goal of philosophy, however, is not to gain power over the Absolute but to know it as it truly is. This is the source of the difficulty of importing into philosophy two metaphors for knowledge which derive from the knowledge-as-power tradition. "In both cases [assuming we are doing philosophy and not engineering] we employ a means which immediately brings about the opposite of its own end; or, rather, the absurdity lies in our making use of any means at all." This is best seen by taking each case separately. "For if knowledge is the instrument to take hold of the Absolute, one is immediately reminded that the application of an instrument to a thing does not leave the thing *as it is for itself,* but brings about a shaping and alteration of it. Or, if knowledge is not an instrument for our activity, but a more or less passive medium through which the light of truth reaches us, then again we do not receive this truth *as it is in itself*, but as it is in and through this medium."[15]

The thoughtless use of the instrument and medium metaphors is not an isolated inadvertance within the critical tradition. That tradition is pictured, not as a miscellaneous conclusion here and an isolated pronouncement there, but rather as a network of interrelated elements. The "fear of error" which is its hallmark has both its "presuppositions" and its "consequences", i.e., it is a system of logically related elements. At least four of these are distinguished: 1) the idea of knowledge as an instrument or medium, 2) the idea of the Absolute as something separated from us and our knowledge, 3) the idea that in addition to the absolute truth and knowledge there are lower kinds of knowledge which can be said to possess "truth of another kind," and 4) for employment in stating these three principles, a whole set of basic categories whose meaning is assumed to be familiar to everyone, such as absolute, knowledge, objective, subjective, etc.[16] Just as Kant finds "a whole nest of dialectical assumptions" underlying and undermining the cosmological argument, so Hegel finds a whole system of presuppositions at the basis of critical finitism.[17]

Hegel's differences with that tradition are thus revealed to be systemic. If we distinguish an external question as "a question which concerns the collective justification of all the true propositions contained in any particular realm of discourse," from an internal question, which is "the question of the justification of a judgment within the particular realm of discourse [at hand]," then the issue between Hegel and critical philosophy begins to look more like an external than an internal question.[18] That is, Hegel's own stress on the systematic nature of criticism's stance suggests that this debate with it is more like discussing the relative merits of Euclidian and Riemannian geometries than correcting a pupil for doing a Euclidian proof incorrectly. The difficulties of carrying on a debate under these circumstances are enormous. Hegel does not underestimate them, but rather gives primary attention to them in the second and third parts of the Introduction. In the Preface he says one must teach the opponent to "walk on his head," so fundamental is the change of attitude that is necessary, but at the same time one must remember that all genuine criticism is internal.[19]

A more immediate result emerges, however, from this

analysis of criticism. It is the discovery that the entire enterprise, *as traditionally practiced,* is as dogmatic in its procedure as
it is sceptical in its conclusions, for it rests on unexamined presuppositions. It sets out to examine the categories and principles of knowledge, but it employs categories whose meaning
has not been clarified and principles whose truth has not been
established. It thereby opens itself to a variety of epithets which
suggest mindlessness and even bad faith: random talk, opaque
distinction, useless ideas, accidental and arbitrary ideas, pretense, fraud.[20] Hegel's language is strong here because he
wants to do philosophy and because he has long been convinced
that this kind of absolute and unanalyzed assumption means
that "all philosophy is routed from the field of battle."[21]

This being the case, "one should not overlook the possibility of reversing this procedure [of distrusting Science] by placing distrust in this very distrust and becoming concerned about
another question: Is not this fear of erring already the error itself?" Since conclusions based on arbitrary presuppositions can
have no normative force, we are entitled immediately to dismiss
the whole business as the fraudulent effort "to avoid the toil of
Science and to give at the same time the impression of earnest
and zealous effort." The fear of error turns out to be the fear of
truth.[22]

This is far from being Hegel's last word on the subject of
critical philosophy. He neither abandons critical questions
completely, as he seems about to do, nor does he leave his
critique of critical finitism in the form it takes here. But he
never abandons this charge that carelessly adopted assumptions
underlie its negative conclusions. This raises the question
whether he has, in Collingwood's terms, discovered the "absolute" or most basic of these presuppositions. Of the elements he
has singled out, the most basic seems to be the idea that the Absolute is an object which stands over against us, escaping our
gaze by escaping our grasp. This leads to the idea that knowledge is an instrument for seizing the Absolute (the verbs used
with this metaphor are *bemächtigen, habhaft werden, fassen,* and
erfassen) and a medium through which to see it; then, since this
is bound to distort the object, the face-saving appeal to that elusive "truth of another kind."

A rigorous questioning must ask on what presupposition, if

any, rests the idea that the Absolute is separated from us and hidden from our view like a bird which we would catch with a lime-twig or a stone under the snow, rather than being "in and for itself already close to us of its own accord."[23] Hegel has not overlooked this question. Underlying this basic theoretical presupposition he finds a more basic pre-theoretical presupposition, the fear (*Furcht*) of error and an anxiety (*Besorgnis*) which is its constant companion. So he introduces the presuppositions mentioned above with the following formula: "In fact, this fear of erring presupposes something, indeed a great deal, as truth." Similarly, it is "the anxiety about falling into error" which "posits a mistrust in Science," just as it is "this anxiety [about grasping clouds of error instead of the heaven of truth]" which "will surely transform itself into the conviction . . . that between knowledge and the Absolute there lies a boundary which completely cuts off the one from the other."[24]

This makes it clear that a full understanding of critical philosophy, upon which any attempt to go beyond it must be based, can only rest on an understanding of its affective roots, its fundamental fearfulness. The critique of criticism will have to uncover both the nature and the origin of the anxiety expressed in all its behavior. A kind of psychoanalysis seems to be called for, but Hegel offers nothing of the kind in his Introduction. Instead, he breaks off his line of thought very abruptly (in the middle of a paragraph in the German text, at *Aber die Wissenschaft . . .*) and begins to reflect on how the branch of philosophical Science he calls phenomenology can mediate between the pseudo-philosophy of the critical tradition and genuine, i.e., speculative philosophy.

Hegel is here seeking to avoid the genetic fallacy. He knows that the theoretical presuppositions of critical philosophy cannot be discredited simply by reference to more basic pre-theoretical presuppositions. Even when his philosophical psychoanalysis is completed and a fuller comprehension of critical philosophy is available the task of generating philosophical Science by deepening critical reflection will only be begun, by no means completed. If we are to be prepared for what is to come Hegel must give us some indication of how he thinks this is possible.

1B. Phenomenology as the Way of Doubt and Despair.

In other places Hegel seeks to dismiss critical finitism briefly and decisively.[25] While the initial paragraphs of the Introduction suggest the same procedure, the sudden shift we have just noted indicates that a different strategy is being adopted. It is based on the belief that a quick battle is not genuinely decisive, whatever its rhetorical success in embarrassing the opponent. At best one silences him temporarily, creating a vacuum as abhorrent to truth as to nature.

The new train of thought begins with the recognition that "Science, in the very fact that it comes on the scene is itself a phenomenon [*Erscheinung*]; it is not yet Science in its fully realized and propagated truth simply by virtue of coming on the scene . . . [Consequently] it cannot simply reject an untrue form of knowledge as a merely common view of things and give assurance that it is a completely different way of knowing . . . By giving this assurance it would declare that its force resides in its being; but the untrue knowledge also appeals to the fact that it is, and gives assurance that to it Science is nothing––one barren assurance carries as much weight as another."[26]

The issue is now posed as a quarrel between Science and "another kind" of knowledge or consciousness, variously characterized as phenomenal, untrue, unreal, incomplete, and natural.[27] Science can conquer its opponent only "by turning against it," i.e., by actually coming to grips with it and engaging it in battle. It cannot in good faith either simply ignore finite knowledge and the philosophy which absolutizes it, or help itself to assumptions which beg the question against them. Science must become the medium which contains natural consciousness and yet invalidates its pretensions to exhaust the scope of human knowledge, showing how natural consciousness transcends itself and leads to Science. "These, then, are the reasons for proposing to undertake a description of knowledge as it appears, a presentation of knowledge as a phenomenon."[28]

There is an elegant ambiguity in the phrase *das erscheinende Wissen*. It can be rendered either by "knowledge as a phenomenon, as it appears," or by "phenomenal knowledge." The former case indicates that knowledge is an object available for investigation, while the latter carries a pejorative connotation derived from Kant. Hegel intends both meanings. It is the first which belongs to the idea of a description or presentation [*Darstellung*] of knowledge in various of its modes, but the second is called for in the immediately following sentence—"In view of the fact that this presentation has for its object only phenomenal knowledge, the presentation itself seems to be unscientific, for unlike free Science, it does not seem to move in a shape peculiar to itself. But it can be regarded . . . as the way of the natural consciousness which is striving toward true knowledge."

The point is this: the whole of the *Phenomenology* is now given as the critique of criticism, not just the Introduction. For it alone is this presentation of phenomenal knowledge as a phenomenon, the "turning against" which is not simple, dogmatic negation. Not only in this Introduction but again and again in the earlier Jena writings Hegel has been telling us about the antithetical relationship between the natural consciousness (sometimes called, following Kant, healthy human understanding or common sense—*der gesunde Menschenverstand*) and genuine philosophy.[29] Now he is accepting the challenge to show us what he has been telling us, namely that human knowledge is not finally subject to the kinds of limitation and finitude attributed to it by Kant and the critical tradition. This he intends to do by placing before us the various finite forms of knowledge validated by this tradition that we may see for ourselves how they lead beyond themselves. Thus at least part of the meaning of the often discussed "we" and "for us" which occurs in the text is Socratic. Hegel seeks as pedagogue to evoke in each of his readers the insights he has already achieved for himself. This carries no implication, as is often charged, that one must already be in the realm of Absolute Knowledge to follow Hegel's argument. It only supposes that like the slaveboy in the Meno, the reader can see for himself what is there to be seen and does not need to take anything on Hegel's authority. How Hegel himself may have come to the insights he seeks to evoke is no more relevant here than the same question about Socrates' geometrical knowledge would be. What matters is the insight, not the occasion under which it arises. In his final chapter Hegel will himself describe the

philosophical understanding to which we are led in terms of recollection, deliberately invoking this Platonic model.

Anticipating the final outcome, Hegel emphasizes above all
else the destructive nature of his presentation. "Natural consciousness will show itself to be merely the concept of knowledge, or unreal knowledge. But since it immediately takes itself
to be real knowledge, this way has a negative significance for it,
and what is actually the realization of the concept [of knowl-
edge] is for it rather the loss and destruction of itself. For on
this road it loses its truth. The road may thus be viewed as the
way of doubt, or more properly, as the way of despair." In this
way philosophy begins with a "thoroughgoing scepticism."[30]

It is not just any old scepticism, however, which marks the
beginning of true philosophy. It is a triply distinctive scepticism
whose determination is a trio of negations. In the first place, it
is not a temporary doubt, "entertaining a disbelief in this or that
presumed truth only to return to that same 'truth' once the
'doubt' has been appropriately dissipated, so that in the end
matters stand pretty much as in the beginning. On the contrary,
this way is the conscious insight into the untruth of phenomenal
knowledge." Temporary doubt is merely the resolve to take nothing on authority but to test everything by reason. But since it
reveals itself to be an empty intention by holding fast to "a system of opinion and prejudice, it matters little whether one bases
himself on the authority of others or on personal conviction;
the only difference is the vanity which is peculiar to the latter."[31]

We are likely to think of Descartes in this context, though
Hegel more likely has Fichte in mind.[32] The point, however, is
not so much to discredit Fichte or anyone else, but rather to
give us the standard by which Hegel wishes to be judged, not
the promises of his Introduction but the performance of the
750 pages which follow. It is only there that his scepticism can
be thoroughgoing in its examination of the various modes of
theoretical and practical knowledge which belong to natural
consciousness.

Secondly, if phenomenological scepticism is not temporary, neither is it paralyzing. It seeks to discover as well as to ne-
gate, and thus to be able to move on. To do this it must avoid
the fallacy of simple negation, the flaw of that ancient scepti-

cism of Pyrrho and Sextus Empiricus which Hegel otherwise so greatly admires.[33] This scepticism "sees in every result only pure nothingness and abstracts from the fact that this nothingness is determinate, that it is the nothingness of that from which it results." Thus it "cannot proceed any further but must wait and see whether anything new presents itself to it, and what this is, in order to cast it into the same abysmal void."[34]

Such a scepticism cannot, like Socratic scepticism in the hands of Plato, become the introduction to metaphysics. But this is just what phenomenological scepticism must be, the negative side of genuine philosophical Science. It must recognize that the negation of one form of consciousness is itself a new form of consciousness which has a positive content of its own. For example, from an abstract point of view critical philosophy is a simple negation of philosophy as knowledge of the Absolute. But as Hegel has already shown, that negation rests on a variety of positive assumptions such as the absoluteness of the finite and empirical and the "undeniable certainty of the common consciousness and its whole realm of finite facts."[35] Because Hegel recognizes that every negation rests on some such position he can describe his phenomenological scepticism as "the way of the soul which is making its way through the sequence of its own transformations as through waystations prescribed to it by its very nature." At each stage "the transition is made by which the progression through the complete sequence of shapes [of consciousness] takes place of its own accord."[36]

This continual movement is guaranteed not only because every negation is itself a position, but also because each new position must measure itself against the philosophical ideal, opening itself to a new negation. "For knowledge, however, the goal is fixed just as necessarily as the sequence of the progression. It is that point where knowledge no longer has need to transcend itself, where it finds itself, and where the concept corresponds to the object and the object to the concept. The progression toward this goal is consequently without halt and at no earlier stage is satisfaction to be found."[37]

This description of the goal is only an account of what Absolute Knowledge would be. We are not told whether this goal is a postulate to be grasped by some sort of philosophical faith, a regulative ideal to be approximated in an infinite process, or a possibility to be realized by actual knowledge. We are only told that short of achieving this goal in actual knowledge there will be the kind of cognitive dissonance required to keep the process moving. For all we know, each new form of consciousness may be cast into the same "abysmal void" already mentioned. Negating will be positing indeed, but nothing positive will be able to sustain itself. Dialectical thought will produce the terror of absolute freedom and the frenzy of self-conceit. Far from being the way to Science, phenomenology will be the way of endless despair. This is not, of course, the conclusion that Hegel reaches. The point is only that he has not precluded this possibility at the start. One need not already have attained the goal in order to set out on the path toward it. One needn't even be persuaded there is a goal to be reached at the end of the path. One only needs to see how movement along the path is possible.

Finally, and most importantly, the scepticism which Hegel calls phenomenology is not a positivistic scepticism.[38] In his critique of Schulze, applied in the Lesser Logic to Hume as well,[39] he distinguishes ancient from modern scepticism. The latter is positivistic in taking as fixed and unshakeable the finite objects of common sense and natural science and consequently doubting anything which cannot be reduced to these spheres. One has only to think of the glorious book burning scene in which Hume plays Grand Inquisitor at the conclusion of the *Inquiry Concerning Human Understanding*. The "grand" and "noble" scepticism of antiquity, by contrast, is directed against "this dogmatism of common sense . . . against the finite and the knowledge of the finite, i.e., the understanding." It knows that "the beginning of philosophy must be the elevation above the truth provided by the common consciousness, and the presentiment of a higher truth." The ancient sceptics listed by Diogenes had "the insight that a true philosophy necessarily has its own negative side, which is directed against all that is limited, including the heap of facts of consciousness and their undeniable certainty . . . against this whole ground of finitude on which this modern scepticism has its nature and its truth." Of these the most brilliant example is Plato's *Parmenides*. "This Platonic scepticism does not lead to doubting these truths of the understanding . . . but to the total negation of all truth of such knowledge . . . It is the negative side of the knowledge of the Absolute, and it immediately presupposes reason as the positive side."[40]

It is just this contrast which Hegel wants to establish between his phenomenological scepticism and the "modern" scepticism of critical philosophy. Hence the cryptic statement with which he expresses the third characteristic of his own "ancient" scepticism—"But through that scepticism which directs itself to the whole compass of phenomenal consciousness, Spirit becomes suited for the first time to examine what truth is. For this scepticism brings about a despair over the so-called natural ideas, thoughts, and opinions."[41]

Both at the beginning of our analysis of Hegel's triply radical scepticism and here at the end we find him describing it in terms of despair rather than doubt. It is indeed a traumatic journey for the natural consciousness, a fact which Hegel goes out of his way to underscore. "Although what is limited to a natural life is by itself powerless to transcend its immediate existence, it is driven out by another power—and thus to be uprooted is its death."[42] This is how natural consciousness will experience genuine philosophical scepticism, and why "healthy common sense not only cannot understand speculation, but must also hate it if it experiences it, and, if it is not wholly indifferent in its security, must also abhor and persecute it."[43]

This clinging by consciousness to its familiar existence shows that it still belongs to natural life and has not yet achieved the life of Spirit. Shortly before writing the *Phenomenology* Hegel told his students that "Spirit exists only as transcending [*aufhebend*] that which it immediately is."[44] Similarly, in the Introduction he continues by contrasting consciousness to natural life. "But since consciousness is for itself its own concept, it immediately transcends [*das Hinausgehen ist*] what is limited, and because this limitedness is its own, it transcends itself . . . Consciousness therefore suffers this violence at its own hands, a violence through which it destroys for itself any limited satisfaction." Anxiety [*Angst*] is sure to result from this process, and a variety of escapes from it will be tried. But it is of the nature of consciousness that short of its goal it can find no rest, and it will continue to suffer this "violence at the hands of reason." As Hegel later put it in the Preface, "not the life that shrinks from

death and keeps itself undefiled by devastation, but the life that
endures, and preserves itself through death is the life of
Spirit."[45] In other words, it is not so much suicide to which
Hegel is calling the natural consciousness as it is initiation, the
process by which one dies to an old life and is reborn to a new.

In the light of this whole analysis of the phenomenological
journey with its emphasis on the attachment to an infinite goal
which produces only restlessness and negativity in the face of
everything finite,[46] it is no wonder that the *Phenomenology* has
been so frequently compared on the one hand to Goethe's *Faust*
and on the other to St. Bonaventure's *Itinerarium Mentis in
Deum*. What we do not learn from the Introduction is how seriously we are to take these comparisons and Hegel's use of
such terms as fear, anxiety, despair, violence, and death. When
Jean Wahl tells us that Hegelian doubt is more like that of Pas-
cal and Nietzsche than that of Descartes, and when Jean Hyppolite suggests that we have to do here with *une angoisse exis-
tentielle,* is it Hegel or the intellectual atmosphere of France in
the forties which is speaking to us?[47] Is Hegel dealing here with
the conflict between philosophical systems or with something a
little closer to where we all, even as philosophers, live, and
move, and have our being? The answer to this question about
what might be called the existential import of the *Phenomenology*
is, along with the analysis of criticism's fearfulness, the unfinished business with which the Introduction leaves us as it
moves on to its third and final part.

1C. Phenomenology as Criticism without Presuppositions.

The discussion of method which concludes the Introduction grows directly out of the first two parts. Hegel has tried to
show that critical philosophy brings with it a lot of presupposi-
tional baggage, which is not surprising if every negation also involves a position. What then about his own sceptical project?
We may have carelessly read him to say that Science "takes up
its work and actually knows without any hesitations," dispens-
ing with the critical task entirely. But it has become clear that
this is not the case, and what he actually says is that Science
"takes up its work and actually knows without any *such* hesita-

tions,"[48] i.e., such hesitations as stem from the anxiety over falling into error. Since the *Phenomenology* invites itself to be read as a long series of hesitations which must be dealt with before Science in its full and proper sense can get under weigh, Hegel puts the issue to himself sharply. "For if this presentation is viewed as a description of the way Science is related to phenomenal knowledge, and as an investigation and critical examination into the reality of knowledge, it does not seem possible for it even to take place without some presupposition which will serve as the fundamental criterion . . . Here, where Science first comes on the scene, neither it nor anything else has justified itself as the essence or as the in itself; and without some such basic principle it seems that an examination cannot take place."[49]

The dilemma is sharp. Criticism calls for criteria, but any choice of criteria involves either dogmatism or faith, in either case the abrogation of criticism. How can there be criticism without presuppositions?

The answer is found by attending carefully to the object of our investigations—consciousness. As it turns out, "consciousness provides itself with its own criterion, and the investigation will be a comparison of consciousness with its own self."[50] This happy discovery is really simpler than Hegel makes it sound. Every mode of knowledge distinguishes itself from its object or truth. It has at least a general idea of its object, of what would fulfill its intention or verify its assertion, and this serves as the criterion by which all putative knowledge is measured. Thus the question about each form of consciousness is not whether it conforms to our expectations, or Hegel's, but whether it satisfies its own demands. The self-understanding of natural science, for example, is significantly altered when reflection on the problem of induction or the paradoxes of confirmation reveals that it cannot live up to its own previously professed promises.

Hegel goes a step further. It is not just that consciousness provides its own criterion. It also compares itself with that criterion and thus examines itself. In this respect as well no contribution [*Zutat*] is needed from the phenomenological investigator, whose task becomes simply "the pure act of observation [*reine Zusehen*]."[51]

This is criticism without presuppositions. Though we are

given no concrete examples by Hegel, they are not hard to supply. The critical scepticism of Hume and Kant—what is it but the metaphysics of continental rationalism comparing itself with its own demands and coming up with a negative verdict? And what is romanticism, at least in one important aspect, if not the philosophies of faith and intuition which were offered in place of that metaphysics, confessing that they cannot keep their promises of satisfying the human spirit concerning the Eternal? A different sort of example was tucked away somewhere in Hegel's files when he wrote the *Phenomenology*. We now know it as *The German Constitution*. Like Voltaire's *bon mot* about the Holy Roman Empire being neither holy, nor Roman, nor an empire, Hegel's political criticism is wholly internal. Germany *qua* Holy Roman Empire claims to be a state. But then it puts itself to the test by going to war and proves to anyone who cares to watch that it is no longer a state but a living lie. "If Germany were to profess to be a state and a constitution, although its constitutional forms were without life, and the theory of them without actuality, it would be speaking an untruth."[52]

Instead of such examples, however, Hegel summarizes his discussion of method with the following most peculiar definition of experience: "This dialectical movement, which consciousness exercises on itself—on its knowledge as well as its object—is, insofar as the new, true object emerges for consciousness as a result of it, precisely that which is called experience."[53] Concern over the unusual use of the term 'experience' which Hegel employs (though he is after all talking about the way in which objects are given to consciousness) must not distract from the really substantive dimensions of this definition.

In the first place there is the emergence of the new object for consciousness. Consciousness compares itself with its own criterion and in the process alters itself. But since each different form of consciousness is a new kind of knowing and each new kind of knowing is new just because it is the knowledge of a new kind of object, the process is one in which neither our concept of knowledge nor our concept of its object remains constant.[54] If Absolute Knowledge does not turn out in Chapter Eight to be what we expected it to be, and the Absolute which is the object (and the subject) of that knowledge is also a bit surprising, we should not be surprised. If we understand Hegel's method we will expect to be surprised, for it is a method of watching the familiar repeatedly self-destruct and replace itself with a new mode of consciousness to which new objects correspond.

Secondly, the process by which a new form of knowledge and its new objects arise occurs repeatedly. This is "the dialectical movement which consciousness exercises on itself."[55] In other words, it is consciousness and not Hegel's method which is dialectical. Both here and in the Preface, where the discussion of dialectic is more directly related to the Logic than to the *Phenomenology,* this is the case.[56] The dialectical movement belongs to the subject matter of philosophy, whose task it is simply to describe this movement. Marxists sometimes speak of employing a dialectical method whose purpose is to change reality. But Hegel is suspicious of all methods, just because they are employed for someone's purpose, thereby introducing concerns extraneous to the subject matter into the process of knowing.[57] In his discussion of his own method he remains faithful to this distrust of method. His "method" is the *reine Zusehen* of human consciousness, the pure description of its dialectical restlessness and its striving to transcend its own finitude.

A further consequence of the fact that consciousness itself is dialectical is that the emergence of each new form of consciousness is no mere fact but has a rationality or intelligibility to it. This is because, as we already know from the discussion of scepticism, the new form is "the nothingness of that whose result it is, a result which contains what is true in the previous knowledge." It doesn't just come from nowhere. It comes from an "earlier" form of phenomenal knowledge by means of a feeling for its untruth. Since this feeling is not necessarily the conscious insight which Hegel seeks to evoke, the intelligibility of the transition may go entirely unnoticed. So he assigns to the phenomenological enterprise the task of pointing it out. Even if phenomenology is to be a descriptive science, this description is something other than the "gaping which always sees the opposite of what takes place before its eyes."[58]

The phenomenologist in this way has a role to play after all, even if he is deprived of the philosopher's favorite toy, a method. "This way of observing the subject matter is our contribution [*unsere Zutat*]; it does not exist for the consciousness we observe. But when viewed in this way the sequence of experiences constituted by consciousness is raised to the level of a scientific progression." Hence phenomenology can be called "The Science of the Experience of Consciousness."[59]

In making the distinction between observed and observing consciousness basic to his philosophical enterprise Hegel is placing himself within the tradition of transcendental reflection which stretches from Descartes to Fichte, who explicitly builds his *Science of Knowledge* around this distinction. This is one sense in which his own philosophy, which is the determinate negation of that tradition, "contains what is true in the previous philosophy." But in this respect Hegel is that tradition comparing itself with its criterion and thereby transcending itself. For the criterion which leads to transcendental reflection is the requirement that philosophy shall be without presuppositions. Descartes and Fichte, at opposite ends of the historical development are most explicit about this. But from the opening words of Descartes' Third Meditation, "I shall now close my eyes . . ." to the opening words of Fichte's *First Introduction to the Science of Knowledge,* "Attend to yourself: turn your attention from everything that surrounds you and towards your inner life," transcendental reflection had rested on this distinction of itself from knowledge of the external world and on the assumption which entitles the Second Meditation, that the mind is better known than the body, that inner sense is more reliable than outer sense.

This introspective orientation has a dogmatic character about it, for it rests on unexamined psychological assumptions about the directness and purity with which the self is available to its own inward look. Hegel counts it among the greatest sins of the critical tradition that it is so naive about its psychological assumptions,[60] not because this violates the canons which Hegel would impose on transcendental philosophy from without, but because it violates that tradition's own loudly proclaimed standards. The prejudice toward introspective inwardness is conspicuously missing from the way in which Hegel distinguishes observed and observing consciousness. To emphasize the point he explicitly tells us that "the phenomenology of Spirit is to replace psychological explanations as well as the more abstract discussions of the foundation of knowledge." In fact, this is the first thing Hegel wanted the public to know about his book beyond the fact that it presents "the becoming of knowledge."[61]

The Introduction concludes with a promissory note, that "consciousness will reach a point where it casts off the semblance of being burdened by something alien to it, something which is only for it and which exists as an other." In other words, the distinction between observed and observing consciousness will be overcome in a fully transparent self-consciousness. " . . . at that point where its appearance becomes equal to its essence, consciousness' presentation of itself [the *Phenomenology*] will converge with this very same point in the authentic Science of Spirit [the System]. And finally, when consciousness itself grasps this its essence, it will itself indicate the nature of Absolute Knowledge."[62]

This final part of the Introduction leaves no new unfinished business other than getting on to the text itself to see whether Hegel can produce what he has promised and in the way he has promised it, i.e., whether he can overcome critical philosophy by turning against the various forms of natural consciousness in a criticism which is without presuppositions. But there remain the earlier unanswered questions about the analysis of criticism's fearfulness and the existential import of phenomenological negation. Even a preliminary indication of what Hegel has to say about them would be a real asset in working through the text. Perhaps the Preface will supply what the Introduction has left undone.

NOTES

1. *Glauben,* GW, 4:325-26, 316. *das absolute Aufgehobensein des Gegensatzes.*

2. SL, I, 25/45.

3. Upper case will be used for these and other terms which Hegel uses as quasi-proper names for the modes or forms of consciousness he describes. Where Science appears in upper case it designates Hegel's conception of systematic philosophy in contrast to natural science. The justification for putting Spirit in upper case can only be the interpretation of that concept as given in Chapters Five through Seven below.

4. PhG, 3/63/131.

5. Hegel's first university appointment was at Jena, where he began in 1801 as *Privatdozent.* He was promoted in 1805 to *Ausserordentlicher Professor* but left in 1806 as Napoleon's armies approached for the fateful Battle of Jena, the official end of the Holy Roman Empire. It was not until ten years later that he had another university appointment, this time at Heidelberg.

6. Quite appropriately a recent collection of essays on Hegel's theory of knowledge, edited by Frederick G. Weiss, is entitled, *Beyond Epistemology.*

7. *Rules for the Direction of the Mind,* discussion of rule 8.

8. *An Essay Concerning Human Understanding*, Introduction, Section 7. Hegel quotes from a translation by Poleyen. I have given Locke's original. The ellipsis indicates an omitted sentence of which Hegel gives no indication.

9. PhG,3/63/131.

10. *Skepticismus,* GW, 4:201.

11. HP, SW, 19:555/III, 428.

12. B XXII.

13. HP, SW, 19:278/III, 170. Hegel gave his lectures on the history of philosophy for the first time while he was still in Jena. Whether the discussion of Bacon which is included in the editions we have was included at that time or comes from later versions of the lectures, long after the *Phenomenology* was written, it is impossible to tell at this time. So we cannot be sure that Hegel had Bacon in mind while writing his Introduction.

14. *On the Aesthetic Education of Man,* tr. Snell, New York, 1954, p. 26.

15. PhG, 3-4/63-64/131, my italics.

16. PhG, 5-7/64-65/132-34.

17. *Critique of Pure Reason,* A 609 = B637 f.

18. The distinction is Carnap's. These modified definitions are from Lewis White Beck's essay, "The Fact of Reason: An Essay on Justification in Ethics," in his *Studies in the Philosophy of Kant,* Indianapolis, 1956, pp. 200-01.

19. PhG, XXVIII-XXXI/23-25/85-87.

20. PhG, 5-7/65-66/133-134.

21. *Glauben,* GW, 4:350.

22. PhG, 5-7/64-65/132-34. In the interlude on misology in the *Phaedo* Socrates considers the possibility that someone might get so exasperated in the face of sophistical argumentation that he spent his life loathing and decrying argumentation "and so missed the chance of knowing the truth about reality—would it not be a deplorable thing?" 90d, Tredennick translation.

23. PhG, 4/64/132. cf. *Differenz,* GW, 4:15, "[The Absolute] is already at hand. How else could it be sought?"

24. PhG, 3-5/63-64/131-33.

25. See my essay, "In Defense of the Thing in Itself," *Kant-Studien,* 1968, Heft 1, 118-41.

26 PhG, 7-8/66/134.

27. PhG, 7-11/66-68/134-37. 'Natural consciousness' comes to be the most used designation. Included in its compass are not only our everyday awareness of the world and the knowledge of natural science but also the highly reflective activity of critical philosophy. There is a kind of gnostic or mystical perspective at work here which designates as merely natural all consciousness not engaged in actually knowing the Absolute. Thus everything short of Science is natural consciousness.

28. PhG, 8/66/135.

29. For example, *Differenz,* GW, 4:20-23, *Skepticismus,* GW, 4:206-16, *Glauben,* GW, 4:322-23, 355-57.

30. PhG, 9/67/135. Hegel has fun here with a word play on *Zweifel* and *Verzweiflung.*

31. PhG, 9-10/67-68/135-36.

32. The opening pages on doubt in *The Vocation of Man* are a classic expression of doubt as the public resolve to take nothing on authority.

As for the conceit which is supposed to go with this kind of doubt, one need only join the following statements from the *Science of Knowledge* and its *First Introduction*: "For my personal position I have no regard whatever. But I am hot for truth." "I thought and still think myself to have discovered the way in which philosophy must raise itself to the level of a manifest science." With reference to "these final results of idealism"—"Anyone who thinks otherwise simply does not know what he is talking about." *Science of Knowledge (Wissenschaftslehre)*, trans. Heath and Lachs, New York, 1970, pp. 90, 89, 26. *Sämmtliche Werke,* ed. I. H. Fichte, I, 87, 86, 447.

33. *Skepticismus,* GW, 4:213.

34. PhG, 11/68/137. cf. Preface, LXXIII-LXXIV/49/117-18.

35. *Skepticismus,* GW, 4:201-03. The first formula is typical of *Glauben.*

36. PhG, 9/67/135, 12/69/137.

37. PhG, 12/69/137-38. *über sich selbst hinausgehen.*

38. Though it is anachronistic to describe pre-Comptean positions as positivistic, I believe it is useful to do so to highlight their affinity with nineteenth and twentieth century views which repudiate metaphysics in favor of empirical science.

39. LL, #39-40 and *Zusätze* to #24 and #81. Perhaps Hegel is unfair to Hume here, though I think not. It is true that along with his twentieth century heirs, the logical empiricists, he has very sophisticated views of the ambiguous status of our scientific knowledge and does not share the naiveté of someone like Schulze. But he does share with all forms of positivism the view that empirical science and common sense (so far as it is assimilable to empirical science) are genuine knowledge, while metaphysics is spurious.

40. *Skepticismus,* GW, 4:215-16, 207.

41. PhG, 10/68/136.

42. PhG, 12-13/69/138.

43. *Differenz,* GW, 4:21.

44. *Realphilosophie,* 179.

45. PhG, XXXVIII/29/93.

46. See Fichte, *op. cit.,* pp. 231-33, 265-67. *Werke,* I, 261-65, 301-04.

47. Wahl, *Le Malheur de la Conscience dans la Philosophie de Hegel,* Paris, 1951, p. 7. Hyppolite, *Genèse et Structure de la Phénoménologie de l'Esprit de Hegel,* Paris, 1946, p. 10.

48. PhG, 5/64/132, my italics.

49. PhG, 13-14/70/139.

50. PhG, 15/71/140.

51. PhG, 16-17/72/141. cf. Fichte, *op. cit.*, 30, 120, *Werke*, I, 454, 123-24.

52. *The German Constitution, Werke*, I, 473/154. For context see 461-85/143-64.

53. PhG, 18/73/142.

54. PhG, 17/72/142.

55. PhG, 18/73/142. Dialectic might here be defined as self-transcendence through inner tension.

56. PhG, LXXX/53/123 f.

57. PhG, IV/11/69, LXVI/45/112. The entire second half of the Preface, from XLIV/33/97 on, is an extended treatment of this issue.

58. *Skepticismus,* GW, 4:199. The philosophical activity which Husserl calls phenomenology is also concerned with pure description and presuppositionless philosophy. The relationship between the two kinds of phenomenology is complex. Two important differences should be noted. What Husserl means by transcending the natural standpoint in order to philosophize is very different from what Hegel means by transcending natural consciousness for the sake of true philosophy. Second, where truth and certainty tend to coalesce for Husserl, Hegel constantly and deliberately holds them apart, claiming instead that truth is the whole, not the certain.

59. PhG, 19-21/74/143-44.

60. *Skepticismus,* GW, 4:200, *Glauben,* 4:322, 330-31.

61. From Hegel's own announcement of the PhG, which appeared in the October 28, 1807 issue of the *Jenaischen Allgemeinen Literatur-Zeitung.* The German text is found in the Ullstein edition of the PhG, p. 588. There is an English translation in Walter Kaufmann, *Hegel: Reinterpretation, Texts and Commentary,* Garden City, 1965, p. 366.

62. PhG, 21/75/145.

CHAPTER TWO: The Task of the *Phenomenology:*

B) The Preface

For the most part the Preface is best read as it was written—after the rest of the text. Unlike the Introduction, nearly every paragraph of which is crucially important for understanding what follows, most of the Preface does not provide the same sort of advance help for the reader. Indeed, parts of it are all but unintelligible apart from the substance of what follows; so one can say that the Preface requires the main text for its own understanding more than that text requires the Preface, a reversal of the usual relationship. For this reason, and because the Preface is four times the length of the Introduction, a close analysis of the whole Preface like that just given of the Introduction would not be appropriate.

At the same time there are a few central passages in the Preface which contribute significantly to the reader's preparation for the main argument. Furthermore, reflection on these helps us develop a fuller picture of the intellectual ferment which culminated for Hegel in the writing of the *Phenomenology*. So we cannot ignore the Preface entirely at this stage, even if we cannot treat it in the same way as the Introduction.

2A. The present standpoint of Spirit

On the basis of the Introduction alone it would be easy to suppose that Hegel was a philosopher's philosopher; that he took his problems from philosophers and addressed his answers to them, something in the style of G.E. Moore; that it was simply his attempt at Jena to come to grips with the dominant philosophical epistemology of his day that led him to write the *Phenomenology*. Since the task of phenomenology is given in such heavily epistemic language, it would not be arbitrary to suppose that the "existential" overtones detected by some readers are the result of taking too seriously the metaphors of a would-be literary stylist or of projecting their own interests and situation into the text. Such a view cannot be sustained past the first few chapters of the text, however, and it is the Preface which prepares us for this discovery.

To be sure, it still describes the goal in noetic terms. "To help bring philosophy nearer to the form of Science—that goal where it can lay aside the name of love of knowledge and be actual knowledge—that is what I have set before me."[1] Or again, "The goal is Spirit's insight into what constitutes knowledge."[2] Although the separation of knowledge and its object (truth, being) infects all the forms of consciousness through which phenomenology passes and is the defect which moves the process along, we are promised a vision of that state in which "the separation of knowledge and truth is overcome . . . With this the phenomenology of Spirit is concluded. What Spirit prepares for itself in this phenomenology is the element of knowledge. In this element the moments of Spirit spread themselves out in the form of simplicity which knows its object as itself. They no longer fall apart into the opposition of being and knowledge but abide in the simplicity of knowledge."[3] Statements of this sort stand in closest connection with the Introduction's idea that phenomenology is a re-doing of critical philosophy in such a way that the story has a happy rather than a sceptical ending.

Side by side with such statements in the Preface are others which formulate phenomenology's task in radically different language; language more likely to suggest Marx or Nietzsche than Hume and Kant; language which leads Kroner to say that the issue in the *Phenomenology* is no longer merely *Erkennen* but *Erlebnis* and Marcuse to say that the dualisms of subject and object, understanding and sense, thought and existence, are "not primarily an epistemological problem for Hegel."[4]

For example, it is essential to consider "what stage self-conscious Spirit occupies at present. It has passed beyond the substantial life that it formerly led in the element of thought, beyond this immediacy of its faith, beyond the satisfaction and security of the certainty which consciousness possessed about its reconciliation with the divine [*mit dem Wesen*] and its . . . presence . . . Not only has Spirit lost its essential life; it is also conscious of this loss and of the finitude which is now its content. Turning away from the husks, confessing that it lies in wickedness, and despising its situation, it now demands from philosophy not so much self-knowledge as that philosophy should help it to restore that substantiality and the solidity of being."[5]

We have yet to learn more precisely what Hegel means by Spirit, but it is clear from this passage that he refers to the historical life of the human spirit. To say that the human spirit has lost its substantial and essential life is to say that "the times are out of joint" and that "things fall apart—the centre cannot hold." By evoking the image of the prodigal son Hegel suggests the experience of exile and estrangement, while at the same time underscoring the religious dimension of Spirit's loss. Having lost touch with the Divine Spirit the human spirit has lost its way.

This religious experience is juxtaposed to the scientific revolution of the preceding three centuries as Hegel continues: "Formerly men had a heaven, furnished with abundant riches of thoughts and images. The significance of all that is used to lie in the thread of light that tied it to heaven; and following this thread, the eye, instead of abiding in the present rose above to the Divine Being [*zum göttlichen Wesen*], to, if one may say so, a present beyond. The eye of the Spirit had to be directed forcibly to the things of this earth and kept there. Indeed, it took a long time to work that clarity which only the supernatural possessed into the must and confusion in which the sense of this world lay, and to make attention to the present as such, which was called experience, interesting and valid. Now the opposite need meets the eye . . . Spirit appears so poor that, like a wanderer in the desert who languishes for a simple drink of water, it seems to crave for its refreshment merely the bare feeling of the divine in general."[6]

Speaking for philosophy, Hegel accepts these demands. It is true that he vigorously repudiates those who think that philosophy can meet them with edification, ecstasy, and fermenting enthusiasm rather than with insight, the concept, and the coldly progressing necessity of the subject matter.[7] But this concerns only the form appropriate to Science, not whether it must address itself to the present predicament of Spirit. That predicament Hegel here interprets in terms of a scientific secularism which has tended to undermine "the significance of all that is," or at least radically alter it so that the human spirit has come to feel deeply impoverished. The *Phenomenology* is to concern itself with this historical-cultural crisis of the times and not merely with critical philosophy.

So perhaps Wahl and Hyppolite are not projecting their Paris into the Introduction when they give an existentialist reading to Hegel's focus on despair rather than doubt. Perhaps Hegel's references to death and to *Angst* do not concern the luxurious anxiety of the professional philosopher whose system has just been declared dead by the learned journals, but rather, as the texts just cited suggest, the experience (by no means unique to scholars) of living in the Wasteland.

It is not that Hegel has abandoned his confrontation with critical philosophy. It is rather that, like Husserl more than a century later, he is convinced that the intellectual crisis of his day is a "radical life-crisis of European humanity," which concerns "the total meaningfulness of its cultural life, its total *Existenz*." Both see the development of modern philosophy with all its epistemological concerns as simply "humanity struggling to understand itself."[8]

Hegel's earliest Jena writings insist on this most clearly. For example, if critical philosophy separates its conceptual activity from the unconditioned and supernatural as something absolutely beyond it, this involves the separation of man from himself.[9] Philosophy is needed when this sort of estrangement [*Entzewiung*] prevails in the life of men from whom the power of unification [*Vereinigung*] has disappeared. The forms which estrangement takes are varied and they come to philosophy as contingently given. Such oppositions as those between spirit and matter, soul and body, faith and understanding, freedom and necessity, which involve "all important human interests" can be transposed into the form of such oppositions as that between subjectivity and objectivity. In the "northwest" the prevailing form is the opposition between thought and actuality, and the stronger this opposition grows "the more meaningless become the strivings of life to give itself a rebirth of harmony."[10] In other words, when critical philosophy talks about the relation of thought as subjectivity to actuality as objectivity it is only the abstract and technical form which makes this seem remote from all human interests. Just as Kant took note of "the interest of reason in these conflicts," when speaking about the antinomies, so Hegel tells us that the interest of reason is "the transformation of such congealed oppositions." Reason is not here conceived as an abstract psychological faculty which lives man like the Freudian id, but simply as human life in its totality seeking wholeness. The essential question, which sometimes takes epistemic form, concerns the meaningfulness of this search, whether man is a useless passion or not.

In order fully to appreciate the concreteness of the concern underlying Hegel's allusions to the loss of substantial life and a sense of the divine presence, however abstract the epistemological form in which these matters may be discussed, it is necessary to ask what sort of society is the archetype of health in relation to which the present cultural sickness is diagnosed. This question takes us back from the Jena period to the "early theological writings" of Tübingen, Bern, and Frankfurt. A detailed analysis of these papers and of Hegel's development during these years (1793-1800), on which there is a large and growing literature, will not be necessary in order to extract what is most helpful for reading the *Phenomenology*. But it will be helpful to mention briefly the two objections which have been raised to the publication of these materials, both in German and in English, as "theological" writings. There is first the claim that these papers are political rather than theological, and second the claim that they are more nearly anti-theological than theological. To the first contention it must be granted that political issues are prominent throughout the papers, but one only needs to read them to see that for Hegel this in no way lessens their theological significance. One might say that for Hegel they could only be theological if they were political as well, and this discovery is not unimportant for understanding the *Phenomenology*. It is also true that the fragments published by Nohl as "Folk Religion and Christianity," not included in the English translation, unfavorably contrast theology with religion in order to express Hegel's preference for a religion of the heart over religion of the cold, lifeless understanding. But the distinction is between two kinds of religion, which he calls subjective and objective, and the discussion is no less theological for its insistence that true religion is more than systematic theology. Hegel's intent is by no means secular, and this, too, is important for understanding the *Phenomenology*, where he once again will refuse to cast the conflict between orthodoxy and secularism in an either/or mold.

What pervades and unites these essays and fragments is the

contrast between Greek and Judeo-Christian culture. In the former Hegel finds unity, harmony, joy, and beauty; in the latter separation, estrangement, sorrow, and ugliness. In fact, he goes so far as to say that Christianity was able to conquer the ancient world because that world, in the time of the Empire, had lost the substantial life and sense of the divine presence which characterized city-state Greece and republican Rome. The success of Christianity was not due to its intrinsic spiritual superiority but to its congruity with the decadence of the period. The Empire meant that "the picture of the state as a product of his own activity disappeared from the citizen's soul." In that situation "without a fatherland, the citizen lived in a state with which no joy could be associated and all he felt was its pressure. He had a worship to whose celebration and festivals he could no longer bring a cheerful heart, because cheerfulness had flown away out of his life."[11] To such a miserable people, Christianity offered a "miserable sort of culture."[12]

The primary categories for drawing this cultural contrast are those of slavery and freedom, with the result that there is a striking resemblance to Nietzsche's contrast between slave morality and master morality. Like Nietzsche, Hegel looks behind Christianity to Judaism as the source of the slave mentality which permeates Christian culture. At the heart of Judaism lies not only a "mechanical slavery" but also a "pedantically slavish spirit of the people," an "obstinate pride in slavish obedience," a "maniacally servile disposition," and a "frenzied slavery of spirit." The Jews have a sense of their nothingness, but not of their selfhood.[13] All this is in reference to the Jewish ethic, based on the absolutely authoritative command of God and not on man's own reason, in Kantian language the heteronomy of practical reason.

By the time Hegel wrote this account (1800), which is also found in earlier papers, he had come to have severe reservations about Kant's theory of practical reason. But this Jewish heteronomy remained the very essence of depravity. "There is one God . . . What deeper truth is there for slaves than that they have a master? But Mendelssohn is right not to call this a truth . . . For truth is something free which we neither master nor are mastered by; hence the existence of God appears to the Jews not as a truth but as a command. On God the Jews are depen-

dent throughout." With a fervor that even Nietzsche never surpasses, Hegel describes Judaism as a tradegy which can arouse
neither fear nor pity, but only horror.[14]

Christianity represents no improvement. Jesus was largely
free from the spirit of Judaism, it is true, but it was his fate,
both because of the overwhelming force of the spirit of his time
and place and because he was not himself totally free from that
spirit, to become the founder of a religion which not only took
over in theory and practice the "perverted and immoral concepts of the Jews"[15] but increased their heteronomy. For to the
authority of the Lord was added the authority of the church,
and the church "has not stopped at prescribing a number of external actions whereby we are supposed to do honor to the
Deity . . . It has also directly prescribed laws for our mode of
thinking, feeling, and willing . . . While in Judaism only actions
were commanded, the Christian church goes farther and com-
mands feelings, a contradiction in terms."[16]

A crucial point at which Jesus succumbed to the Jewish
spirit was his willingness to let religion be a private matter. This
failure of nerve opened the door to one of the worst forms of
dualism, the separation of religious and political life. The disciples are to some degree responsible, since it was they who "had
no interest in the state like that which a citizen of a free republic
takes in his fatherland" to whom the founding of the church
was entrusted.[17] But Jesus himself is not innocent. When he
told the young man to sell all he had and give it to the poor he
showed "how much [he] was concerned in his teaching only
with the education and perfection of the individual man, and
how little this was extended to society at large."[18] And when he
said, "Render unto Caesar the things that are Caesar's," he announced that Christianity was a religion of inwardness which
could co-exist with all forms of political alienation. It does not
require that dimension of freedom which for Hegel is the pre-
requisite of an "association of beauty." Rather it is an association of private persons submitting passively to a hostile state.
Since it is obviously not a kingdom of this world, its only recourse is "separation from the world, and flight from it into
heaven; restoration in the ideal world of the life which this
world turned away empty handed."[19] Thus the whole Jewish
tradition of Messianic and apocalyptic ideas comes into play.

Heaven and the church take the place of fatherland and a free state.[20]

This separation of religious from political life, however, is but one of the dualisms which constitute Christian culture. *The Spirit of Christianity and Its Fate* concludes with a more complete account of the ways in which Christian consciousness is separated from actual life: "In all the forms of the Christian religion which have developed themselves in the advancing fate of the ages, there lies this fundamental characteristic of opposition in the divine, which is supposed to be present only in consciousness, never in life ... And it is its fate, that church and state, worship and life, piety and virtue, spiritual and worldly action, can never dissolve into one."[21]

In starkest contrast to the spirit of Judeo-Christian culture is the harmonious and happy humanism of Greece. The religion of Hellenic folk culture was the spontaneous creation of free men, and it stood in intimate relation to the whole of life. Man lived in a whole which was at once religious, ethical, and political, and the individual felt himself to be an inherent part of that whole. His religion stemmed from the traditions of his people, and expressed itself in their folksongs, their monuments of art, their daily religious rites, and their periodic festivals, all of which were public. His faith in the gods was "interwoven by a thousand threads" into the web of daily life. No feelings of life were excluded, but the prevailing atmosphere was that of joy and ecstasy. Thus even the bacchanalia were sacred to the gods. "If the imagination of the Greek priestesses of Bacchus slipped over into madness and to the wildest eruption of anarchic drunkenness in order to see the divinity himself present, still this was an enthusiasm of joy and jubilation, an enthusiasm which soon returned again to common life."[22]

To the terror and awe of Sinai and Calvary this beauty and joy of Olympus bear no resemblance. The Jewish cultus was a reminder of "the nothingness of man and the littleness of an existence maintained by favor" and of an emancipation which the people did not accomplish for themselves but passively received with a "most slavelike demeanor." The Christian sacrament in turn was the reminder of a Lord no longer present, a cold and lifeless private exercise and by no means a celebration of delight in society. But Greek festivals celebrated the solidarity of the people with their gods and with nature, expressing their exuberance for life.[23] Whereas the Germans, "who never were a nation," have only Luther for a national hero and celebrate his Reformation only with the wearisome annual reading of the Augsburg Confession and the dull sermon which follows, "anyone who did not know the history of the city, the culture, and the laws of Athens could almost have learned them from the festivals if he had lived a year within its gates."[24] Not surprisingly the important religious concept of sacrifice comes to radically different forms of expression as well. On the one hand there is the Judeo-Christian concept grounded in the notions of sin, punishment, and regaining the lost favor of one's supreme Lord. On the other is a softer and milder conception grounded in cheerfulness, thanks, and good will directed toward the being who, though he transcends man, does not despise whatever man may bring as an offering and needs no appeasing.[25]

Hegel's enthusiasm for the Greeks belongs to the larger story which has been told by E.M. Butler as *The Tyranny of Greece over Germany* and by Henry Hatfield as *Aesthetic Paganism in German Literature.* Like the literary figures they discuss, he was influenced by Winckelmann's idealization of Greek experience, particularly through the mediation of Goethe and Schiller. But these influences came to soil already well prepared. Hegel began his reading of Homer, Euripides, and Sophocles, as well as Plato and Aristotle, during his gymnasium years. His sister tells us that during his student years the Greek tragedies were his favorite reading, and of these, Sophocles, whom he read uninterruptedly for several years and translated as well, his favorite author, and *Antigone* his favorite play. His high school papers include one on the religion of the Greeks and Romans and another on the characteristic distinctions of the ancient poets.[26]

This interest continued through his seminary days at Tübingen, where his friendship with Hölderlin only served to intensify it. The translation of Sophocles continued, and when he had to spend some time at home due to illness, he spent it reading the tragedians. He even presented a revised version of his last high school paper on the ancient poets.[27] He tells us himself that he went to seminary at his parents' wish and insofar as he pursued theological studies of his own accord it was due to their connection with classical literature and philosophy. So it was natural that his seminary training led him, vocationally, not to the parish but to the academy, where he could devote himself to ancient literature and philosophy. The choice of philosophy over literature, incidentally, coincided with his Jena appointment.[28]

In the earliest fragments of the early theological writings, which probably date from Hegel's last year in Tübingen, his name for the Greek experience is folk religion. His references to the simplicity or naivete of their customs [*Einfalt der Sitten*] foreshadows the term he came to use instead of folk religion during the Jena period, *Sittlichkeit* or Ethical Life, an important term in the *Phenomenology*.[29] It is in terms of the first of these that he formulates the basic question of the Bern and Frankfurt period: "What are the requirements of a folk religion . . . Do we meet with them in the Christian religion?"[30]

There is no need for further comment on Hegel's answer to the second part of the question, except to note that by the time he comes to write the *Phenomenology* his view is less one sided. While he continues to link the Christian religion with the alienation pervading modern culture, he also finds it to be integrally bound up with the possibility of a new cultural harmony.

It is the answer to the first part of the question which reveals the principles at work in his admiration of the Greeks. The requirements for folk religion are three:

"I.   Its doctrines must be grounded on universal reason.
II.   Imagination, the heart, and sensuousness [*Sinnlichkeit*] must not be left empty handed by it.
III.   It must be so constituted that all needs of life, including the public acts of state, belong to it."[31]

To the first requirement belongs the distinction between autonomy and heteronomy. It is precisely the acceptance of political, ethical, and religious heteronomy which leads Hegel to label Judeo-Christian culture a slave culture. By autonomy, on the other hand, Hegel does not mean that a genuine folk religion would stay within the limits of mere reason, for such an attempt leaves only lifeless abstractions. Rather, its teachings should be "so human that they are suited to the stage of

spiritual culture and morality which a people have reached."
Both will gradually develop together.[32] The important thing is
not that there be nothing historically conditioned and particular in the religion, as opposed to the timelessly universal, but
that there be nothing which has to be imposed on the people by
theologians rather than arising from the people themselves.[33]
The contrast between heteronomy and autonomy resides in the
difference between "forcible institutions" and the "common
life" with its "spontaneous interest," between what is "given
throughout" and what is "given as something free to be freely
received."[34]

To the third requirement belongs the contrast which Hegel
gradually develops between Ethical Life [*Sittlichkeit*] and
Morality [*Moralität*], so crucial to the *Phenomenology's* sixth chapter. Folk religion is a public matter, and much of the meaning
of Ethical Life derives from its contrast with the connotation of
Morality as a private and personal affair. But Morality is not
only private; it is also abstracted from other dimensions of life,
the religious, and legal, and the traditional [*die Sitten*]. Ethical
Life and folk religion, by contrast, represent that simplicity of
customs in which these separations have not yet been made.
Man is not yet divided into moral and legal, religious and
worldly, rational and emotional, theoretical and practical components. In short, the conclusion of *The Spirit of Christianity and
Its Fate* (see note 21 above) serves as a negative definition of
Hegel's folk religion-Ethical Life ideal.

Where then does the second requirement of a folk religion
fit in—the demand that the heart, imagination, and feelings be
satisfied and not starved? The important thing here is not so
much Hegel's repeated emphasis on the role of an indigenous
imagery growing out of a people's history and traditions in
achieving this goal, as his making this goal the end to which the
first and third requirements serve as means.[35] The reason why
a people's religion should be autonomous, public, and integrated with all of life is that human experience should not be
what Hegel finds it to be in his Preface, "so poor that, like a
wanderer in the desert who languishes for a simple drink of
water, it seems to crave for its refreshment merely the bare feeling of the divine in general. By that which suffices Spirit one
can measure the extent of its loss."[36]

We have indeed returned to our point of departure for this discussion of Hegel's Greek ideal, his diagnosis of the present standpoint of Spirit. The irrationalism against which he proposes his concept of philosophy as Science, the "prophetic talk [*prophetische Reden*, Schleiermacher, et.al.]" which "deliberately keeps its distance from the concept and from necessity as if they were the reflection that makes its home in the finite,"[37] and which seeks to respond directly to the demand of the age for edification, ecstasy, and fermenting enthusiasm—this irrationalism is not wholly unwarranted, even if it is not to be accepted. For it recognizes the present position of Spirit as one in which the non-rational (better: non-theoretical) components of man have been starved, and it accepts the responsibility of addressing hungry and thristy men, not transcendental egos. It is this same recognition and acceptance which started Hegel on his diagnosis of the present situation as the loss of substantial life and the sense of the divine presence. Although the story of his love for the Greeks can be told in much more detail, this brief sketch is enough to give some initial understanding of his otherwise all too cryptic diagnosis.

2B. The Life-World of Critical Philosophy

Assuming that the text supports this reading of the Preface, there can be no further question about the existential import of the Phenomenology. At issue is nothing less than the meaning of human life, especially in its social and religious dimensions. But a new question arises. By now the phrase 'task of the *Phenomenology*' seems to designate nothing unambiguously. Are there two accounts of its purpose, an epistemological one in the Introduction and a cultural-existential one in the Preface? Something like this is implied by Haering and those who follow him in arguing that the *Phenomenology* is non-organic due to the way it was written. It is argued that the original intention was to break off somewhere in the section entitled "Reason" and make a direct transition to the Logic. The entire second half of the text, Chapters Six through Eight, in which the central concept of Spirit is developed, was added in the process of writing, for some reason, and the Logic was relegated to a separate work.

Of these two parts the first is quite easily related to the epistemic orientation of the Introduction, but because the last three chapters or so venture off in new directions, Hegel had to write a Preface oriented primarily to them. In other words, the *Phenomenology* began as a reply to Kant and company, but this concern fell into the background as Hegel felt impelled to get his philosophy of Spirit into print. Having lost sight of his original purpose he abandoned the debate with critical finitism, which had occupied him at Jena, and returned to the religious and social concerns of his days as tutor in Bern and Frankfurt.[38]

But even if Hegel did not have the entire plan for his book in mind when he began to write, it does not follow that the final product is a piece of patchwork. Hegel himself rejects this interpretation, since the Preface clearly reaffirms the noetic concerns of the Introduction and develops many of them as well. Nor can he mean that he will first deal with the critical philosophy and then, putting on another hat as it were, deal with cultural crisis, folk religion, etc. We have already seen from the earliest Jena writings that he refuses to separate the epistemic and the existential in this way. We have also seen that in the Preface he prescribes "the concept" as the genuine cure for the present cultural malaise. In other words, the issues discussed in critical philosophy are intimately related to the possibility of experiencing folk religion. The Introduction and the Preface are correlative descriptions of the task of the *Phenomenology*.

I have argued in another place that Kant's dualism and finitism are the expression of a religious world-view, since the thing-in-itself is so clearly defined as the thing-for-God.[39] If this is true, we will have to conclude that as the problem of the *Phenomenology* developed and took on dimensions transcending the narrowly epistemological, Hegel moved closer to the spirit of Kant and to real engagement with his thought. For both of them the question of knowledge becomes the question of man in relation to God.

The Preface is Hegel's bold attempt to relate this enlarged concept of his undertaking to the permanent noetic orientation of one for whom "humanity exists only in the accomplished community of consciousness," though animals are able to communicate only through feeling.[40] The phrase 'community of

consciousness' itself contains the implication that human consciousness or knowledge can never be wholly independent of
human social life.

Both these dimensions are involved in Hegel's answer to
the question around which the Preface moves, What is Science?
If one asks about its form and content the answer is given exclusively in terms of knowledge. Formally, Science is mediated,
organized, systematic knowledge. Its subject matter [*die Sache
selbst*] is substance as subject. Form and content are internally
related, since the form is required by the content it seeks to express. The union of the two is crucial to Hegel's idealism. "That
the true is actual only as system, or that substance is essentially
subject, is expressed in the conception which speaks of the Absolute as Spirit . . ."[41]

But all this is directly related to the more concrete concerns
on which the Preface dwells, for the passage just quoted continues, "This is the most sublime concept, and it belongs to the
modern age and its religion." The knowledge which is Science
belongs to a new religion, one which no doubt involves the restoration of substantial life and a sense of the divine presence.
Science not only has a form and content which can be described
in noetic terms; it has a purpose and result which break
through the limits of any narrowly theoretical conception of
knowledge. This two-fold but unified nature of the Preface and
of the *Phenomenology* itself is elegantly summarized at the conclusion of the paragraph whose opening has just been cited.
"Spirit, when it knows itself developed in this way as Spirit, is
Science. Science is the actuality of Spirit and the kingdom which
it builds for itself in its own element." Science is the kingdom?
What kingdom? Since we have to do here with the new age and
its religion it may well be the Kingdom of God which Hegel has
in mind. The full confirmation of this can only come in the long
journey through the text, but we do know that such an identification of Science and the Kingdom of God can be found as
early as a 1795 letter to Schelling and as late as the 1816 inaugural lecture at Heidelberg.[42]

It is not enough, however, for Hegel simply to assert this
unity of his project. He must give us some indication of how
such a unity is possible, especially since we, like his original
readers, are more inclined to separate what he insists on unit-

ing. To find Hegel's response to this demand we need only backtrack to the point at which he began reflecting on "the present standpoint of Spirit" (his heading for the second section of the Preface), its loss of substantial life and sense of the divine presence. What motivates this discussion? First, it is Hegel's awareness that the "conviction of the age" is not in sympathy with his conception of the scientific system as the true form in which the truth exists, and that the demand of the age is not for "the concept" but for feeling and intuition. Second, and this is the crucial move, is the suggestion that such a demand should be "considered in its more general context," which is to say that "one should see what stage self-conscious Spirit occupies at present."[43]

The point is that Hegel's description of the present standpoint of Spirit is given precisely as the context out of which arises "such a demand." But such a demand has the critical philosophy for its basis, whether in the romantic form here described with reference to intuition and feeling, or in the earlier form described in *Faith and Knowledge* as faith-philosophy. Hegel makes no distinction between a Kant, Jacobi, or Fichte telling us that he has denied knowledge in order to make room for faith, and a Schelling, Schleiermacher, or Schlegel telling us that we must abandon conceptual knowledge for feeling and intuition. Nor need he, since the negations of critical finitism are presupposed by both of these traditions.

Now if "such a demand" is made on the basis of critical philosophy and Hegel's investigation of the "present standpoint of Spirit" concerns the context from which such a demand arises, it is nothing less than an inquiry into the nature of the life-world in which critical philosophy can flourish. Such a procedure assumes that abstract and theoretical thought is not autonomous but is intimately related to everyday life with its familiar and obvious contours. It only deceives itself in thinking it dwells in its own isolated and insulated medium. More concretely, Hegel is suggesting that what comes to expression in the *Critique of Pure Reason* is nothing less than society's loss of substantial life and of a sense of the divine presence.[44]

Hegel knows that reflection on the life-world out of which critical philosophy arises does not refute that philosophy. It may help to explain it, but never to explain it away. The jux-

taposition of the critical philosophy with an analysis of how "the
times are out of joint" reminds us that the deficiencies of the
former are not simply theoretical. More importantly, it warns
us that any possibility of genuinely transcending the critical-
sceptical point of view depends upon getting the times back in
joint.

It follows that when Hegel tells us that "the time has come
for the elevation of philosophy to a science,"[45] he means this in
a very strong sense. It is not that others have tried their hand at
such a task and done it clumsily, so that it's now time to quit
fooling around and do it right. It is rather that "the present
standpoint of Spirit" is undergoing a change, that a new soil is
being prepared in which new philosophical flora can thrive.

At times Hegel can speak as bitingly as Kierkegaard about
"the almighty age and its culture," which he sees as a kind of
spiritual sickness. At the same time, however, he is persuaded
that "our age is an age of birth and transition to a new period.
Spirit has broken with what was hitherto the world of its existence and ideas and . . . is at work giving itself a new form."[46] In
Baillie's rendering of *der bisherigen Welt seines Daseins and Vorstellens* Spirit's break is with "the old order of things hitherto prevailing, and with the old ways of thinking." This is perhaps a
rather free translation, but it is entirely in the spirit of the passage, for Hegel's point is the correlation between thought and
the world from which it arises.

What Hegel sees happening in his time is a comprehensive
cultural revolution. The period of preparation in which Spirit
"matures slowly and quietly toward the new form, dissolving
one particle of the edifice of its previous world after another,"
is nothing less than "a far-reaching revolution in ever so many
forms of culture."[47] By culture [*Bildung*] Hegel does not mean
simply the fine arts, the theater, and the *New York Review of
Books*. He includes the most basic and original transcendence of
man's natural life by means of ideas [*Gedanke*] which achieve
some form of universality. Beyond the mere presence of language, the catechisms and proverbs of a people are examples of
culture in this sense, for they are the wisdom which even a
young child possesses and by which he is socialized into the
spiritual world to which he was born. "Children are to be seen
and not heard," "In Adam's fall we sinned all." "I pledge allegiance to the flag . . ."

After the gradual and largely invisible revolution of culture the appearance of the new world of Spirit is as sudden as lightning or the birth of a child after months of gestation. Like the newborn child, the new world is not fully developed at the beginning. It takes still more time for it to develop its "perfect actuality," just as it takes time for an acorn to become an oak. Only then can Science, "the crown of a world of Spirit," itself be complete and anything more than an unfulfilled promise.[49] But of course, at the top (crown) of an oak tree one will find acorns and not pine cones. Just the same, at the crown of a world from which substantial life and a sense of the divine presence have departed one will not find Science as the systematic, actual knowledge of the Absolute. Since the "unsurpassable horizon [*feste Standpunkt*] which the almighty age and its culture have fixed for philosophy is that of a sense bound reason, such philosophy can proceed to know, not God, but what is called man."[50] Note well! The notion of reason as finite is not something which philsophy seeks to impose on its age but something which is given to philosophy by its age. It is as if critical philosophy were the dreams and symptoms in which the collective unconscious of the age comes to the light of day. We are reminded of Hegel's later formulations of the idea that philosophy is its age comprehended in thought.[51]

In his Jena essay on natural right Hegel had already developed this motif in direct connection with the concept of Ethical Life. Science, he says, is the empirical condition of the world reflected in the mirror of thought [*ideelen Spiegel*]. The form of Ethical Life in which a people develop themselves is bound by the limits of their geographical-climatic and world-historical location, just as the life of fish and birds is bound to the elements of water and air. As these elements condition the development of a people's life together, so that life in turn conditions the higher levels of spiritual expression, not excluding philosophy. It too must learn to honor its necessity and to overcome the individuality and contingency of its world by penetrating and enlivening it, not by fleeing from it.[52]

The reason for this is the organic character of spiritual life, expressed in the Preface by the metaphors of the oak tree and the newborn child.[53] Not only is there continuity of development in time, such that each stage must be seen as part of the whole process, but at any given stage of development the parts are organically related to one another in the whole. Thus the Germans, who (in 1803) are "a dissolved people" whose political institutions are only the "dead husks" of a form of life no longer present, live in political heteronomy and untruth. But since such an untruth is an "inner untruth of the whole" one cannot expect to find truth anywhere among them, in their social life, their religion, or their philosophy.[54]

What we have before us is a full-fledged theory of ideology, which can hardly be said to have originated with Marx. For it was Hegel to whom we owe the discovery that "a radical critique of knowledge is possible only as social theory."[55] Habermas, whose formulation this is, argues that Hegel was too much in the grip of the philosophy of identity to carry out such a program consistently or even formulate it clearly. Whether the *Phenomenology* carries out such a program consistently we cannot tell without reading it. But that Hegel failed to formulate such a program clearly, giving it as the standard by which his work is to be measured, does not seem to be a fair reading of his Preface against the background of his earlier writings.

Of course this is not a materialist theory of ideology. One will look in vain for any consistent ordering of the various elements as basis and superstructure. A careful examination of Hegel's usage will turn up more than enough evidence to make him into Marx or Weber, but only as long as the contradictory evidence is ignored. His practice, which suggests the model of mutual interaction within an organism, is consistent with his earliest formulation: "The spirit of a people, their history, religion, and level of political freedom should not be considered in isolation from either their influence on one another or their own constitution. They are interwoven into a single cord." Perhaps with reference to his friendship with Schelling and Hölderlin at Tübingen, Hegel compares the different moments to three colleagues each of whom can do nothing on his own apart from what he has incorporated from the others.[56]

Now it is no longer puzzling why Hegel should think that "the seriousness of the concept" presupposes "the seriousness of that fulness of life which leads to the experience of the Absolute [*die Sache selbst,* used in this context repeatedly for the subject matter of philosophy]."[57] Nor is it puzzling that the heart of his philosophy, the concept of the Absolute as Spirit, should belong to "the new age and its religion;"[58] that epistemological discussions about the relation of thought to actuality should involve "all important human interests," especially the effort to achieve a harmonious human life;[59] that Science and the Kingdom of God should be so intimately connected;[60] that the difference between religious autonomy and heteronomy should be so closely bound to the difference between political freedom and slavery;[61] that the faith-philosophy of Kant, Jacobi, and Fichte is a fundamentally Protestant form of thought, whose discussions about finite and infinite, real and ideal, sensible and supersensible, etc., belong to the ongoing debate over faith, as positive religion, and reason;[62] and that the metaphysical discussion of finite and infinite is identical with the theological question of nature and grace.[63]

2C. The Medical Function of Philosophy:
a) Midwifery

At the heart of the idea of ideology is the claim that theoretical thought is not autonomous, that our ideas are conditioned by our interests and our situation. In the twentieth century this has come to be almost taken for granted. While the term 'ideology' is used only in special contexts, the basic insight finds some sort of expression in almost every philosophical tradition. It is, of course, fundamental to Marxism and pragmatism. It is implicit in Wittgenstein's suggestion that language is a form of life, and it underlies the turn from "ideal language" philosophy to "ordinary language" philosophy. It has received detailed development in the phenomenological tradition, and a whole new discipline, the sociology of knowledge has arisen on its foundation. Especially in these last two traditions insight into the social and existential conditioning of thought, including philosophical thought, entailing "the historically changing nature of mind," has brought with it "the vertigo of relativity."[64] Whether it is called historicism, psychologism, perspectivism, or whatever; and whether it is seen as a peril to be avoided at all costs, as a fate to be courageously accepted, or as a tough question to be sidestepped so that research can continue—relativity is the shadow under which the heteronomy of theory is discussed. Platonism is alive and well in our day, at least in its assumption that truth and becoming make poor bedfellows.

Hegel sees things, if the expression may be forgiven, from a different perspective. He too, as we have seen, recognizes the dependence of thought on its life-world, and he does not seek to escape the consequence of this, the historically particular nature of all theory. As Merleau-Ponty puts it, "There is not one of our ideas or one of our reflexions which does not carry a date." Even the thought of the philosopher is "not without roots," but "is always situated and always individuated."[65] But Hegel is not embarrassed by this fact and he is not smitten by "the vertigo of relativity." In contrast to the Platonism of our contemporaries, his thought, at least on this point, can be described as biblical, for he finds history to be the medium for divine revelation. So rather than focusing on the timelessness which philosophy cannot have and should not seek, he directs us to the timeliness it can and should achieve if it is willing to think its present world rather than trying to be the formaldehyde in which a passing form of life is preserved. Rather than asking whether thought can ever be absolute in being unconditioned by life, he asks whether the human existence which ever comes to expression in thought can itself become absolute by becoming the Kingdom of God. After all, the relativity of thought conditioned by a world which is the Kingdom of God is a relativity which even the most ardent Platonist might be willing to accept.

The question, then, is where the Kingdom of God is breaking into human history. Hegel did not view the Holy Roman Empire during the last years of its existence as that Kingdom. So he said of his analysis of its internal contradictions, "The thoughts contained in this essay cannot have any other aim or effect upon publication than the understanding of that which is, and thus to promote calmer contemplation as well as the ability to endure it . . ."[66] But he does not believe that calm endurance is the appropriate reaction to every possible state of affairs. Rosenkranz gives us a fragment from the Jena period in which Hegel looks forward to a new, post-Protestant religion "in which the infinite pain and the entire weight of Spirit's disharmony is acknowledged but at the same time serenely and purely dissolved, if there should be a free people and reason's reality should be born again as an ethical [*sittlichen*] Spirit which can have the audacity to take its pure form from its own soil and its own majesty." If individuals are not to participate in this new spiritual life blindly, they require a knowledge of what is going on. "This knowledge which comprehends the whole energy of the suffering and disharmony which has ruled the world and all forms of its cultural development for some thousand years and at the same time rises above it—this knowledge philosophy alone can provide."[67]

Philosophy's immersion in history does not mean that it can create the new religion and the free people *ex nihilo,* giving birth itself to the Kingdom of God. Rather, its role is to provide insight instead of blindness before the historical process, which does not proceed at the philosopher's beck and call. It brings the new age and its religion to the form of the concept.[68] But in this instance the result of an "understanding of that which is" cannot be calm endurance. The knowledge which philosophy provides at such a moment of birth does not exclude the memory of morning sickness and labor pains with all their agony. But its keynote is the joyous realization, "Unto us a son is born."

By giving insight into historical developments philosophy serves in a Socratic way. The historical process is an organic development which continually gives birth to new forms of life and thought. In the difficult and even unhappy times of birth,[69] philosophy assists as midwife, not as the giver of life. As Socrates examines the newly born thoughts of individuals to see whether they are genuine or spurious ($\alpha\lambda\eta\theta\eta\varsigma$ or $\psi\epsilon\nu\delta\eta\varsigma$), and, as he tells Theaetetus, if he finds them to be but phantoms ($\epsilon\iota\delta\omega\lambda\sigma$), "I take the abortion from you and cast it away," so Hegel sees philosophy as examining the new offspring of the age to see whether they are viable forms of human life, whether the appropriate response is endurance or enthusiasm, whether they should be nourished or starved.[70] In this way philosophy can serve its contemporaries, needing neither to flee from its time nor to succumb to it.

Fichte had reintroduced this motif into philosophy when, decrying the shallowness of the age, he described the current form of the Kantian philosophy as "the most fantastic abortion that has ever been produced by the human imagination."[71] In *Faith and Knowledge* Hegel suggests the same verdict for Kant

himself, not just the Kantians, along with Jacobi and Fichte.[72]
Then in the Preface he not only announces that "our time is a
time of birth and transition to a new period," indicating that a
genuine birth has taken place; he also practices his art of critical
midwifery on those romantic enthusaists who flee conceptual
thought and believe themselves to be "His beloved to whom
God gives wisdom in sleep. What they thus conceive and give
birth to in sleep are, naturally, dreams."[73] In other words, to
the age which gave birth to both critical finitism and romantic
irrationalism his message is that of Socrates, "I take these abortions from you and cast them away."

2D. The Medical Function of Philosophy:
b) Socioanalysis

Midwifery can be a dangerous art, as Socrates discovered.
Like a bear robbed of her whelps the age is likely to turn on any
midwife who does not treat all its offspring as a campaigning
politician would. Yet Hegel knows he has no choice but to rely
on the one weapon which failed Socrates, persuasion. Like all
the arts, this one requires knowledge; but unlike most arts, this
one cannot be practiced unless it can be taught. That is, the
philosophical midwife can perform his services only by implant-
ing in the patient his own understanding of the situation.

Psychoanalysis is such an art. We are reminded that in the
Introduction Hegel seemed to commit himself to something
like a psychoanalysis of the anxiety critical finitism displays
about its capacity to be in touch with the Absolute. It is now
clear that this depth diagnosis of the age will be absolutely essential to the practice of philosophical midwifery espoused in
the Preface, though it now looks as if socioanalysis would be a
better name for the process. Here the Introduction and Preface
are united. Coming from the direction of the Introduction and
its epistemological concerns, the necessity for socioanalysis is
linked to the task of deepening the reflections of transcendental philosophy. Coming from the direction of the Preface and its concerns about the historical crisis of the era, this
necessity derives from the responsibility of philosophy to serve
its times without simply being their child. But there is only a

single task—to show the age its sickness, freeing it from its doting on the phantoms and dreams it takes to be glorious progeny, thereby freeing it for something better.

Hegel has one enormous advantage over Socrates, who, in his famous ignorance found nothing but abortions in the Athenian wisdom. Hegel has bad news for his contemporaries too, but like John the Baptist he calls them to repentance out of the persuasion that the Kingdom of God is at hand.

Only the sketchiest glimpse of this Kingdom which Hegel announces is available to us before we plunge into the text; but a more nearly complete picture of the diagnosis which grounds his call to repentance can be given. Its elements are already before us, though not in the form of a systematic answer to the Introduction's question about the deepest roots of contemporary scepticism.

The life-world of critical philosophy is structured by Judeo-Christian religious traditions and the newer traditions of the modern scientific revolution. The linking of critical philosophy to these two factors is an echo in the Preface of the argument of *Faith and Knowledge*. Critical finitism is there described as the systematic expression of a culture of common sense [*gemeiner Menschenverstand*],[74] a culture in turn repeatedly described as, on the one hand, Protestant, and on the other, a Lockean-Humean culture, i.e., one intoxicated with the exploits of Newton.

A third dimension of the same world has also been uncovered, present but less conspicuous than the other two in both the Preface and *Faith and Knowledge*. It is the political-social sphere, without which neither Hegel's conception of substantial life nor his idea of the divine presence can be understood. This is because politics and religion are not independent variables for Hegel, but are like the convex and concave sides of an arc.

In these terms we can summarize Hegel's view of the old modernity quite simply. It was structured by protestant Christianity, the new scientific outlook, and a political perspective best described as privatism. What remains is to indicate how each of these elements contributes to the social neurosis Hegel seeks to diagnose.

If we ask what sort of religious life would come to philosophical expression as an anxiety about the remoteness of the Absolute and the possible inability of reason to grasp it, the answer is easy. Any form of religious heteronomy is likely to do so. By the time Hegel wrote the *Phenomenology* he had come to view Christianity as reconciling rather than alienating in its essence. But he still retained the view, so outspoken in his earlier writings, that both its original and subsequent historical manifestations had the form of extreme heteronomy.

On this score Protestantism is seen as an intensification of the heteronomous elements of Christianity. Catholicism at least borrowed some of the beautiful elements of paganism.[75] In its concern for orthodoxy, Protestantism enforced correct belief from above, by the theologians if possible, by the police and army if necessary.[76] In this respect there was an equality of heteronomy, but only a formal one. Materially there was an important difference. On Hegel's view the inner motif which makes the enforcement of orthodoxy necessary to Protestantism is bound up with one of its most fundamental distinctives, its view of nature and grace. It is the total depravity of man and his total dependence on divine grace which requires his particular dependence on divine revelation for knowing God and the good.[77] For Hegel (as for Luther) no aspect of Protestantism is more prominent or distinctive than man's sinful impotence before God and his complete dependence on divine mercy. "Theological prejudices about a congenital depravity of human nature," which are derived from "artful exegesis," are "constantly pounded into the memory and conscience of the common man," with the result that what is healthy, powerful, and active in him is destroyed.[78] As the life-world becomes Protestant human self-confidence is undermined and God becomes *Deus absconditus,* the Wholly Other.

This is why Hegel sees the *Critique of Pure Reason* as a palimpsest on which Luther's experience of guilt and grace can still be read beneath arguments about synthetic a priori judgments. After all, the epistemological implications of Protestantism did not have to await Kant for their formulation. Luther himself drew them in his own scathing denunciations of human reason. The peculiarity of Kant's position, on this view, is that he accepts Protestantism's bad news about the capacities of human reason without accepting the corresponding good news about revelation and grace.

The political and social character of the modern world can scarcely be unrelated in Hegel's mind to this religious character. At Jena this is put in terms of Ethical Life rather than folk religion, but the point is the same. The living customs of a people should be expressed both in universal form as their laws and institutions, and in particular form as the God of the people, who is intuited and worshipped in their cultic life. But when a nation is losing its spiritual life and "is not able to sense and enjoy the image of divinity in itself, but places this outside itself . . . then vassalage and bondage have absolute truth, and this condition is the one possible form of Ethical Life, and thus the necessary, the right, and the ethical [*sittliche*] form."[79]

It is this same correlation which had earlier enabled Hegel to explain the triumph of Christianity as a slave religion over the pagan religions of free men in terms of the disappearance of political freedom and participation under the despotism of the Roman emperors. The loss of public virtue among the Romans, together with the corresponding success of Christianity, mean that private life comes to be all important for the individual, the security and expansion of his property his major worldly project.[80]

Since the triumph of private over public, of independence over participation, has this economic dimension, political despotism is not its only possible origin. It can arise directly from economic conditions, and in the modern world it is the rise of the bourgeoisie which Hegel pinpoints as the source of that individualism which dissolves a people into the war of all against all; though at times he simplistically blames the "stubborness" of the German character, which has always defined freedom as independence rather than participation. In making this analysis he does not neglect to mention the happy harmony between bourgeois economic privatism and Protestant religious inwardness.[81]

What this dimension of the life-world contributes to critical finitism should not be too hard to see. The altogether finite individual pursuing his private economic advantage does so at the mercy of two impersonal, remote, and at times apparently hostile powers, the Market and the State. They are the infinite whose workings are neither comprehensible nor controllable, especially during the period under consideration. The lesson of religious humility which was taught on Sunday was reinforced by a lesson of political-economic humility during the rest of the week. Not even economic success worked to counteract this. It was more natural to see this too in terms of the grace of God.

There is another, possibly more important consideration. If, as Hegel suggests, the divine is simply the living customs of a people or their national genius intuited in the form of particularity, then the replacement of common participation in public life by competition in private life can hardly increase man's sense of the divine presence. The absence of the divine becomes less a religious teaching than an everyday experience. Such experience might well take epistemic form as a theory of knowledge as the instrument for grasping a recalcitrant Absolute not already with us from the start; all the more so if the gradual rationalizing of economic life, in Weber's sense, involves an everyday familiarity with a thoroughly instrumental sort of economic know-how.

Finally, if the value of instrumental knowledge belongs to what is taken for granted in the economic zones of the early modern world, this is even more true in the scientific realm. For Hegel there is a strong link between modern science and Protestantism, viewed as a religion of the heart, of feeling, of yearning after an absent God. And why is God absent? At least in part because his intuition has been denied by the understanding, which knows what is intuited only as a thing, the sacred grove only a timber. [82] Timber is very useful in countless ways, and the reason understanding can see the forest only as timber and not as a sacred grove is that it is that form of man's intellectual capacity which has learned to understand things in terms of their usefulness, to produce the kind of knowledge which will extend man's power over nature.

This instrumentalism is only part of what Hegel is getting at here. He is equally concerned about what we would call positivism, the view which makes the natural sciences the paradigm of knowing and tends to discredit all knowledge claims which cannot be assimilated to that model. In this context it is man's power and accomplishments rather than his weakness and finitude which are front and center. The results of the exact sciences are so impressive in their clarity, their certainty, and their usefulness, that they are easily taken to be the highest use of reason. When this happens a reality that is finite and a knowing that is empirical tend to be absolutized. It is no wonder then, that the sacred grove is reduced to timber, a potentially useful object of empirical knowledge. When it is a question of knowing what is infinite, for which empirical methods are demonstrably unsuited, it is natural that there should be a fear that this might not be possible; and it is just as natural that this fear should become the dogmatic conviction that whatever cannot be known by the application of knowledge as a formal instrument (categories, logical-mathematical calculi, etc.) to a sensible subject matter is unreal, and that all other attempts at knowing are sophistry.[83]

It may be that "the eye of the Spirit had to be directed forcibly to the things of this earth and kept there," and that the scientific revolution took a long time to make itself felt in common sense.[84] It is not easy to get people to live in the cave once "the significance of all that is" has derived from "the thread of light that tied it to heaven." But when people have lived in the cave long enough to make it their home and have learned how to furnish it with an ever increasing standard of living, we know how they will respond to anyone who challenges the cave's ultimacy by, e.g., seeking to develop another form of knowing in terms of the ontological argument or claiming that nature is not only *natura naturata* but also *natura naturans.*[85]

Humility before God, the Market, and the State. Confidence concerning the certainty and usefulness of instrumental knowledge in economics and natural science. Such in brief is Hegel's view of the old modernity he bids his contemporaries abandon in favor of the new modernity whose John the Baptist he purports to be. The old modernity is the Protestant, bourgeois, scientific life-world out of which critical philosophy arose. Its critique can only be the examination of this life-world, and its transcendence can only come about through the actual transcendence of this life-world. When Fackenheim claims that the Hegelian philosophy assumes the ultimacy of "the modern bourgeois Protestant world," and views this as "in principle final and indestructible," the seminal form of the Kingdom of God, we shall ask whether this is intended to apply to the *Phenomenology.*[86] As we come to the main body of the text we have every reason to expect that it is precisely as the modern world is becoming post-Protestant and post-bourgeois (as well as post-positivist) that Hegel is able to detect any seminal ultimacy in it.

The stages of Hegel's argument follow from this analysis. First, there will be an analysis of natural scientific knowledge to see whether the imperialistic majesty attributed to it is justified. (Chapters Three and Four) There will follow an examination of man's political and social life to see whether community and freedom are as irreconcilable in essence as they have come to be in fact. The religious dimension of social life will emerge in this examination. (Chapters Five and Six) Finally, there will be a description of religious life itself, not neglecting its social dimensions, and the implications of the whole project for philosophy will be drawn. (Chapters Seven and Eight) Only if a new life-world has shown itself to be in the making can there be any promise of a new philosophy in the system to which the reader is introduced by the *Phenomenology*.

If all goes as planned the three examinations which lead to whatever conclusions we find at the end will not be carried out by either Hegel or the reader. "Consciousness examines itself." In other words, Hegel will only be calling our attention to things that are happening in the modern world. Our contribution is simply to watch carefully in order to see what is there to be seen.

NOTES

1. PhG, VI/12/70.
2. PhG, XXXV/27/90.
3. PhG, XLII-XLIV/32-33/96-97.
4. Kroner, *Von Kant bis Hegel,* Tübingen, 1961, II, 374. Marcuse, *Reason and Revolution,* Boston, 1960, p. 23.
5. PhG, VIII/13/71-72. In this paragraph Hegel uses both *das Wesen* and *der Substanz* as synonyms for the Absolute. For a similar use of the former see *Volksreligion,* HTJ, 3, 5, 25, and Fragment #3, HTJ, 361.
6. PhG, X-XI/14/73.
7. PhG, IX/13/72. When Hegel speaks of "the concept" he does not mean any particular concept in the usual sense, but the whole of Science, conceptual knowledge of what truly is.
8. *The Crisis of European Sciences and Transcendental Phenomenology,* tr. Carr, Evanston, 1970, pp. 2, 12, 14.
9. *Glauben,* GW, 4:360.
10. *Differenz,* GW, 4:12-14.
11. PCR I, HTJ, 223-24/156-58. cf. *Volksreligion,* HTJ, 71.
12. PCR I, HTJ, 177/101.
13. PCR II, HTJ, 148-50/178-80.
14. SC, HTJ, 253-54/196, 260/204-05.
15. Fragment #2, HTJ, 359.
16. PCR I, HTJ, 208-09/139-40.
17. PCR I, HTJ, 163/82.
18. Fragment #2, HTJ, 360.
19. SC, HTJ, 327-29/283-87.
20. PCR I, HTJ, 227/162. cf. 224-25/158-59.
21. SC, HTJ, 341-42/301.
22. PCR I, HTJ, 220/152; *Volksreligion,* HTJ, 26-27, 54; Fragment #1, HTJ, 357.
23. SC, HTJ, 249-51/190-92; *Volksreligion,* HTJ, 26.
24. PCR I, HTJ, 215/146-47. cf. Fragment #2, HTJ, 359.
25. *Volksreligion,* HTJ, 24-25; Fragment #1, HTJ, 355.
26. Rosenkranz, *Georg Wilhelm Friedrich Hegels Leben,* Darmstadt, 1963, pp. 10 f. For the letter from Hegel's sister see Kaufmann (as cited in Ch. 1, n. 61), p. 299.
27. Rosenkranz, *op. cit.,* pp. 11, 25-27.
28. From the *Lebenslauf (curriculum vitae)* submitted by Hegel in

1804 for his promotion at Jena. The text appears in HTJ, IX, and in *Briefe von und an Hegel*, IV, 91-92.

29. The development of the Greek ideal at Jena comes primarily in *Naturrecht* and *Sittlichkeit*. As a technical term *Sittlichkeit* comes to be practically synonymous with Hegel's whole view of the Greek experience, at least during the Jena period. This whole section (2A) can be taken as its extended contextual definition, especially the sentence on p. 32. "Man lived in a whole which was at once religious, ethical, and political, and the individual felt himself to be an inherent part of that whole."

30. *Volksreligion*, HTJ, 62.

31. *Volksreligion*, HTJ, 20.

32. *Volksreligion*, HTJ, 14, 21, 23. cf. all of PCR II.

33. PCR I, HTJ, 194-95/122-23.

34. PCR II, HTJ, 139-44/167-74.

35. *Volksreligion*, HTJ, 26,39.

36. PhG, XI/14/73. See note 6 above.

37. PhG, XI-XII/15/74.

38. For a brief discussion see the editor's introduction to Hoffmeister's edition of the PhG. Though he quarrels with the specifics of this Haering-Hoffmeister thesis, Otto Pöggeler gives, if anything, more emphasis to the tension between the Introduction and the Preface. See *"Zur Deutung der Phänomenologie des Geistes,"* Hegel-Studien, Band 1, 1961, and *"Die Komposition der Phänomenologie des Geistes,"* Hegel-Studien, Beiheft 3, 1966.

39. See Ch. 1, n. 25.

40. PhG, LXXXVII/56/127.

41. PhG, XXVIII/24/85-86.

42. *Briefe von und an Hegel*, I, 18; HP, SW, 17:20/I, XII.

43. PhG, VI-VIII/12-13/70-71.

44. In the title essay of *Traditionelle und kritische Theorie*, Hamburg, 1968, Max Horkheimer writes of the Kantian philosophy that in it *"die gesellschaftliche Aktivität erscheint als transzendentale Macht, das heisst als Inbegriff geistiger Faktoren . . . Das Zusammenwirken der Menschen in der Gesellschaft ist die Existenzweise ihrer Vernunft . . ."* pp. 24-25.

45. PhG, VI-VIII/12-13/70-71.

46. *Glauben*, GW, 4:323 and PhG, XIII/15/75. This theme of a new age was expressed in Hegel's final Jena lecture. "We stand at the gates of an important epoch, a time of ferment, when Spirit moves forward in a leap, transcends its previous shape and takes on a new one. All the

mass of previous representations, concepts, and bonds linking our world together, are dissolving and collapsing like a dream picture. A new phase of the Spirit is preparing itself. Philosophy especially has to welcome its appearance and acknowledge it, while others, who oppose it impotently, cling to the past." As he returned to university life ten years later, this theme was much on his mind. In an address from 1815 we read, "We must oppose this mood which always uselessly misses the past and yearns for it. That which is old is not to be deemed excellent just because it is old . . . The world has given birth to a great epoch." In 1816 Hegel writes to Niethammer, "I stand by my belief that the world spirit has given [our] time the order to advance. This order is being obeyed." And in an essay on the proceedings of the Württemberg Estates, published in 1817, Hegel writes, "One might say of the Württemberg Estates what has been said of the returned French emigres: they have forgotten nothing and learnt nothing. They seem to have slept through the last twenty-five years, possibly the richest that world history has had, and for us the most instructive, because it is to them that our world and our ideas belong." Quoted from Schlomo Avineri, *Hegel's Theory of the Modern State,* Cambridge, 1972, pp. 64, 71, 72, and 74.

47. PhG, XIII-XVII/15-17/75-77. For both aspects at once, see the conclusion of the Preface, LXXXVIII-XC/57-58/128-29.

48. PhG, VI/11/70, LXXXIV-LXXXVI/55-56/125-27. cf. XXXIX/30/94.

49. PhG, XIV/16/76.

50. *Glauben,* GW, 4:323.

51. See the Preface to *The Philosophy of Right* and HP, SW, 17:82-86/I, 51-55.

52. *Naturrecht,* GW, 4:419, 479.

53. PhG, III-IV/10/68.

54. *Naturrecht,* GW, 4:483.

55. Jürgen Habermas, *Knowledge and Human Interests,* tr. Shapiro, Boston, 1971, p. VII.

56. *Volksreligion,* HTJ, 27.

57. PhG, VI/12/70.

58. See note 41 above.

59. See note 10 above.

60. See notes 41 and 42 above.

61. See the first section of this chapter.

62. *Glauben,* Introduction.

63. PCR II, HTJ, 146/175-76.

64. Karl Mannheim, *Ideology and Utopia*, tr. Wirth and Shils, New York, 1936, p. 67, and Peter Berger and Thomas Luckman, *The Social Construction of Reality*, Garden City, 1966, p. 5. These are two important works in the sociology of knowledge. From the phenomenological tradition perhaps the most important works are Heidegger's *Being and Time*, especially sections 12-16 and 29-33, Husserl's *Crisis*, and Merleau-Ponty's essay, "The Primacy of Perception" (see following note).

65. *The Primacy of Perception and Other Essays*, ed. Edie, Evanston, 1964, pp. 41, 48, 51.

66. *The German Constitution, Werke*, I, 463/145. For this translation see Kaufmann (as cited in Ch. 1, n. 61), p. 107.

67. Rosenkranz, *op. cit.*, p. 141.

68. See note 41 above.

69. *Naturrecht*, GW, 4:484.

70. *Theaetetus*, 149a-151c, Cornford translation.

71. *First Introduction to the Science of Knowledge*, in Fichte (as cited in Ch. 1, n. 32), 12n., *Werke*, I, 430n.

72. *Glauben*, GW, 4:315.

73. PhG, XII-XIII/15/74-75.

74. *Glauben*, GW, 4:322.

75. Fragment #1, HTJ, 359.

76. *Volksreligion*, HTJ, 42; Fragment #1, HTJ, 356; PCR I, HTJ, 194-95/122.

77. PCR I, HTJ, 161-62/79-80.

78. *Volksreligion*, HTJ, 43. cf. pp. 63-69; PCR I, HTJ, 157/74, 205-10/135-42; *Glauben*, GW, 4:405-08. All this sounds as if Hegel had been subjected to the strenuous sort of religious upbringing which Kierkegaard received, filled with intense emotional crises in childhood and adolescence. The evidence is quite to the contrary.

79. *Naturrecht*, GW, 4:470, 480; *Sittlichkeit*, pp. 54-55.

80. *Volksreligion*, HTJ, 70-71; PCR I, HTJ, 219-230/151-65; SC, HTJ, 273/221, 327/284; "Fragment of a System," HTJ, 349/315; *Naturrecht*, GW, 4:456-57. Note especially the quotation from Gibbon in this last reference.

81. *Naturrecht*, GW, 4:458, 468; *The German Constitution, Werke*, I, 516-17/189-90.

82. *Glauben*, GW, 4:316-17.

83. This is the heart of Hegel's argument in *Glauben* and *Skepticis-mus.*

84. See note 6 above.

85. *Glauben,* GW, 4:35-38; *Skepticismus,* GW, 4:223.

86. Emil Fackenheim, *The Religious Dimension in Hegel's Thought,* Bloomington, 1967, pp. 232-33.

CHAPTER THREE

The Knowledge of Nature:

A) **Sense Perception**

3A. "The Truth is the Whole" as Hermeneutical Guide

In view of the scope and boldness of the phenomenological task as described in the Introduction and Preface it is surprising that Hegel's book should be as short as it is. It is, nevertheless, a very long book, and it is not surprising that the old saw about Mom's hash being so good because "She put everything she had into it" could so easily be used to caricature comments frequently directed against the *Phenomenology*. Hegel made hash out of what might have been a good book, so the story goes, because under pressure of the imminent disruption of life at Jena by Napoleon's armies, he threw into one book just about everything he was thinking about at the time.

But Hegel's claim is that "the truth is the whole." This means not only that his philosophy can only supersede other philosophies by including them, but also that philosophy as such can validate its truth claims only by including those non-philosophical forms of experience which make a claim on the truth.[1] Just as the truth about the plant is neither the bud, nor the blossom, nor even the fruit by itself, but rather the whole process in which each plays its necessary part, thereby retaining its radical difference from the others, so the whole truth about knowledge may turn out to be quite complex.[2] It may have to include not only the discussion of such obvious topics as sense perception and physical science, but even the analysis of "the madness of Diderot's musician . . . [and] the fanaticism of Marat and Robespierre."[3]

We can at least be thankful that Hegel begins where we would expect a treatise on knowledge to begin, with sense perception and our knowledge of the external world. But even here we run into the problem of totality and inclusion; for there is more philosophy going on in the three chapters collectively entitled Consciousness than the reader can possibly dream of in a single reading. To begin with, at least three major moments in

59

the history of philosophy are narrated here simultaneously. Each of them provides a different but indispensable perspective for understanding the significance of Hegel's descriptions.

One way of reading these chapters is as a re-telling of Plato's *Theaetetus*. The parallel is threefold. With natural consciousness in the role of Theaetetus, Hegel's method is that of Socratic dialogue. At least his claim would be that "the arguments never come out of me, they always come from the person I am talking with. I am only at a slight advantage in having the skill to get some account of the matter for another's wisdom and entertain it with fair treatment . . . So I will have recourse to the wisdom of Theaetetus."[4] The result is equally Socratic. At the end of the chapters on Consciousness we can say that we have learned a lot, but not that we know what knowledge is, which was, of course, the question at issue.

The final and most important parallel is that between the three answers given by Theaetetus to the question What is knowledge? and the three answers given by natural consciousness under Hegel's questioning. When Theaetetus says first that knowledge is perception he means to identify knowledge with the direct and unreflected having or enjoying of the rich, concrete, sensory content given in perception. It is such a view which Hegel describes as Sense Certainty. When Theaetetus is reminded that such a view makes it impossible to preserve the connection between knowledge and truth, since one can "see" what isn't there, he replies that knowledge is true judgment. Already this implies that knowledge is complex enough to involve the difference between subject and predicate, referring and describing, substance and quality. It is no longer the passive having of sheer sensations, but involves the active discrimination by the knower of features in the field of knowledge. It is this view of knowledge which Hegel calls Perception. Finally, Theaetetus is led to see knowledge as true judgment with the addition of an account or reason [λογος]. Merely to assert the truth is not to know, for that can happen quite by accident. To know is to be able to ground one's correct judgments, to recognize their truth by relating them to other truths, thus weaving them into the whole fabric of truth. This is the project Hegel calls Understanding.

To follow only these clues, however, would be to miss entirely another story that Hegel is here re-telling. This is the story of modern natural science. The transition from Perception to Understanding highlights the way scientific knowledge is rooted in our everyday perception of the external world, which perception it in turn uproots. The development within Understanding traces the replacing of the Aristotelian physics of forces with the Galilean-Newtonian physics of laws. An integral part of this story is its first philosophical telling by Bacon and Descartes, Locke and Hume. In this tradition epistemology becomes identical with philosophy of science. For the question—What is knowledge?—is answered not so much by establishing the claim of the exact natural sciences to be knowledge as by assuming them to be and simply analyzing their method. The question about knowledge becomes the question—How is science possible?

By recapitulating this tradition Hegel is led, as the wording of the last question suggests, to a third story which Hegel wants us to re-hear, the one about Kant and his Copernican Revolution. The analysis of the Here, the Now, and the I of Sense Certainty can be read as another deduction of space, time, and the transcendental unity of apperception as a priori conditions of the possibility of experience. The constitution of objects in space and time by and for the transcendental ego, and particularly the role of the category of substance in this constitution are the Kantian themes underlying the discussion of "things" and their "properties" in the chapter on Perception. Then the chapter on Understanding restates Kant's discovery of the importance of rules and the concept of nature in general for the way we experience objects. It can thus be read as a further deduction of the categories of cause and reciprocity.

The dialogue between Hegel and natural consciousness in the section on Consciousness is not identical with any one of these three stories, but it can be read fruitfully from the standpoint of each, for each is included in that dialogue. In fact, since for Hegel the truth is the whole, we will understand these chapters as he wants them understood, only if we somehow manage to see them from all three standpoints at once.[5]

This is not, however, the only demand made of the reader

by Hegel's principle of totality. It is not loosely that his narrative is described as a dialogue, for it represents both the experience of natural consciousness and the meta-experience which occurs "for us" as "we" observe the dialectical movement of natural consciousness. To grasp the totality of Hegel's account we must recognize the different levels on which it operates, grasping not only their discreteness but also their interrelation.

Two passages from the Preface throw light on this requirement. Both contrast the movement of natural consciousness, even in some of its highest forms, with another movement of thought which can only be that of the philosophical observer. "The beginning of culture [*Bildung*] and of the struggle to pass out of the immediacy of substantial life has always to be made by acquiring knowledge of universal principles and perspectives, by first working oneself up to the thought of the subject matter in general. It is equally important to support or refute these thoughts with reasons, to grasp the concrete and rich fullness in its determinateness, and to know how to furnish an orderly account and a serious judgment about it."[6]

This movement of thought from original immediacy to the knowledge which grasps its object through the mediation of universals, i.e., in judgment, and then goes on to support its judgments with reasons is the movement of natural consciousness as traced in the *Theaetetus*. Hegel stresses its abstractness. Since thought's labor is *herausarbeiten* and *heraufarbeiten*, thought's movement to the thought of the subject matter in general, *die Sache überhaupt*, is a movement away from *die Sache selbst*, away from the concrete and rich fullness which it set out to think.

"This beginning of culture will, however, very soon make way for the seriousness of life in its fullness, which leads to the experience of the subject matter itself [*die Sache selbst*], and when in addition the seriousness of the concept descends into the depths of the subject matter, knowledge and judgment of the previous kind will keep their due place in conversation."

Over against the thought which owes its achievements to its abstractness there inevitably arises the appeal to concrete experience, to immediacy, to intuition, etc., in the name of seriousness. Enlightenment and Romanticism always go together. But there is another seriousness which distinguishes itself from both. It claims to be more serious than romantic seriousness, for it recognizes the deficiencies of the first attempt to think without assuming that this exhausts the possibilities of conceptual thought. This seriousness of the concept acknowledges the genuineness of the appeal to "the experience of the subject matter itself," but it boldly claims that it is just this experience and this subject matter which it will think. Since it is on the phenomenological path of doubt and despair that the seriousness of the concept is born, it will already begin to appear alongside various modes of natural consciousness. The insights which "we" derive from observing natural consciousness are the initial elements of a different level of conceptual achievement.

A second passage in which the same two modes of thought are contrasted gives a fuller indication of what the second, the seriousness of the concept, is like. Here the abstract mode of thought is attributed to antiquity. "The manner of study in ancient times is distinct from that of the modern world, in that the former was the development of natural consciousness. Testing life carefully at all points, philosophizing about everything it came across, the former created an experience permeated with universals. In modern times, however, an individual finds the abstract form ready made. In striving to grasp it and make it his own, he rather strives to bring forward the inner meaning alone without any process of mediation; the production of the universal is abridged instead of the universal arising out of the concreteness and multiplicity of existence."[7]

Hegel is not willing to rest with this antithesis between two modes of abstractness, the thinking which in its formality and universality abstracts from the subject matter it purports to think and the inevitable reaction which abstracts from conceptual thought in order to restore concrete encounter with the world. "Hence nowadays," he continues, "the task before us consists not so much in getting the individual clear of the stage of sensible immediacy, and making him a substance that thinks and is grasped in terms of thought, but rather the very opposite, namely by breaking down and superseding fixed and determinate thoughts to actualize the universal and infuse it with Spirit . . . Through this movement the pure thoughts become concepts and are then what they are in truth . . . that which is their substance, spiritual entities."

Hegel's remedy for sterile and lifeless thought is not to give up on reason but to transform it by moving from pure thought to concept, or, more specifically, from pure thought to Spirit. Hegel here coins the term *begeisten*. It is translated "enfuse with Spirit" because on the one hand it suggests *begeistern*, to animate, enthuse, or enliven, while on the other hand its own form is *be-Geist-en*. To enfuse the universal with Spirit is not only to enliven otherwise dead thought. It is to re-establish the connection between pure thought and its own living source by showing that pure thoughts belong to Spirit and are indeed *geistige Wesenheiten*, spiritual entities. Once again we must be able to move back and forth between two distinct levels of rational activity.

The full significance of this can only come with the development of the concept of Spirit (in Chapter Five below). But the following important implications are given in the paragraph already before us. "Thought determinations get their substance and the element of their existence from the ego," and "thoughts become fluent when pure thinking, this inner immediacy, knows itself as a moment, when pure certainty of self abstracts from itself. It does not 'abstract' in the sense of getting away from itself and setting itself on one side, but of surrendering the fixed quality of its self-affirmation, and giving up both the fixity of the purely concrete—which is the ego as contrasted with the variety of its content—and the fixity of all those distinctions, which are present in the element of pure thought and share that unconditionedness of the ego."[8]

This movement is twofold. First comes the Copernican Revolution, the discovery of the transcendental role of the thinking subject. The Cartesian ego, the "substance that thinks and is grasped in terms of thought," comes to know itself as a moment of its own knowledge, as the origin of the thought determinations which make its knowledge possible. But this is only half of what it means to *begeisten* the universal. When thought recognizes itself as a moment in the process of knowledge it also recognizes its own relativity. In abandoning the fixity of its self-affirmation both as the transcendental unity of apperception and as the determinate categories by which that unity is maintained, it abandons "that unconditionedness of the ego" which it claims for itself in the element of pure thought.

Just as the transcendental turn deprives the object of its fixity by showing that it is not simply given, this second move is the discovery that the subject is not simply self-posited.

In this sense one can ask within the Hegelian context a question which is meaningless in the Cartesian, Kantian, and Fichtean context—*Who is the transcendental subject?* It is precisely the meaningfulness of this question which brings us to the realm of Spirit. At least part of the secret of this crucial but elusive concept is found in the idea that a phenomenology of Spirit will be a transcendental philosophy which sees the transcendental ego as conditioned. While it is too early to say that for Hegel "the achievements of the transcendental subject have their basis in the natural history of the human species,"[9] one can at least begin to see how some such formula might be necessary.

What these two passages indicate is that we must distinguish three different levels in Hegel's analysis of our knowledge of the external world. 1) There is the presentation of the different ways in which the object is grasped, first by pre-scientific everyday consciousness as the thing and its properties, and then by the two forms of scientific understanding as the interplay of forces and as the exemplification of universal laws. 2) There is then the reflective discovery of the active role of consciousness in all of that first order knowing. 3) Then there is the further reflective discovery of the contingent character of that transcendental activity, however necessary it may be in relation to the objects constituted by it.

These last two levels are what make up the "descent into the depths" which is the *Be-Geist-ung* of thought. Here thought overcomes the fallacy of misplaced concreteness and ceases to mistake the product of its own abstracting acts for the independently and genuinely real. It then learns to view those acts themselves concretely in the context from which they arise. These discoveries are, on the one hand, the introduction to the realm of Spirit; on the other hand, they are the scepticism of which the Introduction speaks, the "conscious insight into the untruth of phenomenal knowledge," and the "despair over notions, thoughts, and opinions which are called natural." The untruth of phenomenal knowledge is due to its incompleteness, whereas the truth is the whole. Everyday perception and

natural science are genuine modes of knowing. But until they
are seen as parts of the whole which makes them possible, they
remain untrue from a philosophical point of view. Their object
cannot be understood apart from their subject and their subject
cannot be understood apart from the historical life of Spirit.

3B. The Mediated Character of Sense Perception

Sense Certainty has not yet learned any of these lessons,
but Hegel's task is not exactly to teach. His "method" here as
elsewhere is to observe the contradiction between the criterion
by which a form of natural consciousness seeks to validate its
knowledge and the actual knowledge which it produces. Such a
contradiction comes to light in the first sentence on Sense Certainty. On the one hand it wishes to be "immediate knowledge."
On the other it purports to be "knowledge of the immediate or
of what is [das Seinde]." Having this object it claims to be the
"richest" knowledge, for it has an infinite wealth of concrete
content available to it, all that is to be seen, heard, smelled,
tasted, and touched. The tree here, the house over there, and
the whole world to which they belong—these are the riches of
Sense Certainty.

At the same time Sense Certainty claims to be the "truest"
knowledge and not only the "richest". For as immediate knowledge it has its object complete and unadulterated. Nothing has
been added to it or taken from it by the knowing subject, to
whom it is simply given. Since Sense Certainty is in this way the
"truest" knowledge in relation to the riches of its content, it
leaves no room for error and is also the "truest" with respect to
form. That is, it is the most certain knowledge and deserves to
be called Sense *Certainty*.[10]

But the criterion of immediacy by which Sense Certainty
seeks to elevate sense perception to be both the truest knowledge in itself and the unshakable foundation of all other
knowledge stands in sharpest contradiction to the richness of
the actual knowledge which it takes to be its own. The knowledge which takes this criterion seriously is not the richest, but
the "abstractest and poorest" knowledge of all. It can completely express itself by saying, It is. The rich content of its ob-

ject has been reduced to its mere being, the most indeterminate of all predicates. Sense Certainty knows and can say *that* its object is, but not *what* it is. Any attempt to get beyond this indeterminacy runs afoul of the immediacy criterion, for every determination is a negation, and every negation is a mediation.[11]

Since Hegel seems to presuppose rather than deny that we sometimes do perceive trees, we may suppose that the "it" which "is" is a tree, and that it is perceived as a tree. But for the object of perception to be a tree, it has to have certain qualities which determine it as a tree and distinguish it from say, a computer or an igloo. But this is already to introduce mediation, for the tree can be a tree and not merely an "it is" only by virtue of its negative relation to other things. At the same time, to perceive the tree as a tree is to perceive it as not a computer and not an igloo. The determinate is given as such to consciousness only by the mediating act which distinguishes it from what it is not. Once again immediacy is lost.

This is not what Sense Certainty had intended. From its perspective, "I, this particular I, am certain of this thing, not because I develop myself as consciousness in relation to it and in manifold ways set thought to work on it; nor because the thing of which I am certain, in virtue of having a multitude of distinct qualities, is a copious relation to itself or a manifold relation to other things. Neither has anything to do with the truth of Sense Certainty. Neither the I nor the thing has in this domain the meaning of a multi-faceted mediation."[12] But the simple immediacy which avoids these mediations is only the "pure being" or the bare "it is" from which all content has departed. Such knowledge owes its certainty to its emptiness. As with the "knowledge is perception" thesis in the *Theaetetus,* the possibility of truth disappears with the possibility of error.[13]

The contradiction within Sense Certainty is a glaring one. It refutes itself in its opening statement. But just as Plato allows Protagoras to carry on a defense of the knowledge-as-perception view further than Theaetetus is able to, thereby developing his own argument in considerably more detail, so Hegel does not dispose of Sense Certainty without careful examination of its further attempts to extricate itself from the seeming contradiction involved in its claim to be simultaneously determinate and immediate. It suspects that it has let mediation get its nose in the tent by carelessly assuming that subject and object are equal partners in perception. In that case, "I have certainty through an other, namely the thing; and it is correspondingly in that certainty through an other, namely through the I." Both are thoroughly mediated through the other in perception. (What they may be outside of perception is, very importantly, not pertinent to the examination of Sense Certainty and its claim that *within* sense perception immediacy and determinacy can be combined.)[14]

Sense Certainty now seeks to avoid the previous difficulties by eliminating any suggestion of partnership between subject and object. In an asymmetrical relation in which one element is unessential and conditioned, the other might well be essential and unconditioned. In that case its presence in perception would not be mediated through the other. The realistic form of this defense is the first to be tried. It is the object which is to be the essential, conditioning, unmediated element of perception.

It is not realism as a metaphysical thesis which is here in question. The issue is not whether for a tree "to be is to be perceived," but only whether the suggested asymmetrical relation adequately describes the way the tree is present in sense perception for the perceiving subject. Since it is clear that to be present is to be here and now, we must ask what it means to be here and now for consciousness, or, in Hegel's locution, What is the Now? and What is the Here?[15]

Sense Certainty first discovers that the Now is not a particular, existing thing [*ein Seiendes*], but something negative, something which remains and preserves itself, something universal, and thus something mediated. What this means is not quite as forbidding as Hegel's language suggests, but in the background is the familiar argument of Kant's Transcendental Aesthetic.

For a thing to be present to consciousness now it must have a temporal location defined by its being later than some moments of time and earlier than others. More specifically, to locate the event of a thing's presentness as now is to place that event in a determinate relationship with the whole of time, the totality of moments to which the moment of this event belongs. The nowness of the perceptual event is not a function of a particular, the moment in which it occurs, but only of the totality within which this particular moment occurs and first becomes possible. The totality is neither this moment nor that one. One can say that it is the whole it is by virtue of its negative relation to its parts. It is what remains and maintains itself in and through the passing away of its moments. That Hegel should call this sort of negative, remaining, self-maintaining totality a universal sounds strange to modern usage for which the term is used to distinguish type from instance rather than whole from part. But that he should call the presentness of the object to perceptual consciousness something mediated can no longer be surprising, for the Here is evidently the same sort of universal as the Now, and together they are essential to perceptual experience. If we try to think of a perceptual content apart from the time and space which it normally occupies, to represent a perceptual foreground apart from its perceptual background, it is clear that we have abandoned what Sense Certainty wanted to talk about, our everyday perception of the tree here and the house over there, if indeed we are talking about anything at all.[16]

What has come to light in analyzing the here-and-nowness of the perceptual content is only slightly different from the discovery made in the preliminary examination of Sense Certainty. The principle there was that every determination is a negation, that for an object to be given in perception as determinate it must be taken as such, mediated by an act of consciousness which distinguishes it from what is not. Hegel's transition to the chapter on Perception is thus more than a pun on the term *Wahrnehmung,* for it succinctly locates the Achilles heel of Sense Certainty. "I point it out *as* a here which is a here among other heres . . . I take it *as* it is in truth, and instead of knowing something immediate, I take it truly [*nehme ich wahr*]."[17] There can be no unmediated givenness in perception, for to perceive is to take something *as* something. The analysis of the Now and the Here shows how this is true even for the least conceptual and most intuitive aspects of perception, for reference as well as description. In relation to space and time the logical principle that every determination is a negation becomes the explicitly perceptual principle—the object is always distinguished within perception as a foreground against a background. In both cases the result is the same. It is only by means of the judgmental act

of the perceiving subject which takes the object as here and not
there, now and not then, and, e.g., tree and not computer or igloo, that the object can be determinately given in perception.

Since Hegel is not here concerned with how mathematics is
possible a priori his treatment of the transcendental character
of space and time has a different emphasis from Kant's. It is not
limited to the formal aspects of experience, but exemplifies a
principle which applies to the content as well, to the greenness
of the tree as well as its nowness.[18]

With this discovery of transcendental subjectivity Sense
Certainty experiences a dialectical reversal, for the realistic
asymmetry by which it sought to preserve immediacy with determinacy has turned into its opposite. "The object, which was
to be the essential reality, is now the non-essential element of
Sense Certainty; for the universal which it has become is no
longer such as the object was to be for Sense Certainty. The certainty is now found to lie in the opposite element, namely in
knowledge, which formerly was the non-essential element. The
truth of Sense Certainty lies in the object as my [*meinem*] object,
or in the intending [*Meinen*] of it. The object is because I know
it."[19]

Again nothing can be inferred from the last sentence about
the existence of unperceived trees, for the issue is still only the
object as it is present in perception. But this also means that the
subject, which is now taken to be the essential element, the unmediated giver of the given, cannot be deprived of its immediacy by reference to the physics of perception, for the impact of
light waves on the retina is as inappropriate to the present discussion as is the existence of unperceived trees. In the language
of later phenomenology, the natural standpoint has been brack-
eted. In the language of Anglo-Saxon empiricism the language of sense data has replaced that of physical objects. As
Sense Certainty seeks to preserve itself "in the immediacy of my
seeing, hearing, etc.," this no longer has reference to the relation of empirical subject to physical object.

Having been forced to withdraw from the familiar, everyday world in which it was completely at home to the rarefied
atmosphere of sense data and noemata, Sense Certainty can
now hope at best to salvage a highly qualified victory. But even
this is not to be. Mediation raises its ugly head once again and

forces Sense Certainty to one final desperate defense. The I, which is now taken to be the essential element, turns out to be the same sort of universal as the Now and the Here. The particular I which sees the tree and takes it to be a tree disappears and is replaced by another particular I which sees the house instead as the object present to consciousness. What does not disappear is the I as universal, the I which is not the particular seeing of any particular object but seeing in general, the totality of the perceptual capacity which makes possible the perceiving of both the tree and the house. Only the I which can also intend a house can intend a tree, for to intend an object as a tree is to intend it as not a house, as not the ground in which it grows, as not the birds who build their nests in it, and so forth. Hegel only says the obvious when he says that "Sense Certainty experiences in this connection the same dialectic as in the former case," i.e., as in the case of the realistic asymmetry. Both cases illustrate the contradiction which came to light in the opening sentences on Sense Certainty between its criterion of immediacy and the determinateness of its actual knowledge.

The final capitulation of Sense Certainty takes the form of one last desperate defense, the attempt to think a consciousness devoid of all the mediating universals which have come to light. It will be a consciousness whose Now and Here are unrelated to any other Nows and Heres and whose content is thus unrelated to any other content, if that makes any sense. As intentional act it will not relate itself to any other intentional act. In short, it will have the character of what is sometimes called the solipsism of the present moment. Loewenberg has tried to describe it in this way: "A consciousness dominated by an intense sensation completely withdraws from all distinctions and all relations. While the sensation lasts, the content present and the self aware of it constitute a miniature world."[20] One must hasten to add that the distinction between the self and the content of its awareness is one of the distinctions from which this consciousness has completely withdrawn.

Something like this minature world can occur during the moment of transition from fainting to fully regained consciousness.[21] There is no sense of personal identity or of location in space and time. Only after the "experience" and not during it is the "I think" able to accompany it. But in spite of this

complete lack of orientation, there is a feeling which can subsequently be vaguely described as a pressure or a pain. These
determinations of the "experience" as mine and as of pain are
absent from the "experience" itself. For a moment I become a
pure feeling, unowned, unlocated, and indescribable. As this
"experience" gradually becomes my experience of pain it completely changes its character. As Hegel says, "Were we to concern ourselves afterwards with this truth, or stand at a distance
from it, it would have no meaning at all, for that would do away
with the immediacy which it essentially is."[22]

In attempting to think a consciousness like Loewenberg's
minature world or this not quite conscious consciousness, Sense
Certainty concedes the untenability of its position. In thinking a
consciousness which strictly adheres to its criterion of immediacy it shows how fully indeterminate and empty that consciousness must be, if it can legitimately be called consciousness at all.
If such a consciousness could speak, absurd as such a supposi-
tion is, its assertion "It is" would sound, if anything, like an
exaggerated account of its experience.

That such states of pure immediacy exist, in infancy, in
semi-consciousness, in mystic trances, and so on, Hegel does
not deny. That they are as devoid of truth as of falsity, since
they lack all determinate content, Hegel does not need to affirm. Sense Certainty has discovered this for itself. It will return
to the world of everyday perception, whose richness remains,
quite unchanged by the now completed dialogue. Sense Certainty, however, has changed so radically in abandoning its immediacy criterion, that it is no longer Sense Certainty, but what
Hegel calls Perception.

3C. Language, Sense Certainty, and Feuerbach's
Critique

It is too soon, however, to turn to the chapter on Perception, for what is most often taken to be the heart of the chapter
on Sense Certainty has been completely overlooked to this
point, namely the discussion of language in relation to sense
perception and the notorious claim that we cannot say what we
mean. That this can hardly be the key to Sense Certainty's self-

refutation should be clear from the foregoing, where that self-refutation occurs without so much as a reference to the three passages where the so-called argument from language is found.

The first and most important of these passages is the following paragraph, which occurs between the analysis of the Now and that of the Here: "It is *also* as a universal that we express [*aussprechen*] the sensible. What we say is, This, i.e., the universal this. Or we say, It is, i.e., being in general. Of course we do not have in mind [*vorstellen*] the universal this or being in general when we speak in this way, but we express what is universal. In other words, we simply do not say what we mean in this Sense Certainty. But language, as we see, is truer than our meaning or intention [*Meinung*], which we ourselves immediately refute when we speak. And, *since the universal is the truth of Sense Certainty, and language merely expresses this truth,* it is not possible at all for us to express in words any sensible particular [*sinnliches Sein*] which we mean."[23]

For the understanding of this paragraph it is crucial whether we take the (italicized) protasis of its last sentence or its apodasis as our point of departure. The latter calls attention to the *discrepancy* between what we mean and what we say. The italicized statement, by contrast, points to the striking *congruity* between language and perception, thereby echoing the "also" of the paragraph's first sentence. That the universal is the truth of Sense Certainty is the discovery of the preceding paragraph in which the Now is found to be a universal. That we *also express* the sensible as universal and now wish to discover the consequences of this (in the last sentence of the paragraph) indicates first, that the self-refutation of Sense Certainty occurs in the discussion of the Now (and subsequently of the Here and the I) rather than here in the discussion of language, and second, that we are here concerned with expanding our understanding of those other parts of the dialogue. For example, it might be intended that from the isomorphism of language and perception, together with the discovery that we cannot say what we mean, we should draw the conclusion that we also cannot even perceive what we mean.

This intriguing possibility could be uninterruptedly pursued at this point only by ignoring the loud protest from Feuerbach. Not entirely unlike Thrasymachus in the *Republic*, he insists that Hegel has made a farce out of dialectic by reducing what should be a dialogue between Speculation and Empiricism to a monologue between Speculation and itself in the form of a pseudo-defender of Empiricism who presupposes the results of Speculation and is entirely unable to get inside the perspective of Sense Certainty and think the way it thinks. Feuerbach volunteers to act as the advocate of Sense Certainty, and promises to play a real *Du* to Hegel's *Ich*. He promises not to capitulate obediently as the previous defenders of Sense Certainty have done in the face of Hegel's all too Socratic word games.[24]

If only because Feuerbach's critique has been so regularly repeated, wittingly or unwittingly, down to the present day, it is worthy of examination. His point of departure is the apodasis of the final sentence of the paragraph cited above. Thus he finds the heart of Hegel's critique of Sense Certainty in the claim that we cannot say what we mean, that verbal expression never adequately captures the unique particularity of the sensible particular.

This leads to a double misunderstanding of Hegel's text. The first concerns the criterion by which Sense Certainty is to be examined. Feuerbach reminds Hegel that it is a nominalistic consciousness which knows that "language by no means belongs to its object . . . How then should sensible consciousness find itself to be refuted or actually be refuted by the fact that the particular does not allow itself to be said? Sensible consciousness rather finds in just this fact a refutation of language."[25] If Hegel thinks that Sense Certainty is refuted by showing that we cannot say what we mean, this can only be because he attributes to it the claim that we can say what we mean. Feuerbach's point is that Sense Certainty need not make such a claim, and that Hegel's refutation rests on tricking some pseudo-representative of Sense Certainty into making that claim and then showing the absurdity of his position. What Feuerbach fails to notice, largely because of his almost exclusive focus on the discussion of language, is that it is quite a different criterion by which Sense Certainty is examined, namely that of immediacy, and that its refutation takes place in those analyses of the Now, and Here, and the I to which he pays almost no attention. It is not Sense Certainty in Hegel's critique, but Hegel in Feuerbach's who is judged by a criterion imposed from without.

The curious phrase "refutation of language" expresses Feuerbach's second and equally basic misunderstanding. What does it mean for language to be refuted? Feuerbach finds the *Phenomenology* to begin with the contradiction between word as universal and thing as particular. "But no more than the word is the thing as spoken or thought being actual being." This actual being to which language and thought are opposed is "*Existenz*", and it is before its court that they are "refuted". For Feuerbach as for Kierkegaard the term *Existenz* gathers around itself three interrelated themes: particularity inaccessible to thought, reality as opposed to mere possibility, and practical, or as we have come to put it, existential interest. These are the basic categories of Feuerbach's "existentialist" critique of Hegel on Sense Certainty.[26]

His point is clearest in the examples he gives. According to Hegel's critique the bread I eat may be "unsayable" because of its particularity, but it is a matter of life and death to me that I have the real unspeakable bread rather than the linguistic or logical bread which, just because it can be spoken cannot be eaten. Similarly, I have a brother named Johann Adolph. Since many other persons have that name, even his proper name does not distinguish him from them. "But does it follow from this that my Johann is unreal and that truth is found only in Johann-ness?"[27] Again, "This woman is, for example, my wife, this house my house, although everyone says the same thing about his house and wife that I say about mine: this house, this woman. But the indifference and absence of distinction which characterize the logical This is here broken through and transcended by the sense of right. If we were to apply the logical This in the realm of natural rights, we would come directly to the community of goods and wives where there is no difference between this and that . . . [but] right is grounded precisely on the reality of this distinction."

If it be objected that these examples introduce the realm of the practical whereas Hegel was only concerned with the theoretical, the reply is "that the practical standpoint is entirely in place here. The question of being is indeed a practical question, one in which our being has a share, a question of life and death."[28]

Feuerbach has located the decisive objection to his existentialist critique, for the practical point of view is surely out of place where the question of the independent reality of the objects of perception has deliberately been set aside so as to focus exclusively on the question of the way objects are present to consciousness in perception. As if to remind the reader of this Hegel does not end the chapter on Sense Certainty without an anticipatory reference to his own upcoming discussions in which eating and drinking as well as life and death will be considered. And as if to refute Feuerbach's interpretation directly Hegel indicates here that what he means by the unreality of the sensible particular is illustrated and confirmed by the phenomenon of eating.[29]

Feuerbach knows all this, but objects that it is illegitimate to postpone the practical perspective when it is a question of being. Perhaps so. But Hegel is not here discussing the question of being, only the very limited question of the being of something for consciousness in perception. Such reflection in no way implies the unreality of Feuerbach's brother or his bread; and far from implying that he is suddenly unable to distinguish his wife from other men's wives, it stresses the determinateness of the perceptual object and assumes that we can at least distinguish trees from houses. Rather than denying our capacity to refer to individuals, Hegel is asking how it is possible for us to do so.

Actually Feuerbach is a better Hegelian than he knows, for he ends up arguing for rather than against the two major results of Hegel's dialogue with Sense Certainty: the mediated character of sense perception and the concrete humanity of the perceiving subject.[30] We have already seen that the mediated character of sense perception is the heart of Hegel's analysis of Sense Certainty. Similarly Feuerbach sees a double mediation in sense perception. Our certainty of the existence of external objects is mediated through our dialogue with other persons, and the way in which we perceive them is a function of the expectations and hopes we bring with us, which in turn are a function of our degree of culture and of our historical context. Any "immediate" sensible intuition could only be the result of a purification of these factors and thus an abstraction. It would thus be what Hegel calls "that immediacy which does not leave mediation outside itself but which is mediation itself."[31] This means that man is distinguished from the animals in his whole being, including the senses, that "even the lowliest senses, smell and taste, rise up in man to perform spiritual, scientific acts."[32]

This is already to affirm the concrete humanity of the perceiving subject. Idealism had asked, "What are the eyes without consciousness?"[33] Feuerbach now answers with idealism, Animal eyes, not human eyes. But if sense cannot be abstracted from consciousness, consciousness or thought must not be treated as an abstraction either. From the principle that "Man thinks, not the I," Feuerbach derives the following categorical imperative: "Don't think as a thinker . . . think as a living, actual being . . . think in *Existenz,* in the world as a member of the world . . ."[34]

That Hegel also wishes to go beyond the abstract ego of earlier transcendental philosophy to something like Feuerbach's "Man thinks, not the I," is indicated clearly in the Preface (see sections 2B. and 3A. above). But that he does so in the dialogue with Sense Certainty, that we are to learn from it that it is man who perceives, not the senses, or even the Kantian tandem of senses and transcendental ego, intuitions and concepts—this is not yet clear. It is necessary to return to the question of language and ask what its contribution to the chapter may be, since the refutation of Sense Certainty has proven not to be its task.

Prior to the Feuerbachian interruption the hypothesis had been developed that since language and perception are isomorphic in that "the universal is the truth of Sense Certainty, and language merely expresses this truth," and since on the linguistic side this means that "it is not possible at all for us to express in words any sensible particular which we mean," it would seem to follow that on the perceptual side we also cannot even perceive what we mean. Does this make any sense?

It is usually not noticed that every time Hegel says we cannot say what we mean he reaffirms the obvious fact that in sense perception we mean, intend, or refer to the particular. In this sense, namely as intended or referred to, the particular is present to perception. To say that we cannot perceive what we mean is only to say that this intention is never completely fulfilled, that this reference is never completely unambiguous. The object we mean is a fully determinate particular, but in and for perception it is never more than partly determined, partly determinable. In this respect the perceived object and the spoken object are alike. When Urban says that "poetry says what it means, but it does not say all that it means,"[35] what he says may be true not only of language as such, but, *mutatis mutandis,* of perception as well. After pragmatism and the debate over phenomenalism this discovery can hardly be said to be the esoteric possession of either Hegelian or twentieth century phenomenology.

Such a reflection on the isomorphism between language and perception completes two of the three moments described at the conclusion of section 3A. above. As far as the object is concerned, Hegel has first stressed its determinacy and now its indeterminacy. This determinate-indeterminate object is precisely the thing and its properties of the chapter on Perception. The thing is the fully determinate and thus fully particular object we intend. Its properties are the many different and incomplete ways in which it is determinate for consciousness. The difficulties of Perception are simply that the gap between the thing and its properties, its oneness and its manyness, its determinacy and its indeterminacy is never actually bridged in Perception.

The determinate-indeterminate character of the perceptual object has this further consequence, that as a mode of knowledge sense perception is both uncertain and incomplete. The attempt to maintain immediacy was from the start an attempt to maintain or regain certainty, and the inability of Sense Certainty to sustain its claim to immediacy has cost it its claim to certainty. On the other hand, the necessary indeterminacy of the object for perception means that this knowledge is never adequate to its object (as meant) and is thus essentially incomplete.

In the same process by which the nature of the perceptual object has been clarified, the active role of the perceiving subject has come to light. This object is only present to the consciousness which intends it in its full determinacy and particularity, permitting it to be given in actual perception by taking it to be what its various properties show it to be.

To this point, however, no insight has been gained concerning the third moment described in 3A., the manner in which the essential acts of perceiving consciousness may themselves be conditioned. It is not yet clear who the transcendental subject may be. Along with this unanswered question there remains the unexamined phenomenon of the isomorphism of language and perception. Reflection on the "fact" of this isomorphism has helped to clarify the indeterminacy of the perceptual object, but the "fact" itself, the structural similarity of perception and language, has not been discussed. Is it merely a fact, an accident, that we *also* express the sensible as universal, that we can and do say what we see, even if we cannot say what we mean?

When this unexamined phenomenon is juxtaposed to the unanswered question about the identity of the transcendental subject, an hypothesis suggests itself. The transcendental subject is the speaker of a language. This in turn suggests that the relation of language to perception may not be an accidental one, that for the human perceiver it is above all his language which makes possible his perception, which enables him to intend the particulars he intends and to take them in the way he does as variously determined. This would be a special way of saying that it is man who perceives, neither the animal senses, nor the transcendental ego, nor the two in conjunction. For man distinguishes himself from the animals by language, and language is always a language, carrying with it its own history and tradition, structuring the expectations and hopes we bring with us to perception.

None of this is explicit in the text. Sense Certainty has long since moved on to Perception and is about to become Understanding. Since it is still an unsophisticated form of natural consciousness it keeps all its attention on the object, and so far from worrying about who the transcendental subject may be, it forgets about transcendental subjectivity altogether as quickly as possible. Fully resubmerged in its object, it employs a whole variety of categories which it does not recognize as such. When philosophy tries to reflect on them and win some sort of mastery over them, perceptual common sense reproaches it for wasting its time on mere lifeless thoughts. It does not realize that it is tossed about like the prey and plaything of these *Gedankendinge*, which it takes to be unreal abstractions. Since it never becomes aware "that there are such simple realities operating within it and dominating its activity," it remains a thoroughly alienated, false, pre-Copernican consciousness.[36]

But we who observe the experience which consciousness makes are supposed to see what goes on behind its back and need not close our eyes to what is going on right before them. Nor did Hegel. The hypothesis which suggests itself more or less between the lines of the *Phenomenology* is one which he had already developed with some care just previously in the Jena *Realphilosophie.*[37]

3D. Language and the Double Mediation of Theoretical Consciousness

Man's mastery over nature is both theoretical (ideal) and practical (real). To deal with either in isolation from the other and from the context of social interaction in which they take place, that of family and people [*Volk*], is to deal with an abstraction. For, to take the case at hand, the speaking perceiver of theoretical consciousness is always at the same time a member of a family and society who shares in their socially organized labor. When Marx, for example, insists that the abolition of private property has implications for sense perception he is simply refusing to treat theoretical consciousness in abstraction from the rest of man.[38]

It is just such abstractions with which natural consciousness feels most at home. It assumes that the distinction between theoretical and practical as well as that between sense and intellect is fixed and immoveable. In seeking to lead natural consciousness to see that it is man who perceives and not the senses, Hegel must begin where natural consciousness is, with theoretical activity abstracted from the total man. He must think it so concretely that the rigid distinctions of natural consciousness break down. This is the strategy in both the *Phenomenology* and the *Realphilosophie.*

Natural consciousness is proud of man's superiority over the animals. But at the theoretical level it tends to conceive of this as the pasting together of sub-human animal sensation with a formal ego which is too abstract to be human. In the *Realphilosophie* Hegel wants to show that the mediation which humanizes pure sensation is not that of the ego, which he describes as a formal universal, but that of Spirit, which is truly universal since it contains the particular within it. To do this he develops the linguistic character of perception, for language is "the true being of Spirit as Spirit in general."[39]

A two-fold mediation is involved here, between subject and object and within the subject itself, conceived of as Spirit. We have first to observe "how Spirit intends the thing," that is, "how the object comes to be something universal for it, or how it makes it to be what it is, intends it as what it is." At the same time we are to see that "Spirit is that which is self-mediating. It exists only as withdrawing from and thus transcending what it immediately is." In language this self-mediation of Spirit has its extremes in the individual consciousness and the universal consciousness which contains the individual consciousness within it and comes to expression by means of it.[40]

In both cases "the middle is the essential"—neither subject nor object, individual nor universal consciousness maintain their discrete and identifiable particularity. They rather become united in a third reality. Using the syllogism as a metaphor Hegel calls this third reality their middle, for like the middle term in a syllogism it so unites the other two terms that we can say that the one *is* the other (Socrates is mortal).[41] The mediation of subject and object is the process by which thing [*Ding*] becomes ego [*Ich*]. The mediation of individual and universal consciousness is that by which ego becomes thing, that is, takes on an empirical, objective character. At the heart of both processes lies language.

The first of these mediations corresponds to the analysis in the *Phenomenology* of the mediated character of sense perception, except that it makes explicit the linguistic character of perception. The "overcoming of the indeterminacy of sensation" is accomplished even in the child's apprehension of something as, e.g., a large nose.[42] Already this involves language and its presuppositions, imagination and memory. In imagination the original intuition becomes the object of consciousness. The image is "being as mine, as transcended." Like the first stage of experience within Plato's cave, the realm of images can only be compared to night-time, dreaming consciousness. Waking consciousness involves the "power to call up images out of this night or to leave them submerged in it." Through this mastery which consciousness wins over the realm of its images, the image becomes a sign which refers back to the original object, which, in the process, "has come under the mastery of the self and has lost the significance of being immediate and independent." This image-sign, which has become the essence [*Inner-*

lichkeit] of the thing does not remain wholly inner. It becomes a
thing itself and wins outward existence as language when the
subject names the thing. The perceptual process completes itself only in this bond between name and image made possible
by the cooperation of imagination and memory. It is what Kant
called the schema.[43]

This is a kind of linguistic idealism. But it is not the "laugh-
able idealism" which opposes itself to realism. Both parties to
this irrational conflict, about which there is nothing rational to
say, assume that subject and object sustain themselves unchanged in perception, that no mediation takes place. But perception is "a synthesis of object and self, of content and ego."
The essence is their middle, and it does not make sense to ask
what the contribution of each party may be. The truth is the
whole and the human perception of a large nose belongs to the
totality from which sensation (passivity) and naming (activity)
cannot be isolated as discrete realities.[44] It is to counteract the
crude realism of common sense that Hegel invokes idealistic
language to make his point; as when he says the thing becomes
ego, or more specifically, "Thus it is through the name that the
ego gives birth to the object as the thing it is. This is the first
creative power which Spirit exercises. Adam gave all things
names. This is . . . the creation of nature out of Spirit. λογος is
reason, the essence of things and of speech, of telling and of
what is told [*Sache und Sage*]. In short, reason is category. Man
speaks to things as to his own and lives in a spiritual nature, in
his own world, and this is the being of the object."[45]

We are brought in this way to the second mediation, that of
Spirit with itself. For while transcendental subjectivity has just
regained the spotlight, the linguistic character of its presentation in the Jena lectures leads directly to reflection on the identity of this transcendental ego, the "bearer, space, and substance" of names, which creates the world in which man lives.[46]
Language as the namegiving power is "the true being of Spirit
as Spirit in general" because "it is there as the unity of two free
selves." It takes two (or more) to play a language game. This
clarifies Hegel's claim that in seeing how the thing is intended
we get beyond the formal universality of the transcendental ego
to Spirit as the true, self-mediating universality which contains
the particular within itself.[47] Again universality signifies whole

in relation to part rather than type in relation to instance. The perceiving subject is the player of many language games. Since each of these involves living interaction with at least one other human individual, the speaking-perceiving subject stands in relation not only to the object of his perception but also to the linguistic community of which he is a part. This community is the universal consciousness which stands over against the individual consciousness. But language is the middle in which the two are united and lose their abstract opposition to one another. Just as there is no language without an individual who speaks, so no individual speaks except in a language already there, given to him and imposed on him by his society.

When one asks, against the background of the linguistic character of perception, Who is the transcendental subject?—the most accurate answer would be, Language. For the perceiver who intends the object of perception does so as the speaker of a language. This means that he is not the abstract, ahistorical transcendental ego of Kantian thought, but the concrete, historically conditioned bearer of a given language and all of the cumulative tradition built into the language.[48] This concreteness of transcendental subjectivity is neither that of the empirical ego as a discrete, isolable individual nor of a social totality somehow distinct from the individuals which make it up. For, to repeat, the essence of language is the middle where the individual is simultaneously master and slave of his linguistic tradition, where a people's linguistic self-expression is servant to and served by the speaking individual.[49]

The socialization process by which the individual becomes the bearer of this historically specific transcendental subjectivity is described by Hegel in his own inimitable way: the ego becomes thing. The formal possibility of the ego to be the "I think" by which experience is possible becomes a concrete actuality as the ego becomes determinate and in this respect thinglike. The namegiving power was free and arbitrary for Adam, but we are confronted by a relatively fixed "order of names." Transcendental subjectivity is thus the result of the historical process in which consciousness "forms itself and constitutes itself as Spirit existing for itself and withdrawing itself from nature." The ego becomes thing not by relapsing into nature, but by taking to itself a second nature which is itself the

product of human activity. Hegel calls this man's unorganic nature to distinguish the socially-historically conditioned aspect
from the biologically given aspect of his nature.[50] For him as for
Marx, "the nature which comes to be in human history, in the
activity which founds human society, is the actual nature of
man."[51] For both of them this means that "the education of the
five senses is a work of all previous world history."[52]

In this way theoretical consciousness is denied autonomy.
Both the subject, as Spirit, and its relation to the object, have a
history. Furthermore, consciousness does not preside over that
history but plays a servant role. As Hegel puts it in a Jena fragment, "Through consciousness Spirit intervenes in the way the
world is ruled."[53]

3E. Sense Certainty and the Phenomenology as a Whole

The truth is the whole for Hegel, and it follows that the
part is the false so far as it is merely part. But the part is also
true in the degree that it expresses in its own limited way the
whole. It is legitimate to ask in what ways, if any, the whole of
the *Phenomenology* is expressed in its first chapter. The question
is a timely reminder that Hegel is not simply trying to develop a
theory of perception but is engaged in the complicated task described in the Introduction and Preface.

The first such reflection of the whole in the part concerns
the unity of the transcendental and historical perspectives, the
epistemic and the existential. Whereas Haym and so many
others following him have been able to see only a hopelessly
confused mixture of two thoroughly distinct types of investigation, the preceding analysis of Sense Certainty shows exactly
how the transcendental and historical perspectives arise simultaneously and how only an artificially abstract tran-
scendentalism can avoid reflection on Spirit and its history.

No doubt it would have helped if Hegel had made these
connections as explicitly in the *Phenomenology* as in the *Realphilosophie*. He seems to have ignored his own advice that the
successful phenomenology cannot be a hurried one but must be
willing to take its time over each moment.[54] But when the chap-

ter on Sense Certainty is read against the background of the lecture materials it is possible to see one of the ways in which Hegel discovered "that a radical critique of knowledge is possible only as social theory."[55]

The first and central theme about Sense Certainty, however, is not the linguistic nature of perception but its mediated character. It seems likely that the silencing of immediacy also has a significance for the work as a whole, especially since so much of the Preface is devoted to an attack on the appeal to immediacy at the highest levels of religious and philosophical knowledge. It doesn't matter whether our immediate knowledge of the Absolute is entitled intellectual intuition, as in Fichte and Schelling, faith, as in Jacobi, or feeling, as in Schleiermacher. In each case "beyond Kant" means "back to the immediate itself."

We have already seen Hegel's analysis of this. Kant's destruction of traditional metaphysics is the authentic expression of an age which "has passed beyond the substantial life that it formerly led in the element of thought—beyond this immediacy of its faith, beyond the satisfaction and security of the certainty which consciousness possessed about its reconciliation with the divine . . ."[56] This is not a loss Spirit can dispassionately observe. When it becomes conscious of this loss, as it did so forcefully in Kant, as the price for its movement beyond the immediacy of its faith, it is not surprising that a "back to immediacy" cry should be raised. Philosophy is now asked to come to the rescue "not by returning the chaotic consciousness to the order of thought and the simplicity of the concept, but rather by confounding the distinctions of thought, by suppressing the discriminating concept, and by establishing the feeling of the divine, granting not so much insight as edification."[57]

This "suppressing" [*unterdrücken*] is an almost psychoanalytic concept, and Hegel's interpretation suggests that it is indeed a defense mechanism. Similarly, the appeal to immediacy has the form of a wish-fulfilling illusion. It is not only an act determined more by interest than by insight. It also involves systematic self-deception.

To see this we must begin again with Kant. He not only undermined traditional metaphysics. He also generalized the negative character of thought. "Our age is, in especial degree, the age of criticism, and to criticism everything must submit. Religion through its sanctity, and law-giving through its majesty, may seek to exempt themselves from it. But they then awaken just suspicion . . ."[58] Kant's everything was no hyperbole. It became all too clear that the foundations were being shaken, not only of the world beyond, but of this world as well.

Such a situation generates not only the hope for instant metaphysics but also a sudden fondness for the familiar. It is then possible for the appeal to immediacy to function as an absolutizing of the familiar in the following manner. The accomplishments of the people and tradition to which the individual belongs at first confront him as external and objectively given. But socialization is a process of "acquiring what is thus given to him [*das Vorhandene*], digesting his unorganic nature, and taking possession of it for himself." This inheritance includes what is here called *das Aufheben* of existence and was previously called "the thought of the subject matter in general." In other words, mediation has already taken place. But "existence, taken back into the substance, has merely been transposed immediately by this first negation into the element of the self. This possession which the self has acquired thus still has the same character of uncomprehended immediacy and unmoved indifference as does existence itself . . . At the same time it is thus something familiar, something that the existing Spirit has mastered so that its activity and interest no longer abide in it . . . But knowledge is directed against the way of thinking that arises in this way, against this familiarity. It is the activity of the universal self and the interest of thinking. What is familiar is not known simply because it is familiar."[59]

Ignoring Hegel's warning, natural consciousness takes what is familiar in this way to be self-evident truth. It is essentially a dogmatic form of thought, for it rests upon unexamined presuppositions. The contingency of the familiar is hidden from natural consciousness by its very familiarity, its relative immediacy to consciousness. Consequently the appeal to the immediate often ends up as an attempt to go beyond criticism by returning to dogmatism. In this absolutizing of the familiar what began as wish-fulfillment ends up as ideology.[60]

The irony of the situation is not noticed by natural consciousness. The conservative substance of the appeal to immediacy is masked by its radical appearance. Described as a return to nature it sounds like a return to the primal and archetypal, the overcoming of the disharmonies of mediated existence by return to the original harmony. But when this nature is seen to be only what has contingently become man's second nature at a given stage of historical development within a particular society, and when immediacy is seen to designate the familiar rather than the primordial, the whole project is condemned by its own criterion. It claims to capture the archetypal and absolute. It only dogmatizes the consequent and contingent.

Hegel's Science, to which the *Phenomenology* belongs, can be more than merely an alternative to this project of his contemporaries only if he can show it to be self-refuting. He cannot appeal to external criteria. Here lies the significance of the critique of Sense Certainty for the whole of the *Phenomenology*. For like Sense Certainty all the contemporary philosophies of immediacy claim to unite a rich content with the form of immediacy. When the lessons of Sense Certainty are applied to these philosophies of intellectual intuition, faith, and feeling they can be shown that their content comes from the familiar, which is only relatively immediate. A philosophy which took its own immediacy criterion seriously would be utterly silenced. It would expose itself as sheer emptiness, "the night in which all cows are black," the "monochromatic absolute painting," which drowns all the distinctions of reflection "in the emptiness of the Absolute," and whose masterpiece is "pure identity, formless whiteness."[61]

The only alternative would be to acknowledge that whatever content consciousness possesses has been historically mediated. This brings with it the anxiety that what is familiar and relied upon will turn out to be abortions that should be cast away. But it also opens the door of hope—openness to the possibility that somewhere in the historical process one will encounter something new and unfamiliar which deserves to be called the Kingdom of God.

NOTES

1. It is thus an Hegelian principle which Feuerbach directs against Hegel when he writes, "The philosopher must include in the text of philosophy what Hegel reduced to only a footnote, that in man which does not philosophize, but is rather against philosophy and opposed to abstract thought." *Vorläufige Thesen zur Reform der Philosophie*, in *Kleine Schriften* (henceforth KS), ed. Karl Löwith, Frankfurt, 1966, p. 135.

2. PhG, III-IV/10/68.

3. Rudolf Haym, *Hegel und seine Zeit*, Berlin, 1857, p. 241. The reference is to Section B of Chapter Six.

4. Theaetetus, 161b-162b, Cornford translation.

5. Hints of the Kantian story are already found in the Theaetetus at 184d ff. One of the rocks on which the knowledge-is-perception thesis founders is the discovery that in knowing we employ concepts which are not derived from sense experience.

6. PhG, VI/11-12/70.

7. PhG, XL-XLI/30-31/94-95.

8. Hegel often uses the adjectives *fest* and *fix* when describing unexamined presuppositions which are dogmatically taken to be self-evident, eternal truths. Here the fixity, *das Fixe*, which is to be replaced is the assumption that the a priori or categoreal features of experience are such self-evident, eternal structures, free of all historical conditioning. Kant is the primary, if not the only target of these remarks.

9. Jürgen Habermas, "Knowledge and Human Interests: A General Perspective," (Frankfurt inaugural address of June, 1965) translated by J. Shapiro in *Knowledge and Human Interests*, Boston, 1971, p. 312.

10. PhG, 22/79/149. cf. 43/93/166.

11. For this and the following paragraph, PhG, 23/79-80/149-50. In the *Science of Logic* the first category, Being, is defined as the indeterminate immediate, indicating that Hegel is speaking of immediacy in its absolute sense and not in the relative sense which neither precludes mediation nor determinacy. The familiar is immediate in this latter sense. See section 3E. below.

12. *Idem*. Baillie's rather free translation of part of the next sentence is right to the point. " . . . the I here does not think."

13. This provides a helpful commentary on Hegel's identification of the fear of error with the fear of truth in the Introduction.

14. For this and the following paragraph, PhG, 24-25/80-81/150-51.

15. For this and the following paragraph, PhG, 25-27/81-82/151-52.

16. See Introduction, 12/69/138. "With the intending of something individual the beyond is also intended, even when it is only next to what is limited, as in spatial intuition."

17. PhG, 37/89/160, italics mine. This same discovery leads in the *Theaetetus* to the thesis that knowledge is true belief or judgment. Kant's identification of experience with empirical knowledge also expresses the judgmental character of perception. Much of what contemporary phenomenology discusses under the rubric 'intentionality' is treated in the Wittgensteinian tradition in terms of 'seeing as'. Where the former is chosen over the latter in what follows this is for stylistic and not philosophical reasons.

18. In this respect the theory of transcendental subjectivity which emerges from the discussion of the Now and the Here is, in spite of its obvious Kantian overtones, closer to the Husserlian principle of strict correlation between intentional act and intentional object, of noesis and noema.

19. For this and the following two paragraphs, PhG, 28-29/83-84/153-54.

20. J. Loewenberg, *Hegel's Phenomenology: Dialogues on the Life of Mind*, LaSalle, 1965, p. 33.

21. I am trying here to describe an "experience" I have had on several occasions.

22. PhG, 31/85/156.

23. PhG, 26-27/82/152, my italics.

24. Ludwig Feuerbach, *Zur Kritik der Hegelschen Philosophie* (henceforth *Kritik*), KS, 99, 104-07. cf. *Grundsätze der Philosophie der Zukunft* (henceforth *Grundsätze*), #62, KS, 218.

25. *Kritik*, KS, 105.

26. *Grundsätze*, #28, KS, 187.

27. *Idem.* and *Kritik*, KS, 104-05.

28. *Grundsätze*, #28, KS, 186-87.

29. PhG, 34-35/87/158-59. cf. 25/81/151.

30. For the second of these see the next paragraph but one and ff. Agreement between Feuerbach and Hegel on these points does not establish their correctness. It is stressed only to indicate how deeply Feuerbach misunderstood Hegel, thereby rendering himself incapable of a cogent critique.

31. PhG, XL/30/94.

32. *Grundsätze*, #41 and #43, KS, 203-05; #53, KS, 214-15.

33. *Ibid.*, #17, KS, 169.

34. *Ibid.*, #50-51, KS, 212-13.

35. W. M. Urban, *Language and Reality*, London, 1939, p. 500.

36. PhG, 56-57/100-01/176-77.

37. In 1931-32 J. Hoffmeister edited and published in Felix Meiner's *Philosophische Bibliothek* series two volumes entitled *Jenenser Realphilosophie I* and *Jenenser Realphilosophie II*. The latter, which includes lecture manuscripts from Hegel's 1805-06 lectures on the philosophy of nature and Spirit was reprinted in 1967 with the simple title *Jenaer Realphilosophie* and is designated elsewhere in the present essay simply as *Realphilosophie*. The former was not reprinted, due to the discovery that Hegel gave separate lectures on the philosophy of nature and Spirit only in 1805-06 and that the first volume contains fragments mostly related to the 1803-04 lectures which included logic and metaphysics. For details see the essays by Heinz Kimmerle in *Hegel-Studien*, Volume 4. Since these materials come from the Jena period their exact date and setting is not crucial for the use to which I am putting them. I shall draw on both volumes and, for the following section only (3D.), designate them simply as I and II.

38. Karl Marx, from the 1844 Paris manuscripts, *Die Frühschriften*, ed. Landshut, Stuttgart, 1968, pp. 239-45. An English translation is available in *Karl Marx: Early Writings*, Bottomore, trans., New York, 1964, pp. 159-64.

39. II, 179, 183.

40. II, 179.

41. II, 192; I, 213.

42. II, 188.

43. II, 179-83. cf. I, 207-12. Careful study of these passages shows that Hegel is blending Aristotelian and Kantian accounts of perception.

44. I, 213-16; II, 182.

45. II, 183. cf. I, 211. A similar linking of categories and language is found in *Theaetetus*, 185-86, where Plato describes the mind as "the faculty that works through the tongue." For discussion in the PhG of the thing becoming ego, see 168/179/277 and 174-76/183-84/281-83.

46. II, 185.

47. See note 39 above.

48. This is true even if there is a deep structure which is common to all languages.

49. Cf. I, 200-02, 206.

50. I, 197. For discussion in the PhG of man's unorganic nature, see XXXIII-XXXVI/26-28/89-91 and 240-42/225-27/333-36.

51. Marx makes this statement, interestingly enough, at the conclusion of the spectacular and often quoted passage in which he discusses the implications for *sense perception* of the abolition of private property. *Die Frühschriften*, pp. 239-45; Bottomore, pp. 159-64. He distinguishes not only human from non-human eyes, but also emancipated human eyes from not yet emancipated ones.

52. *Die Frühschriften*, p. 242; Bottomore, p. 161.

53. Quoted in Schlomo Avineri, *Hegel's Theory of the Modern State*, Cambridge, 1972, p. 64.

54. PhG, XXXV/27/90-91. cf. Kant, *Critique of Pure Reason*, A xviii-xix. "If the size of a volume be measured not by the number of pages but by the time required for mastering it, it can be said of many a book, that it would be much shorter if it were not so short."

55. Habermas, *op. cit.*, p. VII. See Ch. 2, n. 55.

56. PhG, VIII/13/71-72. cf. Ch. 2, n. 5.

57. PhG, IX/13/72.

58. *Critique of Pure Reason*, note to A xi.

59. PhG, XXXIV-XXXVI/27-28/90-92. cf. n. 6 above. Perhaps Hegel is thinking of Augustine's comment on time. "What, then, is time? I know well enough what it is, provided that nobody asks me; but if I am asked what it is and try to explain, I am baffled." *Confessions*, XI, 14, Pine-Coffin translation. The discussion of scepticism in 1B. above and of surprise in 1C. are both pertinent to Hegel's attitude toward the familiar.

60. Hegel returns to this theme in its political overtones in the Preface to the *Philosophy of Right*, where he writes that truly rational thought "does not remain stationary at the given, whether the given be upheld by the external positive authority of the state or the agreement of mankind, or by the authority of inward feeling and emotion and by the 'witness of the spirit' which directly concurs with it . . . The unsophisticated heart takes the simple line of adhering with trustful conviction to what is publicly accepted as true [*die öffentlich bekannte Wahrheit*] . . ."

61. PhG, XIX/19/79 and LXII/43/110/ cf. 74/112/192 on absolute darkness and pure light. These passages form a helpful commentary on the treatment of Being and Nothing in the Logic.

CHAPTER FOUR

The Knowledge of Nature:

B) Natural Science

4A. Preliminary Sketch of Hegel's
Phenomenological Philosophy of Science

The movement of the first two chapters of the *Phenomenology* is not so much from Sense Certainty to Perception as it is the discovery that consciousness is always inescapably at the level of Perception. Sense Certainty is an unreal abstraction. Our knowledge of the external world does not begin in the rarefied atmosphere of pure sensation but in the everyday world of things and their properties.

But if all our knowledge begins in the familiar world of Perception, it does not follow that our knowledge always stays at home. "Spirit exists only as transcending that which it immediately is, stepping back from it;" and since its life is "not the life that shrinks from death and keeps itself undefiled by devastation, but the life which endures and preserves itself through death" and "gains its truth only by finding itself in absolute dismemberment,"[1] everyday life is not immune to the wanderlust which calls it to find new life through self-destruction. It is in the natural sciences that our knowledge of the external world finds its most impressive new form of life. After the previous chapter we are eager to move on from the theoretical to the practical and from the transcendental to the historical. But Hegel will linger long enough to examine this new form of theoretical consciousness. Since its description will inevitably involve transcendental reflection, the question will become, How is science possible?

The question has a Kantian ring, but Hegel's understanding of Understanding differs in two important ways from Kant's. The first is expressed in Dilthey's description of Wilhelm Scherer: "He was a modern man, and the world of our ancestors was no longer the *home* of his spirit and his heart but his historical *object*."[2] Though it is the *Geisteswissenschaften* which are here in question, the issue is their enthrallment with the methodology of the natural sciences, especially as formulated by Mill. For it was the natural sciences which first achieved the methodological dismemberment of the everyday world by which nature ceased to be man's home and became his object.

The story is told brilliantly by Descartes.[3] Probably no more dramatic reminder of the gulf between the world of common sense and nature as conceived by modern science is to be found than his analysis of the piece of wax in the Second Meditation. Kant's tribute to the scientific revolution retains the Cartesian emphasis on method in one of its most elegant expressions. The scientific revolutionaries "learned that reason has insight only into that which it produces after a plan of its own, and that it must not allow itself to be kept, as it were, in nature's leading-strings, but must itself show the way . . . constraining nature to give answer to questions of reason's own determining."[4]

Implicit in this formulation is Dilthey's contrast between nature as home and as object. But Kant tended to equate the question—How is science possible?—with the question—How is experience possible? The result was to narrow the concept of experience, and, perhaps even more important, to blur the difference between the life-world and science. Correspondingly, when in the Jena Logic (1804-05) Hegel treats essentially the same materials as belong to Perception and Understanding in the *Phenomenology* as a discussion of the Kantian categories of relation (substance, cause, reciprocity), the same merging of science and everyday perception occurs.

But in the *Phenomenology* the fuller Cartesian perspective is restored. The difference between Perception and Understanding is not that the former operates with the category of substance while the latter thinks in terms of cause and reciprocity. The two are rather entirely different forms of consciousness. Taking his cue from Descartes, Hegel makes the point with considerable rhetorical flourish. Substituting a cube of salt for the piece of wax, he distinguishes the sensible world of ordinary perception from what he calls the supersensible world of the natural sciences. The sensible salt is the familiar salt which we sprinkle on our food and on icy sidewalks. The supersensible salt is, most simply, NaCl, an object which does not directly appear to sense perception. Dilthey's contrast between home and object expresses Hegel's perspective most succinctly.[5]

Having stressed the mediated character of Perception over against the claims of Sense Certainty, Hegel is now stressing the immediate character of Perception in contrast to the mediated and indirect relation of Understanding to its object. We have here a splendid example of the relativity of immediacy and mediation in Hegel's usage. In this contrast Hegel's affirmation of the primacy of Perception is enriched. It becomes clear that Perception is not only the inescapable and irreducible starting point for natural consciousness, but also that when it leaves this home for the new world of Understanding it does not really leave the latter behind. For its presence to the supersensible world of scientific explanations is always mediated through its immediate presence in the world of everyday Perception.[6]

There is a second important difference between the Kantian and Hegelian ways of asking, How is science possible? This one is expressed in Gadamer's comment that "for Helmholtz the methical character of the natural sciences required neither an historical derivation nor an epistemological restriction."[7] For Hegel (as for Husserl, Gadamer, and Whitehead after him) the triumph of method which gave birth to the scientific revolution was doubly finite, for it was both an historical accomplishment and an epistemological restriction. This brings to focus a question which lies at the heart of Hegel's philosophy of science, Is method the way to truth? or does one pay too high a price for its services?

It is just by keeping the gap between science and our everyday perspectives that this question is not lost sight of. It is not possible to ask how science is possible without beginning on the road to transcendental philosophy. But it is possible to leave this road quite quickly. Already in Kant's "Appendix to the Transcendental Dialectic" this transformation of the transcendental question into the methodological question—How does one go about doing science?—begins to take place. Neo-Kantianism and positivism are but the heirs of this tendency in Kant.

When, however, science is recognized as a radical demolition of and withdrawal from natural consciousness' home in its pre-scientific sensible world, the question of the possibility of science cannot be reduced to the how-to-do-it question of a methodologically oriented philosophy of science. The method question becomes less important than the motive question, and instead of asking how to do science we ask how it comes about that science occurs. For to see science as both an historical accomplishment and an epistemological restriction is to see it as praxis, as a special form of human behavior. This raises questions about the purpose and results of this activity in relation to other human behavior. What is it that inspires consciousness to claim its inheritance and set out from its father's house seeking fame and fortune in a far country? Will consciousness turn out to be a prodigal son indeed, forced to return from the husks of the supersensible to the father's house once scornfully abandoned?[8]

Here as in the analysis of Sense Certainty transcendental philosophy is led beyond itself and the boundary between the theoretical and the practical is blurred. "We", at least, are to see that the transcendental perspective in the Kantian sense is an unstable one, either relapsing into methodology, thereby reducing knowledge to know-how, or transcending itself by reflecting on the historical derivation and epistemological restriction involved in the human activity called science. As the question about the possibility of science becomes the question—Why and with what results does consciousness abandon nature as its home in order to make nature its object?—the whole network of issues is brought into play which in the previous chapter were summarized by the question—Who is the transcendental subject? In this way Hegel seeks to discredit, not science, but those philosophical perspectives which are overawed by science and have come to worship it.

We have now to see that this preliminary sketch actually describes what is found in Hegel's text, briefly in the transition from Perception to Understanding, then in the analysis of Understanding (Hegel's Chapter Three) and Observing Reason (Chapter Five-A). That it is scientific consciousness which is described in Chapter Three is clear from the detailed account of the postulation of forces and the search for laws, in spite of Hegel's allusions to similarities between scientific consciousness and other forms, particularly Platonic and religious, and in spite of the fact that in other writings Hegel often uses the term Understanding in distinction from Reason to characterize a genus of thought which has science as only one of its species.

The inclusion of Chapter Five-A at this point is more problematic. Apart from the Kantian tradition which sharply distinguishes Understanding from Reason, it at first appears as if any joint treatment of Understanding and Observing Reason involves excessive violence to Hegel's own format, in which the two are separated by all of Chapter Four on Self-Consciousness. In the process the realistic attitude of Understanding has been replaced by the idealism of Reason. It is nevertheless neither desirable nor necessary to separate the two. It is undesirable because so much of the latter is a repetition of the former, or rather, the application of the same insights to new illustrative material. This is especially clear in relation to the search for laws of nature, which characterizes both Understanding and Observing Reason. It is unnecessary because the theoretical differences between realistic Understanding and idealistic Reason actually play no significant role in the analysis of science. Observing Reason is repeatedly described as merely the instinct of Reason, a description equally appropriate to Understanding.[9]

4B. The Supersensible Character of Scientific Thought

Since he is seeking to lead natural consciousness to understand its own self-transcending tendencies, Hegel takes the bold step of reformulating the question—How is science possible?—by asking instead—Why is science necessary? Is it a mere accident that Perception becomes Understanding? Or is there something about the former that somehow generates the latter? Most of the chapter on Perception is devoted to showing how the answer to this last question must be affirmative.

Hegel directs our attention to a cube of salt, just as Descartes directed it to a piece of wax. Both these familiar objects are used to illustrate the movement of consciousness to the world of scientific thought. It is entirely typical of Hegel that while Descartes points out the changeability of the wax in our *sensory* experience of it, he focuses on the volatility of our attempts to *think* the salt. It is not the changing appearance of the salt from one moment to the next but its contradictory character at any given moment which drives consciousness beyond Perception.[10]

The cube of salt is the determinate-indeterminate object which emerged in the discussion of Sense Certainty. As intended in its full determinateness it is an entirely unique particular. As actually present to consciousness, however, it is only partially determined in a process of determination which is never completed. In precisely these two aspects it is the thing and its properties, the former as intended, the latter as actually intuited. There seems to be no contradiction here, for the determinacy and indeterminacy of the object are parcelled out to different aspects, namely to the in-so-far-as-intended and the in-so-far-as-intuited. It is in fact the function of the category, thing-and-properties, to avoid contradiction by distinguishing respects in this way.

This distinguishing of respects is crucial. For contradiction arises when conflicting predictions can be made of the same subject matter at the same time and in the same respect, and the salt is clearly at the same time *qua* thing something one and simple and *qua* properties something manifold and diverse.[11] If it should turn out that there is a single respect in virtue of which the object both is a thing and has its properties, Perception would be in trouble. Thinghood and property having would be revealed as not genuinely different aspects of the object, but simply the artificial attempt of natural consciousness to hide the contradiction between the thing's oneness and its manyness, its determinacy and its indeterminacy. This would be fatal to Perception, whose criterion Hegel discovers to be self-sameness or self-consistency [*Sichselbstgleichheit*], by which he means to say simply that for common sense a thing is what it is and not another thing.[12]

Hegel finds that there is indeed a single respect by means of which the perceptual object is a thing and has its properties. The very determinacy which distinguishes Perception from Sense Certainty is now its Achilles' heel. For the object is the one thing it is just in so far as it is determinate, while it is also the many properties it "has" just in so far as it is determinate. "Healthy common sense" is here betrayed by the very "in so far" that it uses to preserve the integrity of its objects. Since it is in respect to its determinateness that the object is a thing and has properties, is one and many, Hegel finds a genuine contradiction. "The object is rather *in one and the same respect* the opposite of itself: for itself in so far as it is for another, and for another in so far as it is for itself."[13]

Since consciousness "experiences"[14] this contradiction between its criterion and its actual knowledge, though without knowing exactly what is happening, it develops itself into another form of consciousness. Perception is distinguished from Sense Certainty by the universality of its object, i.e., by its mediated character in a variety of whole-part contexts.[15] "But this universal, since it is derived from sense, is essentially conditioned by it, and hence is, in general, not a genuine self-identical [*sich selbstgleich*] universality, but one affected with opposition." Consciousness therefore seeks for the "unconditioned absolute universality" in opposition to this "merely sensible universality."[16]

Typically for Hegel the adequate statement of the problem practically provides its own solution. The trouble with the things of Perception is that they can neither be nor be understood apart from their relation to other things. They are in this sense both mediated and conditioned. Their full comprehension can only come through grasping the whole of which they are a part. This whole is the unconditioned universal which can both be and be understood in terms of itself. It is mediated and therefore both real and determinate, but it is self-mediated and therefore intelligible in itself. It is Spinoza's substance, or what Kant calls the concept of nature in general.[17] It is clearly an object of thought, for this sort of totality is not given in sense experience.

This distinction between conditioned, sensible universality and unconditioned universality, free from the limits of sense, is clearly a categoreal issue. It involves the basic conceptual framework within which the object of consciousness is determined. But the transition is not simply from the category of substance to those of cause and reciprocity, as the parallel sections in the Jena Logic would suggest.[18] Still less is the difference between empirical concepts and a priori categories, for it is already clear that 'thing-and-properties' is no less categoreal than such concepts as force and law. The transition from the sensible to the supersensible world is one from the categoreal framework appropriate to everyday perceptual experience to a system of categories which systematically reinterprets that experience. Descartes' wax becomes matter in motion, Hegel's salt NaCl.

Hegel's task is now to describe two different but closely related modes in which Understanding ascends to its supersensible world, force postulating science and law formulating science. The former corresponds roughly to Aristotelian science, the latter to Galilean-Newtonian science. The boundary between them is not sharp, since the concept of force did not die out quickly but continued to play an important role even for Newton.

When consciousness begins to think in terms of forces and their expression (whether these be Aristotelian entelechies or gravitational and magnetic forces) instead of in terms of things and their properties, "the unconditioned universal emerges as the unobjective or inner aspect of things."[19] Since it is the universal aspect of things in Hegel's own distinctive sense which is their truth or essence, the truth of things is no longer their immediate, familiar presence to everyday perception, but something related to this presence as inner reality to outer experience. Remember Descartes' wax. Baillie is quite justified here in introducing "unperceived" as a gloss on "inner".

Hegel stresses the indirect and non-perceptual relation of consciousness to what is now its object. "This true being of things has here the characteristic of not existing immediately for consciousness; rather consciousness has a mediated relation to the inner and as Understanding looks through this middle, the play of forces, into the true background of things. The middle [die Mitte] which unites the two extremes, Understanding and the inner of things, is the developed being of force, which Understanding itself now takes to be that which disappears. It is therefore called appearance [Erscheinung] . . . The being of the object is mediated for consciousness through the movement of appearance, in which the world of Perception and sensible objects in general have only the negative significance that consciousness thus reflects itself out of the sensible into itself as the true, but as consciousness makes this truth into an objective inner realm . . . an extreme over against it . . . It is only in this inner realm of truth, as the absolute universal . . . that a supersensible world now opens up as the true world above the sensible world of appearance, the permanent beyond [das *bleibende Jenseits*] above the disappearing present [*das verschwindende Diesseits*], an in itself which is the first and therefore incomplete appearance of Reason."[20]

It is no different when Understanding seeks to discover laws of nature. Such a law is the "changeless image of changing appearance. The supersensible world is in this way a peaceful kingdom of laws, no doubt beyond the world of Perception, for this exhibits the law only through constant change, but likewise present in it and its immediate unmoving image."[21] This definition of laws as the unchanging or unmoving image of the temporal flux is a deliberate inversion of Plato's definition of time as the moving image of eternity. For Hegel as for the neo-Kantian, the law formulating scientist is a kind of Platonist.

The analysis of the quest for laws in Chapter Five repeats these motifs with special emphasis on the link between scientific method and the abandonment of the everyday life-world. Scientific consciousness is anything but a passive receptacle to whom experience happens. "Here it settles itself the observations to be made and the experience to be had." Nature must answer questions of Reason's own determining. Science thus consciously takes the perceptual world as *aufgehoben*. It claims to know the truth about the "things" of that world, bits of wax and salt, for example. In doing so "it transforms their sensibility into concepts, i.e., precisely into the kind of being as thought [*gedachtes Sein*] and asserts in fact that things have truth only as concepts." For this reason the perception of a penknife lying beside a snuffbox does not count as a scientific observation, nor do the tradesman and housewife express a law of nature when they complain that it always rains at the fair and on washday.[22]

What these forms of everyday knowledge lack is the experimental procedure by which reason "purifies the law and its moments and makes them concepts. It puts the law to the test of experiment. As the law first appears, it presents itself impurely, enveloped in particular, sensible being, and the concept which constitutes its nature is submerged in empirical subject matter." In experiment "the law seems only to be plunged still deeper into sensible being, but instead it is the sensible aspect which is lost in the experiment . . . As the truth of this experimenting consciousness we see that pure law which is freed from sensible being. We see it as a concept, which while present in sense, operates there independently and unrestrained, while sunk in sense is free from it and is simple concept."[23] This purification of law takes place primarily as the purification of its moments, i.e., by the development of such concepts as positive and negative electricity, acid and base. The object is to be understood not in terms of the features it immediately offers to everyday perception, but in terms of precisely defined concepts developed for the purpose of making nature answer questions of Reason's own determining. In this way scientific method replaces the sensible with the supersensible object.[24]

4C. The Tautological Character of Scientific Explanation

In spite of its supersensible character science is at least as worldly as the original Prodigal Son. For its interest in the supersensible world is nothing but the desire to make sense of the sensible world, or, as it is often put, to explain it.[25] The examination of science's claim to be paradigmatic knowledge now takes the form of testing its explanatory power. As in the Jena Logic, the thesis which emerges is that scientific explanations are tautologies.[26]

A sense of the explanatory emptiness of Aristotelian science contributed significantly to the rise of modern science in the sixteenth and seventeenth centuries. The developing critique of its substantial forms as occult causes was effectively summed up by Molière's witticism about opium causing sleep by means of its dormitive virtue. This translates into the rather unilluminating assertion that opium causes sleep by means of its capacity to cause sleep.

That Hegel's critique of force is directed against Aristotelian science is particularly clear in the Jena Logic where the link between the category 'force-and-its-expression' and the category 'actuality-potentiality' is explicit. In that context he even gives his own version of Molière. "That the stone falls to the ground, i.e., posits itself as one with the ground, is not expressed by scientific explanation by saying that it posits itself as one with the ground because it posits itself as one with it, but rather by saying that a force in the stone posits it as one, namely the force which posits it as one with the ground." Nor does explanation describe a magnet by saying "that the magnet orients itself to north and south because it orients itself that way, attracts iron filings because it attracts them, and repels its like poles because it repels them; rather because in the substance which shows itself in this way there is something else than itself, namely a magnetic force, and this magnetic force has the power to orient the substance in this way, to attract such filings to it and to repel like poles."[27] In this way the tautology is hidden.

Modern science did not immediately abandon the concept of force, however. Even Newton, the prime target of Chapter Three, was not entirely of one mind about the matter. At times he speaks of the "deduction" of forces, while at other times his concern is for descriptive laws, accompanied by an agnosticism about any causal forces behind the regularities described. Compare the following:

1a) By the propositions mathematically demonstrated in the first book, we then derive from the celestial phenomena the forces of gravity with which bodies tend to the sun and the several planets.

1b) But hitherto I have been unable to discover the cause of those properties of gravity from phenomena, and I frame no hypotheses.

2a) By this way of analysis we may proceed from compounds to ingredients and from motions to the forces producing them; and in general, from effects to causes.

2b) To tell that every species of things is endowed with an occult specific quality by which it acts and produces manifest effects is to tell us nothing. But to derive two or three general principles of motion from phenomena, and afterwards to tell us how the properties and actions of all corporeal things follow from those manifest principles, would be a great step in philosophy, though the causes of those principles were not yet discovered.[28]

These passages express a movement of thought which Hegel takes up in the *Phenomenology*, an ambivalence in modern science. On the one hand squeamishness about occult causes leads from force to law as the principle scientific category. On the other hand the distinction between the expression of force appearing as effect and force proper as hidden inner cause is not abandoned. Instead it is simply maintained that "the inner being of things cannot be known." To be sure, Hegel replies, there can be no knowledge of the inner, so conceived, "but not because reason is too shortsighted or limited . . . but because of the nature of the matter itself, namely that in the void there is nothing known, or to put it from the other side, because the inner is determined precisely as that which lies beyond consciousness."[29] In other words, the unknowability of the inner realm is as tautological as the previous claim to explanation by reference to it. Having defined the inner as unknowable, Understanding wisely frames no hypotheses and confesses that the substance of things is "something I know not what."

That which explains nothing and is itself unknowable seems to be more than useless. But rather than seeking to reduce the concept of force to absurdity, a la Molière, Hegel seeks to understand it.[30] The problem is that the distinction of force proper from its expression "exists only in thought" so that "the truth of force thus remains only the thought of force." In this way "consciousness has reflected itself out of the world of Perception and sensible objects and into itself as the true . . ." But consciousness doesn't realize this and so "it again makes this truth an objective inner reality . . ."[31]

Hegel's point is fairly simple. Consciousness begins with substances externally related to each other, the things of Perception. In seeking to think these things it develops a concept, force, in which the processes of the perceptual world are conceived in terms of a distinction between two internally related moments, force proper and its expression. But consciousness forgets that its thinking has not left the perceptual world unchanged, and it takes its own conceptual distinction of internally related elements for a distinction of externally related substances. It then treats force proper as a cause and its expression as an effect. At first this results in pseudo-explanation; then, as the explanatory claim is withdrawn, it results in the idea of an unknowable inner world hidden behind the appearances which somehow both conceal and reveal it. Lacking self-consciousness, Understanding is snared by what Whitehead calls the fallacy of misplaced concreteness. That is to say, when it finds certain conceptual devices useful for some purpose it immediately and without further ado takes these for the definitive expression of the real. While it is proud of its radical transformation of the perceptual world, it continues to treat its newly developed concepts as if they belonged to that long since abandoned sensible world. It is all too half-hearted about leaving home.

There is nothing very original in this critique of Aristotelian science and its residual presence in Newtonian science. Where Hegel's discussion of science is untimely, relative to "the present standpoint of Spirit," is in the discovery that law formulating science as such is plagued by the same problems as force postulating science. Understanding claims that in uncovering the laws of nature it achieves a genuine, non-tautological form of explanation. Hegel finds this to be a delusion just because "Understanding has not yet transcended the process of framing laws."[32]

Rather than impose an external criterion on science, Hegel compares the actual laws of nature it puts forth with the "pure concept of law" (which he curiously wants to identify with Newton's universal law of gravitation) and finds a contradiction. Science does not conform to its own criterion, and "the concept of law is turned against the law itself." The variables related in the law are to be, in Hegel's language, "mutually indifferent and inherently real entities." But at the same time "the pure concept of law . . . must, to get its true significance, be so apprehended that in it as something absolutely simple, the variables [*Unterschiede*] which are present in the law as such return again themselves into the inner as simple unity. This unity is the inner necessity of the law."[33] Had Hegel mentioned Hume here as he does in a similar passage in the Jena Logic, it would have been easier to see that this is his way of posing the problem of finding any necessary connection between independently specifiable variables.

If the two components of the concept of law, independent specifiability and necessary connection, are as incompatible as they seem to be, science can only vacillate between them. Its laws will either possess necessity without independence or independence without necessity. But it will no more be able to combine both in the same law than Sense Certainty was able to combine genuine immediacy with determinacy. This is what Hegel finds, though his formula is once again less than Humean in its lucidity. "Either the universal, force, is indifferent to the division into elements which is found in the law, or the variables, the elements of the law are indifferent toward each other."[34]

Fortunately there are examples. Electricity is used to illustrate the first case, where the force in question is said to be indifferent to the analysis used in formulating laws. Since it represents a series of phenomena to be caught in a nomological network, it may be spoken of as a force distinct from the laws which describe it. It is analyzed into positive and negative electricity, and the laws about the relation of these two elements seem to express a necessary connection. But such necessity is "an empty word," for there is no necessity that electricity should be analyzed in this way. To reply that this is the way electricity is defined is to let the cat out of the bag. It is to confess that necessity has been purchased at the cost of independent specifiability. Within the context of a certain analysis positive and negative electricity are necessarily related to one another in various ways, but this necessity is a function of the theory, not of anything in nature. For there is no reason apparent to Hegel why electricity should be conceptualized in this way.[35]

In the second case the elements into which a phenomenon naturally divides are seen as indifferent to one another. The division of motion, for example, into spatial and temporal determinations, distance and velocity, belongs to the subject matter in a way in which positive and negative do not belong to electricity. But these elements are indifferent to one another and resist the attempt to discover any necessary connection between them. This is not to deny that Understanding can observe regularities in nature. It is only the reminder that observed regularity is one thing, necessary connection quite another. Hegel's point is the same as Hume's, even if the style is not.

Laws of nature, then, pose this dilemma: either they achieve the necessity their concept calls for, only to discover that it is a definitional necessity and "it is thus only its own necessity to which Understanding gives expression," or they fail to find that necessity and are reduced to summarizing empirical data. "While explanation makes as if it would say something different from what is already said, it really says nothing at all, but merely repeats the same thing over again."[36] When a law-like statement must be interpreted as merely a summary of the data on which it is asserted, it loses the nomological, as opposed to the accidental universality, which is required of a law of nature. It can no longer support subjunctive conditionals. To do so and thus to conform to the idea of a law of nature some sort of necessity would have to be regained. But the only available necessity is tautological.

The materials with which Hegel illustrates this dilemma in Chapter Five are obscure for historical reasons, but not hopelessly so. The horn of the dilemma on which only contingency and indifference are to be found is illustrated at great length in the discussion of Physiognomy and Phrenology. They represent extreme cases of Observation coming upon a genuinely indifferent subject matter and becoming ludicrous in the attempt to extract necessity from it.

On the other hand, when Observation turns to an organic subject matter or to the relation of individual human personality to its environment, it is dealing with a subject matter where genuinely internal relations are present. But here where the parts have their meaning only within the process of the whole and are not thus indifferent to one another, "the law wants to grasp and express the opposed elements as independent variables [*ruhende Seiten*] and to give them in their independence the determinacy which is their relation to one another . . . [The moments] lose their organic significance in being kept apart in this way. And at the bottom of the idea of law lies just this, that each of its two aspects should have a subsistence on its own account indifferent to the other."[37] For Hegel this means simply that we murder to explain, that Observation can apply its method to a living subject matter only by first turning it into a cadaver. For Observation it means that all hope of finding non-tautological necessity is lost. It is in this context that Hegel calls special attention to the quantifying dimension of scientific method.

One example from this domain of the organic is of particular interest. It concerns the analysis of organisms into three systems: sensibility, irritability, and reproduction. Irritability, the strange looking member of the trio, is simply the power of an organism to respond to stimuli. Structurally it refers to the muscular system, while functionally it is the complement of sensibility, the capacity to receive stimuli. When observation seeks to formulate laws about the relation of these functions it may seek to quantify the qualitatively complementary elements of sensibility and irritability and come up with a neat looking inverse proportion, "Sensibility and irritability stand in inverse quantitative relations." Hegel's opinion of this is expressed in the parallel he suggests, "The size of a hole increases the more we decrease what it is filled with." The tautological character of these affirmations lies in the fact that the two elements are so related conceptually in each case that "the one has any significance at all only in so far as the other is present." Like north and south poles of a magnet, positive and negative electricity, acid and base, one element is defined by its relation to the other. Hence the tautological character of the necessity discovered.[38]

It is not impossible, of course, to define the organic functions independently of one another. This would be necessary for finding a non-tautological law. But at the same time all hope of finding necessity is lost. The functions then become indifferent to one another and "defy the attempt to reduce them to law. For their character as sensible being consists in existing in complete indifference to one another . . . in exhibiting nature's irrational way of playing up and down the scale of contingent quantity . . . ."

Here again is the dilemma of contingency and tautological necessity. But this time the two horns are represented by one and the same subject matter, not by different fields of scientific endeavor. Here Observation vacillates in its treatment of a single phenomenon between finding its variables contingently related and finding them necessarily related, though the latter is possible, in Carnapian language, only because the proper meaning postulates have been added to the system.

The witticisms which Hegel sprinkles throughout his analysis of science will suggest to some that in this area he was reduced to ridiculing what he could not understand. But the problems he pinpoints have merited serious discussion in our own century quite outside Hegelian circles. What he calls the supersensible character of scientific thought lies at the heart of the problematic of Whitehead's *Science and the Modern World* as well as Husserl's *Crisis.* At the same time contemporary philosophy of science concerns itself with what he calls the tautological character of scientific explanation. We take it to be a law of nature that copper is a good electrical conductor, that if equal weights are placed at the extremities of a homogeneous rigid bar suspended in the middle the lever is in equilibrium, and that a body moving without the influence of external forces maintains a constant velocity. But while these laws were at first asserted on experimental grounds and were presumably falsifiable by counter evidence, they now most often function as logically necessary truths, expressing in whole or in part the definitions of copper, equal weights, and freely moving bodies.[39] Similarly, when the conservation of energy was challenged by beta-ray decay, instead of taking the law to be refuted, it was "saved" by positing the neutrino. When this sort of thing happens, "we are along the road to transforming the meaning of some of the terms employed in the premise, so that its empirical content is gradually absorbed into the meaning of those terms."[40]

Hegel's critique of the quest for Laws of nature can be summarized as follows:

1) Science is not able to find the necessity it seeks for its laws, for the concept of law requires that the related elements be independently specifiable whereas necessity resides in internal relations. Where science comes upon internal relations, it first destroys them by its mathematical analysis, and then bemoans the problem of natural necessity.

2) What necessity science does profess is only apparent or tautological. It comes from identifying nature with its own conceptual framework, where all necessity is definitional.

3) These difficulties and the consequent vacillation between contingency and tautology result from science's attempt to force nature to answer its own questions, to impose its own purposes on the world.

This last way of putting it indicates that the time has come to move on from the pre-transcendental analysis of the object of science, nature as the interplay of forces and the realm of lawful processes, to consideration of the transcendental and post-transcendental insights which have come to light "for us."[41]

4D. The Transcendental Source of Science's Supersensible Tautologies

We have already noted the naive objectivism of Perception. Its object and the process of perceiving it stand in strictest correlation. "The object is in its essential nature the same as the process." But healthy common sense, instead of being aware of the categories by which its own activity is carried out and thereby coming to master them, is unconscious of them and is thus tossed about as their plaything and prey.[42]

Understanding resembles its common sense counterpart in this respect. "We" who watch its object emerge out of the world of Perception see that it "has arisen through the movement of consciousness in such a way that consciousness is implicated in its development, and the reflection on both sides is the same, i.e., there is only one reflection. Intentional act and intentional object are inseparable. The given is what is taken. Understanding, however, is still consciousness, focused on its object, not self-consciousness, aware of itself. Its transcendental subjectivity is hidden from it and "it does not know itself in that reflected object," i.e., in the object developed by the systematic reinterpretation of the perceptual world.[43] This recurring assertion from Chapters Three and Five-A that science doesn't know itself in its object or that it finds itself there but doesn't recognize itself means simply that Understanding is a systematically false consciousness. Not recognizing its own creative activity in its own products, it becomes enslaved to them as if they were independently and eternally given.[44]

This objectivism is not merely the absence of a certain self-awareness. It involves a mistaken self-image on the part of Understanding. In taking its object [Gegenstand] to be something objective [gegenständlich] it not only views the object as simply given. It views itself as having no role in the result of the knowing process. It merely looks on and mirrors [ihr nur zusieht und sie rein auffasst].[45] There is no quarrel here between Hegel and the Understanding about the criterion to be invoked. Hegel, too, knows that "scientific knowledge, however, demands precisely that we surrender to the life of the object or, and this is the same, that we confront and express its inner necessity." The only question is whether science adheres to this

criterion sufficiently to be genuinely scientific, or whether it is
the kind of knowing which "instead of abiding in the subject
matter and forgetting itself in it . . . always reaches out for
something else and really remains preoccupied with itself instead of sticking to and devoting itself to the subject matter."
Hegel finds it to be the latter, the kind of formal understanding
which "instead of entering into the immanent content of the
matter always looks over the whole and stands above the individual existence of which it speaks, i.e., it simply overlooks it."[46]

At issue here is the significance of scientific method. Science claims to be objective in an honorific sense because it has a
method which frees its knowledge from private and collective
prejudice and provides it with intersubjective verifiability.
Hegel, on the contrary, finds that it is precisely science's
method which precludes its giving itself in a listening way to its
subject matter and results in its imposing itself on its subject
matter. Its questions and its categories determine the way in
which the world can be given to Understanding. It is not nature
who offers herself as a network of necessary connections between independent variables. It is scientific method which requires that she appear that way. Being unaware of all this,
Understanding is objective in a pejorative sense. The
phenomenological task is to assist natural consciousness in this
stage of its development by bringing to light the transcendental
subjectivity without which scientific explanation is impossible.

It is not that Understanding is entirely unreflective. But its
philosophy of science, like Hume and unlike Kant, recognizes
problems like that of necessary connection without winning its
way through to an explicit and systematic transcendental self-
consciousness. Like the early Wittgenstein it recognizes the difficulty of developing a language which is isomorphic with reality, but unlike the late Wittgenstein it doesn't see that language
constitutes the world and is no mere attempt to mirror it.
Understanding must first be brought to the Kantian or transcendental perspective and then to the late Wittgensteinian or
post-transcendental perspective. In this latter perspective language is recognized as a form of life, theory as a form of praxis.
There it is possible to see science as both an historical accomplishment and an epistemological limit, and, in seeing both together, to transcend the positivistic tendencies of Kantian tran-
scendentalism.

Hegel returns to the problem of necessity in laws of nature. The spatial and temporal variables dealt with there, distance, velocity, etc., are indifferent to one another and sustain no necessary relation. But in the law they are *begeistet*, and assume, like positive and negative electricity, a necessary relation. In the process of explanation Understanding transcends the independence of the variables and posits them in necessary relation. But the movement and necessity here is that of Understanding. This is why "there is so much satisfaction in explanation, because consciousness, being there, so to speak, in conversation with itself, enjoys only itself. No doubt it seems to be occupied with something else, but in fact *it fools around only with itself.*"[47] The moments of the law may be abstractions in the sense of being products of the activity by which Understanding deliberately withdraws from the perceptual world. "By its way of looking at the matter, Observation transforms the opposition into one which conforms and is *adapted to its own point of view.*"[48]

With this insight "we see that in the inner world over against appearance Understanding experiences nothing other than appearance itself," but in such a way that at the same time it "in fact only experiences itself. Raised above Perception, consciousness reveals itself united and bound up with the supersensible world through the mediating agency of the world of appearance, through which it gazes into the background. The two extremes, the pure inner world and the inner world which looks into this first inner are now merged together . . . In this way the curtain of appearance no longer hides the inner world, which, instead, is present to the gaze of the other inner world . . . It is manifest that behind the so-called curtain which is to hide the inner world there is nothing to be seen unless we ourselves go behind it, as much in order that we may thereby see as that there may be something behind there which can be seen."[49]

Hegel is entitled to speak of "inner" worlds here for one very simple reason: he is talking about what is not given in the "outer" world of Perception where consciousness first makes its home. It is only by transcending this patent and palpable world of outward sensory awareness that consciousness discovers the two inner worlds which here unite. The first is the world of theoretical entities and laws postulated by science. The second is the world of scientific intelligence whose theorizing brings

the first to light. To say that these two "are now merged together" and that in experiencing the first inner world consciousness "in fact only experiences itself," i.e., the second inner
world, is to say that the two belong inextricably together.
Hegel's way of putting it suggests a fictionalist or conven-
tionalist account of scientific theory. But his point is not so
much to settle the ontological status of science's objects as to call
epistemological attention to the importance of science's activity.
The totality of nature as the object of scientific theory turns out
not to be the unconditioned universal after all, for in its presence to consciousness it is thoroughly conditioned by consciousness itself. The totality which could claim to be a
genuinely unconditioned universal will have to include not only
the object of consciousness but consciousness as well, in all the
modes of its active encounter with its object. It follows that the
knowledge of nature cannot be Absolute Knowledge, for it does
not include the conditions of its own possibility.

This is the result of the whole dialogue with Sense Certainty, Perception, and Understanding, a movement from Consciousness to Self-Consciousness. Its full meaning has yet to be
disclosed, for it is only a transcendental perspective which has
here been achieved, and the post-transcendental attitude for
which Hegel has been preparing us has not yet emerged. We
have reached a half-way house between the simple and sophisticated forms of objectivist consciousness with which we began
and the standpoint of Spirit to which Hegel wants to lead us.

The Idealism whose description prefaces Chapter Five is a
permanent resident of this half-way house. It has achieved
transcendental self-consciousness and knows that the "I am I"
or the transcendental unity of apperception is the foundation
of all knowledge. But having forgotten the path by which this
insight has been achieved and the evidence which could support its claim, it not only cannot go further but comes on the
scene as a dogmatic and unintelligible assurance.[50]

An even more serious consequence of this forgetfulness is
that this Idealism (Hegel seems to have Fichte in mind more
than Kant) does not fully understand its own insight and cannot
even articulate its full meaning. What needs to be unfolded and
developed is the claim that "all objects are in a deep sense
mine."[51] But it is only in a very shallow sense that this newborn

Idealism is able to see all objects as its own. "Its first declaration is merely this abstract, empty phrase that everything is its own ... Reason knowing itself in this sense in its object is what finds expression in abstract, empty Idealism, which only grasps reason as it appears at first, and by pointing out this pure mine [*Mein*] of consciousness in all being [*Sein*] ... it fancies it has shown that mine to be complete reality. It is bound, therefore, to be at the same time absolute empiricism, because for the filling of this empty mine ... its reason needs an impact [*Anstoss*] from without in which alone lies the diverse content of sensing or representing. This idealism is thus just such a self-contradictory equivocation as scepticism."[52]

In identifying this Idealism with empiricism and scepticism and discussing it simply as a preface to the description of Observing Reason, Hegel gives us part of the socio-analysis of critical finitism which was called for by the Introduction.[53] That finitism, with which Idealism is here associated, sees clearly that a knowing which consists of bringing together highly formal (mathematical-logical) a priori categories with sensibly given subject matter cannot know the Absolute. Yet it absolutizes this finite knowing because it is so bedazzled by its spectacular achievements as natural science. It claims to be philosophy but is overawed by a knowledge it knows cannot fulfill philosophy's task. Had it pursued its transcendental insights more doggedly it would have avoided dogmatically absolutizing a mode of knowledge whose method bars it from the truth.[54]

This empirical, sceptical Idealism has learned with Kant that the "I think" must be able to accompany all my representations, and that they are all in this sense mine. And it has learned with Descartes that I, who think, am a thinking being. But it has not reflected deeply enough on the Cartesian question, What am I, in so far as I am a thinking being, *res cogitans*? In the Third Meditation Descartes' answer is that a thinking being is one who, among other things, doubts, believes, imagines, and chooses. While transcendental analysis of these activities can be given, it is important to notice that the transcendental ego never doubts, believes, imagines, or chooses anything. Hegel's account reminds us that only concrete persons do these things, and that how they do them depends at least in part on where they stand in history. "Consciousness will determine its relation to otherness or its object in various ways, according as it is at one or another stage in the development of World Spirit to self-consciousness. How the World Spirit immediately finds and determines itself and its object, or how consciousness is for itself, depends on what World Spirit has already come to be . . ."[55]

This is to suggest that the transcendental ego must be placed in the context of Spirit and its history. Spirit is not Aristotle's Unmoved Mover which thinks itself outside of any relation to the processes of our world and its history. Its self-consciousness is not immediate, but mediated through its own external expressions. What Hegel says of individual Spirit is no less true of universal Spirit. "Language and labor are expressions [*Äusserungen*] in which the individual no longer retains possession of himself, but lets the inner get completely outside of him and exposes and abandons it to another." This has the consequence that "in order to know what a specific individual is in himself" one must acknowledge the wisdom of Solon, "who thought it possible to know this only from and after the course of one's whole life."[56] Spirit is known through the interpretation of its words and deeds, i.e., through historical understanding.

To place transcendental subjectivity in this context is to adopt the post-transcendental perspective. It is to talk about the history of intentionality, of how consciousness takes what is given, thereby bridging the alleged gulf between the transcendental and historical points of view. This calls for an explicit development of the concept of Spirit and a comprehensive interpretation of its history.

NOTES

1. *Realphilosophie*, 179 and PhG, XXXVIII/29-30/93. This latter passage comes in the context of Hegel's critique of the familiar.

2. Quoted from Hans-Georg Gadamer, *Wahrheit und Methode*, 2nd ed., Tübingen, 1965, p. 4. My italics.

3. Also see the opening chapters of E.A. Burtt, *The Metaphysical Foundations of Modern Science*, and of A. N. Whitehead, *Science and the Modern World*.

4. *Critique of Pure Reason*, B xiii.

5. So does Heidegger's distinction between *Zuhandenheit* and *Vorhandenheit*.

6. The importance of this dependence has been developed with great subtlety as a major theme of twentieth century phenomenology, not only in the work of Merleau-Ponty, from whom the phrase "primacy of perception" is borrowed, but earlier in Heidegger's *Being and Time* and Husserl's *Crisis*.

7. *op. cit.*, p. 3.

8. It is in the Preface that Hegel himself invokes the image of the Prodigal Son while describing the poverty of Spirit underlying the reversion to immediacy. In the following paragraph he relates this directly to the scientific revolution. See section 2A. above. The metaphor is particularly apt, since he seeks to show that like the original prodigal, scientific consciousness comes by itself to recognize its poverty and to return home from the far country. This return is at first without repentance, however, since it appeals to an immediacy which absolutizes the familiar, i.e., tries to act as if nothing had happened.

9. See note 20 below.

10. An explicitly practical "deduction" would not be in place here, since the form of natural consciousness which is our object here has not yet come to question the rigid boundary between theory and praxis. That science is not pure theory but a form of behavior is something which "we" are to see in the course of the description.

11. PhG, 41/91/164. *zugleich*.

12. PhG, 44/93/167.

13. PhG, 54-56/99-100/175-76. Hegel italicizes the phrase here in italics as well as the remainder of the sentence. In this context "for itself" implies oneness, "for another" manyness.

14. In both the Introduction and the Preface Hegel develops the

concept of "the experience which consciousness makes" to refer to its transitions from one form to another rather than to its life within each form. This sense of "experience" is developed more explicitly in the chapters on Perception and Understanding than anywhere else in the *Phenomenology*.

15. On the link between universality and mediation, see PhG, 39-40/90/163-64.

16. PhG, 54-55/99-100/175-76.

17. Spinoza defines substance as "that which is in itself and is conceived through itself." *Ethics*, Part I, Definition III, Elwes translation. In terms of the Kantian categories of quantity, Hegel is here looking for the Totality which will keep Unity and Plurality from falling apart.

18. GW, 7:38-75. For Kant the category of substance is already a determination of the whole, of nature in general.

19. PhG, 65/106/185.

20. PhG, 71-73/110-11/190-91.

21. PhG, 78/114-15/195.

22. PhG, 174-77/183-85/281-84. cf. Ch. 3, n. 45 and 256/236/349.

23. PhG, 186-89/191-93/291-93.

24. This discussion should be read in conjunction with C.G. Hempel, *Fundamentals of Concept Formation in Empirical Science*. Although Hegel almost expresses the notion of operational definitions here, he ignores the important role of quantification and calculation in concept formation until a later passage. See note 37 below.

25. See Ch. 2, n. 6.

26. GW, 7:48-50, 58-61.

27. *Ibid.*, pp. 59-60.

28. Quoted from E.A. Burtt, *The Metaphysical Foundations of Modern Science*, Garden City, 1932, pp. 210, 226, 225, and 223. The first pair is from *The Mathematical Principles of Natural Philosophy*, the second from the *Opticks*. Burtt does not call attention to the striking ambivalence of these passages, widely separated in the former work, but only four pages apart in the second.

29. PhG, 74/112/192. Though Hegel may be alluding to a poem of A. v. Haller, Book III of Locke's *Essay* and Newton's refusal to hypothesize are the original formulations of the position in question. Haller's poem from 1730 includes the lines, *"Ins innre der Natur dringt kein erschaffner Geist,/ Zu glücklich, wenn sie noch die äussre Schale weist!"* See GW, 7:372, note to page 63.

30. The contemporary reader can appreciate Hegel's patience in

dwelling with this form of scientific consciousness. Science has turned back on itself, and the once despised practice of an ontologically oriented science has returned in new dress. See J.J.C. Smart, *Philosophy and Scientific Realism*. So much is this the case that Wilfrid Sellars is able to define the scientific outlook not in terms of the quest for laws, which he sees as merely a sophisticated form of common sense, but in terms of the postulation of imperceivable entities. See "Philosophy and the Scientific Image of Man," in *Science, Perception, and Reality*. Whether the postulating of theoretical entities in this sense can be said to provide an explanation of phenomena which is non-tautological is the discussion of a long essay by C.G. Hempel, "The Theoretician's Dilemma," *Minnesota Studies in the Philosophy of Science*, Vol. II, edited by Feigl, Scriven, and Maxwell.

31. PhG, 63-72/105-11/183-90.

32. See quotation 2b) from Newton above, and PhG, 214-15/209/313.

33. PhG, 80-81/116/197. cf. 183-89/189-92/288-93 and GW, 7:47-51.

34. PhG, 84/118/200.

35. PhG, 81-82/117/198-99. cf. GW, 7:61.

36. PhG, 84-86/119/200-01. The parallel between the former alternative and Poincaré's conventionalism on the one hand, and between the latter alternative and the Mill-Mach economy theory of scientific laws is striking.

37. PhG, 210-15/206-09/309-13. On quantification see 216-21/210-17/313-23. On human personality and its environment see 240-42/225-27/333-36.

38. For this and the next paragraph, see PhG, 202-09/201-05/303-08.

39. Ernest Nagel, *The Structure of Science*, London, 1961, Ch. 4. For similar discussions see N.R. Hanson, *Patterns of Discovery*, Cambridge, 1961, Ch. 5, and T.S. Kuhn, *The Structure of Scientific Revolutions*, Chicago, 1962, pp. 78, 132.

40. Nagel, *op. cit.*, pp. 66-67. Also see the Hempel essay cited in n. 30 above and Quine's essay, "Two Dogmas of Empiricism," in *From a Logical Point of View*.

41. See section 3A. above.

42. PhG, 38/89/162, 56-58/100-02/176-78. cf. Ch. 3, n. 36.

43. PhG, 59-60/103/180-81.

44. While this language suggests Marx, one could also use Freud-

ian metaphors; for the neurotic is enslaved to processes going on within him largely because he is unaware of them. In PhG, 193-96/195-97/296-99 and 231/220/326 these formulas about knowing oneself or finding oneself in the object have a different meaning and belong more to the philosophy of nature than the philosophy of science.

45. See note 43 above.

46. PhG, V/11/69 and LXVI/45/112. These passages from the Preface deal with philosophical thought, but they express Hegel's view of science and its method most succinctly. This is true of the entire second half of the Preface and is especially clear in the critique of pure mathematics. For similar passages dealing directly with science, see notes 47 and 48 below.

47. PhG, 93-97/124-27/207-10, my italics.

48. PhG, 183/189/288 and 198/198/300, my italics.

49. PhG, 99-100/128-29/211-13.

50. PhG, 164-65/176-77/273-75.

51. J. N. Findlay, *Hegel: A Re-Examination,* New York, 1962, p. 101, his italics.

52. PhG, 170-71/180-81/279.

53. See section 1B. above.

54. This critique is developed at length in *Glauben* and *Skepticismus.*

55. PhG, 166/178/275-76. Some editions would substitute "World Spirit" for the last mention of consciousness in the quotation, reading *er* instead of *es.* I have followed the first edition, which is retained by Hoffmeister. The "correction" by earlier editors doesn't significantly change the meaning, but it tends to underplay the interplay between individual and universal consciousness which comes to expression, for example, in the following passage: " . . . consciousness takes as the middle term between universal Spirit and its individuation in sensible consciousness the system of the forms of consciousness, as a life of Spirit which orders itself to totality [*zum Ganzen*],—the system which is dealt with in this treatise and which has its objective existence as world history." PhG, 231/220/326.

56. PhG, 246-49/229-31/340-42. The link between *Äusserung* in this passage and *Entäusserung* in Chapter Eight is crucial for the entire *Phenomenology.*

CHAPTER FIVE: The Concept of Spirit

5A. The Official Introduction to Spirit

It is not uncommon that we become acquainted with someone and learn to interact with him in various ways without ever being officially introduced. This does not always render such an introduction wholly useless. Indeed, when it finally comes it can significantly alter the relationship which has developed. Hegel's reader has by this time developed some such acquaintance with Spirit, but the time for an official introduction has clearly come. We'd love a simple definition. But Hegel insists upon a long and detailed derivation designed to defend the definition he ultimately gives us from the charge of being merely stipulative. The procedure by which Hegel derives the concept of Spirit is so thoroughly Kantian that it could usefully be called the transcendental deduction of Spirit. The point of contact with Kant's famous deduction is not merely procedural but also substantive. For Hegel wants to lead natural consciousness to an understanding of Spirit through a deepened reflection on self-consciousness as foundational to all our experience.

Having completed his description of the forms of consciousness collectively entitled Consciousness, Hegel has two apparently quite different tasks to perform. Most immediately his task is to develop the insight that "consciousness of an other, of an object in general, is indeed itself self-consciousness." This is the lesson which natural consciousness has derived from its experience at the end of Chapter Three. "The necessary advance from the previous forms of consciousness, which found their true content to be a thing, something other than themselves, brings to light this very fact, that not merely is consciousness of a thing only possible for a self-consciousness, but that this self-consciousness alone is the truth of those forms."[1]

The other task rests on Hegel's earlier promise to overcome the severe abstraction of theoretical from practical consciousness which characterizes the reflections on Consciousness.[2] It is clear from the way this promise is made that he does not mean practical reason in the Kantian sense, but rather a

121

phenomenological orientation to desire.[3] The philosophy of Spirit cannot begin with Spirit. Its highest principle must be its developed result, not its presupposed starting point. Just as the analysis of theoretical consciousness begins with sense perception, that of practical consciousness begins with desire. In both cases, and here Hegel is thoroughly Aristotelian, perhaps even Feuerbachian, the starting point is not man as rational but man as animal, as embodied. The task is to discover what is distinctively human in human perception and desire, never to find Spirit by disembodying man. From the perspective of the *Phenomenology* idealism is a philosophy of Spirit incarnate. After all, the guiding principle of Hegel's Jena work is that philosophy is to overcome such dualisms as that between mind and body, reason and sense, freedom and nature, etc., not to initiate them.[4]

It is through the combination of these two tasks that a distinctively Hegelian analysis of self-consciousness emerges. A phenomenology of desire is to be built into the phenomenology of self-consciousness. The fruitfulness of such a combination for Hegel's project is immediately evident. It would provide an initial answer to the question which he sought to evoke as a question throughout the description of Consciousness—Who is the transcendental subject? The transcendental subject is (perhaps more but not less than) embodied desiring consciousness. The way we take the world is conditioned by those interests we have in it which are called desire. If the categories which structure our intending of the world are the conditions for the possibility of experience, our interest in the world is in turn the condition for the possibility of those categories. What we are likely to find in the world is not independent of what we are looking for.

This would be the beginning of a meta-critical theory of knowledge, one which achieves the transcendental standpoint in such a way as immediately to transcend it by finding a larger context for its insights. It is what Hegel has been preparing his readers for.[5]

The question, then, is not the fruitfulness of combining the two tasks before Hegel, but the possibility of such a combination. This possibility is already hinted at in Hegel's promise not to abstract permanently from the practical. In the critique of

Sense Certainty he seeks to undercut the alleged "truth and certainty of the reality of the objects of sense," i.e., their absolute independence and dominance, by showing that they can be objects of sense only through the activity of consciousness. He finds a curious confirmation of this thesis in the phenomena of eating and drinking. In the mysteries of Ceres and Bacchus the initiate "not only comes to doubt the being of sensible things, but also to despair of it; and in dealing with them he partly himself brings about their nothingness, partly sees them bring about their own nothingness. Even animals are not shut off from this wisdom, but show themselves to be most deeply initiated into it. For they do not stand still before sensible things as if these had their being in themselves. Rather, in despair of this reality and in the full certainty of the nothingness of these things, they help themselves without ado and eat them up."[6]

The sense in which transcendental subjectivity and eating both undermine the independence of the object is formally expressed at the opening of Chapter Four. "In the kinds of certainty so far considered, consciousness takes the true to be something other than itself. The concept of this true, however, vanishes in the experience of it. Though the object was immediately [taken to be] in itself . . . it shows itself instead not to be this in truth. Rather, this in itself proves to be a way in which it is only for an other."[7] It is this abstract characteristic of being for another, of having its essential meaning in its relatedness rather than in its autonomy, that the intentional object shares with the eaten object.[8]

More than this formal similarity is implied, however, in the concept of a self-consciousness which a) is understood to be the truth of consciousness and b) at the same time is understood as desire. This implies some identity of intending consciousness with desiring consciousness such that desire can be said to be the truth or essence of intentionality.

That self-consciousness is the truth of consciousness is the result of Chapter Three. For Consciousness the object was something other than itself. But since it always showed itself to be for consciousness, attention is switched from it to a new "object," the consciousness before which the supposed autonomy [*Ansichsein*] of the first object always turned out to be a being-for-an-other [*für-ein-Anderes-Sein*]. Consciousness is thus no

longer knowledge of an other but knowledge of itself, and thus
Self-Consciousness, the successor not just of Understanding but
of the whole domain of Consciousness. The knowledge of nature, or more precisely, of the external world, has led beyond itself to another kind of knowledge. Because this new knowledge
is reflection in which the object is not alien to the subject but
identical with it, Hegel can say, "With Self-Consciousness then,
we have now passed into the native kingdom of truth." But far
from being at the end of our journey we have only really begun.
"We have to see how the form of Self-Consciousness first enters
the scene."[9]

Hegel now proceeds to show that Self-Consciousness is
only to be understood in terms of desire. It appears that Self-
Consciousness first enters the scene as the Kantian "I think,"
for it is a restatement of the deduction of the transcendental
unity of apperception which introduces it. But Kant's transcendental deduction is a two-edged sword which argues not
only that consciousness of an object is only possible for a self-
consciousness, but also the converse, that self-consciousness is
only possible through the consciousness of an object. For this
reason transcendental self-consciousness is not actual self-
consciousness. In the first flush of the discovery of self-
consciousness it is forgotten that self-consciousness is simply the
movement of reflection upon and out of object-
consciousness.[10] For this reason it "seems" that the "essential
feature" of Consciousness has been lost, namely "the simple independent reality [selbständige Bestehen]" of its object. "But when
Self-Consciousness distinguishes only itself as itself from itself,
the distinction is immediately taken to be transcended
[aufgehoben] in so far as it involves otherness. The distinction is
not, and Self-Consciousness is only the motionless tautology, I
am I. When the distinction does not also have for Self-
Consciousness the form of being, it is not Self-Consciousness.
For Self-Consciousness then, otherness [Anderssein] is there in
the form of being [als ein Sein] or as a distinct moment. But the
unity of itself with this difference is also there for Self-
Consciousness as a second distinct moment. In that first moment Self-Consciousness has the form of Consciousness, and
the whole expanse of the sensible world is retained for it, but at
the same time, only as related to the second moment, the unity
of Self-Consciousness with itself. And consequently the sensible

world has for Self-Consciousness a reality [*Bestehen*] which, however, is only appearance [*Erscheinung*]. It is something distinct from consciousness which in itself has no being."[11]

Here again the truth is the whole. Self-Consciousness is neither of these moments alone but the two together, *Bestehen* and *Erscheinung*, the relation of consciousness to what is other and its relation to itself.[12] To hold the two together is to remember both lessons of Kant's transcendental deduction, the mutual interdependence of consciousness and self-consciousness. In the language of the Transcendental Aesthetic this means preserving not only the transcendental ideality but also the empirical reality of the objects of experience. Having devoted a major effort to analysis of the former in the description of Consciousness, Hegel urges us not to forget the latter just because it is not the whole truth.

Hegel is Kantian here not only in substance but also in method. The following description of Kant's method in the transcendental deduction applies as well to Hegel's procedure here. As opposed to the deduction of consequences entailed by the concept of self-consciousness, this method "specifies the presuppositions of the *possibility of the existence* of self-consciousness. But using this method, one can come to a knowledge of the conditions which, although they are not already given in the structure of self-consciousness itself, must precisely in virtue of this structure be presupposed if a self-consciousness is to become actual."[13]

But just at the point where Hegel is most Kantian he is suddenly beyond Kant. For he claims on the basis of strictly Kantian premises not only that transcendental apperception is only the idea of Self-Consciousness and not actual Self-Consciousness (to which Kant might agree in terms of his own distinction between transcendental and empirical apperception), but also that actual Self-Consciousness first enters the scene as desire.

The first conclusion is relatively simple and is already before us. Transcendental apperception is derived from the relation of consciousness to its object *as present to consciousness*.[14] In this relation it loses its character as radically other than consciousness, *Sein* as *Anderssein*. Self-Consciousness is therefore only the immediate and empty relation to self which Hegel calls a "motionless tautology." It is a tautology because it expresses identity without difference. It is motionless because the mediating process between self and other has been excluded. In support of his conclusion that Self-Consciousness can be actual only if mediated through an object genuinely other than itself, Hegel appeals not only to Kant's argument, but to his own phenomenological derivation of Self-Consciousness in which it is "the reflection out of the being [*Sein*] of the sensible and perceptual world and essentially the return out of otherness [*Anderssein*]."[15]

Somewhat less evident is the second thesis, the crucial one for going beyond transcendental philosophy, that it is in desire that Self-Consciousness is first actual. To begin with desire has the form of Self-Consciousness. It is the inseparable unity of self-relation and relation-to-another. That desire is actual Self-Consciousness in contrast to transcendental apperception means, as the foregoing indicates, that the moment of empirical reality, *Sein* as genuinely *Anderssein,* is retained in its experience of the object. This is exactly what Hegel finds to be true of desire. To desire an object is to experience its otherness. Desire is Self-Consciousness, since for it the object has "the significance of a non-entity [*Character des Negativen*]." Its own satisfaction is the essential thing; the object is merely a means to that end, material for its use. Desire is consequently that form of Self-Consciousness "which is absolutely for itself and immediately takes its object to have the significance of a non-entity," but which will at the same time "experience the independence of its object."[16] It is this dual experience of the object as there for consciousness yet independent of it which makes desire actual Self-Consciousness.

These two aspects of conscious desire are intimately intertwined. Desire is aware of the object as its own, as something for it. It is therefore "certain of itself only through dominating [*das Aufheben*] this other, which presents itself to Self-Consciousness as an independent living being . . . Certain of the nullity of this other, and taking the position that this nullity is the truth of this other, it annihilates the independent object and thereby gives itself the certainty of itself which is true certainty, a certainty which has won objective status." It is just this moment of satisfaction, however, in which the independence of the object is experienced. The self-certainty achieved in the satisfaction of desire is dependent on the object "for it exists through the dominating of this other. In order that this dominating may occur, this other must be there . . . It is in fact something other than Self-Consciousness, the essence of desire, and it is through this experience that Self-Consciousness learns this truth." Which is to say that Hegel knows as well as Feuerbach that one could starve on merely thought or imagined bread.[17]

It is in animal desire, then, the eating and drinking mentioned above,[18] that Self-Consciousness is an actual fact. But it is not fully actualized at this level. Animal desire is not the fully developed concept of Self-Consciousness, or, to speak more phenomenologically, desire is a richer phenomenon than the analysis of eating and drinking can reveal. What remains to be found if the *Phenomenology* is to proceed is not a form of Self-Consciousness independent of desire but a form of Self-Consciousness in which desire is distinctively human.

Hegel is simply seeking to interpret given phenomena here, not to deduce them *more geometrico*. But there is a principle suggested by his analysis which gives intelligibility not only to the movement just completed, from transcendental apperception to animal desire, but also to the movement now to be considered, from animal desire to human desire. Hegel states that principle this way: "The independence of the object of consciousness in itself is proportional to that of consciousness itself."[18] The object that is eaten is surely more independent than sense data. Still it has a relatively low grade of independence, and the Self-Consciousness of the eater achieves a rather minimal self-certainty from its triumph. Hegel actually calls it self-feeling rather than Self-Consciousness.[19] A higher grade of Self-Consciousness could only be achieved by victory over a more thoroughly independent object. In order to get a qualitative difference from the victory which depends on superior force, Hegel turns to the extreme case in which the object is so independent that desire can find satisfaction "only when this object itself carries out the negation of itself," i.e., offers itself for the sake of desire's happiness. This capacity for self-negation which the object incorporates into its independence means that it must itself be consciousness of some sort. In fact, since it relates to itself as self-negating while relating to the other for whose satisfaction it gives itself, it is Self-Consciousness. In the fullest sense "Self-Consciousness attains its satisfaction only in another Self-Consciousness."[20]

It is only as this new level, which Hegel calls the doubling of Self-Consciousness that Self-Consciousness is able to experience "the unity of itself in its other." In animal desire Self-Consciousness is actual, for its object has the genuine otherness of empirical reality. But the other of animal desire does not survive the negating act of Self-Consciousness. With its disappearance Self-Consciousness also ceases to be, and satisfaction must give way to a new desire for a new object in order constantly to renew the sense of self-certainty. Since the object has independence without permanence, Self-Consciousness can have no lasting experience of unity with its other. The object of desire whose empirical reality consists in its own ability to give or not to give itself for the other's satisfaction and self-certainty is different. It does not disappear in the moment of satisfaction. Since this satisfaction is a happy relation to otherness which is not self-destroying, Hegel says that Self-Consciousness can only here find "the unity of itself in its other."[21]

Hegel is about to turn to his famous description of Lordship and Bondage, an account of the difficulties involved in actualizing this satisfaction which is here but a conceptual possibility. But there are two reasons why we need not hurry on quite yet. The first is that the analysis of Lordship and Bondage only renders concrete the principles already contained in the preceding discussion. The inherently destructive nature of domination for the one who dominates is already before us. In such a project the other is reduced to the object of animal desire. He has no meaning other than the satisfaction of my desires and it is I who will bring about that satisfaction. The unsatisfactory nature of this kind of satisfaction is what moves the dialectic from animal desire to the doubling of Self-Consciousness. This move requires the qualitative transcendence of desire and domination, for at this new level satisfaction is something that can be given but not taken. Even at the purely human level *eros* must give way to *agape*.[22]

The second reason for not rushing right ahead is that Hegel himself lingers long enough to enlarge on the thesis that with Self-Consciousness in its fully developed form "we have now passed into the native kingdom of truth."[23] In doing so he informs us that we have also, without realizing it, been introduced to the concept of Spirit. In the analysis of Self-Consciousness "we already have before us the concept of Spirit. What remains for consciousness is the experience of what Spirit is—the absolute substance which is the unity of the distinct, self-existing [*für sich seiender*] self-conscious individuals in the perfect freedom and independence of their otherness to one another. Spirit is that I which is We and that We which is I. Consciousness first finds in Self-Consciousness as the concept of Spirit its turning point, where it leaves the colorful show of the sensible present [*Diesseits*] and the empty night of the supersensible beyond [*Jenseits*] to enter the spiritual daylight of the present."[24]

It may not be too bold to call this definition of Spirit *the* clue to the *Phenomenology*. The following distinctive characteristics of Spirit which it introduces are fundamental to the remainder of Hegel's argument:

1) Spirit is a social reality, a unity of individual human selves, not a timeless metaphysical reality akin to the world of Platonic forms or Aristotle's Unmoved Mover. It is something present, not a supersensible beyond. As the immediately following discussion of Lordship and Bondage shows, it is to a crude and primitive stage of human social experience that Hegel here applies the name of Spirit. Where the experience of I and We is to be found, there is Spirit.[25]

2) Yet Hegel speaks of Spirit, without having yet traced its development to its fulfillment, as absolute. The recurrence of such references to a determinate form of human social experience as absolute emphasizes both the temporal nature of Spirit and the fundamentally adjectival role of the term 'absolute' in the *Phenomenology*. One must not say with Royce, "The Absolute must be a self that by virtue of its inmost principle appears to itself as an interrelated unity of selves without being the less one self. From this point of view Hegel calls the Absolute *Geist*."[26] While this is a valuable commentary on Hegel's talk about I and We, subject and predicate have been reversed. Spirit is that interrelated unity of selves which is at the same time one self, a We that is also an I, and in so far as this is the case Hegel speaks of Spirit as absolute.

3) Spirit is substance. This means that it must be understood as having such characteristics as self-sufficiency, permanence, and individuality in the sense of determinateness; further, that it must be understood as the bearer of "attributes" or "accidents," components which in isolation from the substance to which they belong do not themselves have the characteristics of substance just mentioned.

4) Yet Spirit needs to be for itself what it is in itself. Substance must become Subject. Not only must each I know itself also as We, but the We must know itself as I. The social whole must become conscious of itself.[27]

5) Finally, we have to do here with a turning point, an entry into the native land of truth, in so far as the concept of Spirit makes possible the treacherous voyage between the Scylla of one dimensional this-worldliness and the Charybdis of an appeal to the transcendent which flees to the emptiness of what is wholly Wholly Other. In this thinly veiled allusion to the Enlightenment and Romanticism we have a reminder of the historical timeliness of a philosophy which takes Spirit for its central category. Our own time, too, knows the extreme worldliness of scientific-technological rationality and the military-industrial complex pitted against the extreme repudiations of all that which we know somewhat too simply as "the Counter-Culture." But we know little of what might mediate between them. Perhaps we might learn something from Hegel.

5B. The Priority of Love Over Life and Labor.

Looked at in the context of Hegel's personal development it is clear that the concept of Spirit is not only the attempt to unify Kantian apperception with Aristotelian appetition; it is also the fruition of his efforts at Frankfurt (1797-1800) to develop the concepts of love and life into fundamental philosophical categories. Dieter Henrich has written, "Hegel's system came forth without a break out of his assumption of love as the key word of his reflection. This required only that the theme of love be replaced, for reasons which can be specified, with the richer structure of life and then again with that of Spirit, which implies still more than life." The importance of the first sentence can hardly be exaggerated, though the second is somewhat doubtful, as we shall see.

According to a fragment from 1797-98, "Where subject and object or freedom and nature are thought as so united that nature is freedom, that subject and object are not to be separated, there is the divine." But this ideal, which belongs to every religion, is not available to either theoretical or practical consciousness (the latter understood as simple desire). "The theoretical syntheses become fully objective, entirely opposed to the subject. Practical activity annihilates the object and is entirely subjective. *Only in love are we one with the object,* neither dominating it [*beherrschen*] nor dominated by it."[29] This phenomenon of love shows itself to be "a reciprocal giving and taking," but "the lover who takes is not thereby made richer than the other. He is enriched indeed, but only so much as the other is. So too the giver does not make himself poorer. By giving to the other he has to the same extent enhanced his own treasure. Juliet in *Romeo and Juliet:* the more I give to thee, the more I have, etc."[30]

Already the concept of Self-Consciousness in and through another self is present here, and Hegel is careful not to let the unity of those who love each other eliminate their difference. "The beloved is not opposed to us but is one with our essence. We see only ourselves in the beloved, whom we in turn, nevertheless, see as not ourselves—a wonder which we cannot comprehend."[31]

In the so-called "System Fragment" of 1800 Hegel suggests the following formula for such a relation: "the union of union and non-union."[32] Here, however, it is life rather than love which is the immediate subject of reflection. The first of the two surviving pages of this essay begins with the last three words of a sentence, " ... absolute opposition prevails." Kroner's speculation that this refers to the realm of the dead makes good sense.[33] For Hegel maintains that the idea of the living individual "includes opposition against the infinite manifold [of other living beings] and union with this manifold. A human being is an individual life in so far as he is something other than all the elements and the infinity of individual lives outside himself. But he is only an individual life in so far as he is at one with all the elements, with all the infinity of life outside

himself. He exists only in so far as the totality of life is divided
into parts, he himself being one part and all the rest the other
part; he exists only in so far as he is no part at all and nothing is
separated from him. If we presuppose undivided life as fixed,
then we can regard living beings as expressions or manifestations of that life . . . If on the contrary we presuppose an individual life, namely ourselves as the observers, then that life
which is posited outside our own limited life is an infinite life of
infinite multiplicity, infinite opposition, infinite relation. As a
plurality it is an infinite plurality of organizations or individuals. As a unity it is one unique organized whole, divided and unified in itself—Nature."[34]

Though this statement comes from the tradition of romantic philosophy of nature, if it is compared with the one in which
Spirit is introduced in the *Phenomenology* it will come as no surprise that Hegel says of this infinite life that we can call it Spirit,
"for Spirit is the living unity of the manifold . . . an animating
law in union with the manifold which is then itself animated."[35]
Conversely, it is no surprise that in the *Phenomenology* Hegel
should anticipate the concept of Spirit by devoting four paragraphs to the restatement of this concept of life, according to
which "the independent members exist for themselves. This
being for themselves, however, is really just as immediately
their reflection into the unity as this unity is the breaking asunder into the independent forms. The unity is sundered because
it is absolutely negative or infinite unity; and because it is what
endures the members correspondingly have their independence only in it."[36]

Life so conceived serves as a conceptual model or
metaphor for understanding Self-Consciousness as Spirit. But
it can be no more than this, for while both are reflections of the
same basic structure, the unity of what is distinguished, life
simply is this unity while Self-Consciousness has this unity for
itself. It knows itself to be this unity.[37] This means that of the
two Frankfurt categories, love is more adequate to the concept
of Spirit than life. For love is not simply the unconscious structure of Self-Consciousness. Those who love know themselves to
be the unity of what nevertheless remains distinct, an incom-
prehensible wonder. Thus the unity which can be described as
love can also be described as the substance which is also subject.

This privileged character of love over life is already to be seen in the Frankfurt period if one compares the "System Fragment" not just with the love fragments of 1797-98 but also with *The Spirit of Christianity and its Fate*. There love is every bit as sophisticated a category as life is in the "System Fragment," and one would not be tempted to call the latter the richer of the two. Both categories continue in the Jena period to be important ones, but with this important difference, which further establishes the priority of love: in the *Realphilosophie* life is relegated to the philosophy of nature, while, love, interpreted in terms of a new category, recognition, becomes the central category of the philosophy of Spirit.[38]

We use the term 'recognition' in two rather different senses. "I saw you sitting there some time ago but until just now I didn't recognize you." "It was not until just after his death that he finally won the recognition he deserved." In the first case recognition is simply a matter of properly identifying someone. In the second to recognize is to esteem, to value, to acknowledge a certain worth. It is always in this second sense that Hegel uses the term. According to the concept of Self-Consciousness human desire is fully satisfied only when the self "is in and for itself *for an other*."[39] To be in itself is to be autonomous, to be something independent of relation to an other. (For example, the Kantian thing in itself is the thing independent of its relation to our experience of it.) To be for itself is to preside over this autonomy, to have it as the active principle of self-maintaining and self-developing self-movement. To be something in and for itself for another is to be acknowledged by another self to be everything that 'in and for itself' connotes, or, as Hegel puts it simply, to be fully Self-Consciousness is to be recognized. It is not difficult to see why Hegel identifies recognition with love or to see the close connection between this concept and Kant's notion of the person as an end in himself.[40]

It is by means of this concept of recognition that Hegel returns in the *Phenomenology* from the pure concept of Self-Consciousness to the concrete experience for which that concept serves as criterion. The question is whether recognition is a reality and not just a fascinating concept, whether the consciousness in which this desire is at work can find the satisfaction it seeks.[41] The self wishes to be loved, to be acknowledged as an end in himself. He desires recognition. But this desire clearly cannot be satisfied as hunger is satisfied in annihilating the other. Here force is impotent. Satisfaction can only come about in so far as the other "itself carries out the negation of itself," the negation involved in not taking himself to be the absolute end in itself.[42] But the independence of the other, so crucial to surpassing animal self-feeling, consists precisely in the power to recognize or not recognize. It is anything but automatic that Self-Consciousness in the fully developed sense of Spirit will be actualized in accordance with its concept. In fact, it is just the opposite that is phenomenologically more "natural".

In Sartrean language, love first appears only as the desire or demand to be loved. Both selves are so given to demanding love from each other that neither is in a position to give what the other demands. The lack which each self is, needing the other's love simply in order to be himself, makes of each self a primordial emptiness.[43] Two emptinesses encounter each other as the demand to be filled, but since there is no overflowing fullness anywhere on the scene, only a plurality of emptinesses, love turns out to be a useless passion. Out of reciprocal emptiness there is no immediate path to reciprocal recognition.

This is what the celebrated life and death struggle which culminates in master-slave relationships is all about. The attempt to kill the other is fundamentally confused, for it rests on the assumption either that the desire for recognition can be satisfied like hunger through annihilating the other, or that the self-negation of the other can be coerced. Both assumptions are patently at odds with the concept of recognition, for it is clear that a dead man cannot recognize his conqueror and that a conquered man's coerced "recognition" of the conqueror is no genuine self-negation or love at all. For "there is no fear in love, but perfect love casts out fear . . . he who fears is not perfected in love."[44]

Hegel doesn't dwell much on the absurdity of the resort to violence in the attempt to extract recognition from the other. For him the more interesting (and more easily overlooked) aspect of the struggle for recognition is the fact that each party risks his own life in seeking to take the life of the other. This brings to focus the distinctly human character of the desire for recognition in contrast to animal desire. The desire which consciously risks life in the pursuit of satisfaction cannot be interpreted within the horizon of life, either as self-preservation or species preservation. The desire for recognition is qualitatively different from the hunger and sex drives, biologically interpreted. Hegel's conclusion is that "it is solely by risking life that freedom is obtained. Only thus is it tried and proved that the essential thing for Self-Consciousness is not mere existence [*das Sein*], not the immediate way in which it makes its appearance, not its immersion in the expanse of life—but rather that for Self-Consciousness nothing is present that might not be taken as a vanishing moment, and that Self-Consciousness is nothing but pure being for itself. The individual who has not staked his life may, no doubt, be recognized as a person. But he has not achieved the truth of this recognition as an independent Self-Consciousness."[45] In other words, "Give me liberty or give me death" belongs to the essence of human desire. Since love and freedom are here identified, we can say that the unloved life is not worth living.

A further aspect of the Lordship and Bondage discussion needs to be considered if Hegel's concept of Spirit is to be fully understood, especially in its relation to Marxian materialism. It is the notion of labor, of which Marx writes in the 1844 manuscripts, "The greatness of the Hegelian *Phenomenology* and its final result . . . is thus . . . that Hegel grasps the essence of labor and conceives of objective man, true man because actual man, as the result of his own labor . . . Hegel occupies the standpoint of modern national economy. He grasps labor as the essence of man which proves itself indeed to be such."[46]

It is true that Hegel finds in labor a distinctively human form of desire. "Desire has reserved to itself the pure negating of the object and thereby unalloyed feeling of self. This satisfaction, however, just for that reason is itself only something that vanishes, for it lacks the aspect of objectivity or endurance. Labor, on the other hand, is restrained desire, delayed vanishing. In other words, it forms the object. The negative relation to the object becomes the form of the object, something that remains, because it is precisely for the laborer that the object has independence." Clearly the human significance of labor is not to be found in consumption. Labor surpasses simple desire in that a more satisfactory form of Self-Consciousness is thereby achieved. Hegel continues, "In forming the thing being for self comes to be taken by the laborer as his own, and he becomes conscious that he is in and for himself."[47]

But while it is true that for Hegel labor involves creation and not just consumption, Self-Consciousness and not just self-preservation, it is just as clear that the object of labor cannot mediate as complete a mode of Self-Consciousness as another self can. The definitive characteristic of human desire is not labor any more than it is life. It is love. The essential thing is not the postponement of satisfaction but the nature of the satisfaction which recognition involves. Hegel would find Marx's account of his accomplishment one-sided and incomplete.[48]

In keeping with this priority of love over labor in Hegel's understanding of man as Spirit, he sees history as grounded in original sin rather than in the division of labor. While his account of original sin in the life and death struggle for recognition suggests Cain and Abel rather than Adam and Eve, it is clear that the master-slave relation is something subsequent, a superstructure whose basis is found in the directly interpersonal and non-economic domain of the quest for recognition. The relations of dominance and dependence within economic institutions are *Schein*. The desire to be loved and the hatred of the one who instead of loving me demands that I love him are *Wesen*. Correspondingly Hegel's analysis of the historical process will focus attention on the quest for love as recognition rather than on labor and the economic process, which in turn can only be understood in terms of the former.[49] This does not mean that Hegel will have to be an idealist in the sense of one who thinks the world's problems are solved when they are understood. Marx's 1844 critique of the *Phenomenology* is misdirected in this respect. To find the search for recognition as the horizon within which not only labor and the economic process but the whole of human history are to be understood is not equivalent to letting thought swallow up being. For the manifold encounters between persons desiring to be loved and thus ratified as persons are very real events and not merely thought processes in the mind of some philosopher.

Despite these important differences, Hegel stands with Marx over against the transcendental tradition and Kant. One might even borrow Adorno's formula to express this: "Since the author has trusted his own spiritual impulses, he has found it to be his task to break through the deceit of transcendental subjectivity with the power of the subject."[50] This would not adequately express the tension in Hegel's position, however, which seeks not so much to deny transcendental subjectivity as to discover the conditions of its possibility and thereby its conditionedness. The formula borrowed earlier from Habermas comes closer to expressing this: "The achievements of the transcendental subject have their basis in the natural history of the human species."[51] It should now be clear both why this formula is appropriate and why Hegel, too, would have to add a qualification like that of Habermas: "Taken by itself this thesis could lead to the misunderstanding that reason is an organ of adaptation for men just as claws and teeth are for animals. True, it does serve this function. But the human interests that have emerged in man's natural history . . . derive both from nature and from the cultural break with nature." In Hegel's terms, human desire is not just animal desire but the desire which restrains itself in labor and re-directs itself in the quest for recognition. It is in such desires that the achievements of the transcendental subject have their basis.

Once again we are brought to the crucial Hegelian question—Who is the transcendental subject? The question itself is directed against Kant's kind of transcendental philosophy, for it presupposes that the transcendental subject is concrete, not an abstract network of timeless, perhaps even bloodless categories. That man in the concrete, thus man as desire, is the transcendental subject means that for Hegel as well as for Marx, "It is not consciousness that determines life but rather life that determines consciousness." From this point of view "one begins with the actual living individual himself and considers consciousness only as *his* consciousness."[52]

The point of these formulas from Adorno, Habermas, and Marx is not to show that Hegel is someone other than himself but simply to indicate the implications of his concept of Spirit. His own formula, if one must be found, comes at the beginning of the 1805-06 lectures on the philosophy of Spirit where he characterizes the ego as only formally universal, Spirit as truly universal.[53] This carries with it the clear implication that a philosophy oriented to the ego is abstract and incomplete until it becomes a philosophy of Spirit, that transcendental philosophy in the Cartesian and Kantian sense finds its own foundation beyond itself.

5C. Spirit and Ethical Life.

Beginning with the epistemological issues discussed in the Introduction Hegel has developed them or watched them develop to the point where transcendental philosophy is forced to become philosophy of Spirit. If the concept of Spirit which emerges in this context is to have relevance to the issues raised in the Preface, it will have to be shown that it stands in an intelligible relation to the issues of "substantial life" and "sense of the divine."[54] After introducing the concept of Spirit in Chapter Four and before tracing its historical career in Chapter Six Hegel develops the concept further in two brief but crucial passages which fulfill this expectation.[55]

The first of these passages serves as the introduction to Sections B. and C. of Chapter Five on the practical dimensions of Reason. Hegel takes up where he left off in Chapter Four, with the concept of Self-Consciousness. "The object, therefore, to which Self-Consciousness positively relates itself, is a Self-Consciousness. This object has the form of thinghood, i.e., it is independent. But Self-Consciousness has the certainty that this independent object is nothing foreign to it. It knows itself herewith to be in itself recognized by the other Self-Consciousness. Self-Consciousness is Spirit which has the certainty of having its unity with itself in the duplication of its Self-Consciousness and in the independence of both selves."[56]

A rather dramatic change has taken place while the reader was away reading Section A of Chapter Five on Observing Reason. When he left Self-Consciousness at the end of Chapter Four recognition was only a utopian dream, a mere concept without reality in a society of masters and slaves. How different it all sounds in the passage just cited. To be sure it is only the certainty of being recognized which Self-Consciousness has, and Hegel regularly contrasts certainty as claim from truth as fulfillment. Further, Self-Consciousness knows itself to be recognized, but only "in itself." This is one of the few places where

Hegel's *an sich* requires translation as "implicitly" or "potentially." Nevertheless, the atmosphere has changed. This confidence on the part of Self-Consciousness can hardly stem from an experience which knows nothing but the futile desire of Chapter Four.

Even so, we are not quite prepared for the boldness of the question Hegel asks: Where does this concept of recognition have its "complete reality," where does it come to light as "an existing, flourishing substance"? Answer: "in the life of a people [*Volk*]," in "the realm of Ethical Life [*Sittlichkeit*]."[57] The concept of recognized Self-Consciousness opens up this realm for us "because Ethical Life is nothing other than the *absolute* spiritual unity of the being of individuals in their independent reality. It is an in itself *universal* Self-Consciousness which is so fully itself in another consciousness that this latter has complete independence for it, is looked on as a thing, and the universal Self-Consciousness is aware precisely therein of its unity with the other, and is only then Self-Consciousness when in such unity with this objective being. This ethical [*sittliche*] substance, taken in its abstract universality is only law as posited [*das gedachte Gesetz*], but just as much it is immediately actual Self-Consciousness, i.e., custom. Conversely, the individual consciousness is this existing unit only by being conscious in his individuality of the universal consciousness as his being, only by acting and existing in accord with universal custom."[58]

This crucial passage calls for careful comment, especially in light of the fact that as early as 1803 Hegel had identified absolute Spirit with Ethical Life in its perfection.[59]

In the first place Ethical Life involves the concept of universal Self-Consciousness. While Hegel sometimes uses the term universal to signify an abstract concept, his normal usage describes as universal only what is in some sense a concrete totality and in this sense particular. Thus he speaks, with Kant in mind, of space and time as universals, of the thing with its properties as universal, of the organism, and then again of the species as universal. In the present context where the particular is the self-conscious individual, it is well to remember that Spirit is not the unity of I with I-ness, but of I and We. That which can be described as We is the concrete totality which is universal, "the absolute spiritual unity of the being of individuals in their independent reality." Independent individuals, without ceasing to be such, form a unity which Hegel calls absolute and spiritual. Since this unity, concretely speaking a people, has its own form of self-awareness, Hegel calls it universal Self-Consciousness. It is not the abstraction which Kant called pure reason, but rather "the real substance, into which the preceding forms of consciousness return and in which they find their ground."[60]

This is the second point: Ethical Life is substance. The analysis of the thing and its properties has indicated that to speak of qualities or properties is to speak of parts or aspects in isolation from the whole to which they belong, while to speak of a thing or substance is to speak of the togetherness of the parts or aspects, and thus of something concrete. The concreteness of Ethical Life as a universal consciousness which must be described as substance can be expressed in terms of language. " . . . this universal substance speaks its universal language in the customs and laws of its people. But this existing unchangeable being is nothing else than the expression of the individuality which seems opposed to it. The laws give expression to what each individual is and does."[61] Ethical Life is thus the substantial life of a people as it is expressed in their customs and laws.

If the concept of a people as substantial subject defines the scope of Ethical Life, Hegel's refusal to separate customs from laws indicates its form, the third element of this concept. The separation of customs and laws would signify the separation of morality from legality, of private from public person, in short, of man from citizen. Ethical Life is the life of a people in so far as these distinctions do not arise.[62]

Finally, this means that the concept of individuality in the context of Ethical Life is not that "modern" concept, already present at the dissolution of the Greek *polis*, which presupposes these distinctions as ultimate.[63] In Ethical Life the individual stands in a relation of immediate unity with the social whole. He is I only as he is We. He knows himself only in the customs and laws of his people; and he knows only himself in them.

Since this dialectic of individual and society, which Hegel here introduces into the concept of Spirit, occupies more space than any other single topic in the *Phenomenology*, it is important to see that their relation is not that of simple otherness. It has already been suggested that the universal is primarily a concrete totality. Correspondingly, to be an individual is to be a part of a whole.[64] Since a totality is not merely an aggregate, being part of a whole means more than being one of a bunch. In the life of a people reason appears "as the fluid universal substance, as the unchangeable, simple thinghood which, just as light bursts asunder into stars as innumerable self-illuminating points, likewise breaks up into many entirely independent beings which in their absolute being-for-self are dissolved in the simple independent substance, not only in themselves but also for themselves. They are conscious of themselves as being these individual independent beings through the fact that they sacrifice their individuality and that this universal substance is their soul and essence, just as this universal is, on the other hand, their deed as individuals, the work which they have produced."[65]

Once again the question is inescapable—Where is this beautiful concept actualized? It comes as no surprise that our attention is directed toward antiquity. "Among a free people, therefore, reason is in truth realized. They are Spirit, living and present, where the individual . . . finds his destiny, i.e., his universal and particular nature . . . The wisest men of antiquity for that reason declared that wisdom and virtue consist in living in accordance with the customs of one's people."[66]

In Chapter Six Hegel will describe in detail the Greek experience of Ethical Life. But he knows that he is dealing with a concept which is not universally realized, even in antiquity. There are forms of interaction between individual and society which can be looked at as either not yet having achieved this harmony or as having lost it. The latter view is especially significant, for it indicates that Ethical Life is an inherently unstable harmony, limited both in scope and form. In terms of its scope it is limited to one people among many. As the life of a free people "this universal Spirit is also itself an individual. It is the totality of customs and laws of a determinate ethical substance, which casts off this limitation only when it reaches the higher moment, namely when it becomes conscious regarding its own nature. Only in this knowledge does it have its absolute truth, not immediately in its being."[67]

The limitation of Ethical Life in terms of its form is equally serious. The unity of individual and society is an immediate confidence which is easily and necessarily broken by reflection, in which the individual and not the universal Spirit becomes the essential moment. Then "the individual has set himself over against the laws and customs. They are only a thought without absolutely essential significance, an abstract theory without reality. The individual, however, as this ego, is in his own view the living truth."[68]

The forms of consciousness which pass in review through Sections B. and C. of Chapter Five are but variations on this theme. They portray a variety of ways in which perversely abstract individualism destroys any hope of a satisfactory relation to the social environment (unorganic nature) by being unwilling or unable to be part of a whole. While they indirectly illuminate the concept of Spirit, their role in Hegel's overall argument is peripheral.

More important is the question—What has the concept of Ethical Life added to our understanding of Spirit? It clearly represents an expanded conception of the We of the original definition. This is of double significance. First, while Spirit is defined as substance in its first appearance, it is not entirely clear why this should be. Two individuals appear seemingly ready made out of nowhere to struggle for recognition. We cannot be sure Hegel has avoided the state of nature *cum* social contract type thinking he otherwise repudiates.[69] Such thinking forgets that to speak of individuals apart from their social milieu is to speak of the barest abstractions. Consequently it loses half of the dialectic of individual and society. It notices that society is produced by the individual, but not that the producing individuals are first produced by society.[70] The link between Spirit and Ethical Life corrects this impression with the reminder that the struggle for recognition takes place in a social context. It is not just the relation of one individual to another, but more fundamentally of their relation to society, for all their inter-relations take place in the context of customs and laws. This is true even of the extreme case suggested by the original struggle for recognition—war.

Second, by making it clear that recognition is not to be understood in terms of social contract but of society as substance, the concept of Ethical Life links the concept of Spirit to the cultural crisis of Hegel's present with its concern for the substantial life which has been lost. Ethical Life is Spirit in its immediacy. As such its loss is inevitable and irrevocable. But at the same time it gives content to the concept of Spirit in such a way as to make clear what must be regained in a mediated way if romantic yearning and rigoristic imperatives are to give place to the enjoyment of the ideal as present.[71]

The Preface, however, speaks not only of the loss of "substantial life" but also of the desire for a renewed "sense of the divine." So far the concept of Spirit has been related to the former, since it is presented as a thoroughly historical and human reality, the life of a free people. But what of the divine? In his essay on natural right (1802-03) Hegel writes that Ethical Life comes to self-knowledge through a twofold self-representation. In the form of universality it expresses itself as the system of laws. In the form of particularity it is to be seen in the God of a people. This indicates the closest of connections between Ethical Life and the divine.[72] Only hints of such a link are found in the passage just considered, where the universal substance which is a people is twice characterized as the unchangeable substance.[73] This is the primary designation for God in the earlier analysis of the Unhappy Consciousness.

It is only when we turn to the second of the passages mentioned at the beginning of this section that we find the religious aspect more fully expressed. Just before launching into the description of Spirit's historical career, Hegel pauses to reflect on the concept of Spirit as Ethical Life. "The self-contained and self-sufficient being, however, which is aware of being actual in the form of consciousness and at the same time presents itself to itself is Spirit. Its spiritual essence has already been designated as the ethical [*sittliche*] substance. But Spirit is the ethical actuality. Spirit is the self of actual consciousness, to which Spirit stands opposed, or rather, which appears over against itself as an objective actual world, which likewise, however, has lost all sense of having a dependent or independent existence by itself, cut off and separated from that world. Being substance . . . Spirit is the immoveable and irreducible ground and starting point for the action of everyone. As the essence of all Self-Consciousnesses for thought, Spirit is their purpose and goal."[74]

Spirit is here described with four characteristics of the divine. 1) It is *causa sui,* self-sufficient, self-contained, self-supporting. 2) It is transcendent, a substantial self which stands over against the individual self as an other. 3) It is the ground of the individual's action. 4) It is also the goal and purpose of that action.

The manner in which the social whole may be said to be the ground and goal of human activity is relatively unproblematic. It is illustrated by the way in which a team is the ground and goal of an athlete's activity. The team is the ground of his activity as that without which he could not perform. You can't pitch without a catcher. And the team is the goal of the athlete's activity in that it is the team's success that finally matters most. Being voted Most Valuable Player is never a satisfactory substitute for the team's winning its way to the World Series or Super Bowl. What Hegel has in mind as Ethical Life is a mode of social experience in which individuals relate to their society in the same way a real team player relates to his team. His language serves to transfer to society in this relation a function traditionally thought of as God's. For theologically speaking it is God who is the ultimate ground without which the individual cannot even be, much less act, and it is for his glory that life is to be lived.

The other two characteristics of Spirit, transcendence and aseity, must be treated with special care, least they be confused with the very different doctrines of classical theism which involve the same kind of language. The manner in which Spirit is immanent to human experience is sufficient to distinguish its transcendence from that of the theistic view. In terms of Spirit as here conceived, what stands over against the individual as a transcendent spiritual self or world is nothing other than himself. This is true for two reasons. "The substance is likewise the universal product, wrought by the action of all and each as their unity and identity." That is, Spirit is as much the individual's creation as his creator. In addition, Spirit's subjectivity is actual only in its constituent individuals. " . . . as being-for-itself the continuity of this substance is resolved into discrete elements; it is the self-sacrificing goodness in which each fulfills his own work, tears the universal being apart and takes his own share of it. This resolution of the whole into parts [*diese Auflösung und Vereinzelung des Wesens*] is precisely the moment of the action and selfhood of all the parts . . . Just because this substance is a being resolved into selfhood, it is not a lifeless essence, but actual and alive."[75] In this respect Hegel can say of the ethical substance that "it is Spirit which is for itself by maintaining itself in the reflection [*Gegenschein*] of the individuals of the community. It is in itself or substance by preserving them within itself. As actual substance Spirit is a people. As actual consciousness it is the citizens of a nation."[76] Findlay has good reason to describe Spirit as "a self-consciousness which is dispersed among a number of distinct centers."[77]

The individual participates in Spirit both as its creator and as the sole locus of its consciousness. That is to say that the transcendence of Spirit is simply that of society to the individual. Yet we have seen that Hegel is not hesitant in this very context to speak of Spirit as absolute. The theological language is important, for it serves to identify Hegel's ultimate concern. But it is also misleading, for the divine is neither God in any traditional Judeo-Christian sense, nor the metaphysical absolute of the later so-called Hegelians (including, perhaps, Hegel himself). As social substance with collective self-consciousness Spirit is more akin (to follow up the previous analogy) to team spirit than to the Holy Spirit of Christian theology or the Brahman of Hindu mysticism.

Finally, to speak of Spirit as self-contained, self-sufficient, and self-supporting is not to designate a being prior to and independent of the world of finite reality. Rather, it is to say that societies create themselves and that, unlike their constituent elements they are not abstractions in the sense of being essentially parts of a larger whole. (It is not a contradiction to speak of a universal society.)

It is instructive at this point to compare two three-point summaries of Hegelian idealism, each of which is followed by a highly significant comment. Sidney Hook writes that for Hegel 1) Reality is spiritual, 2) Reality is systematic, and 3) Reality is rational, adding that the idea of a corporate social consciousness is a deduction from these theses.[78] Jean Hyppolite's Hegel holds that 1) Spirit is a *nous* (French, not Greek), 2) Spirit is history, and 3) Spirit is knowledge of itself in its history. He adds the comment that this latter point tends to lead Hegel beyond strictly phenomenological concerns to an ontologizing of

Spirit.[79] Both Hook and Hyppolite distinguish the socio-historical elements (Spirit as *nous*, French) from the speculative or metaphysical elements (Reality as *nous*, Greek). But for Hook the former are deductions from an a priori metaphysical construction of Reality, whereas for Hyppolite Hegel's thought is first and foremost concerned with Spirit, even if at times he gets carried beyond the historical and cultural world of Spirit as phenomenon. Between the first Hegel, a Platonist who deduces things from thought, for whom time is unreal and the sensible world a mere appearance,[80] and the second, for whom time is a fundamental category and concrete social experience the starting point for philosophy, there is scarcely a family resemblance. Nor is it hard to identify the more faithful portrait so far as the *Phenomenology* is concerned.

NOTES

1. PhG, 98-99/128/211-12.
2. PhG, 34-35/87/158-59. cf. Ch. 3, n. 29. What here follows can be read as Hegel's developed reply (in advance) to Feuerbach's critique of his treatment of Sense Certainty, especially as the challenge to mediate between philosophy and what is not philosophy. See *Vorläufige Thesen zur Reform der Philosophie*, KS, 135, and *Kritik*, KS, 99-100.
3. This is just what one would expect from the *Realphilosophie*.
4. This is the leitmotif of the earliest Jena writings, *Differenz* and *Glauben*.
5. This linkage of knowledge and interest links Hegel not only to the American pragmatists but also to Heidegger's analysis of Being-in-the-world as Care, though the language in both cases is very different.
6. PhG, 34-35/87/158-59. cf. *Realphilosophie*, II, 120, "Eating and drinking make unorganic things into what they are in themselves, in truth. They are the unconscious comprehending of these things." And II, 160, "Animal desire is the idealism of objectivity, the certainty that objects are nothing foreign . . . It is the self-feeling that what is lacking to it is itself . . ."
7. PhG, 101/134/218.
8. Cf. *Realphilosophie*, I, 197, where the theoretical process is described as the ideal and the practical process as the real mastery of nature.
9. PhG, 102/134/218-19.
10. This same charge of forgetfulness is central to the critique of Idealism at the beginning of Chapter Five. Due to this forgetfulness Observing Reason is not significantly different from the Understanding of Chapter Three. See especially PhG, 164-66/176-78/273-76.
11. PhG, 103-04/134-35/219-20, Hegel's italics.
12. Cf. Hegel's early formulas in this respect from the so-called Frankfurt "System Fragment" and *Differenz* respectively: "*die Verbindung der Verbindung und der Nichtverbindung,*" *Werke*, I, 422, English translation in *Early Theological Writings*, p. 312, and "*die Identität der Identität und der Nichtidentität,*" GW, 4:64. These phrases serve as predicates, in the first instance of Life, in the second of the Absolute.
13. Dieter Henrich, "The Proof-Structure of Kant's Transcendental Deduction," *The Review of Metaphysics*, June, 1969, p. 657, his italics.

14. In Husserlian language Hegel is dealing with the relation of intending consciousness to intentional object. Something like the *epoche* of the natural standpoint is involved in reflecting on the objects of perception simply *qua* present to consciousness. Such objects have no independence for they are only the wholly immanent correlate of the intentional act which constitutes them.

15. PhG, 103/134/219.

16. PhG, 102-05/134-35/219-21.

17. PhG, 110-11/139/225. I have translated *das Aufheben* as "dominating" partly as a signal that the basic structure of the master-slave relationship is presented in the immediately following paragraph. *Re* Feuerbach, see Ch. 3, n. 27 and *Grundsätze*, #25 and #37, KS, 182 f. and 199 f.

18. PhG, 105/135/221.

19. PhG, 126/148-49/238. cf. 108/137/223.

20. PhG, 111/139/225-26.

21. PhG, 112/140/226-27. This analysis of animal desire merits comparison not only with Plato's critique of hedonism in the *Gorgias,* but also Kierkegaard's critique of aesthetic existence in the first volume of *Either/Or.*

22. Where Kant tried to show that it was logically self-defeating to treat others simply as means to our own happiness, Hegel tries to show that it is practically or existentially self-defeating.

23. See note 9 above.

24. PhG, 113/140/227.

25. See the discussion of language in section 3D. above.

26. Josiah Royce, *Lectures on Modern Idealism,* New Haven, 1919, p. 174.

27. In his lectures published in 1859 as *Philosophie der Kunst* but given in 1802-03 at Jena and in 1804-05 at Würzburg, Schelling writes, "Mythology can be the work neither of an individual person nor of a race [*Geschlecht*] or species (in so far as these are only a collection of individuals) but only of a race so far as it is itself individual and the same as an individual person . . . It requires, thus, as a necessary condition of its possibility, a race that is an individual like a person. The incomprehensibility which this idea may have for our time cannot deny it its truth. It is the highest idea for all of history in general." *Sämmtliche Werke, 1859, I. Abt., 5. Bd., 414-15.* In comparison with Hegel's concept of Spirit this formulation lacks explicit reference to the independence of the parts which make up the whole and to the need of the whole to become self-conscious if it is to be subject and not merely substance.

28. Dieter Henrich, "Hegel und Hölderlin," in *Hegel im Kontext,* Frankfurt, 1971, p. 27. cf. "Historische Voraussetzungen von Hegels System," *op. cit.,* p. 67.

29. *Werke,* I, 242, my italics.

30. *Ibid.,* p. 248. This is from another Frankfurt fragment, one included in the *Early Theological Writings.* See p. 307.

31. *Ibid.,* p. 244.

32. "System Fragment," (see note 12 above), *ibid.,* 422/312.

33. In *Early Theological Writings,* p. 309, note 2.

34. "System Fragment," *Werke,* I, 419-20/310.

35. *Ibid.,* 421/311.

36. PhG, 106/136/222. The first of these paragraphs is the one beginning *"Die Bestimmung des Lebens . . ."* Baillie has divided this passage into five paragraphs, the first of which begins "The determination of the principle . . ."

37. Hegel makes this clear just before his extended discussion of the structure of infinite life (see previous note), PhG, 105/135/221. This corresponds to the relation between philosophy of nature and philosophy of Spirit as expressed in the Jena *Philosophy of Nature* (1804-05). "The Spirit of nature is a hidden Spirit. It does not come forth in the form of Spirit. It is Spirit only for knowing Spirit, in other words, it is Spirit in itself but not for itself . . . It is Spirit as the other of itself." GW, 7:185.

38. The category of recognition first appears briefly in *Sittlichkeit,* pp. 32 ff. and 89 ff., but achieves a central place only in the *Realphilosophie,* both volumes. Its link with love is explicit in such passages as II, 204, "Love is that spiritual recognition itself which knows itself." Such a relation, Hegel adds on the margin, is the "actuality of love."

39. PhG, 114/141/229, my italics.

40. In his *Grundlage des Naturrechts* Fichte had introduced the concept of recognition in a thoroughly Kantian manner. At one point of his argument he presents the following three propositions: "I. I can expect a particular rational being to recognize me as a rational being only in so far as I treat him as such . . . II. But I must expect all rational beings outside of me in every possible instance to recognize me as a rational being . . . III. The conclusion is clear.—I must recognize the free being outside of me in every case as a free being, i.e., I must limit my freedom through the concept of the possibility of his freedom." *Werke,* III, 44-52. Later the concept of reciprocal recognition is introduced in response to the question, "How is a community of free beings as such possible?" III, 85 ff.

41. Cf. *Realphilosophie*, II, 205, where Hegel explicitly distinguishes between the mere concept of recognition as love and the task of realizing this concept.

42. See note 20 above. cf. *Realphilosophie*, II, 201-02, "Precisely by knowing himself in the other, each one has renounced himself [*auf sich selbst Verzicht getan*]: Love." This knowing of self in the other takes place when each one "*sich aufhebt,* gives up his independence as existing for himself and in distinction from the other." A similar passage is found at I, 230. In the Jena *Metaphysics,* where Leibniz's *Monadology* is the model for developing the concept of Spirit, it is this same *sich aufheben* which is the key to the harmony in which the parts retain their individuality while relating to the whole. GW, 7:169-73.

43. That desire indicates an ontological lack is suggested by *Realphilosophie*, II, 195-96.

44. I John 4:18, RSV.

45. PhG, 119/144/233.

46. *Die Frühschriften,* ed. Landshut, Stuttgart, 1968, p. 269. English translation in *Karl Marx: Early Writings,* Bottomore, trans., New York, 1964, p. 202. Marx had no way of knowing how extensive Hegel's study of modern political economy had been by the time he wrote the *Phenomenology.*

47. PhG, 126/148-49/238.

48. That human desire is distinguished from animal desire both in terms of labor and love, and that the latter of these has primacy over the former is already Hegel's view in the *Realphilosophie.* See I, 220-21 and II, 196-202.

49. This expresses a connection not only with the Augustinian tradition but also with the Aristotelian, for which *praxis* has priority over *techne.*

50. Theodor Adorno, *Negative Dialektik,* Frankfurt, 1966, p. 8. cf. pp. 20-22.

51. See Ch. 3, n. 9.

52. *op. cit.,* p. 349, Marx's italics, from *The German Ideology.* In this sense Hegel's philosophy has the same presuppositions as Marx's, men in their concrete individuality. cf. pp. 346-47. For both of them concrete individuality is socially conditioned.

53. *Realphilosophie*, II, 179. Now it is clearer why Hegel could also say on p. 183 that "language is then the true being of Spirit as Spirit in general. It is there as the unity of two free selves . . ." That is, even language involves reciprocal recognition. That it is nevertheless not

possible to comprehend Spirit adequately within the limits of the theoretical, which is the point of the cited contrast between ego and Spirit, is also expressed in the Jena *Metaphysic,* GW, 7:165, 171.

54. See section 2A. above.

55. PhG, 287-97/255-61/374-82, and 376-83/313-18/457-63.

56. PhG, 287/255/374. There follow two other formulations of this concept: "Recognized Self-Consciousness, which has the certainty of itself in the other free Self-Consciousness and finds its truth precisely in this relation . . ." What is required is "intuiting complete unity with the other in his independence, or of having the given, free thinghood of the other, which is the negative of myself, for my object as my own ˌbeing-for-myself." 289-90/256-57/375-76.

57. This question and answer appear in connection with the two formulations of recognized Self-Consciousness cited in the previous note.

58. PhG, 289/256/375-76, my italics. This is a good example of Hegel's somewhat promiscuous use of the term 'absolute'. But we must take him seriously. If he calls the knowledge which a "determinate" society gains of itself "absolute" we must not assume that he must have meant something else, since *we* do not use the term in that way. See note 67 below, especially *Naturrecht,* p. 479. Speaking there of the plurality and conditioned nature of Ethical Life he says that "the World Spirit in each of its forms has its duller or more developed but nevertheless absolute self-feeling. Among every nation and within each totality of customs and laws it has its essence and its enjoyment of itself."

59. *Naturrecht,* GW, 4:484.

60. PhG, 288/256/375. This characterization of pure consciousness as the a priori We expresses succinctly Hegel's critique of the transcendental tradition.

61. PhG, 291/258/377.

62. In *Naturrecht,* where these distinctions are the subject of a sustained critique, Hegel's explicit orientation is to the political thought of Plato, Aristotle, and Montesquieu. He calls any incongruity between customs and laws a "barbarity". GW, 4:470.

63. Cf. *The German Constitution, Werke,* I, 516-17/189-90.

64. See note 42 above. In the *Monadology* to be an individual is to have a unique perspective ˀn the world.

65. PhG, 290/257/376. cf. the discussion of life, note 34 above, and the discussion of man's unorganic nature, Ch. 3, n. 50. In the next

paragraph of the PhG, this structure is developed in terms of abstract labor. cf. *Realphilosophie*, II, 213 ff.

66. When Hegel speaks of this wisdom of antiquity in *Naturrecht* he also mentions the Pythagorean notion that the best education for a young man is to become the citizen of a nation with good institutions. GW, 4:469.

67. PhG, 292-93/258-59/378. On the determinate particularity of Ethical Life and the relation of this to the issue of war see *Naturrecht*, GW, 4:449-50, 479-81.

68. PhG, 293-94/259/379. For Hegel's discussion of this phenomenon in connection with attitudes toward war see PCR I, HTJ, 222-24/155-58 and 229-30/164-65.

69. For example, see *Naturrecht*, GW, 4:424-27.

70. Just in those passages where Hegel describes the social substance as unchangeable he emphasizes this reciprocity. See notes 61 and 65 above.

71. That *Sehnsucht* and *Sollen* express an imperfect relation of the self to the social whole is emphasized in the Jena *Metaphysics*, GW, 7:170.

72. *Naturrecht*, GW, 4:470.

73. See notes 61, 65, and 70 above.

74. PhG, 377/314/458. The rendering of *das an-und-fürsichseiende Wesen* as "the self-contained and self-sufficient being" is supported by Hegel's characterization of Spirit as *das sich selbst tragende absolute reale Wesen* and as *der die Existenz ist*. 378/314/459.

75. PhG, 377-78/314/458-59. See note 70 above.

76. PhG, 385/319/467.

77. J. N. Findlay, *Hegel: A Re-Examination*, New York, 1962, p. 95.

78. Sidney Hook, *From Hegel to Marx*, Ann Arbor, 1962, p. 41.

79. Jean Hyppolite, *Genèse et Structure de la Phénoménologie de L'Esprit de Hegel*, Paris, 1946, II, 312-14. He adds, "Spirit is precisely the We in so far as it simultaneously actualizes the unity and the separation of the I's."

80. Hook, *op. cit.*, pp. 18, 30-35, 54, 62.

CHAPTER SIX: The Career of Spirit

6A. The Legal Self as the Destiny of the Ancient World

The concept of Spirit is the linchpin which holds the *Phenomenology* together. It has been developed out of epistemological reflection through a deepened questioning into the "I think" of Descartes and Kant, the self-consciousness which is presupposed in every consciousness. Hegel's conclusion is that this self-consciousness is concrete and that it is rooted in the social interaction of persons seeking recognition. This inseparability of the I from the We is what brings the concept of Spirit into vital contact with the other problem area to which Hegel has addressed himself, the present spiritual crisis. This crisis is so plainly an historical event that Hegel's description of it will have to be a kind of narrative. It is none other than the concept of Spirit which permits Hegel at this point to take up the historical perspective. We must see how this is possible.

The transition to Spirit is qualitatively different from earlier advances, for Spirit, understood in terms of Ethical Life, is "the real substance, into which the preceding forms of consciousness return and in which they find their ground."[1] More specifically, "Spirit is thus the self-supporting, absolute, real being. *All the previous forms of consciousness are abstractions from it.* They are constituted by the fact that Spirit analyses itself, distinguishes its moments, and dwells on each of these. The isolating of such moments presupposes Spirit itself for its own reality. In other words, this isolation of the moments exists only in Spirit, which is existence."[2] Like Consciousness, Self-Consciousness, and Reason, Spirit represents a dimension of human experience within which a movement from immediacy and mere certainty to mediation and truth must take place. But whereas the first three dimensions are abstract, Spirit is concrete. This means that the forms through which Spirit passes on its way from immediacy to self-knowledge "distinguish themselves from the preceding forms in being real spiritual totalities [*Geister*], authentic actualities. They are forms of a world, not merely forms of consciousness."[3]

The most important consequence of this is that while the *Phenomenology* up to this point has called increasingly explicit attention to the historicity of man in developing the concept of Spirit, it turns in Chapter Six for the first time to the question of human history as such. The movement from Consciousness to Self-Consciousness to Reason to Spirit is not a temporal progression. Nor is the movement within each of the first three dimensions to be understood in that way. "It is only Spirit in its entirety that is in time, and the forms of the totality of Spirit as such present themselves in a temporal succession. For it is only the whole which has authentic actuality and hence the form of pure freedom relative to anything else, the form which expresses itself as time."[4]

We know that Hegel wants to concentrate his historical account of Spirit on the transition from the old modernity to the new modernity, the revolution he believes to be occurring as he writes. This will involve a structural analysis of the old modernity as well as an account of both its demise and the new forms that seem to be replacing it. The structural analysis will function as the socioanalysis of critical finitism, for it is by understanding this world that we will understand the philosophical dogmatism which denies that we can know the Absolute. But this will not be the "refutation" of that antiphilosophical philosophy. That can come only in the account of the demise of the old modernity and the birth of the new, for it is Spirit and not Hegel who refutes that tradition. To broaden our understanding of the old modernity Hegel will first take us back in time beyond it to the world from which he believes it arose and which provides striking typological contrasts with it.

There will therefore be three stages to Hegel's narration of the historical career of Spirit in Chapter Six: Ethical Life—True Spirit, Culture—Self-Estranged Spirit, and Morality—Self-Certain Spirit. These represent three historical epochs which culminate in three types of selfhood or three kinds of social self-knowledge: the legal self, the revolutionary self, and the conscientious self.[5] Each epoch represents a determinate form of "the essential opposition between individual and universal."[6] Each form of selfhood represents that relation as it structures individual consciousness. The legal self is the culmination of Greco-Roman paganism, the process that leads from

Ethical Life to empire. The revolutionary self marks the end of the development of medieval and early modern Christian Europe. Hegel's analysis, under the rubric 'Culture', concentrates on France. The conscientious self is Hegel's attempt to understand the world-historical significance of the new world whose birth pains were the French Revolution. The orientation here is to German Idealism and Romanticism.[7]

At the beginning of this longest chapter of the *Phenomenology* we are told that the goal and result of this historical progression is "that the actual self-consciousness of absolute Spirit will come forth."[8] That would be no minor result, for if the self-consciousness of absolute Spirit is not Absolute Knowledge, it's hard to say what would be. In this sense Hegel promises to complete his phenomenological task by the end of Chapter Six. But since he describes this with the very idea which is basic to his understanding of religion, Spirit's self-consciousness, we have a preliminary clue why the result of Chapter Six might not be fully understood apart from a further chapter on religion.

The story begins, however, not with the self-consciousness of absolute Spirit but with Spirit in its immediacy. As Ethical Life, the beautiful simplicity of social wholeness, it is not aware of itself as Spirit. Just for that reason it is not fully absolute. But the process of coming to self-consciousness destroys Ethical Life by disrupting the immediacy which defines it. "Spirit, so far as it is the immediate truth, is the ethical life of a people . . . It has to advance to the consciousness of what it immediately is, transcend the beautiful ethical life, and come to a knowledge of itself by passing through a series of forms."[9] When this has happened "the ethical substance has by this process become actual self-consciousness. In other words, the particular self has come to be in and for itself. But precisely thereby is Ethical Life ruined."[10]

In his earlier discussion of Ethical Life Hegel describes its lability in terms of a two-fold immediacy.[11] Immediacy for Hegel means relation solely to self, excluding relation to an other. Thus Sense Certainty seeks to maintain immediacy in the relation of perceiving subject to perceived object by making first the one term and then the other fully unessential, thus leaving the essential moment to determine the perceptual result entirely apart from its relation to the unessential moment.[12] The two-fold immediacy of Ethical Life, therefore, is to be understood as the failure of the whole to be grasped in terms of its relations to other similar wholes and to its parts. Ethical Life is immediate in so far as it lacks the awareness of its determinate character, that is, fails to see itself as just one society among many and takes itself to be, as it were, the center of the world.[13] It is also immediate in so far as the relation between the social whole and the personal parts is not seen to be just that, a relation, presupposing at least a relative difference and independence.

It is this second immediacy which distinguishes Ethical Life from Morality in Hegel's technical usage. The laws and customs of Ethical Life are immediately valid and immediately effective. It is not for the individual to examine and validate them. His station defines his duties. The tragedy of Antigone is thus unlike that of Hamlet. As a moral person his conflict is an inner one. He reflects on his situation and tries to bring action out of soliloquizing meditation. She, however, like her antagonist, Creon, does not reflect. Both experience the conflict between the duties of their respective stations in the family and state, but not an inner conflict of soul. Each is directly identified with the role he or she is to play. Just because the social norms do not require the individual's insight and sanction they are also immediately effective. They are not a master whom the individual might disobey. Hegel expresses this double immediacy of laws and customs by saying of them simply, "They are." Neither as the question—What is my duty?—nor as the question—Shall I do it?—does reflection separate the individual from the principle of his action. But when the laws and customs of the whole have this validity and effectiveness in the parts it is difficult to speak of a relation between parts and whole, for the difference between them has vanished. One is left with the immediacy of the whole and can speak of society, but not of the individual.[14]

For Ethical Life to pass out of its immediacy and come to self-consciousness it must become aware of its relatedness as a whole to other similar wholes and to its own constituent parts. Hegel finds this double experience exquisitely expressed in Sophocles' *Antigone*.[15] First of all the social substance "tears its moments asunder." Just as the immediacy of Sense Certainty turns out to be a part of Perception, in which the moment of universality, the one, conflicts with that of particularity, the many, so Spirit's immediacy is found to involve spheres or powers which represent these same abstract aspects, the state and the family respectively. By dividing itself in this way Ethical Life plants the seeds of its own destruction, creating an enemy within its own gates. Since each of the spheres into which the substance divides itself takes itself to be the whole, the whole becomes a living contradiction.[16]

Actually each of the parts is, in an important sense, the whole. The family as well as the state is a community [*Gemeinwesen*] in which reciprocal recognition takes place. Apart from the question of size the categories of Ethical Life apply at least as well to the family as to the state. Though family and state are reciprocally dependent, it is easy for each to see the other simply as a means to its own ends. Thus the family becomes "the rebellious principle of individuality" vis-a-vis the larger community, which in turn becomes the violator of the divine law which expresses the sanctity of the family.[17]

Antigone illustrates this nicely. She comes into conflict with the state, not in virtue of the particularity presupposed by social contract theory, but in terms of her own immediate identity with another, smaller universal, the family. Creon, too, acts as the executive of the state, not a private individual. Both agents become guilty through the one-sidedness of their action. It is not merely they who perish, however, (Creon does not survive his victory over Antigone) but Ethical Life itself.[18]

Still following Sophocles, Hegel finds war to be the catalyst of their experience. It is through war that both aspects of Spirit's immediacy are overcome. To begin with war is a counter force to the centrifugal tendencies of family and economic life. "In order not to let these get rooted and settled in this isolation and thus break up the whole into fragments allowing Spirit to evaporate, the government from time to time has to shake them to the very center through war."[19] By claiming the life and wealth of its citizens the state makes clear the tension between the whole and the parts. In this respect Ethical Life passes out of its immediacy.

But war is also the struggle for recognition between communities. Each community seeks to be for itself, as Hegel would

put it, by negating the other communities and reducing them to
the status of something for it. The dialectic of master and slave
repeats itself at the collective level. Whether as the master or
slave community the ethical totality in this way becomes aware
of the other totalities and thus of its own determinate and limited character.

In these two ways war enables Ethical Life to come to self-
consciousness and thus achieve its "absolute truth."[20] But in
doing so it destroys the *polis* and the form of Spirit associated
with it. In overcoming the first immediacy war signifies only
the victory of the national spirit over the household gods. As a
confrontation between peoples, however, war has deeper consequences. " . . . the living nations [*Volkgeister*] are ruined
through their individuality and pass over into a universal community, whose bare universality is spiritless and dead, and
whose living activity is found in the particular individual as particular. The ethical form of Spirit disappears and another takes
its place." Ethical Life is overrun by empire.[21]

Hegel discusses the Roman Empire as a form of human
experience which he entitles "Legal Status" [*Rechtszustand*]. Instead of the unity of law and custom we have here the primacy
of law.[22] Hegel finds in the notion of a legal person the form of
recognition and corresponding self-consciousness which are
the destiny of the ancient world. In antithesis to the immediate
unity between the individual and the social substance which
characterizes Ethical Life, the two are here in total separation
and opposition to each other. "The substance comes forth as a
formal universal over against its component individuals and no
longer dwells within them as living Spirit. Rather the simple solidarity of their individuality is dispersed into a plurality of
separate points . . . The universal unity into which the living,
immediate unity of individuality and substance regresses is the
spiritless community which has ceased to be the un-self-
conscious substance of individuals. In this community they now
count in their individual being-for-self as selves and substances on their own account. The universal, split up into the
atomic units of the absolute plurality of individuals, this dead
Spirit, is an equality in which all count for as much as each, that
is, have the significance of persons." To be a legal person is to
be an instance of a kind, not the part of a whole.[23]

It is true that as a legal person the individual is recognized. But Hegel finds this to be an abstract recognition since it is only as the bearer of legal rights and thus for all practical purposes as the owner of property that the individual is recognized, "only as this brittle or obstinate [*spröde*] self, not the self dissolved in the substance . . . as the bare, empty unit of the person."[24] Whatever the individual may be beyond his property, that is, his personhood in the non-legal sense, is not recognized. Only the Emperor is more fully recognized. Since he is recognized without having to recognize his citizens except as legal persons, he is rightly called the Master of the World, suggesting that legal persons, in spite of their rights as slave owners, are themselves little more than slaves.

But this is no ordinary master. "This Master of the World takes himself in this way to be the absolute person, comprising at the same time all existence within himself, for whom there exists no higher Spirit." The overtones of divinity here are not accidental. "Knowing himself in this way to be the sum and substance of all actual powers, this Master of the World is the numinous [*ungeheuer*] self-consciousness which knows itself to be the actual God." He is not, however, the God of love. It is only a "destructive power which he exercises against the selfhood of the subjects over against him. For his power is not the harmony of Spirit in which each person would perceive his own self-consciousness . . ." Rather the individuals relate as externally to him as to each other. He is a "foreign content" and a "hostile being" in relation to them. Individuality, defined in economic-legal terms, finds the state to be substantial and divine, but at the same time an alien and hostile power in which it has no share.[25]

The form of recognition realized in legal personality is thus an intense form of the alienation Hegel seeks to overcome, by no means its solution.[26] Yet this is presented as "the truth of the ethical world."[27] Antiquity founders on the problem of the individual and society. Their relation swings violently from the extreme of immediacy to the extreme of reflection, from identity to difference, without being able to find the classical ideal, expressed by Aristotle as the mean, more profoundly by Hegel as the identity of identity and difference, of immediacy and reflection.

Whereas at first one can hardly speak of individuals at all, Antigone and Creon being merely the executives of family and state, the classical world ends in such an extreme and alienated form of individualism that Hegel can describe the larger process he is tracing as the movement from independence to freedom.[28] Because the world of legal persons is structured by a "spiritless independence" which is not freedom but slavery, Hegel finds it to be the fulfillment of the "slave ideologies" (Kojeve) presented in conjunction with the Lordship and Bondage section of Chapter Four, namely Stoicism and Scepticism. Just as these develop into Unhappy Consciousness, "so here the actual truth of that view has made its appearance. This truth consists in the fact that the universal worth of self-consciousness is reality estranged from self-consciousness . . . The actuality of selfhood which was not found in the ethical world has been gained by this world's regression into the world of the legal person. What was harmonious in the former now comes on the scene as developed but self-estranged."[29] With this we have entered a new world, that of Self-Estranged Spirit. This world is the truth of Unhappy Consciousness, or, put the other way around, Unhappy Consciousness tells us the truth about this world. The transition from Stoicism and Scepticism to Unhappy Consciousness only mirrors at the ideological level the way in which Roman civilization is transformed into Christendom. This is the background of the old modernity.

6B. The Revolutionary Self as the Destiny of Christendom

In *Differenz* (1801) Hegel writes, "Estrangement [*Entzweiung*] is the source of the need of philosophy, and as the culture [*Bildung*] of the age, the unfree, given aspect of philosophy's form. In culture the appearance of the Absolute isolates itself from the Absolute and fixes itself as something independent."[30] This definition of culture in terms of estrangement guides Hegel's interpretation of the modern national Christian state in France from its feudal origins through the Revolution. It appears in the title of Chapter Six's second section: Self-Estranged Spirit—Culture.

There seems to be something of a gap in the historical narrative here, for Hegel does not narrate the transition from the Roman Empire to the feudal world to which he now turns. But the world he calls Culture spans the entire career of the Holy Roman Empire and is in essence the world of that peculiar political entity, though not in any geographically exclusive sense. Since the Holy Roman Empire took itself to be not merely the successor to the Roman Empire but in large measure its continuation, Hegel's jump is less abrupt substantially than it is chronologically.

Hegel takes seriously his own suggestion that Unhappy Consciousness is the model for the estrangement which defines the world of Culture. This means that the individual takes what is essential [*das Wesen*], the substantial and divine, to be external and negative to him, excluding his participation. Yet he knows the essential to be Spirit and thus essentially to be "the interpenetration of being and individuality. This its existence is the work of self-consciousness, but likewise an immediately given actuality, foreign to self-consciousness, with a being of its own in which self-consciousness does not recognize itself." The essential world is the "work" of self-consciousness because this world "acquires existence by self-consciousness of its own accord alienating itself [*Entäusserung*] and giving up its own essentiality [*Entwesung*] . . ." The substance becomes actual through "the estrangement of selfhood, for the immediate self, that is, the self whose validity is in and for itself apart from estrangement, is without substance . . . Its substance is thus just its alienation, and the alienation is the substance, that is, the spiritual powers forming themselves into a coherent world and thereby maintaining themselves."[31]

Because the production [*Erzeugung*] of the actual world comes about through the renunciation [*Entsagung*] by self-consciousness of its being-for-itself, this world has an objectivity over against its maker, who therefore "treats it as something foreign of which it must take possession [*sich bemächtigen*]." Culture is this taking possession. It becomes the basis of recognition. Since the self is actual only through self-estrangement, its recognition is based, not on its mere being, but on the further self-estrangement in which it overcomes its natural self by conforming itself to the universal, the world it has already helped to produce. "This individuality forms itself [*bildet sich*] to that which it is in itself." It takes possession of its world by taking as its essence or second nature that by which it has made the world the essential reality in giving up its own essentiality. Socialization creates both the individual and society, "for the power of the individual consists in conforming himself to the substance."[32]

For Culture this process of repossession remains essentially incomplete, just as with Unhappy Consciousness the essential remains irreducibly other. Culture is thus the world of dualism. In the ethical world all reality belonged to the present and nothing was understood to be radically transcendent. But for Culture the world divides into the world which is present here and now and the world beyond, the actual world and the world of pure consciousness or thought, the real world and the ideal world, the profane world and the sacred world. Over against the present, actual, real, profane world there arises a transcendent world, the distant world where the harmony so conspicuously missing here and now is restored. These two worlds, out of harmony with each other, are also out of harmony with themselves. By dividing itself into conflicting forces each is estranged from itself. The actual world becomes the struggle between State Power and Wealth, while the ideological world becomes the struggle between Faith and Enlightened Insight.[33]

The description of Culture thus divides into three subsections. The inner tensions of the actual world are presented in terms of the rise of absolute monarchy and capitalism. The revolutionary potential of these developments is noticed, but not seen as leading directly to revolution. The immediate result, the second moment, is the intellectual revolution known as Enlightenment. Out of it arises the third moment, the revolutionary self as the destiny of the estranged world of Culture. Since the immediate ground of the Revolution is found in the Enlightment, one must say that for Hegel ideas change the world. But these ideas themselves have their basis in the world that is to be changed. Ideology is not impotent. The world of the old modernity gives rise to ideas which are the vehicles of the historical change which ushers in the new modernity. Among these ideas are those which Hegel wishes to repudiate. Instead of seeking to refute them directly, he traces the path by which they undercut their own worldly basis.

The division of the actual world into spheres or estates is not peculiar to Culture. It is as natural as the division of nature into earth, air, fire, and water,[34] and was already present in the ethical world as the distinction of family from state. Nor is the fact that it is now the economic domain rather than the family which stands in conflict with the state what distinguishes the world of Culture. It is rather the non-immediate relation of the individual to these conflicting spheres of interest. Antigone was born to her role. The medieval nobility, original bearers of the world of Culture, must choose whether they shall serve State Power or Wealth.[35]

The former choice is "the heroism of service, the virtue which sacrifices the being of the individual to the universal and thereby brings the universal into being . . . Through this alienation the existing consciousness makes itself [*bildet sich*] something essential . . . Through this culture it acquires self-respect and respect from others."[36] State Power is at first this collective undertaking, and the proud vassal finds no conflict between serving the common good and his own interests, even where this service costs him his life in feudal warfare.

But State Power in the full sense involves the concept of particular will, and only with the emergence of unlimited monarchy is it fully *begeistet*, fully in possession of the union of universal and particular which typifies Spirit. Hegel stresses the linguistic character of royal authority and introduces the monarch as the linguistic creation of the nobility. He is the king because he is called the king, because they pledge him their allegiance. "Through the name the universal power is the monarch." Of course the king is not the alienated independence of just anyone. Only the speech of those with the power to confer kingship can make a king. That power resides in the wealth of the nobility. It is the ultimate source of State Power.[37]

When the nobility is seen to be wealth pursuing its own interest its nobility is somewhat tarnished. While it poses as in service to the common good, "its true nature lies rather in retaining its own being-for-itself through its service. Its spontaneous renunciation of its selfhood is actually the breaking up and tearing asunder of the universal substance. Its spirit is the attitude of thoroughgoing discordance."[38] As this comes to consciousness the distinction on which medieval society was based, between noble and base, is undercut, and the modern world takes shape in the tension between State Power and Wealth, absolute monarchy and the bourgeoisie.

The bearers of the world of Culture are now caught in an acute predicament. They have created not one but two powers which now confront them as independent and indifferent to their purposes. Not only the political power of the monarch but also the economic power of the market have this character. The wealth which began as the very principle of self-esteem has become something foreign. In both the economic and political realm bourgeois consciousness "sees itself in the power of an alien will on which it depends, which may or may not transmit being-for-itself to consciousness." Because selfhood and recognition have become so identified with political and economic power, the bourgeoisie "sees its selfhood as such dependent on the contingent individuality of an other, on the accident of the moment, of an arbitrary choice, or some other utterly indifferent circumstance."[39]

At the stage of Legal Status the self was at least recognized, imperfect as this recognition may have been. "But here the self sees its self-certainty as such to be the most unessential thing, its selfhood to be the absolute lack of selfhood. It is grateful [for its wealth] in the spirit of one who feels the deepest reprobation as well as the deepest rebellion. In this inner strife in which the pure ego sees itself outside itself and torn asunder, everything which has continuity and universality, all that bears the name of law, of good, and of right, is at the same time dispersed and destroyed . . . The pure ego itself is absolutely disintegrated."[40]

There is an important difference between the spirit of beneficent Wealth and the spirit of those who receive its benefits. Hegel has in mind the distinction from classical political economy between the capitalist whose wealth is seen as producing goods and employment for the community at large and the wage laborer in his dependence on the entrepreneur.[41] But the difference is not what it might appear to be. "Wealth thus shares reprobation with its clientele, but in the place of rebellion appears arrogance. For, on the one hand, it knows as well as the self it benefits that its being-for-itself has the character of contingent thinghood. On the other hand, it is itself this contingency in whose power selfhood is placed. In this arrogance, which thinks it has sustained an alien self through a meal and thus obtained the submission of this self in its innermost being, Wealth overlooks the inner rebellion of the other . . . It stands directly in front of this innermost abyss, this bottomless pit in which all stability and substance have vanished. It sees in this pit nothing but a common thing, a plaything for its whims, a chance result of its own caprice."[42]

Over against this arrogance is the rebellion of alienated labor. Its language is "the linguistic epitome of this whole world of Culture, the spirit of this world in its truth and objective reality." If you want to know what the world of Culture is all about, listen to the proletariat. The revolutionary attitude of this group is to be understood in terms of its experience of selfhood. "This self-consciousness, the rebellion which reprobates its reprobation, is immediately absolute self-identity in absolute dismemberment, the pure mediation of pure self-consciousness with itself." That is to say that it has been reflected out of its social substance. Social rules no longer have any value for it, and it can no longer find recognition or fulfillment through participation in the economic, political, or family life of its people.[43]

While Hegel finds proletarian consciousness to be the revolutionary truth of the world of Culture, he does not proceed directly to a description of the revolutionary self. He knows that the French Revolution was not a proletarian revolution. It is clear from this passage as well as from the earlier analysis of the master-slave relationship that Hegel understands the character of alienated labor. But though he brings this phenomenon to our attention on two separate occasions, he does not find it to be the vehicle of historical change. It is clear that on his analysis there can be no "happy consciousness" as long as alienated labor remains. But he does not see the laborer as an effective revolutionary. The world of Culture is not revolutionized directly through itself, but indirectly through that other world which reflects it, the world of pure but by no means proletarian consciousness.

The house of Culture is, as we have already seen, divided against itself. Hegel now directs our attention to the ideological world which lies beyond the world of State Power and Wealth he has just been describing. "The first world is the actual world where Spirit's estrangement is realized. The other is that which

Spirit constructs for itself in the ether of pure consciousness, raising itself above the first. Set in opposition to that estrangement, this second world is just for that reason not free from it, but rather only the other form of that very estrangement, which consists precisely in having one's consciousness divided between two worlds. Thus both worlds are included in this second world. It is therefore not the self-consciousness of absolute being as it is in and for itself, that is, not Religion which is considered here, but Faith, in so far as it is a flight from the actual world and thus not something in and for itself. This flight out of the realm of the present is therefore immediately divided against itself. Pure consciousness is the element into which Spirit raises itself, but it is not only the element of Faith but just as much of the concept. Consequently both appear on the scene together at the same time, and the former comes before us only in opposition to the latter," i.e., Faith in opposition to Enlightened Insight, religion in conflict with philosophy.[44]

This pivotal paragraph introduces the second stage of Hegel's account of Culture with three important points. First, Hegel is dealing here, as in the case of Unhappy Consciousness, with a form of religion which does not fulfill its own aspirations. The faithful desire to experience the presence of the divine, but find their present devoid of divinity. The use of the term 'Faith' to describe this experience is introduced in Hegel's earlier discussion of Ethical Life under the heading, Reason as Testing Laws. Ethical consciousness does not believe in the laws it obeys, "for faith, while it surely intuits the divine [das Wesen], sees it as something alien. The ethical self-consciousness is immediately one with the essential [das Wesen] in virtue of the universality of its own self. Faith, on the other hand, begins with the individual consciousness. It is the process in which this consciousness is always approaching this unity without ever entering the presence of its own essence."[45] For Faith, then, the divine has the character of positivity which was the subject of Hegel's earliest theological critiques.[46]

Second, faith is presented as ideology. As a reflection out of the world of Culture it is at the same time a reflection of that world. Thus its worship can be described as the "obedience of service and of praise," precisely the language used to describe the earthly role of the feudal nobility.[47] But ideologies are never exact mirrorings of the real world. The object of faith is, "according to the concept of Faith, nothing else than the real world lifted into the universality of pure consciousness. The structure of the real world, therefore, also constitutes the organization of the object of faith, except that in this case the parts have the character of Spirit without being estranged from each other."[48] The world beyond is simply this world purified of its flaws. Much of Enlightment's critique of Faith revolves around this point. Anticipating Feuerbach and Freud, it seeks to discredit Faith by interpreting it as a wish-fulfilling projection of its own self-image. God is but the fictitious product of its own undisciplined imagination.

Hegel describes this familiar Enlightenment critique, but he finds Enlightenment to be every bit as ideological as Faith. This is the third and perhaps crucial element of his account of self-estranged Spirit as pure consciousness. If Enlightenment wins out in the struggle with Faith it is not because it is any less a reflection of the world of Culture than its opponent. Hegel does not overlook the real differences between the two, which he seeks to express in formulations like these: Faith has the content without insight, while Enlightenment has insight without content, or, Faith is consciousness without self-consciousness, Enlightenment the reverse. But having a common origin, the two views end up looking more similar than different to Hegel. "Insight therefore is victorious over Faith, because in relation to Faith it validates what is necessary to and contained in Faith."[49] As reflections out of the world of Culture both find the world here and now to be unacceptable. Both point beyond it to a world in which estrangement is overcome. The beyond of Enlightenment is that of the "not yet," while that of Faith, in the form presented here, is the beyond of "once upon a time" and of "somewhere else, not here." Even here Hegel finds identity, for he suggests that the "here, but not yet" hope of Enlightenment is not really alien to a Faith which prays, "Thy will be done in earth as it is in heaven."

Enlightenment's commitment is to a secularized form of the Kingdom of God. "Both worlds are reconciled and heaven is transplanted to the earth below."[50] It is a secularized version of this dream because man alone is to do the transplanting. Yet Hegel sees Enlightenment as reminding Faith of its own claim that "God sent his son into the world, not to condemn the world, but that the world might be saved through him."[51] A religion with Incarnation at its core cannot be entirely otherworldly. Enlightenment's arguments against Faith are always *ad hominem*, though neither party to the quarrel realizes this.

The this-worldly *Weltanschauung* of Enlightenment, the immediate source of the revolution, is presented in its metaphysical, epistemological, and ethical dimensions. As metaphysics it is either deism or materialism. Hegel finds it hard to distinguish between the two, since on both views "the absolute Being turns out to be a mere vacuum, to which no characteristics or predicates can be attributed." Enlightened insight into the absolute Being is that "which sees nothing in it but just absolute Being, the être suprême, the great void."[52] This is in keeping with Enlightenment's "Feuerbachian" view that the wealth ascribed to the divine world belongs to the human world by nature. It is as if deism and materialism signify the emptiness of a transcendent absolute after man reclaims for himself what was, according to Enlightenment, orginally his.

Enlightenment's empiricism is equally motivated by its this-worldliness. Hegel describes it as a return to Sense Certainty, which we have come to recognize as an attempt to validate the knowledge of Perception and Understanding, the knowledge of this world. This empiricism goes hand in glove with deism or materialism. Just because Enlightenment "conceives all determination in general, that is, every content and filling, to be a finite, human representation,"[53] it accuses Faith of anthropomorphism in its concept of God and in turn refuses to predicate anything of the absolute Being.

Enlightenment's this-worldliness, however, comes to its fullest expression in an ethics oriented to utility. The world is to be a Garden of Eden for man. "As he is immediately, as natural consciousness in itself, man is good. As individual he is absolute, and everything else exists for him . . . everything is for his pleasure and delight. As he comes from the hand of God, he walks in the world as in a garden planted for him. He is bound also to have plucked the fruit of the tree of the knowledge of good and evil. He has a use for this knowledge . . . his individuality has its limits and can overreach itself and destroy itself. Reason is a useful means against this possibility . . ."[54] The usefulness of reason is by no means restricted to the knowledge of good and evil. For Enlightenment this is the important thing about the whole range of empirical knowledge.

We are suddenly brought back to the apparently forgotten link between epistemology and the history of Spirit. Having developed the concept of Spirit as the necessary framework within which transcendental philosophy must be placed, Hegel does not pause in his analysis of the Greco-Roman period to comment on the modes of knowledge made possible by its forms of social experience. Here the situation is necessarily different, for the Introduction makes it clear that Hegel wants to understand critical finitism in terms of the world in which it thrives. That world is now before us as Culture, a world of political, economic, and religious alienation. Culture is the attempt to take possession [*sich bemächtigen*] of this world which has gotten out of hand. This is just the language used in the Introduction to describe that instrumental reason which is by definition unable to comprehend the Absolute.[55] In an epoch when the spiritual or social world has gotten so out of man's control that he finds his own products hostile to him, the knowledge which is power inevitably has a special attraction.[56] If man must be the slave of his own institutions and ideas, perhaps he can at least be master of nature. While spiritual estrangement may not account for the rise of the natural sciences as useful knowledge, it does throw light on the apotheosis of instrumental reason, which is Hegel's starting point in the Introduction.

The sense of impotence which defines the world of Culture not only makes instrumental reason attractive, but also tends to confirm the sense of finitude which knows it cannot know the Absolute. This is not the standpoint of Faith, but as it succumbs to the assaults of Enlightenment it turns into that "pure yearning" whose truth is an "empty beyond," that is, the new "religious" opponent of Enlightenment is Romanticism. But again identity is stronger than difference. "In this way Faith has in fact become the same as Enlightenment, namely the consciousness of the relation of an isolated [*an sich*] finitude to the unknown and unknowable Absolute without predicates." The prevailing conception acknowledges the essential "only in the form of an objective realm beyond and it acknowledges consciousness, distinguished from this realm and thus having

the in itself outside itself, as finite consciousness."[57] It is clear
that only through overcoming the estrangement of Culture will
knowledge of the Absolute be possible. A different philosophy
will be possible only in a different world.

Though Hegel interprets Romanticism as Faith capitulat-
ing to Enlightenment, it appears at first as if there is a significant difference between them. For the Enlightenment seems to
be satisfied finitude, Romanticism unsatisfied finitude. But
Hegel reminds us that utility is the truth of Enlightenment. As
long as only nature but not Spirit has been brought under control, as long as the social world resembles hell more nearly than
the Garden of Eden, Enlightenment cannot remain satisfied.
Through its critique of Faith Enlightenment has created a
thoroughly secular consciousness, one which has repudiated
the longing for transcendence characteristic of both Faith and
Romanticism. But it has a longing of its own. It wants to trans-
plant heaven on earth, but this has not yet happened. The result is that God is nowhere to be found, neither in heaven nor
on earth. Since nothing is holy there is no basis for affirmation.
Enlightenment turns from the battle with Faith to its real
enemy, the actual world which stubbornly refuses to be the
Kingdom of God. It does so as an entirely negative and destructive force. The revolutionary self is before us. "Out of this inner
revolution emerges the actual revolution of the actual world,
the new form of consciousness, Absolute Freedom." This freedom is absolute because for it there is "nothing on hand
separating self-consciousness from its inheritance other than
the empty semblance of objectivity."[58]

The new self whose possession the world is to be is not the
individual but the universal, collective subject "which knows its
self-certainty to be the essence of all spiritual spheres, both of
the real and of the supersensible world . . ." This Absolute
Freedom is the general will of Rousseau. As it takes charge of
the world "the whole system of spiritual domains or powers,
which organizes and maintains itself through the division into
separate spheres, collapses . . ." Through this collapse "each individual consciousness raises itself out of the sphere to which it
was assigned and no longer finds its essence and its role [Werk]
in this separate sphere. It rather grasps itself as the concept of
will and all spheres as the essential expression of this will. Con-

sequently it can realize itself only in that work which is a work of the whole. In this Absolute Freedom all social ranks or classes [*Stände*] . . . are abolished." This abolition is simultaneously the "cancelling of the distinct spiritual spheres and of the restricted life of the individual."[59]

Hegel here stresses the sociological aspects of the Revolution over the political. It is not so much that Absolute Freedom as the general will wants to replace the king with itself on the throne of national sovereignty, for it is not simply power but participation which is demanded. The social structure of society cuts off participation not only in the palace but in many other domains of human endeavor. Whereas the individual had been assigned his own special nook and cranny of human possibility, he now demands to be free to share in the whole gamut of man's life together. This means that the limitations imposed by every form of social hierarchy must be eliminated.

This abolition cannot at first be described as a restructuring of the social whole for two reasons. First, the call is not for a different social structure but for freedom from the limitations of social hierarchy as such. Second, there is for this mode of consciousness nothing objective to be reshaped, only the "empty semblance of objectivity." Presumably it could constitute itself as something objective and enduring. That would involve once again dividing the social substance into such spheres as government on the one hand, sub-divided in turn into legislative, judicial, and executive branches, and on the other hand the various spheres of labor, the different estates. Individuals would once again belong immediately not to the whole but to one of the parts. "They would find their activity and being, however, by this process confined to a branch of the whole, to one kind of action and existence. Placed in the element of being, they would have the significance of something determinate. They would cease to be universal self-consciousness." For the first reason given above Absolute Freedom cannot be persuaded to accept this. The idea that the assignment to various roles is the result of self-imposed legislation or at least of legislation in which it has had a share through representation is regarded by Absolute Freedom as an attempt to steal its birthright by fraud.[60]

This is the attitude which expresses itself in the Terror.

"Universal Freedom can thus produce neither a positive achievement nor a positive deed. There is left for it only negative action. It is merely the fury of disappearing."[61] But the Terror is self-contradictory. Its reality does not correspond to its concept, for while its action is supposed to stem from the general will, it finds that action presupposes individual will, and it turns out to be government by faction. The built-in instability of such a "system" is dramatically illustrated by the guillotine. ". . . thus the organization of spiritual spheres to which the plurality of conscious individuals is assigned, takes shape once more. These individuals, who have felt the fear of the absolute master, death, submit to negation and distinction once more, distribute themselves among the spheres, and return to a restricted and assigned role, but thereby to their substantial actuality."[62]

But restoration is not the truth of revolution. If this were the case one would have to say that Spirit has been thrown back to its starting point, the worlds of Ethical Life and Culture, and that this revolutionary interpenetration of substance and self-consciousness was a process ever in need of repetition in order that Spirit might be "refreshed" and "rejuvenated" by the fear of the Lord and better able to "endure" the objectivity of the world from which its individuality is excluded. But this is not the meaning of the Terror's inability to sustain itself. "All the determinations of the world of culture disappear in the disaster which the self experiences as Absolute Freedom."[63]

Strictly speaking, of course, this disappearance does not take place. There are social structures that survive the Revolution, and one might even find some left-over nobility around afterwards. The point is that Spirit's destiny is not found in whatever may have survived from the world of Culture but rather in a new experience, born in the revolution, in which the general will finds a new and less frenzied career. The demand of consciousness to be immediately identical with the universal will is given up. What is sacrificed "is the abstract being or immediacy of insubstantial individuality, and this vanished immediacy is the general will itself, which consciousness now knows itself to be, in so far as it is transcended immediacy, in so far as it is pure knowledge or pure will. By this means it knows that will to be itself, and it knows itself to be what is essential;

but not as an immediately existing being, nor as will in the form of revolutionary government, nor as anarchy struggling to establish an anarchical constitution."[64]

The one thing that is clear from this passage is that the individual's participation in the general will is not immediate. It is not his empirical preferences at any given moment which share the dignity of the general will, but only his "pure" knowledge and will. Here we are only told what this general will as vanished immediacy is not. The positive account of what it is belongs to the third and final section of Chapter Six, Self-Certain Spirit—Morality. "Just as the realm of the actual world passes over into that of Faith and Insight, Absolute Freedom leaves its self-destroying sphere of reality and passes over into another land of self-conscious Spirit, where in this unreality it is acknowledged to be the truth."[65] We need not panic at this reference to the truth in its unreality. Just as the unreal world of thought defined by Faith and Enlightened Insight mediated between two actual worlds, that of Culture and that of the Revolution, we can expect Morality to mediate between the actual world created (or better, destroyed) by Absolute Freedom and a new world of actuality in which, according to Hegel's promise, absolute Spirit will appear.

6C. The Conscientious Self as the Destiny of the Post-revolutionary World

The new land to which Absolute Freedom migrates is Germany. In its unreality it is, in the first instance, the autonomy of pure practical reason as developed by Kant and Fichte. This form of Morality can be seen as akin to Absolute Freedom in that it involves a dignity and recognition for the individual based on personhood as such, wholly independent of class and social status. By speaking of this practical reason as "knowing will" Hegel makes it clear that his reference is not just to a theory of right action but to an entire outlook on the world, the moral *Weltanschauung*.

Over against the knowing will of Morality there no longer stands a world of objectivity. This has been withdrawn into that knowing will. That is to say that Morality finds duty to be the essential and substantial thing, but that as autonomous, self-legislating practical reason it finds duty to belong to its own pure consciousness and to be nothing foreign or alien to it. The object of its knowledge is its own self-certainty as rational will, and we therefore "seem" to be dealing with a form of knowledge which is adequate to its truth, with a subjectivity which is its own object and its only object in total transparency.

As in the transition to Self-Consciousness the moment of Consciousness is at first missing to this moral freedom which takes itself to be absolute. Of course the world of nature is still there. But Morality has its own purpose and creates its own object. It finds the world entirely unessential and meaningless and takes the attitude of complete freedom and indifference toward nature. Its virtue is as independent of happiness as its duty is from inclination. There is something Stoic about Morality. It wins its freedom by withdrawing into the inwardness of its own intentions and treats the world of consequences as unessential.[66]

But Morality is not Stoicism, and it cannot so easily let the world go its own way. Happiness as well as virtue belongs to its full conception of the highest good. Further, if the self-estrangement of Culture is to be overcome, Morality cannot endure the essential separation of duty and inclination, pure and empirical self, intention and consequence. So reason demands that nature conform itself to Morality, and it postulates the harmony of happiness and virtue, of inclination and duty. It takes their identity to be ultimately certain, even if not yet actual. As a kind of guarantee for these first two postulates, Morality makes a third. It affirms the reality of a God independent of moral consciousness, whose function is not only to validate the specific laws, which cannot be derived from pure reason, but also to bring about the harmony of reason and nature.[67]

With this new "Lord and Master of the world" the previously missing moment of Consciousness or outward objectivity is re-established. But Morality falls in this way into contradiction with itself. On the one hand it claims to have overcome estrangement, while on the other it finds the essential to be fully beyond it both as the "not yet" of freedom and nature's unity and as the transcendence of the God from whom it receives this reward for its virtue as a form of grace. The self-confessed reality of Morality does not correspond to its concept. "The object of its actual consciousness is not yet transparent to it; it is not the absolute concept, *which alone grasps otherness as such, its absolute opposite as its very self.*" Both God and nature become essential but remain fully independent of Morality.[68]

Because of this inner contradiction Morality is given over to a vacillation which Hegel calls dissemblance. Rather uncharitably he interprets its confusion as a lack of seriousness. It is in reaction to the perceived inadequacies of this form of consciousness that a new one arises. "It is pure Conscience, which scorns such a moral world-view. It is in itself the simple, self-certain Spirit which, without the mediation of those ideas, acts in immediate conscientiousness, and has its truth in this immediacy."[69] To understand Conscience as the form in which absolute Spirit makes its appearance we have to understand both the meaning of this immediacy and the nature of the new mediation in which it necessarily disappears. The necessity of its disappearance has already been indicated in Hegel's account of the general will as vanished immediacy.[70] It belongs to the nature of Spirit to be intersubjective and actual. But when moral autonomy in its immediacy seeks to form an actual community of persons, it creates only the destruction of the Terror. If Morality is to get beyond its "unreality" to an actual human community, the immediacy with which Conscience first appears will have to be transcended.

This immediacy of Conscience is its fundamentally anarchistic nature. Its self-mediation can only be the process by which community arises out of anarchy. We have now to understand both dimensions of Conscience. In its so-called "Oldest System Program" German Idealism had begun in praise of anarchy. The idea of beauty and the hope for a re-union of mythology and philosophy are directed against the state. The author of this fragment, whether he be Schelling or Hegel, wants to show "that there is no Idea of the state, because the state is something mechanical, just as little as there is an Idea of a machine. Only the object of freedom is called Idea. We must therefore go beyond the state!—For every state must treat free men as mechanical cogs, and it should not do so; therefore it should cease."[71]

When Hegel wrote the *Phenomenology* he had moved a long way from the uncompromising atmosphere in which this was written. This is surely one of the reasons why it is so hard to see and to take seriously the fact that it is in a setting which can only be described as anarchy that absolute Spirit comes on the scene in the *Phenomenology*. No doubt it sounds strange to characterize in this way so crucial a passage in so important a work of the author of *The German Constitution* and *The Philosophy of Right*. But the structure of Chapter Six gives a three-fold justification for such an interpretation.

First, while the state plays an important role in the discussions of Ethical Life and Culture it has fully disappeared in the analysis of Conscience. Yet it is as Conscience that Morality, the third and last moment of Hegel's phenomenological philosophy of history, achieves its truth.[72] In this connection it should be noted that Hegel sees the world of Ethical Life and its truth, Legal Status, as a fulfillment of Stoicism and Scepticism, just as he finds the world of Culture to realize Unhappy Consciousness.[73] But no slave-ideology stands in such a relation to Conscience. One can say that in the *Phenomenology* slavery and the state are only overcome together. This is not to deny that, as Hegel writes in *Differenz*, "the highest community is the highest freedom."[74] It is just that in the *Phenomenology* Hegel does not find the state to be the only or highest community, nor, consequently, the only or the highest freedom.

Second, it is not only a matter of the state. The community in which absolute Spirit appears is also sociologically anarchic. This is because it is the positive result of the French Revolution. The concluding paragraphs of the preceding section[75] have shown how revolutionary freedom takes the objectivity of the world to be "nothing more than empty pretense [*Schein*]," and how this means that for it the role of social roles is past. Hegel knows that they have not simply disappeared, but he claims that for the new experience he is seeking to describe as Conscience they play no essential role. They cannot be the basis of post-revolutionary community.

Third, Conscience is ethically anarchic as well as politically and sociologically. It acknowledges no obligation to any rule or law whatever, inner or outer. The freedom of Conscience is not that of Luther, which is free from all human authority in order to be subject to the authority of God, nor that of Kant, which is free from all external authority, human and divine, but subject to the inner authority of pure practical reason. For Conscience this is not freedom but bondage.[76] For this reason "Conscience is free from every possible content. It absolves itself from every specific duty which is supposed to be binding as law. In the strength of its self-certainty it has the majesty of absolute autarchy, to bind or to loose."[77] When this autarchy acts "the agent's own immediate individuality constitutes the content of moral action, and the form of moral action is just this very self as pure process, namely as knowing in the sense of personal conviction. It is because "this pure conviction is as such just as empty as pure duty" that the content must come from the immediate individuality of the agent. This natural individuality giving content to the emptiness of conviction is the instincts and inclinations of man's sensible nature and his arbitrary choices. One is reminded of the Old Testament, where we read, "In those days there was no king in Israel; every man did what was right in his own eyes."[78]

It looks as if Conscience has left the realm of Spirit altogether. For Spirit means mediation and Spirit means community.[79] But we have been told that the truth of Conscience is its immediacy, and we have seen that this immediacy is a threefold anarchy which seems to exclude any possibility of community. If absolute Spirit is to emerge a mediation is called for which would simultaneously preserve the truth of Conscience's immediacy and make possible a community of the conscientious. This new mediation was anticipated in the discussion of Absolute Freedom as the means by which its pure negativity could be transformed into something positive.[80] Its concrete form and its emergence out of the anarchic immediacy of Conscience must now be shown.

It is important to remember what the new community cannot be, according to the preceding analysis. In his famous essay, "Hegel and the French Revolution," Joachim Ritter suggests that two ideas from the Revolution are built into Hegel's idea of freedom, "the grounding of political freedom as right in the substantial freedom of being oneself [*Selbstsein*] and the consequent determination of the content of political regulations for the purpose of making possible the realization of human existence in its freedom . . . The problem which the Revolution's demand for political freedom has raised is to find the legal form [*Rechtsform*] of freedom, that is, to construct a legal order which is suited to the freedom of being oneself." For Ritter's Hegel "subjectivity is only able to be actualized when the political and social institutions are the actuality of its action in accord with its being itself . . . the freedom of being oneself, of intention, of conscience, and thus the ethical life of free men is only able to have enduring reality when political and social institutions are in accord with these freedoms."[81] Ritter is speaking primarily about the *Philosophy of Right,* and it is tempting to see that treatise as a kind of completion of the *Phenomenology's* sixth chapter, working out in detail what is only stated in principle in the earlier work. This is simply not possible. In the *Phenomenology* the condition of Legal Status is presented as an independence lacking true freedom, and instead of the construction of new institutions in harmony with freedom it is concerned with man's elevation above those limited identities which institutions and their accompanying roles provide. The truth of Conscience's anarchic immediacy cannot be simply abandoned. We are explicitly told that the new world is not that of "anarchy struggling to establish an anarchical constitution."[82]

The mediating process by which community arises out of anarchic individualism is not that of political reform. It is most adequately described, on Hegel's view, in religious categories, confession and forgiveness. It is in these terms that the reciprocal recognition in which Spirit is fully realized must be understood. Although the pure duty in terms of which Morality defined itself left it an empty formalism, Conscience does not simply dispense with the impetus to universality which underlies the concept of pure duty. This remains rather as essential to Conscience, which thereby realizes its need to relate to the other, to win recognition from him, and thus to be self-consciousness in community, the only freedom that is actual. Conscientious action is not merely the externalization of an inner content but also the seeking of recognition for the self revealed in that action. Only in terms of recognition can Conscience be Spirit.[83]

Language becomes essential at this point. Though it is

through action that the agent enters the public domain in which recognition is possible, it is the agent and not his act which is to be recognized. Since there is no immediate identity between the act and the agent, acts which conceal being as possible as acts which reveal, the agent must affirm his conviction, must tell the world that he is acting out of conscience. It is only through the two-fold self-expression of action and speech that the self becomes sufficiently public to be recognized.[84]

But this recognition is by no means automatic. The act which the self presents as conscientious may be taken as evil, his profession of conscientiousness as deception and hypocrisy. Having rendered itself public in action and speech, the self may find his efforts rewarded by judgment and rejection rather than recognition. There is nothing to keep the other self from withholding recognition in the name of his own conscientious conviction. There seems to be no way from anarchy to community. Nor could this war of all against all be terminated by a social contract, for this would only be the reversion to Legal Status.

Conscience, however, is already two steps beyond this impasse. In *saying* that it acts out of conviction it transcends its particularity and recognizes the necessary universality of the self, its own need for recognition. At the same time, by saying that it acts in accordance with its own private conviction and not according to what is already universally recognized it confesses that it is evil.[85] Forgiveness is now the form which recognition must take. It is no more automatic than before, but when the other recognizes itself in the first self, the hard heart is melted and forgiving recognition occurs. The self-recognition which makes possible recognition of the other is two-fold. The judging self realizes that its judgment rests on private conviction as much as the act it judges, and it realizes that it too must act and that its act, though different in content, will be identical in form to the act judged as evil, that it too will be grounded in the privacy of conscience. The community which comes into being through forgiveness is thus a community of mutual tolerance. "The word of reconciliation is the existing Spirit which intuits the pure knowledge of itself as something universal in its opposite, in the pure knowledge of itself as absolutely self-existing individuality,—a reciprocal recognition which is absolute Spirit . . . The reconciling Yes with which both selves desist from their existence in opposition is the existence of the I expanded into a We [*Zweiheit*], which remains itself in that We, and which has the certainty of itself in its complete relinquishment and its opposite;—it is the appearing God in the midst of those who know themselves to be pure knowledge."[86]

With this sudden appearance of absolute Spirit we are at the end of the long journey through which we were to learn what Spirit has become and what knowledge truly is. What remains is to unpack and clarify this result in order that its definitive character may become evident. It must be made clear that the knowledge of which so much is said, not only in the passage just cited but throughout the entire conclusion of Chapter Six and which is an essential element of the community of tolerance, is Absolute Knowledge, the resolution to the whole problem of knowledge as a philosophical task. This is the job of Chapter Eight.

But before proceeding to this task Hegel feels it necessary to clarify the religious dimension into which Spirit is suddenly cast. It is not just that reciprocal recognition is understood as confession and forgiveness; at issue is the inherent divinity of Conscience which makes possible the identification of the community of tolerance with God. This identification occurs not only in the passage just cited, but earlier as well, where Hegel writes, "Conscience, then, in its majestic sublimity above any specific law and every content of duty puts whatever content it pleases into its knowledge and willing. It is moral genius, which knows the inner voice of its immediate knowledge to be a voice divine; and since in this knowledge it knows existence just as immediately, it is the divine creative power . . . It is just as much itself the worship of God, for its action is the intuition of its own divinity." Since, as we have seen, moral genius moves toward community and reciprocal recognition, Hegel is able to continue, "This solitary worship is at the same time essentially the worship of a congregation." It is now the congregation or community of tolerance which intuits its own divinity. This makes it possible to define religion, so far as knowledge is concerned, as "the utterance of the congregation regarding its own Spirit."[87]

The movement of Chapter Six is from community [*Gemeinwesen*][88] to congregation [*Gemeinde*], from the city of man to the city which is the self-intuition of God. It hardly needs to be argued that the divine self-knowledge is Absolute Knowledge, which is why there is little new in Chapter Eight. What needs clarification is the movement by which the human community becomes not simply a worshipping community but a congregation whose worship is God's knowledge of himself. This is the task of Chapter Seven. It supports the interpretations of Chapter Six by repeating them in the opposite direction. It moves from congregation to community, seeking to show that the tendency of the human community to be a congregation is matched by the tendency of religion to find its final horizon in the human community, in an earthly Kingdom of God. While Chapter Six portrays the deifying of society, Chapter Seven supports this with its interpretation of the humanizing of God.

NOTES

1. See Ch. 5, n. 60.
2. PhG, 378/314/459, my italics.
3. PhG, 380/315/460.
4. PhG, 630/476/689.
5. PhG, 581-84/445-46/644-45. cf. 380-81/315-16/460-61.
6. PhG, 384/318/466.
7. Earlier in *The German Constitution* Hegel had given a different sketch of world history in three stages: oriental, Roman, and Germanic. This earlier scheme is the one to which he returns in the Berlin lectures on the philosophy of history. See *Werke*, I, 533/203. cf. I, 428 ff. for still earlier reflection on the spirit of the oriental world.
8. PhG, 382/316/461.
9. PhG, 379-80/315/460.
10. PhG, 383/318/463.
11. See Ch. 5, n. 67 and n. 68.
12. See section 3B. above.
13. On the "symbolism of the center" see Mircea Eliade, *Images and Symbols,* trans. Mairet, New York, 1969.
14. PhG, 404-06/331-32/484-86. cf. 372-75/310-12/451-53. In the latter passage, "Reason as Testing Laws," it is this contrast between Ethical Life and Morality which is posed as the crucial question for a Kantian type moral theory. The question of an empty formalism is secondary. The religious aspect of this same immediacy is expressed in Wilamowitz's oft cited summary of Greek polytheism, *"Die Götter sind da."*
15. On Hegel's early enthusiasm for Greek tragedy, and especially *Antigone,* see Rosenkranz, *Georg Wilhelm Friedrich Hegels Leben,* Darmstadt, 1963, pp. 11 and 25.
16. PhG, 382-84/317-18/462-66 and 418-21/340-42/496-99. On the relation of parts and whole see 400/329/480.
17. PhG, 386-99/320-28/468-79, and 416/339/494. The elevation of the brother-sister relation over that of husband and wife is partly to be understood from the fact that while Hegel was writing the *Phenomenology* he was awaiting the birth of an illegitimate son. In the *Philosophy of Right,* written after he was happily married, the husband-wife relationship assumes priority again.
18. Compare PhG, 412-13/336/491 with the passage quoted in note 10 above. In the former it is the individual who *"ist zu Grunde gegangen"* while in the latter this is the fate of Ethical Life itself.

19. PhG, 393/324/474.

20. See Ch. 5, n. 67 and n. 68.

21. PhG, 419-21/341-42/497-98.

22. For Hegel's early views of the relation between Ethical Life and Roman law, see *Naturrecht*, GW, 4:456-57 and Werke, I, 439-40.

23. PhG, 421-22/342-43/499-501. In a fragment on love from 1797-98 Hegel notes that equality of rights can mean equality of dependence, and in SC he writes, "The Greeks were to be equal because all were free, self-subsistent; the Jews were equal because all were incapable of self-subsistence." HTJ, 378/302 and 255/198. Though Hegel's enthusiasm for Napoleon and the Napoleonic Code at the time of the *Phenomenology* are well documented, this can hardly be, as is sometimes suggested, what he means by the birth of a new era. The description of Legal Status makes it clear that the revolution he believes to be taking place is not essentially one of legal reform.

24. PhG, 422-24/343-44/502-03.

25. PhG, 426-27/345-46/504-05.

26. From his studies in modern political economy, beginning with a commentary in 1799 on Sir James Steuart's *Inquiry into the Principles of Political Economy* and continuing in his study of Adam Smith while at Jena, Hegel developed an appreciation of abstract right or legal status and its place in the modern world. But this principle was clearly in conflict with his "Greek ideal." On the basis of this part of the *Phenomenology* it would be fair to say that any tendencies toward a romantic longing for a return to Ethical Life, observable in both *Sittlichkeit* and *Naturrecht*, were checked by Hegel's understanding of the economic structure of the modern world. This is already clear in *Realphilosophie*. But it is equally clear that the *Phenomenology* does not find either bourgeois civil society or the bourgeois state to be the basis for a truly human existence. Nor (to repeat note 23 above) would a new emperor in the form of Napoleon be of any help.

27. PhG, 582/445/645. This is in sharp contrast to the idealizing of everything Greek in *Naturrecht* and *Sittlichkeit*. Hegel's mature view of Greek culture is Nietzschean. Beneath the Apollinian peacefulness he sees the Dionysian conflict and tragedy. He sees that "despite its calm there is a conflict in pagan society, tragic conflict which results in the destruction of the individual and of society itself." Alexandre Kojeve, *Introduction a la Lecture de Hegel*, Paris, 1947, p. 102.

28. PhG, 288/255-56/375. cf. *Differenz*, GW, 4:54. The contrast between independence and freedom is also basic to Hegel's critique in *The German Constitution*.

29. PhG, 428/346/506. cf. 423-25/343-44/502-03.

30. GW, 4:12.

31. PhG, 429-30/347-48/509-10. *Entäusserung* is a crucial term in the *Phenomenology*. It has connotations of externalizing what is inner and Baillie quite properly translates it as kenosis when Hegel applies it to the incarnation, alluding to Philippians 2:6-7, which says that Christ, though in the form of God "did not count equality with God a thing to be grasped, but emptied himself, taking the form of a servant, being born in the likeness of men." (RSV)

32. PhG, 435-38/351-53/514-17. cf. XXXII-XXXVI/26-28/88-91. Both these passages are illuminated by Peter Berger's account of society in terms of externalization, objectification, and internalization. See *The Sacred Canopy*, Garden City, 1967, Chapter One.

33. PhG, 430-33/348-49/510-12. cf. *Differenz*, GW, 4:14, 79-80.

34. PhG, 439-40/353-54/517-19.

35. PhG, 443/355-56/521.

36. PhG, 449-50/360/527.

37. PhG, 450-59/360-66/527-35.

38. *Idem.*

39. PhG, 461-62/367-68/537-38.

40. *Idem. Verworfenheit* means both depravity and reprobation. The related verb, *verwerfen* is used to speak of quashing a verdict.

41. See note 26 above.

42. PhG, 463-64/369/539.

43. PhG, 465-66/370/540-41.

44. PhG, 434/350/513. For a longer version see 474-81/376-80/549-54.

45. PhG, 372/310-11/451-52.

46. PhG, 478-79/378-79/552. This passage brings together the concept of positivity with the two concepts crucial for the analysis of religion in Chapter Seven, *Vorstellung* and *Gegenständlichkeit*.

47. Compare PhG 482/381/556 with 447-58/359-65/525-34. Here as in PCR I, Christianity is seen less as the cause than the effect or evidence of underlying social alienation.

48. PhG, 480/480/554. Hegel here employs the Trinity as a model of reciprocal recognition.

49. PhG, 515/402/583. cf. 520/405/587.

50. PhG, 532/413/598.

51. John 3:17 (RSV).

52. PhG, 507/397/576 and 511/400/580.

53. See reference in previous note.

54. PhG, 510/399/579.

55. See note 32 above. For the relation of this passage to the Introduction see section 1A. above.

56. The place of honor given to Francis Bacon in d'Alembert's Preliminary Discourse to the French *Encyclopedia* is most instructive here. To begin with, the *Encyclopedia* borrows its system of organization from Bacon. Then comes a brief Enlightenment hagiography, describing "the principle geniuses that the human mind must regard as its masters and for whom the Greeks would have erected statues." Before a longer list, the four greatest heros, including Descartes, Newton, and Locke is given. "At the head of these illustrious personages must be placed the immortal Chancellor of England, Francis Bacon." Denis Diderot, *The Encyclopedia: Selections,* ed. and trans. by Stephen J. Gendzier, New York, 1967, pp. 10, 26, and 19.

57. PhG, 521-24/406-08/588-91. In *Differenz* Hegel develops the intimate relation between *Bildung* and *Verstand,* the finite understanding. GW, 4:12-13, 15.

58. PhG, 533/414/599. On objectivity [*Gegenständlichkeit*] see note 46 above.

59. PhG, 535-37/415-16/600-02.

60. PhG, 538-39/417/603-04.

61. PhG, 539/418/604. cf. the section in Chapter Five on the Law of the Heart.

62. PhG, 539-43/418-20/604-07.

63. PhG, 543-45/420-21/607-08.

64. PhG, 545-46/422/609.

65. PhG, 546-47/422/610. On this migration of Spirit to a new land, see 433/350/512.

66. PhG, 548-51/423-25/613-16.

67. PhG, 551-59/429-30/616-20.

68. PhG, 559-64/430-33/622-26, my italics. On the question of grace see 573/440/635 and Kant's *Critique of Practical Reason,* pp. 122 ff. (Academy edition pages), especially the note on p. 127. The italicized phrase from Hegel indicates why grace is not the solution which Hegel finds acceptable, why Boehme rather than Luther is his first German hero.

69. PhG, 580/444/641.

70. See next to last paragraph of previous section, 6B.

71. Hegel, *Werke,* I, 234-35.

72. PhG, 583/446/646. For a similar interpretation of the theme of anarchy in Chapter Six, see my essay, "Verzeihung und Anarchie," *Hegel-Jahrbuch,* 1972, pp. 105-109.

73. PhG, 423-28/343-46/502-06.

74. *Differenz,* GW, 4:54.

75. Beginning with the one which includes note 58.

76. Cf. *Differenz,* GW, 4:59.

77. PhG, 598/456/658. cf. Matthew 16:19.

78. PhG, 587/449/648-49, 592-94/452-53/653-54, 597-98/456/657. Judges 21:25 (RSV).

79. Both of these are involved in the definition of Spirit as the I that is We and the We that is I.

80. See note 64 above.

81. *Metaphysik und Politik,* Frankfurt, 1969, pp. 198-99. The second quotation is from another essay in the same volume, "Moralität und Sittlichkeit. Zu Hegels Auseinandersetzung mit der kantischen Ethik," pp. 307-08.

82. See note 64 above.

83. PhG, 589-90/450/650.

84. PhG, 601-05/458-61/660-64.

85. PhG, 612-13/465/670.

86. PhG, 621-24/471-72/677-79. Hegel calls this forgiveness the self's *Verzichtleistung auf sich.* Thus *Entäusserung* is rendered as relinquishment toward the end of the quotation rather than as alienation.

87. PhG, 605-06/460-61/663-65. The deification of the social whole is particularly strong in *Sittlichkeit.*

88. See Kant, *Religion Within the Limits of Reason Alone,* trans. Greene and Hudson, New York, 1960, pp. 85-93, where he describes the Kingdom of God on earth, in contrast to the ethical state of nature as an ethical commonwealth [*ein ethisches gemeines Wesen*].

7A. Spirit as the Object of Religious Knowledge

The abiding goal of the *Phenomenology* is "insight into what knowing is," the discovery of that point where "knowledge is no longer compelled to go beyond itself." With the help of Kant's transcendental method of reflecting on the nature of knowledge, Spirit has been discovered as the concrete source of transcendental subjectivity, and the historical analysis of Spirit's career has illuminated the bond between the transcendental subjectivity which makes instrumental reason possible and the life of Spirit in the modern world. All this provides considerable "insight into what knowing is" but it hardly indicates the point where "knowledge is no longer compelled to go beyond itself." For instrumental reason has both the world of nature which it knows and the Absolute which it does not know beyond itself. Subject and object are distinctly other to each other. Nature is not wholly other to instrumental reason, of course, though it has become the object and not the home of consciousness, and beneath its luminous surface it remains a dark and mysterious unknown about which the prudent Newton dares not hypothesize. At the same time instrumental reason has no surer conviction than that it cannot know the Absolute, being suited only to finite objects. This is just as true of transcendental philosophy, for while it knows instrumental reason in all its finitude, it does not know the Absolute either.

While learning all this we have also learned something else. Spirit is not only the transcendental subject which grounds our knowledge of nature. Spirit knows itself. Here subject and object are not other to each other, for the knower is the known. In this sense knowledge is not compelled to go beyond itself. If Spirit is able to find the Absolute within this knowledge of itself rather than outside it, its cognitive task would not have to remain essentially unfinished. It would learn that nature is not the Absolute and that its knowledge of nature consequently cannot be Absolute Knowledge. Spirit is what is absolute, and only Spirit's knowledge of itself can be Absolute Knowledge.

Now Hegel has characterized Spirit as absolute in so far as it is the community of tolerance characterized by reciprocal recognition. This community is not just a brute fact. It is aware of itself. But the community which is thus aware of itself is absolute Spirit and thus divine. Its collective self-knowledge, being God's knowledge of himself, can only be Absolute Knowledge. Hegel finds Spirit's knowledge of itself to be at once the clue to Absolute Knowledge and the essence of Religion. This is the result of Chapter Six. Its detailed development is the task of Chapter Seven.

If Religion is Spirit's knowledge of itself as Spirit, it follows that Spirit is the object of religious knowledge. This is suggested by the description of religion as "the utterance of the congregation regarding its own Spirit."[1] It is even clearer in the definition of religious truth given in Chapter Seven. "The truth of the belief in a given determination of the religious Spirit shows itself in this, that the actual Spirit [der wirkliche Geist] is constituted after the same manner as the form in which this actual Spirit beholds itself in Religion. Thus, for example, the incarnation of God, which is found in Eastern religion, has no truth, because the actual Spirit of this religion [ihr wirklicher Geist] is without the reconciliation this principle implies."[2]

In the light of Chapter Six it is not difficult to recognize what Hegel intends by the notion of actual Spirit. It is the social reality which he calls the life of a people. Since this social reality must correspond to religious ideas if they are to be true, it must be the real object to which they refer. Incarnation entails reconciliation, but since, on Hegel's view, oriental society is not even developed enough to sense a need for reconciliation, the idea of incarnation is false in that context. It is an idea which, if true at all, is true only where the substantial life of a given society has achieved subjectivity through coming to self-consciousness without losing its substantiality in the process, since this is what Hegel means by reconciliation.

This notion that in Religion Spirit moves beyond its mere being or actuality to the knowledge of itself permeates Hegel's interpretation of Religion. For example, Hegel interprets the use of animal symbols for the divine as appropriate to the experience of Spirit's dispersal into warring tribes which "fight each other in their hatred to the death."[3] Or again, "If we ask

next what the actual Spirit is which finds in the religion of art
the consciousness of its absolute essence, it turns out that this is
the ethical or true Spirit."[4] This last phrase takes us directly
back to the first part of Chapter Six and its description of Greek
social life. It is this which Greek religion, the religion of art,
brings to consciousness.

Since Hegel interprets the Christian religion, upon which
his attention ultimately focuses, more in its relation to Greek religion than to Judaism, it is worthwhile to look more closely at
the correlation between the actual Spirit of Greek experience
and its religious expression. The implication of Greek society
being the object of Greek religion is developed most fully in the
discussion of its highest stage, the literary. The development
from epic through tragedy to comedy is one of increasing
humanism, or, as Loewenberg puts it, of increasing "theoclasm"
and "anthropolatry."[5] The gods of the epic pantheon are already fully humanized (in contrast to the Titans), as is fitting,
inasmuch as they actually represent the variety of the Greek
peoples brought to political unity for the first time in the Tro-
jan war. To the united people [*Gesamtvolk*] corresponds a unified heaven [*Gesamthimmel*].[6]

The religion of the epic is awkward, however, since all
events are attributed to both gods and men. In the language of
E. R. Dodds, they are "overdetermined." This redundancy of
the divine world is largely corrected in the religion of tragedy,
where the gods play a much less prominent role. Tragedy involves the "depopulation of heaven."[7]

The full significance of this is grasped only by comedy.
There the gods are consciously recognized to be mere clouds
(Aristophanes), and it becomes clear to all that the true reality
behind the masks which signify the gods is man himself (the ac-
tor). The truth of anthropomorphic paganism is the discovery
of man's own divinity. On Hegel's interpretation, "the Homeric
poems, the tragedies of Aeschylus and Sophocles, and the comedy of Aristophanes constitute together a dialectical movement
whose general sense is the following: the return of the divine
into the human."[8]

Because this result is misconceived in an individualistic
manner Greek comedy is not absolute religion. This involves
the isomorphism of religious and actual Spirit in Greece. The

final proposition of Greek religion—"The self is absolute Being"—is a statement which belongs, "as is evident on the face of it, to the non-religious, the concrete, actual Spirit." Since "the religion of art belongs to the Spirit animating the ethical sphere," we find that the final statement of Greek religion is the same as the final statement of Greek social experience, expressed in legal personality, which also took the individual to be absolute. Both, when they realize what they are, are unhappy forms of consciousness, subjectivity without substance.[9]

Gerardus van der Leeuw has written, "If God speaks humanly, then either a miracle has occurred, or sacrilege has been committed."[10] In Greek comedy and Roman emperor worship, which is not so different from the former as it may appear to be, antiquity was unable to prevent the miracle from degenerating into sacrilege. Precisely this is the developmental task of Christianity. Its mission is to correct the individualistic error of comedy while preserving its humanistic truth. Against the background of *The Spirit of Christianity and its Fate* this assignment is not quite as unexpected as it might otherwise seem. There the view of Christianity which continues in the *Phenomenology* is derived, not from the necessity for historical development beyond classical antiquity, but from a direct (if highly problematical) interpretation of Jesus' teaching in the light of its own immediate historical context. Jesus is portrayed as opposing to the Jewish conception of subjection to an infinite Lord and Master the idea of God's relation to man as that of father to son. "Father and son are simply modifications of the same life, not opposite essences. . . Even in the expression 'a son of the stem of Koresh,' for example, which the Arabs use to denote the individual, a single member of the clan, there is the implication that the individual is not simply a part of the whole. The whole does not lie outside him. He himself is just the whole which the entire clan is. . . A tree which has three branches makes up with them one tree; but every 'son' of the tree, every branch . . . is itself a tree."[11] Whereas the Jews could see only an "impassable gulf between the being of God and the being of men," Jesus saw something entirely different in true faith. "Faith in the divine is only possible if in the believer himself there is a divine element which rediscovers itself, its own nature, in that on which it believes, even if it be unconscious that what it has found is its own nature . . . Hence faith in the divine grows out of the divinity of the believer's own nature. Only a modification of the Godhead can know the Godhead." Thus when Jesus responds to Peter's confession of faith in Matthew 16 by saying "My Father in heaven has revealed this to you," he is actually saying. "The divine in you has recognized my divinity. You have understood my essence. It has re-echoed in your own."[12]

The heart of this interpretation of Jesus' teaching is taking his statements about his relation to God as his father to be general statements about the relation of man to God. Hegel is explicit about this. "Thus specifically does Jesus declare himself against personality, against the view that his essence possessed an individuality opposed to that of those who had attained the culmination of friendship with him (against the thought of a personal God)."[13] To make it clear just why this concept of friendship is in conflict with that of a personal God, Hegel indicates that this friendship *is* God. In opposition to the overtones of "union through domination" carried by the idea of the Kingdom of God, Jesus preaches love. *"This friendship* of soul, described in the language of reflection as a being, as Spirit, is the divine Spirit, *is God* who rules the congregation. Is there an idea more beautiful than that of a nation of men related to one another by love?"[14]

The consequence of this is that "the objective aspect of God, his form, is objective only in so far as it is the presentation [*Darstellung*] of the love which unites the congregation." It was the fate of the Christian church that it did recognize its own love in the form of its risen Lord, but did not realize that what it adored was its own love. It therefore continued to find the divine to be something given, something positive, something alien.[15]

It is this same notion of the loving community (reciprocal recognition) as divine which culminates Chapter Six and leads to the chapter on Religion. When Christianity is so conceived, the task of preserving the humanism of Greek comedy while correcting its individualistic misconstrual is not an arbitrary assignment. Both appearances of Christianity in the *Phenomenology* prior to Chapter Seven prepare the reader for this interpretation of Christianity. As Hegel presents it Unhappy Consciousness is primarily if not exclusively a Christian experience. But the truth of the Christian religion is not to be found in the far off God for whom Unhappy Consciousness pines in mystical devotion. Hegel's trinitarian speculation suggests that the overcoming of the contradictions which torment Unhappy Consciousness is to be found in the church, in so far as it comes to a proper kind of self-consciousness, not in a transcendent personal deity.

Similarly in Chapter Six Hegel writes, "This action of Faith does not indeed make it appear as if absolute Being is thereby produced. But the absolute being for Faith is essentially not the abstract Being that is supposed to lie beyond the believing consciousness. It is the Spirit of the religious congregation . . The action of the congregation is an essential moment in bringing about that there should be this Spirit of the congregation. That Spirit is what it is by the productive activity of consciousness."[16] Since the truth of Faith is to be found in the religious community and not in some super-human, extra-mundane realm, Enlightenment provides an essential corrective to Faith in rejecting the beyond and focusing all interest on the here and now. "Both worlds are reconciled and heaven is transplanted to the earth below."[17]

It is against this background that Hegel develops the central categories for his philosophical interpretation of Christianity in Chapter Seven: incarnation and community. Whereas for Greek experience God's speaking humanly meant the sacrilege of comedy, for Christian experience it means the miracle of incarnation. For Hegel this miracle reveals that "the divine nature is the same as the human, and it is this oneness which is intuited" in the incarnation, the "simple content of absolute Religion."[18] But there is always the possibility (to say nothing of the historical actuality) that incarnation will be interpreted as uniquely true of Jesus rather than a universal truth about the relation of the human to the divine. This means, in Hegel's terms, that the religion of incarnation lives in perpetual danger of being a religion of consciousness, sorrow, and alienation rather than of self-consciousness, joy, and reconciliation. In other words, Hegel's hostility towards orthodox Christianity has not lessened since the days just following his seminary education. The difference is that now he sees other possibilities in the Christian tradition.

These other possibilities lie in the fact that Christianity is not only a religion of Father and Son, but also of Spirit. It teaches not only incarnation but also community. In the context of this community the immediacy and sensuous individuality in which the truth at first appears as an historical fact is replaced by the mediation and universality in which "God's individual self-consciousness [the incarnation as expressed in Jesus] is transformed into something universal, into the congregation."[19]

With this centrality of the community the individualism of Greek religious humanism is overcome. "Spirit remains the immediate self of actuality, but in the form of the universal self-consciousness of the congregation, a self-consciousness that rests in its own proper substance, just as in this self-consciousness this substance is universal subject. It is not the individual by himself, but the individual along with the consciousness of the congregation, and what he is for this congregation is the complete whole of its consciousness."[20] The content of this religion is thus "the certainty the congregation has of its own Spirit."[21]

In overcoming the individualism in which the classical world dead-ended, there is no reversion from its humanism to the theism of Unhappy Consciousness and Faith. Instead the Christian church is seen to be the universal version of the community of tolerance which appeared with such striking religious overtones as the upshot of Conscience. The Kingdom of God is indeed "a nation of men related to one another by love."[22]

Hegel knows that the religious and social communities do not automatically coalesce, that Spirit's actuality and its self-consciousness are not always perfectly congruent. "There is no doubt one Spirit in both, but its consciousness does not compass both together, and religion appears as a part of existence, of activity, of striving, whose other part is life in Spirit's actual world. As we now know that Spirit in its own world and Spirit conscious of itself as Spirit, i.e., Spirit in the sphere of Religion, are the same, the perfection of Religion consists in the two forms becoming identical with one another."[23] Just as religious falsehood is the incongruity of religious ideas and social reality, so religious truth is the actual identity of religious and secular Spirit. Hegel's interpretation of his historical present, therefore, is that it is through the enlightened Christian church that the community of tolerance is beginning to become the universal community of man. The fundamental identity of the Christian church with the community of tolerance is seen in the fact that the collective self-consciousness of both is presented as the divine self-intuition. The need for religious and secular Spirit to become one explains why the new-born world in which Science is finally possible is to be found not at Bethlehem but in the aftermath of the French Revolution.

7B. Spirit as the Subject of Religious Knowledge

Religion is the knowledge which Spirit has of itself as Spirit. The subject as well as the object is Spirit. Just as religion as such is "the self-consciousness of the absolute Being," so in Christianity as absolute Religion, "the divine Being [das Wesen] is known as Spirit. This religion is the divine Being's consciousness concerning itself that it is Spirit."[24] But Spirit is a We, a universal or collective and not merely individual self-consciousness. That is why Religion has come before us as "the utterance of the congregation regarding its own Spirit," "the universal self-consciousness of the congregation," and "the certainty the congregation has of its own Spirit."[25] On the subject side religion is a mode of knowing quite removed from the individual in his Whiteheadean solitude, from Kierkegaard's Abraham alone before God.

But the social or collective subject of religious knowledge is not immediately aware of its identity with its object. "The object is revealed to the congregation from an alien source, and in this thought of Spirit it does not recognize its own self, does not recognize the nature of pure self-consciousness."[26] So far as this is the case the congregation "is not yet perfected in this its self-consciousness . . . It is not consciously aware what it is."[27] Why this is so and how it leads us beyond Religion are matters for the final part of this chapter. At present it is sufficient to note the fundamentally deceptive character of religious knowledge as a self-knowledge which does not know itself to be that.

Here it is useful to call upon the aid of a psychological model for understanding Hegel's view of Religion, the concept of projection. In its strict Freudian sense projection is a means of avoiding aspects of one's own self which are unacceptable, usually to the super-ego, by transplanting them onto some other person, object, or abstract concept such as fate. The individual sees his own hatred, jealousy, or lust, for example, in another person, but does not recognize it as his own.

With two modifications this concept nicely illustrates Hegel's view of Religion. The first is a loosening of the concept from its individualistic limitations. Just as Jung speaks of a collective unconscious, we can speak of a collective projection. The other modification expands the range of features which may be projected so as to include those acceptable to the subject. This expansion has already taken place in psychological theory in so far as such devices as the Rorschach Test and the Thematic Apperception Test are referred to as projective techniques. "Thus common practice has extended the Freudian concept so that it now includes . . . constituents that are acceptable or even admirable to the subject."[28] Both of these changes have been made in Erich Fromm's humanistic interpretation of religion as collective projection, making it an instructive commentary on Hegel.[29]

One is not to infer from the projective nature of Religion that it is an illusion. It is true that God's *esse* is *concipi*. "God is attainable only in pure speculative knowledge, and he is only in that knowledge, and he is simply that knowledge itself, for he is Spirit."[30] This means not only that the representation in which Spirit uncomprehendingly becomes conscious of itself is produced by the subject of religious knowledge, the congregation, but also that the object itself is constituted by that knowing. Actual Spirit in separation from religious Spirit is but an abstract and incomplete reality. Spirit is only truly Spirit as it knows itself in its gods.[31]

In other words Hegel wishes to speak of God as the product of human activity and thought without implying that God is but a figment of the imagination. In fact it is just in the context of emphasizing this character of God as produced by man that he sharply chides Enlightenment for taking Faith's God to be mere illusion.[32] There is, of course, an important element of falsehood in Religion as such on this interpretation, but as in every other sort of projection, there is also important truth, however distorted and disguised. Hegel finds religion to be neither a hoax perpetrated by priests and despots nor a wildly imaginative and primitive pseudo-science of nature. It is rather an essential element of the social experience which is its foundation; so essential, in fact, that Hegel reverses the order and finds it to be the ground of all human experience. You can tell a people by the gods they keep.[33]

There is perhaps no clearer exposition of this view of Religion than Emile Durkheim's *The Elementary Forms of the Religious Life*. Durkheim is full of "Hegelian" ideas. In this context the most important is his view that religious concepts are collective representations of collective sentiments growing out of social experience, and that the quasi-religious two-world philosophies of Plato and Kant are expressions of the tension between individual and society.

The fundamental question of his book—What is the origin of religion?—Durkheim interprets as asking what the ubiquitous features of human experience are which lead to dividing the world into profane and sacred, the world of the ordinary and the sharply separated world of ultimate significance and worth. Working on the methodological assumption that the most primitive religion will exhibit the essence of religion unencumbered by irrelevant accretions, he argues that totemism is the truly primitive religion. In doing so he not only rejects animism and naturism as candidates for the title of most primitive religion, but more importantly the implication normally associated with the presentation of both, that religion is a prescientific attempt to explain certain natural phenomena. From the outset he agrees with Hegel that Religion is not to be understood as a mode of knowing nature.

Seeking clues from totemism about the origin or essence of religion, Durkheim notes 1) that the separation between sacred and profane in totemism does not demarcate man as profane from certain religious objects as sacred, and 2) that sacred objects are not such in virtue of their own inherent qualities, but in virtue of participation in a power that survives the particulars. For example, the sacred emblems used in totemic ritual are frequently good for only one use and are destroyed after the ceremony is completed. Yet as symbolic of the totemic power, they are sacred. Similarly the human members of a totemic clan and the animal (or vegetable) members of the species from which it derives its name are transient, yet as participating in the impersonal power or life usually known by its Melanesian name, mana, they are sacred.[34]

Mana has a curious twofold significance. It is superior to the individual as that to which he owes veneration and respect. It has what Durkheim calls "moral authority." Yet it is at the same time the source of the individual's strength and vitality. The idea of a power or life which is at once sustainer and lord, sharply set off from the ordinary, immediate appearance of things does not come, Durkheim argues, from observing nature. It is grounded in the experience of social life. "Religion ceases to be an inexplicable hallucination and takes a foothold in reality. In fact, we can say that the believer is not deceived when he believes in the existence of a moral power upon which he depends and from which he receives all that is best in him: this power exists, it is society. . . It is true that he is wrong in thinking that this increase of vitality is the work of a power in the form of some animal or plant. But this error is merely in regard to the letter of the symbol by which this being is represented . . . and not in regard to the fact of its existence. Behind these figures and metaphors, be they gross or refined, there is a concrete and living reality. Thus religion . . . is a system of ideas with which the individuals represent to themselves the society of which they are members, and the obscure but intimate relations which they have with it."[35]

It is not difficult to account for ideas of God in these terms. "But whenever the tribe acquired a livelier sentiment of itself, this sentiment naturally incarnated itself in some personage, who became its symbol."[36] This personage is thus the culmination of a complicated rationalizing of the concept of mana with the help of imagination.

Durkheim's analysis of totemic sacrifice serves well to illustrate a paradox which the sociological theory purports to resolve. On the one hand sacrifice seems to involve the idea of communion and participation in which man finds the strength and confidence which come from divine favor. On the other hand he offers an oblation to his god, as if to say that his god could not get along without him. Who sustains whom?

Durkheim accepts the apparent circle. "It comes from the fact that the sacred beings, though superior to men, can live only in the human consciousness."[37] When it is remembered that the divine beings are symbols of society, the paradox is resolved. Man does create his gods and is yet sustained by them, for he makes his own society, on which he is in turn dependent. The purpose of the rite, be it sacrifice or any other, is "to revivify the most essential elements of the collective consciousness. Through it, the group periodically renews the sentiment which it has of itself and of its unity; at the same time, individuals are strengthened in their social natures."[38]

This digression on Durkheim has been introduced, not because it is free from theoretical difficulties of its own, but because it represents so clearly in non-Hegelian language Hegel's fundamental idea about the relation of religion to society. It shows that there is an interpretation of religion according to which the dialectical transition from Chapter Six to Chapter Seven of the *Phenomenology* is both more natural and necessary than Hegel himself is able to make it seem. For many this transition is the central stumbling block of the entire *Phenomenology*. It is often described more or less as Royce describes it. At the level of Spirit we are involved with "the social order to which I belong . . . a humanity in whose life I take part." But then we leave this to discover a "super-social or religious realm."[39] This may be considered a strength, since it seems to offer Hegel a defense against the charges of statism or historicism; or it may be considered a weakness, since it seems to represent a Stoic sort of retreat from the real world and its problems to the inner world where everything is reinterpreted but unchanged.

In either case this reading leads to a fundamental methodological problem which Hyppolite expresses as the question whether at this point phenomenology turns into noumenology, whether human experience and its description are suddenly abandoned in favor of dogmatic pronouncements about super-human realities.[40] If one assumes that when Hegel speaks of absolute Spirit he is speaking of a super-human Spirit, related but not relative to man, transcending the world of human experience like the God of classical theism or the Platonic Ideas, then references to absolute Spirit can only be an embarrassment to his phenomenological approach and the transition from Chapter Six to Chapter Seven a paradoxical *non sequitur*. Whether or not one finds such a concept of absolute

Spirit intrinsically meaningful, and whether or not one finds its employment an advantage or a disadvantage from the political point of view, one will have to admit that the descriptive project described in the Introduction has broken down and been abandoned.

This is the wrong way to ask the right question. The question of Hegel's faithfulness to his own methodological requirements is nowhere more legitimate than at this point. But the way in which it is usually asked, a la Royce and Hyppolite, suffers from the double disadvantage of ignoring Hegel's own careful development of the concept of Spirit as a distinctly human We while at the same time making nonsense of the transition from Spirit to Religion. When Hegel's analysis of Spirit up to the section on Conscience is taken as the clue for interpreting the emergence of absolute Spirit there, the transition to Chapter Seven is a coherent and natural one, free of any sudden leaps to a super-human realm.

It is puzzling why this latter procedure has not been universally adopted. There appear to be two reasons why it has not. First, Hegel begins to speak of Spirit as absolute, and it is difficult to see how any human social reality could be described in this way, however aware of itself it might be. But when it is remembered that Hegel believed the emerging post-revolutionary world to be in its essence a society whose enlightened Christianity enabled it to be a universal community of reciprocal recognition or love, the difficulty is largely overcome. For if such an event had actually taken place it is not so clear that we would be reluctant to call it absolute Spirit. In any case, Hegel would have the right so to describe it, for it would embody a form of human consciousness whose truth was adequate to its certainty, whose reality was equal to its aspiration. There would be a human community completely free from domination or alienating otherness, whether between man and man or between man and God, and this society would know itself to be what it is. Its collective self-consciousness, having no need to go beyond itself, would be Absolute Knowledge. It would be human consciousness fully and genuinely satisfied, sheer blessedness.

Events have not been kind to Hegel's expectations, and it is appropriate to note that "were he alive today, so realistic a philosopher as Hegel would not be a Hegelian."[41] In other words, the right way to ask about Hegel's faithfulness to his descriptive method is not to suggest that this concept of absolute Spirit betrays that method from the outset; it is rather to ask whether the thoroughly describable event he believed to be taking place during his lifetime was actually taking place. From the perspective of our present the answer to this proper way of asking the question has to be negative. With this negative answer comes the judgment that Hegel was not able to be faithful to his descriptive method to the end. He thought the Kingdom of God had begun to dawn in a new and decisive form and he set about to describe it. But he was mistaken and it was not there.

This is perhaps the most serious criticism that can be made of the *Phenomenology*, especially since it derives from Hegel's own criterion and has such a direct and negative bearing on the possibility of transcending critical finitism and knowing the Absolute. But while these considerations are important for evaluating Hegel's project, they cannot govern its interpretation. That must be guided by the text and not subsequent events. This is all the more important since neither the meaningfulness nor the contemporary philosophical interest of Hegel's project depends on the accuracy of his historical projections. The inseparability of the question of Absolute Knowledge from that of the Kingdom of God is a philosophical thesis worthy of more attention than it usually gets in an atmosphere which is more likely to treat both questions as meaningless a priori. Similarly, to suggest that philosophy *per se*, not just political philosophy, is the expression of an essentially utopian striving is to throw interesting light on the history of the West, including the present moment, when philosophy in this sense has all but died out. Hegel's value to us is not tied to the possibility of our being Hegelians. He does not need to be infallible for us all to learn from him, whether we be Marxists or Christians, positivists or existentialists, language analysts or phenomenologists.

This brings us back to the task of interpreting Hegel and to the only partially answered question why absolute Spirit is so frequently interpreted as a super-human reality in spite of the good reasons against doing so. Beyond the fact that Hegel speaks of Spirit as absolute, he seems to emphasize rather than downplay the notion of transcendence, and this, too, is thought to require something on a theistic or Platonic model, or perhaps the Aristotelian νόησις νοήσεως νόησις which somehow manages to find its way onto the title page of Baillie's translation. But there are two ways in which the more nearly Feuerbachian-Durkheimian interpretation which the text calls for includes all the transcendence Hegel needs. The relation of the individual to God (society's collective self-consciousness) is still analagous to the transcendence of traditional philosophical theology. Durkheim makes this particularly clear. Further, the primacy given to the historical development of Spirit towards its absoluteness gives a horizontal transcendence in time which supplements the vertical transcendence of society to the individual. While this latter transcendence disappears with the dawning of the new world, the latter remains.

In summary, there is no need to treat Religion as the realm of the super-social. To do so is to abandon Hegel's careful development of the concept of Spirit just where he finds in it the solution he is looking for. The result is to render incoherent the transition to Chapter Seven by failing to see how Spirit is simultaneously subject and object of religious knowledge, thereby misconstruing the Hegelian sense in which Spirit can be absolute, transcendent, and divine.

7C. Vorstellung as the Form of Religious Knowledge

It was noted above that even though Hegel finds Christianity to be absolute Religion, he says its congregation "is not yet perfected in this its self-consciousness. . . It is not consciously aware what it is." The reason for this is that "its content, in general, is put before it in the *Form des Vorstellens.*"[42] Whereas Kant uses the term *Vorstellung* and the related verb to speak of representation in the inclusive sense of having some content present to consciousness, Hegel uses them as a technical term in contrast to *Begriff* or concept, often translated as notion. It connotes an essential bond with sense experience, and for this reason it is often translated as "pictorial thinking," "imaginative presentation," or "figurative thought." For Hegel as for earlier philosophical theology there is no way that sense bound categories can adequately express the divine. But for Hegel it is not the pictorial element which is the primary difficulty; it is rather that sense perception itself is the presupposed model for knowing. This means that the object of knowledge is viewed as external to the knowing subject. *Vorstellungen* thus express an externality of spatial and temporal relation which absolute Spirit purports to transcend. The unity and interdependence of Spirit are overpowered by multiplicity and independence in any *vorgestellt* subject matter. Religion, whose form of knowing is always *Vorstellung,* is therefore always consciousness and never self-consciousness.

This is a startling discovery, for Hegel has also been stressing the self-conscious nature of religious knowledge, the identity of subject and object, in direct conflict with what he now says about its form. But that is just the point. The apparent contradiction is avoided only by remembering the structure of projection. What is in fact an awareness of oneself may be taken to be an awareness of something other than oneself. Though the content may be that of self-consciousness, the form remains that of consciousness. Hegel finds this to be true of Religion as such. It is always self-consciousness, since the object apprehended is always identical with the collective religious subject. But from its own point of view Religion is always consciousness, since it takes the object to be an independent other, even if the object of religious awareness is not as wholly other as other objects.[43]

Christianity is no exception to this rule, either in Chapter Seven or in its two earlier appearances. At stake is the meaning of the incarnation.

Unhappy Consciousness views the divine as the unchangeable. In the incarnation the unchangeable seems to be brought down from its splendid isolation and united with man. "In point of fact through the unchangeable assuming a definite form the beyond as a moment has not only remained but is really more securely established. For if on the one hand the unchangeable seems indeed brought closer to the individual consciousness by taking the form of an actual individual, on the other hand it stands henceforth over against him as an opaque sensible particular with all the hard resistance of what is actual.

The hope of becoming one with him must remain a hope without present fulfillment." But religious consciousness requires more than this. "The external relation which at first obtains to the unchangeable in human form as to an alien entity must be raised to an absolute fusion [*Einswerden*]."[44] The presence which becomes absence by the contingency of human death is not the divine presence for which Unhappy Consciousness hopes. But hope is a certainty whose truth is still outstanding, and Absolute Knowledge is not to be found in any religion whose "faith is the assurance of things hoped for, the conviction of things not seen."[45]

Faith is also alienated consciousness, sharply in contrast to the self-consciousness, however insubstantial, of Enlightened Insight. Whereas the latter has only the pure self for its object, Faith is "the consciousness of what is given [*des Positiven*], the form of objectivity [*Gegenständlichkeit*] or of *Vorstellen.*" It takes the divine to be "an objective being that lies beyond consciousness of self." For Faith "the divine falls out of thought into *Vorstellung,* and becomes a supersensible world which is supposed to be essentially other to self-consciousness." Like Unhappy Consciousness Faith seeks a sense of unity through its doctrine of kenosis. It thereby makes the divine an "unintelligible sensible actuality. . . The beyond has thus only been more specifically determined as remoteness in space and time."[46] Faith, too, remains mere consciousness.

Absolute Religion as described in Chapter Seven is still not free from the form of *Vorstellung.* For this reason "spiritual life is still burdened with an unreconciled division between a here and a beyond. The content is the true content. But all its moments, when placed in the element of *Vorstellen* have the character of not being understood [*begriffen*]. They rather appear to be completely independent elements, externally related to each other. In order that the true content may also receive its true form for consciousness, it is necessary for consciousness to rise to a higher plane of mental development, to elevate its intuition of the absolute Substance to the level of the concept [*Begriff*], and to bring its consciousness to the level of its self-consciousness for itself, just as this has already happened for us or in itself."[47] In other words, Religion has not yet caught up with "our" insight into what it is really all about.

The whole of Chapter Seven hinges on this distinction between *Vorstellung* and *Begriff*. Four pairs of contrasts summarize its meaning. As the preceding passage indicates, *Vorstellung* is bound to the dualism between the here and the beyond so that the divine is never fully present for the believer's experience. While he is beyond the desolation of "My God! My God! Why hast thou forsaken me?"—there remains as an essential aspect of faith the Psalmist's cry, "As a hart longs for flowing streams, so longs my soul for thee, O God."[48] This is why *Vorstellung* is associated with consciousness in opposition to the self-consciousness of *Begriff* in which, subject and object being identical, no such rift or absence is possible. In addition to these contrasts between *absence* and *presence, consciousness* and *self-consciousness, Vorstellung* means viewing the incarnation as an event, a *contingent* happening, while *Begriff* means viewing it as the expression of a *necessity*. What this distinction between event and necessity means is indicated by the final contrast, that of *individual* and *universal self-consciousness*. The incarnation means that God is present as observable human self-consciousness. But seen in the form of *Vorstellung* this refers uniquely to the historical event and the historical individual known as Jesus of Nazareth. To see the unity of the human and divine as a necessity, and thus in the form of *Begriff,* is to see the human self-consciousness in which God is present and united with man as the universal self-consciousness of the congregation which, in principle at least, incorporates all of humanity.[49]

Once again the question whether Hegel has kept to his descriptive methodology becomes unavoidable. Where God has become society's projected self-image and the incarnation means that mankind universally is divine, how can one speak any longer of Christianity? Is Hegel not telling us what he thinks Christianity ought to be rather than describing what it is when, as Hyppolite puts it, "the Christo-centric point of view of the Bible tends to disappear to make room for the universal Christ who is the community"?[50] Does not Kierkegaard have the right to be deeply offended, not so much at Hegel's view of the world but at the claim that it represents the final truth of the Christian faith?

We must proceed carefully here, for Hegel is careful not to suggest that he is a Christian theologian in the sense of someone like Anselm, who sought to give a conceptual exposition of the very faith taught in the scriptures and proclaimed by the church. He is most explicit in underscoring the difference between the truth of Christianity as *Begriff* and the way it was originally understood.[51] It is clear from his discussions of Unhappy Consciousness and Faith that Hegel sees the subsequent historical manifestations as more nearly the original understanding than the new understanding he presents. In fact he insists that as long as Christianity remains Religion it will see the incarnation as a unique event occurring once and for all in Jesus of Nazareth. Hegel is not for a moment pretending that his *Begriff* is telling us what the Bible and the church have been telling us for centuries.

But Hegel's descriptive method allows him to describe whatever he finds. If he finds a form of consciousness which calls itself Christian but understands the Christian message in the radically new way which Hegel designates as *Begriff* in contrast to *Vorstellung,* he is entitled to describe that too. That such a consciousness was prevalent in Hegel's time cannot be denied. One needs only to mention the writings of Kant, Fichte, and Schleiermacher during the last decade of the eighteenth century.[52]

Hegel does not hesitate to draw the consequences of this perspective, to which he is obviously sympathetic. At the beginning of Chapter Seven he suggests that Religion, which had previously appeared only in the form of consciousness, will now come forward as the self-consciousness of Spirit. So he describes the movement of Chapter Seven from Nature Religion to the Religion of Art to Absolute or Revealed Religion as a movement not simply to more and more adequate conceptions of the divine but primarily as the movement from consciousness to self-consciousness, that is, as a movement beyond the very form of religious consciousness to a new form of consciousness.[53] From its name, *Begriff,* and from its evident link with Absolute Knowledge, there is nothing surprising in the discovery that this new form of consciousness is the philosophical. The Christian congregation can become the bearer of this new mode of experience (which cannot strictly be called a form of consciousness) and of the Absolute Knowledge it makes possible only by radically transcending itself and ceasing to be what it has historically been. It must become a philosophical community instead of a religious community in the strictest sense. One is reminded of the relation of the Platonic republic to the Pythagorean communities. Neither the Platonic nor the Hegelian communities are to be composed simply of philosophers; yet philosophy is to permeate them as their Form or Idea. In Hegel's case this means that the collective self-consciousness of the community attains philosophic form, throws off the elements of unconsciousness involved in the structures of projection, and recognizes itself to be the truth of prior projections.

It would seem fair to say, then, in defense of Hegel, that his descriptive methodology has remained in tact in so far as 1) he is not purporting to describe traditional Christian faith but something clearly different from it in its essential form, and 2) he is describing something actual in the world, a point of view the essentials of which he did not invent. There remains, however, the claim that while the form is different, the content is the same. This amounts to saying that while the Christian religion is radically transcending itself in the movement from *Vorstellung* to *Begriff* it thereby finds its own true fulfillment. At this point Hegel does seem to have gone beyond the limits of pure description. It is tempting to read this claim as a prescriptive one, telling us how we ought to interpret the basic ideas of the Christian faith. But it is probably more accurate to see it as predictive, as the expectation that mankind's longing for the Kingdom of God and the lasting experience of the divine presence would find their fulfillment in the radical self-transcendence of Christianity.

From Hegel's time to our own there have been countless variations on this theme of salvation through a post-Christian Christianity. Since this gospel continues to be proclaimed even in our own time, it would perhaps be rash to say that history has decisively falsified it. But history's verdict on Hegel's hope has been extremely harsh.

Seen in this light Hegel's view of Christianity in the *Phenomenology*[54] is strikingly similar to Nietzsche's in the *Genealogy of Morals*. There Nietzsche applies to Christianity the principle that "all great things bring about their own destruction through an act of self-overcoming."[55] His argument there is that it was the Christian morality of truthfulness which really conquered the Christian God and that this same morality must end by turning against itself and discovering the deceitfulness of its passion for truth. In this way Christianity transcends itself both as dogma and as morality. Similarly, Hegel's Chapter Seven must be read as the application to Christianity of a major thesis of his about Spirit: "not the life that shrinks from death and keeps itself undefiled by devastation, but the life that endures, and preserves itself through death is the life of Spirit."[56]

Kierkegaard remains offended. And not without reason. For the implication of views like Hegel's and Nietzsche's is that Christianity is wholly an historical phenomenon like feudalism or capitalism. Since it has always claimed to be more than that its fulfillment could only be in the confirmation and not in the falsification of that claim.

NOTES

1. See Ch. 6, n. 87.

2. PhG, 639/482/698.

3. PhG, 644/485/703.

4. PhG, 651/490/709.

5. *Hegel's Phenomenology: Dialogues on the Life of Mind,* La Salle, 1965, p. 333.

6. PhG, 676/506/731.

7. PhG, 691/516/743. See E. R. Dodds, *The Greeks and the Irrational,* Berkeley, 1971, pp. 7, 14, and 30 f.

8. Jean Hyppolite, *Genèse et Structure de la Phénoménologie de l'Esprit de Hegel,* Paris, 1946, p. 533.

9. PhG, 699-702/521-23/750-53. This is in contrast to the religion of nature, which knows substance without subjectivity.

10. *Sacred and Profane Beauty: the Holy in Art,* trans. David Green, New York, 1963, p. 132.

11. SC, HTJ, 302-09/253-61. cf Hegel's speculation on life in Ch. 5 above.

12. *Ibid.,* 312-13/265-67.

13. *Ibid.,* 316/271.

14. *Ibid.,* 321-22/278, my italics.

15. *Ibid.,* 335-36/292-95.

16. PhG, 498/391/568-69. cf. 515/403/583.

17. PhG, 532/413/598.

18. PhG, 709-11/528-29/758-60. cf. *Realphilosophie,* II, 266, "The divine nature is not an other than the human."

19. PhG, 735/545/780.

20. PhG, 715/531/763, not "the complete whole of the individual spirit," as Baillie has it at the end of this passage. The influence of Lessing's *The Education of the Human Race* is to be seen here. On his threefold schema of man's religious history Judaism as the religion of the Father and Christianity as the religion of the Son belong to the childhood of the human race and are to be surpassed by an "eternal gospel" based on reason rather than revelation and as different from traditional Christianity as the latter is from Judaism. His contrast in *On the Proof of the Spirit and of Power* between the accidental truths of history and the necessary truths of reason closely parallels Hegel's distinction between *Vorstellung* and *Begriff.* See section 7C. below.

21. PhG, 718/534/766.

22. See note 14 above.

23. PhG, 628-29/475/688. Hegel had concluded *The Spirit of Christianity* by saying of the Christian church that "it is its fate that church and state, worship and life, piety and virtue, spiritual and worldly action, can never dissolve into one." HTJ, 342/301. Persuaded that Christianity is overcoming this fate, Hegel is not simply hostile toward it in the *Phenomenology*.

24. PhG, 434/350/513 and 709/528/758.

25. See notes 20 and 21 above and Ch. 6, n. 87.

26. PhG, 720/535/768.

27. PhG, 738-39/547/783.

28. Henry A. Murray, in a foreword to *An Introduction to Projective Techniques,* ed. Anderson and Anderson, Englewood Cliffs, 1951.

29. *Psychoanalysis and Religion,* New Haven, 1950, especially pages 49-52. It is not so clear that Feuerbach was as anti-Hegelian as he wanted to be in *The Essence of Christianity.*

30. PhG, 712/530/761.

31. See the citation from Schelling in Ch. 5., n. 27.

32. See note 16 above.

33. PhG, 630-31/476-77/689-90.

34. This is an illuminating perspective to bring to the romantic philosophy of nature and to Hegel's own early use of 'life' as a category.

35. *The Elementary Forms of the Religious Life,* trans. Swain, New York, 1965, p. 257.

36. *Ibid.,* p. 331.

37. *Ibid.,* p. 388.

38. *Ibid.,* p. 420. Hegel's own analysis of totemism and sacrifice fits this account perfectly. See PhG, 643-44/485-86/702-03 and 666-67/500/722-23.

39. *Lectures on Modern Idealism,* New Haven, 1919, p. 177.

40. *op. cit.,* pp. 515 f.

41. Emil Fackenheim, *The Religious Dimension in Hegel's Thought,* Bloomington, 1967, p. 224.

42. PhG, 738-39/547/783.

43. PhG, 635/479/693. Since religion always affirms some sort of bond between man and the divine Hegel says that the *Gegenstand* does not sink to pure *Gegenständlichkeit.*

44. PhG, 145-46/161-62/255-56. Kierkegaard's concept of contemporaneity with Christ is also a recognition that the believer never relates to the incarnation simply as an historical fact. What is puzzling

about Hegel's account is that he should speak of faith as fusion rather than recognition.

45. Hebrews 11:1 (RSV).

46. PhG, 478-83/379-81/553-56. On kenosis see Ch. 6, n. 31. On *Gegenständlichkeit* and *Vorstellung* see Ch. 6, n. 46.

47. PhG, 715-16/532/763-64.

48. Psalm 42:1 (RSV).

49. See especially PhG, 713-21/530-35/761-68 and 729-33/540-43/775-78.

50. *op. cit.*, p. 547.

51. PhG, 716-17/532-33/764.

52. Note especially what is said about the church in Kant's *Religion,* Schleiermacher's *Reden,* and Fichte's *Grundlage des Naturrechts* and *System der Sittenlehre.*

53. PhG, 625/473/683 and 638/482/696-97.

54. Nothing is here implied about Hegel's later views.

55. Third Essay, Section 27, Kaufmann translation. Nietzsche uses both *Selbstaufhebung* and *Selbstüberwindung* in this context.

56. See Ch. 1, n. 45. There is something right, then, in Altizer's attempt to enlist both Hegel and Nietzsche as allies in *The Gospel of Christian Atheism.*

CHAPTER EIGHT: Absolute Knowledge

8A. The Withering Away of Religion and the Marxian Critique

Hegel's final chapter is brief, as it can afford to be in the light of the thorough preparation for it. Complaints about its tantalizing brevity (with the usual explanations about the conditions under which the manuscript was completed) may reflect more on the critic's attention to the text than on Hegel's ability to say what he meant. The opening paragraph reminds the reader that he could by now write the conclusion for himself. At the same time it reminds the non-reader that Hegel's view of Absolute Knowledge cannot be found simply by reading Chapter Eight.

"Spirit as Revealed Religion has not yet overcome its consciousness as such; or what is the same thing, its actual self-consciousness is not the object of its consciousness. Spirit itself in general and the moments which distinguish themselves within it fall within the sphere of *Vorstellen* and in the form of objectivity [*Gegenständlichkeit*]. The content of *Vorstellen* is absolute Spirit. All that remains to be done is to transcend [*Aufheben*] this mere form, or rather, because this form belongs to consciousness as such, its truth must have already come out in the forms of consciousness."[1]

So far as "we" are concerned, nothing remains to be done, for "we" are supposed to have seen throughout the preceding chapter that the truth of Religion lies in correcting its misleading form by recognizing the divine to be nothing beyond us but the social whole of which we are parts. This is the cash value of the move from *Vorstellung* to *Begriff,* from consciousness to self-consciousness.[2] "We" who have carefully followed the development of Chapter Seven do not even need a short Chapter Eight to tell us that. But the truth which must have already come out in the preceding forms of consciousness must become the truth for religious consciousness itself. Hegel's account of Absolute Knowledge can remain within the limits of his descriptive method only if the consciousness he is describing

211

comes to see for itself what "we" are to have seen in Hegel's description of it. In other words, the self-transcendence of religion must in some sense be an historical fact and not simply a philosophical requirement or expectation.

Since that which is to be abandoned, *Vorstellung*, consciousness, and *Gegenständlichkeit* are definitive of religious consciousness as such, one can speak here of the withering away of the religious point of view. For just as Marx sees the prerevolutionary, bourgeois state to be incompatible with truly human society, thus requiring radical transformation in the transition to socialism, so Hegel sees in divine transcendence, traditionally conceived, the last and most strategic stronghold of the philosophy of finitude in human knowledge. Only a radical transformation of that point of view can make the world safe for Absolute Knowledge.

Perhaps without realizing it, Hegel makes at this point his most direct assault on the Kantian thing in itself. For this Kantian doctrine not only entails the absolute, i.e., unsurpassable finitude of all human knowing; it is explicitly tied to the religious point of view which Hegel here seeks to transcend. The thing in itself is the thing as known by an infinite Creator, in contrast to which all creaturely knowledge can only be derivative and imperfect.[3]

Hegel calls this withering away of the religious point of view the "overcoming of the object of consciousness." Since he is dealing here with religious consciousness this object is God. His overcoming involves three elements: first, that the object shows itself as such to consciousness as a vanishing factor, that is, as something that does not remain incorrigibly other; second, that it becomes clear in this way that it is the alienation [*Entäusserung*] of self-consciousness which grounds objectivity [*die Dingheit setzt*], that is, that man makes the world he lives in; and third, that this alienation comes to have a positive significance for self-consciousness, namely in the discovery that man's world is not a brute fact but somehow his own creation. This knowledge is grounded in the pulsating movement of Spirit first outward, then inward. It arises "on the one hand through the fact that self-consciousness alienates itself. For in this alienation it establishes itself as object, or it establishes the object as itself, for the sake of the indivisible unity of being for itself. On the other hand, there is this other moment involved at the same time, that self-consciousness has just as much transcended [*aufgehoben*] this alienation and objectivity [*Gegenständlichkeit*] and has taken them back into itself. Thus it is at home [*bei sich*] in its otherness as such."[4]

Actually this summarizes four different processes which Hegel has presented. The *Gegenständlichkeit* of nature is overcome through knowing and labor, the theoretical and practical modes in which self-consciousness *die Dingheit setzt.*[5] As the argument of the first four chapters makes clear, this overcoming is not an obliteration; it rather presupposes a continuing otherness of the object, though not a brute otherness. The knowing and laboring self is "at home in its otherness as such."

Though knowing and labor may well be said to have a history, it is not man's encounter with nature which Hegel finds to be the heart of the historical process. This is rather found in the *Gegenständlichkeit* of the other self and its overcoming, not through knowing and labor but through love. The otherness of finite selves is overcome in the community of tolerance whose foundation is reciprocal recognition. The otherness of the Infinite Self is overcome in the discovery that the divine is nothing but this "nation of men related to one another by love."[6] Here, too, otherness does not simply disappear. But it loses that strangeness which leaves man estranged rather than at home in the presence of the other.

Marx's 1844 critique of Hegel's chapter on Absolute Knowledge takes the passage we have been examining as its focal point. The primary charge is that Hegel has illegitimately identified *Entaüsserung* and *Gegenständlichkeit*. In developing this critique Lukács suggests that it rests upon an ambiguity which Hegel builds into his use of the former term. On the one hand it has a strong sense akin to Marx's notion of fetishism, in which the meaning is that man's own creations win mastery over him. In this sense *Entaüsserung* has the sense of *Entfremdung;* it is alienation in the sense of estrangement and not simply of objectification. On the other hand there is a "broad philosophical universalizing of this concept: *Entaüsserung* then means the same as *Dingheit* or *Gegenständlichkeit.*" In other words it refers to the object of knowledge as such.[7]

For Marx these meanings are entirely discrete. It is to be

expected that man, as a natural being, will have the object of his
knowledge and desire outside himself, just as he is the object of
the knowing and desire of others. Objectivity is not a problem
for him. His concern is solely with that inhuman self-
objectification which he here calls estrangement and later calls
fetishism.[8] By contrast he finds Hegel to have defined man solely in terms of thought and to be offended by objectivity as
such, finding in it the "scandal of estrangement." Consequently
his dialectic is exclusively that of thought and being. Having
falsely identified *Entfremdung* and *Gegenständlichkeit* in the ambiguous concept of *Entäusserung,* he then offers an epistemological idealism as the solution to the real problems of life. As a
comment on this part of Marx's argument Lukács quotes En-
gels' verdict "that finally the Hegelian system only represents a
materialism whose method and content have been idealistically
stood on their head."[9]

Marx has overlooked two important aspects of Hegel's argument. First, in the passage under consideration the primary
reference is to God and not nature, as Marx constantly assumes.
Since Marx is surely to be counted among those for whom in
this instance any kind of *Gegenständlichkeit* would of necessity be
Entfremdung, it is strange that it fails to see Hegel as a potential
ally.

Second, and equally important, we have just seen that the
"overcoming of the object of consciousness" properly refers beyond the primary reference of the immediate context and
applies to nature as well. And we have been reminded that
Hegel, too, in the earlier analysis of Self-Consciousness takes
man to be a natural being with the object of his knowledge and
desire outside himself. Why does Marx take the discussion of
Absolute Knowledge to be a retraction of that position? It is because he has overlooked the significance of Hegel's language. It
is true that Hegel's use of *Gegenständlichkeit* in Chapters Seven
and Eight tends to equate it with *Entfremdung* as Marx says, for
it is an objectivity which keeps man from being at home in his
otherness which must be overcome. But this means that it is not
objectivity or otherness as such which is the obstacle to human
fulfillment, either in the case of nature or in the case of God.
To repeat Hegel's formula, the goal is to be at home in otherness as such, that is, as other. Hegel's "idealism" leaves man

fully embodied and situated in a world of nature and other selves. What he purports to have discovered is not that the *esse* of that world is *percipi* but that history has reached a point where man can be at home in his world.

Nothing in Hegel's argument suggests that on his view nature somehow ceases to be "out there." It is true that at the end of Chapter Eight he speaks of nature as alienated Spirit, though the same sentence describes nature in as materialist a formula as Marx could want. It is "nothing but the eternal alienation of its own existence, and the movement which produces the subject."[10] Perhaps more important for understanding Hegel's meaning when he speaks of nature as alienated Spirit is the fact that he makes a sharp distinction between the way in which nature and history can be spoken of as alienated Spirit. Nature is Spirit's "living, immediate becoming," while history is its "knowing, self-mediated becoming."

Lukács notices this important distinction that Hegel makes, but fails to see in it any corrective to the Marxian critique. He makes it to blame for the fact that "where Hegel discusses actual history [Chapter Six] the problems of nature are as good as completely gone."[11] He is right in noting that Hegel does not find man's encounter with nature and thus the history of alienated labor to be the motor of the historical process. This is a genuine difference from Marx which needs to be carefully spelled out. But it does not follow from this, as both Marx and Lukács conclude, that Hegel reduces the historical process to the history of knowledge. He finds Spirit's basic problem to be Spirit itself. That is why the historical process is interpreted in terms of the quest for reciprocal recognition and why the object whose "overcoming" is crucial to the emergence of Absolute Knowledge is God. It is strange that when Feuerbach presents a projectionist view of God Marx praises its materialism, but when Hegel does the same he repudiates it as idealist.

Since it is this question of God's status which primarily concerns Hegel in the opening paragraphs of Chapter Eight, they serve to recapitulate the themes of the previous chapter on Religion. But he quickly refers us to Chapter Six as well, describing the recognition achieved in forgiveness and the individual self which is "immediately universal" in the community of tolerance as "the reconciliation of Spirit with its actual consciousness," and as "the reconciliation of consciousness and self-consciousness." We thus have two accounts of what Hegel sometimes calls the overcoming of consciousness by self-consciousness but here describes as their reconciliation. One is in the context of religious Spirit (Chapter Seven), the other in the context of "consciousness itself as such" (Chapter Six). Since this reconciliation has the form of being in itself [*Ansichsein*] in the former and the form of being for itself [*Fürsichsein*] in the latter, the two are at first opposed. The community of tolerance and the church have not yet discovered their common identity. "The unification of both sides is not yet shown. It is this unification which concludes this series of forms of Spirit. For therein Spirit comes to know itself not only as it is in itself, or according to its absolute content, nor only as it is for itself, according to its contentless form or in terms of self-consciousness, but as it is in and for itself."[12]

This confirms our reading of Chapter Six as a sacralizing of the secular and Chapter Seven as a complementary secularizing of the sacred. Only the unity of the two perspectives, each one-sided in itself, permits a further stage of Spirit's development. Both involve the concept of "the self-intuition of the divine." But this concept is actualized "partly as acting, self-certain Spirit [the conscientious self] and partly as Religion. In the latter it won the absolute content as content, or in the form of *Vorstellung*, of otherness to consciousness. On the other hand in the former the form is just the self, for it contains acting, self-certain Spirit. The self realizes the life of absolute Spirit."[13] In other words the community of tolerance which appears at the end of Chapter Six is the fulfillment of the concept toward which it is striving only in so far as it comes to recognize the unity of its own self-constituting activity with the content affirmed by Religion. Its self-positing as the autonomy of the general will must understand itself as the subjectivity which is also the absolute substance known in Religion as God. The emergence of Absolute Knowledge means taking in dead earnest the affirmation of Rousseau's *Discourse on Political Economy:* "the voice of the people is in fact the voice of God."

In a similar way the religious consciousness must incorporate the perspective of Conscience. It must learn that the content which it takes to be basic, the sacred, is the self's own act. In doing this it learns to identify the city of God with the city of man and to overcome the fate which at an earlier time Hegel thought was insurmountable.[14]

As the religious and secular points of view thus confess and forgive one another, as it were, Spirit comes to the end of its long journey. "This last form of Spirit—Spirit which at once gives to its complete and true content the form of self and thereby realizes its concept, while remaining within its concept in this realization—is Absolute Knowledge. It is Spirit knowing itself in the form of Spirit; in other words, it is conceptual knowing . . . Spirit appearing in this element to consciousness, or what is here the same thing, produced by it in this element, is Science."[15]

Although Hegel talks freely here of Absolute Knowledge he has not abandoned his original concept of Spirit as the I that is We and the We that is I. He calls Science the "pure being for itself of self-consciousness. It is the I that is this I and no other I, just as much as the immediately mediated or transcended, universal I."[16] This means that just as it is the self which realizes the life of absolute Spirit,[17] so the bearers of Absolute Knowledge are individuals. But it is not as sheer individuals that they are the locus of Absolute Knowledge. Only as their personal self-consciousness can be said to be a particular expression of the collective self-consciousness which Hegel has been describing as absolute Spirit do they express Absolute Knowledge.

The story of Spirit's developing self-consciousness as presented in Chapters Six through Eight can be summarized in these terms: society is the reality which religion adores, and philosophy is the public discovery that this is so. Spirit's journey comes to its end and Science is born when, in Kojève's words, we learn "to say of man everything that the Christian says of his God . . ."[18] Like Lessing before him and Tillich after him Hegel allows his thought to come to rest only where Enlightenment's demand for absolute human autonomy is satisfied, but in such a way as to preserve some sort of "eternal gospel" or "dimension of depth."

It is understandable that Nietzsche, writing for his contemporaries, should have attacked the form of this compromise most popular in his day. But for us it is unfortunate that the target of his first Untimely Meditation should have been the epigone, David Friedrich Strauss, rather than his master, Hegel. There were thinkers of comparable stature, however, who challenged Hegel's attempted synthesis of Enlightenment and Christianity from the outset, Marx on the secular side, Kierkegaard on the religious. The story is beautifully told in Löwith's *From Hegel to Nietzsche*. Since there is so often an attempt to avoid discussion of these criticisms of Hegel by distinguishing the "existential" Hegel of the *Phenomenology* from the later System, it is well to note that the essential features of the synthesis against which Marx and Kierkegaard revolted are at the very heart of the *Phenomenology*. That Marx's own critique of Absolute Knowledge is seriously flawed in no way detracts from his judgment that "it is necessary to begin with the *Phenomenology*, because it is there that Hegel's philosophy was born and that its secret is to be found."[19]

8B. Science and Eternity

Before concluding his text with a preview of the system introduced by the *Phenomenology*, Hegel makes two crucial remarks about the relation of Absolute Knowledge to time.

First, Science is not ubiquitous with respect to time. It comes onto a stage from which it has been absent, not because it has been patiently waiting in the wings, but simply because it was not. "As to the existence of this concept, however, Science does not appear in time and actuality until Spirit has arrived at this consciousness of itself. As Spirit which knows what it is, it does not exist earlier."[20]

Since Science not only did not but also could not exist earlier than the events Hegel believes to be occurring in his own time, it is radically different from other modes of knowing. The knowledge of nature and the social and religious knowledge of Spirit are present wherever human experience occurs. Science does not have this generic character. It is a specific type of experience which occurs only when its temporal conditions have been met. This does not imply that philosophy is not to be found earlier in human history. The implication is rather that philosophy, so long as it has not achieved its professed goal of becoming Science, is only a highly reflective form of natural consciousness, the love of wisdom rather than its possession. As such it needs to be superseded just as much as the scientific and religious forms of natural consciousness. Philosophy is a task word, Science an achievement word.[21]

The second point about Absolute Knowledge and time is the problematic assertion that Science means an end to time. "Time is the concept itself so far as it is there and represents itself as empty intuition to consciousness. Therefore Spirit necessarily appears in time, and it appears in time so long as it does not grasp its pure concept, i.e., does not annul time [*nicht die Zeit tilgt*] . . . When this concept grasps itself, it supersedes its temporal form [*hebt er seine Zeitform auf*] . . . Time therefore appears as the fate and necessity of Spirit where Spirit is not yet complete within itself."[22]

Here the temptation is all but irresistible to think that whatever has gone on previously in the text, Hegel has finally and abruptly introduced a transtemporal, super-human Absolute, since such a being seems the only appropriate subject for this timeless knowledge. St. Thomas' God, whose eternity is "the simultaneously whole and perfect possession of interminable life," or Royce's Absolute, whose life is "present as a whole, *totum simul*," seem the only possible models.[23] It was only by finding an alternative to the theistic-Platonic model of transcendence that Absolute Knowledge as the synthesis of Conscience and Revealed Religion was possible. Now it is just that view of transcendence which seems to be the inescapable meaning attributed to that synthesis. A radical and inexplicable hiatus appears between the goal and the pathway to it. Worse yet, this conclusion would confirm the finitist view of human knowledge. The presence of a super-temporal absolute knower forms a standard of comparison by which any human knowledge, individual or collective, must be judged finite and imperfect. St. Thomas and Royce agree with Kant in making just this point.

These awkward results can be avoided only if the statements about time's annulment are taken in conjunction with the assertion that Science is an emergent reality. An emergent eternity is an odd bird, to be sure, and merely so to describe it, as we must, is to separate it irrevocably from the two models just mentioned. On the classically theistic model, eternity is thought of as "greater than" time, while on the Roycean type view it is coextensive with time. Neither view permits an emergent eternity, one with temporal prerequisites. When Hyppolite asks—"How is an Absolute Knowledge, in itself atemporal, able to have temporal conditions in the existence and becoming of humanity?"—he unwittingly calls pointed attention to the fact that we are not here dealing with atemporal knowledge in any usual sense.[24]

What then is the meaning of time's annulment which is congruent with the parallel doctrine of eternity's emergence? The answer requires our taking note of the fact that Hegel's chief concern with time is not with either duration or succession as such but with the externality of temporal relations. This is particularly clear and close at hand in the critique of *Vorstellungen* in religious knowledge. In this form the unity of human and divine is conceived as a temporal event. In this sense reconciliation is viewed as a past or future event, in either case remote from all except the few contemporaries. Nostalgia and hope thus play a primary and, on Hegel's analysis, a detrimental role in religious consciousness.

Now if the primary significance of time is separation and externality, its abolition would be identical with the reconciliation with which Hegel's narrative culminates. That the divine is fully present to human experience and not a past memory or future hope does not entail anything negative about the durative and successive aspects of time in other respects. Breakfast still comes before lunch. To speak of time's abolition is simply to refer to the socio-religious event in which man is freed from a world in which his ultimate values and joys are always beyond his reach, whether in some past paradise or in some future utopia, and enters the heavenly world (worldly heaven) in which he is fully at home and fully satisfied. Heaven and eternity maintain their intimate connection on this view, but their significance has little or nothing to do with the durative and successive aspects of ordinary experience, and nothing at all to do with the super-mundane. As in the New Testament they serve as metaphors on the boundary between this age and the age to come.[25]

The obvious advantage of this interpretation is that it gives us a harmonious Chapter Eight and a harmonious *Phenomenology*. It gives the former by taking Hegel's two statements about the relation of Absolute Knowledge to time with equal seriousness. It gives the latter by retaining the humanistic interpretation of Spirit which the text has required up to this point.

While these harmonies are good reasons for accepting such an interpretation, there is a further important consideration. The use of language attributed to Hegel by this interpretation of his comments about time and (by implication) eternity is consistent with his regular demythologizing of other Christian categories.[26] The *Phenomenology* provides ample evidence for Kaufmann's judgment that "when Hegel avails himself of Christian categories, he never implies acceptance of Christian faith in the supernatural, in miracles, or in the incarnation and resurrection; he merely finds the Christian myths more suggestive and more appropriate anticipations of his philosophy than the myths of other religions."[27] Hegel may not be quite that cynical, but he surely is a master at the techniques of persuasive (re)definition. Nowhere is this clearer than in the *Phenomenology*, where the Holy Spirit turns out to be the church and the incarnation means that man generically is divine.

Perhaps it would be fair to compare Hegel's talk about the annulment of time and the emergence of eternity with the Marxian distinction between pre-history and history. In both cases the distinction is between an epoch of human history in which man's existence falls fundamentally short of its ideal and an epoch in which that ideal is concretely realized. At the point of transition Marx says history begins, while Hegel says it ends. Since this difference is purely semantic it is again ironical that Marx should have directed one of his sharpest attacks on Hegel against just this final chapter of the *Phenomenology*.[28]

He praises Hegel's critical analysis of religion, the state, and civil society, but finds the potentially negative dialectic swallowed up in an uncritical positivism at the end. The "philosophical dissolution" is followed by "the restoration of the existing empirical world." This is because Hegel overlooks the concrete human subject, the natural, embodied, sentient, living, drive-oriented, suffering self, and concerns himself only with the abstract subject, defined as self-consciousness. We get a sense of Hegel's perspective when we suppose a being which neither is an object nor has one. In spite of the fact that Hegel

introduces Self-Consciousness into the *Phenomenology* in terms
of animal desire and human intersubjectivity, Marx identifies
self-consciousness with man as thinker, as exclusively knowing
subject. So he finds Hegel to end up as a Stoic after all, retreat-
ing from the real world and its real problems to the inner world
of thought and its more easily soluble problems. Man's true
political existence and the true existence of the state turn out to
be the philosophy of the state, just as his true religious existence
and the true existence of religion turn out to be the philosophy
of religion. Philosophy as such is the overcoming of alienation.
Following Marx on this point Hyppolite describes philosophy as
the "prescription" which Hegel offers to alienated, unhappy
consciousness.[29]

What Marx has failed to notice is the emergent character of
Hegel's eternity. Hegel's clear position is that Science enters the
world only when certain historical conditions have been met,
conditions which are not events in the history of philosophy but
concrete social and religious transformations. Marx insists that
the true overcoming of alienation is only to be found in the
theoretical and practical humanism which he sets forth as
atheism and communism. He fails to notice that what Hegel sets
forth in Chapters Seven and Six respectively as the precondi-
tions for Science could easily be described as atheism and communism. For Absolute Knowledge is only the self-conscious ar-
ticulation of those historical events which involve the death of
God as traditionally conceived and the overcoming of the state.
Hegel's "atheism" is a rejection of theism which does not entail
that nothing should be thought of as divine, and his "communism" involves the abolition of the state and social classes,
but not that of private property. In both cases there are
genuine differences from Marx, but it is not these to which
Marx's critique directs our attention.[30]

One reason Marx does not see the emergent character of
Hegel's eternity, which could also be called the ideological
character of Absolute Knowledge,[31] is that he fails to notice
Hegel's consistent and careful preparation for his conclusion.
He says that Hegel does not see the alienation of self-
consciousness as "the expression, reflected in knowledge and
thought, of the real alienation of human life." In saying this he
overlooks Hegel's explicit treatment of Stoicism, Scepticism,

and Unhappy Consciousness as ideologies in just this sense, expressions in thought of the predominance of master-slave relations in daily life. He similarly overlooks the equally explicit treatment of both Faith and Enlightened Insight as similar expressions of the political and economic alienation of Culture. Consistent with this perspective Hegel could not hope to find Absolute Knowledge elsewhere than as the "ideology" of that human society which has concretely overcome the alienations which previously motivated the historical process, whether it be called the Kingdom of God or the classless society. We have seen, as Marx did not, that this is just what he does. The Stoicism which Marx attributes to Absolute Knowledge is a figment of his own careless reading. It is hard to agree with Hyppolite that "Marx is one of the best commentators upon Hegel."[32]

8C. The Phenomenology and the System

While Hegel does not offer his treatise to the world as a cure for its ills, he does present it as Science.[33] It was originally published with a title page that read, in part: "*System der Wissenschaft . . . Erster Theil, die Phänomenologie des Geistes.*" Towards the end of the Introduction he explains how the pathway to Science is itself Science. In so far as we see the necessity of the transformations which natural consciousness undergoes and which Hegel calls experience, the *Phenomenology* can be called the Science of the Experience of Consciousness. Presumably what is to follow will be Science in some other sense. Now, with the Science of the Experience of Consciousness concluded, Hegel is able to say something more about what it is we have been introduced to in the process. His account of Absolute Knowledge therefore not only seeks to synthesize the developments of Chapters Six and Seven; it also looks ahead to the System. Briefly put, the *Phenomenology* is a discovery; the System its development. Whereas the Phenomenology is our Virgil to lead us to the Kingdom of Truth, the System is our Beatrice to show us the splendors of that kingdom.

What has emerged in Absolute Knowledge is not just a new theory of knowledge but a whole new view of reality, a new ontology. This cannot be without its ramifications in every field of

knowledge. It is the task of Science to develop these by reinter-
preting first the forms of thought and then the contents of experience in the light of the new ontology.

The first of these tasks is what Hegel understands by
Logic. He writes, "In [Absolute] Knowledge then, Spirit has
concluded the development of its forms, so far as they are burdened with the now overcome distinction [of subject and object]
involved in consciousness. Spirit has won the pure element of
its existence, the concept . . . In that Spirit has thus won the
concept, it develops both existence and process in this ether of
its life and is Science. The moments of its movement no longer
present themselves in it as determinate forms of consciousness,
but . . . as determinate concepts, and as the organic, self-
grounded movements of these concepts. While in the
Phenomenology of Spirit each moment involves the distinction between knowledge and truth . . . Science does not contain this
distinction and its supercession. Rather, since each moment has
the form of concept, it unites the objective form of truth and
the form of the knowing self in immediate unity."[34]

Such a Logic will be a theory of categories rather than a
theory of inference. But unlike the Kantian doctrine of the
categories it will not be premissed on the inadequacy of knowledge to its object. Quite the contrary. Hegel's ontologically
grounded Logic will presuppose the unity of thought and being
developed in the *Phenomenology*. The only question will be the
adequacy of thought to its own demands. In this sense the Logic
requires the *Phenomenology,* not for the detailed development of
its categories, but for a proper understanding of their status.

Hegel's use of the term 'Absolute Knowledge' for both en-
terprises is not due to ambivalence, as if there were two separate projects with the same name. The two are parts of a whole
which is Science. Neither by itself is Science as such, but both, as
organic parts, are properly called Absolute Knowledge or Science. Since the ontological discovery and its conceptual development are strictly interdependent, both participate in the
character of the whole.

But even the two together do not exhaust the nature of
Science. For the new ontological standpoint must be brought to
bear not only on the forms of thought but also on the contents
of experience. Hegel no sooner refers to the future Logic than

he remarks that its subject matter is abstract and is only fully grasped in relation to its limit. So as not to suggest an external relation between abstract form and concrete content as its limit, Hegel uses the language of alienation. The content of nature and Spirit as they reveal themselves to our experience is simply the external and outward form of the same inner truth comprehended as Logic. Put a slightly different way, thought is the inner life of Spirit, nature and history its outer life. Now that Spirit is fully manifest there is no longer a gulf between the two. So Hegel writes, "Science contains within itself this necessity to alienate itself from the form of the pure concept . . . Knowledge knows not only itself but also the negative of itself, its limit. To know its limit means to know how to sacrifice itself. This sacrifice is the alienation, in which Spirit presents its process of becoming Spirit in the form of free, contingent, happenings, intuiting its pure self as time outside itself and similarly its being as space." To speak of Spirit's being as space is to speak of nature, "Spirit's living, immediate becoming," while to speak of Spirit's self as time is to speak of history, its "knowing, self-mediating becoming."[35] According to this account one would expect the third part of the *Encyclopedia* to be a philosophy of history rather than the synchronic philosophy of Spirit it is, but the basic threefold structure of the System is plainly present.

These remarks about history and alienation lead Hegel to his final comment on the Scientific character of the *Phenomenology* itself. History has come to be seen as the self-alienation or externalization of Spirit in which it presents the whole wealth of its substance to public view. It reveals itself, but only in so far as Spirit learns to recognize itself in its outward manifestations. "Since Spirit's perfection consists in perfectly knowing what it is, its substance, this knowing is its turning inward [*Insichgehen*], in which it leaves its existence behind and gives its embodiment over to recollection."[36] The whole theory of Absolute Knowledge as Spirit's self-consciousness is summed up in this process of alienation [*Ent-äusserung*] and recollection [*Er-innerung*].

One may wish to call this Platonism, but it is evidently a very new kind of Platonism, for Absolute Knowledge consists in recollecting not the timeless but above all the historical.[37] "The path to the goal of Absolute Knowledge, or Spirit knowing itself

as Spirit, is the recollection of the Spirits . . . Their preservation, as free existence appearing in the form of contingency, is
history; but as comprehended [*begriffen*] organization it is the
Science of phenomenal knowledge. Both together, history
comprehended, form the recollection and the Golgotha of absolute Spirit, the actuality, truth, and certainty of its throne,
without which it would be something lifeless and lonely; only

> from the cup of this realm of spirits
> foams to him his infinity."[38]

To all of which Marcuse responds, "History, however, when
comprehended, shatters the idealistic framework."[39] History's
unkind treatment of Hegel's hopes has been stressed in the earlier sections of this chapter, and there is no need to rub salt into
the wound by further accounts of how his did not turn out to be
the definitive and ultimate epoch of human history. But it is not
so clear that the problem is properly diagnosed as idealism.
Over against the "materialist" view that history is primarily to
be understood in terms of economics and alienated labor,
Hegel's "idealistic" view sees master-slave domination in the
economic domain less as the basic reality than as the expression
of a deeper non-economic urge to dominate rooted in the need
for recognition. Hence the priority of love over labor in his historical dialectic. While it takes little comprehension of history to
see that the problematic of recognition or love was not resolved
even in principle by the revolutionary developments of Hegel's
time, it is harder to say that history has given a clear verdict between the "idealist" and "materialist" diagnoses of the problem.

Would it be fair to say, then, that the only major demonstra-
ble defect of Hegel's argument is its imperfect midwifery, its
radical overvaluing of the new births his age brought forth? I
believe not. It is not only that the actuality of reciprocal recognition is missing from Hegel's world; its possibility is missing from
his argument. As we have seen earlier, the original demand for
recognition is unmet because each individual is too concerned
with winning recognition to be able to give it. There is no love,
only the demand to be loved. Hegel does not present this as an
accidental situation of a few egocentric individuals but as the
universal and primordial relation of man to his fellow men.
Like Plato before him and Sartre after him he portrays human
existence as erotic. It is an emptiness needing to draw from a

fullness outside itself the resources it needs to be itself. Until it receives recognition it is too poor to give it.

Against the background of this analysis in Chapter Four the announcement in Chapter Six that reciprocal recognition has been achieved is sudden indeed. No account of how the vicious circle created by the demand to be loved may be escaped is given. No source of overflowing fullness which breaks into the circle is designated. Suddenly, like magic, individuals who have given themselves up to domination (if they are strong) or submission (if they are weak) and who have objectified these patterns in the form of social institutions cease to be what they have been. They become loving, accepting, tolerant, forgiving individuals, the founders of an entirely different type of human society.

If it had actually happened we might have been too happy to ask for an explanation. But since it didn't, the theoretical inadequacy of Hegel's analysis can scarcely be overlooked.[40] He has given us an Augustinian interpretation of history, joined to a Pelagian theory of its culmination. The latter is an unbelievable *Deus ex machina* just to the degree that the former is taken seriously. That is why the "idealism" of the *Phenomenology* has tended to become one or the other of two conflicting modes of existentialism. Sartrean existentialism takes the erotic structure of human intersubjectivity to be unsurpassable. It says of man, whose love is the demand to be loved and whose deepest project is to become his own foundation, no longer needing to be loved, that he is a useless passion. Kierkegaardian existentialism finds in the very God whom both Marxian materialism and Hegelian idealism took to be a major obstacle to human fulfillment that source of overflowing fulness which overcomes man's erotic emptiness and makes it possible for him to love.

Neither alternative would have much appeal for Hegel. He wanted to avoid this sort of either/or. But history seems to have disappointed his hopes in this respect as well.

NOTES

1. PhG, 742/549/789. cf. Ch. 7, n. 43 and n. 46.

2. Again in Chapter Eight the contrast between *Vorstellung* and *Begriff* is regularly assimilated to that between consciousness and self-consciousness.

3. This view is particularly strong in the second edition. cf. Ch. 1, n. 25.

4. PhG, 742-43/549/789-90.

5. This follows Hegel's 1805-06 analysis of language and labor as essential moments in Spirit's transcendence of animal nature. See *Realphilosophie*, II, 179-99.

6. See Ch. 7, n. 14.

7. *Der junge Hegel*, Zürich, 1948, pp. 684-86.

8. Marx's critique is found in *Die Frühschriften*, ed. Landshut, Stuttgart, 1968, pp. 270 f. English translation in *Karl Marx: Early Writings*, trans. Bottomore, New York, 1964, pp. 195-219. The critique of Absolute Knowledge is somewhat scattered in the Landshut volume, since he follows the original order of the manuscripts as given by Marx's own pagination.

9. *op. cit.*, p. 686.

10. PhG, 763-64/563/807.

11. *op. cit.*, p. 687.

12. PhG, 747-48/552-53/793-94.

13. PhG, 749-50/554/795.

14. See Ch. 7, n. 23.

15. PhG, 753/556/797-98. It is interesting to compare this passage with the one cited in note 13 above. Here he speaks of Spirit realizing its concept, there of the concept realizing itself. These seem to be interchangeable ways of describing the same process.

16. PhG, 753-54/556/798. cf. note 12 above where Hegel speaks of the "immediately universal" self.

17. See note 13 above.

18. *Introduction a la Lecture de Hegel*, Paris, 1947, p. 267. This passage is included in the English translation of selected portions, *Introduction to the Reading of Hegel*, ed. Bloom, trans. Nichols, New York, 1969, p. 73.

19. *Die Frühschriften*, p. 252. Bottomore, pp. 198-99.

20. PhG, 754/557/798-99.

21. See the Preface, PhG, VI-VII/12/70-71. For the distinction between task and achievement words see Gilbert Ryle, *The Concept of Mind*.

22. PhG, 756/558/800.

23. St. Thomas Aquinas, *Summa Theologiae,* I, Q. 10, Art. 1. Josiah Royce, *The World and the Individual,* New York, 1959, I. 341.

24. *Genèse et Structure de la Phénoménologie de l'Esprit de Hegel,* Paris, 1946, p. 575.

25. Oscar Cullmann has called attention to this characteristic of the New Testament in *Christ and Time.*

26. The implied comparison with Bultmann is fitting. He recognizes that the thrust of his work is to transform theology into anthropology, for "I am interpreting theological affirmations as assertions about human life." *Kerygma and Myth,* trans. and ed. Bartsch, New York, 1961, pp. 107-08. In this context Bultmann draws the parallel between Feuerbach and himself.

27. *Hegel: Reinterpretation, Texts, and Commentary,* Garden City, 1965, p. 274.

28. Here and in the following paragraphs reference is again made to the Marxian critique as designated in note 8 above.

29. *Studies on Marx and Hegel,* trans. O'Neill, New York, 1969, pp. 82 and 84.

30. When Marx says of communism that "it is the solution of the riddle of history and knows itself to be this solution," the Hegelian structure of his idea is manifest. *Die Frühschriften,* p. 235. Bottomore, p. 155.

31. Absolute Knowledge can be called ideological in the sense of being derivative, but not in the sense of being false consciousness.

32. *op. cit.,* p. 70.

33. Hegel's fullest discussion of what he means by Science comes in the Preface, which should be read in conjunction with Chapter Eight.

34. PhG, 761-62/561-62/804-05.

35. PhG, 763-64/563/806-07.

36. PhG, 764/563/807. cf. XXXIII-XXXIX/26-30/89-94.

37. At the end of Chapter Seven above Hegel's Kingdom is compared with Plato's Republic. Though there are no philosopher kings in the former, both societies are rooted in philosophical recollection.

38. PhG 765/564/808. On phenomenal knowledge see the paragraph in Chapter One following note 28.

39. *Reason and Revolution: Hegel and the Rise of Social Theory,* Boston, 1960, p. 16.

40. Here as earlier the disappointment of Hegel's expectations has no direct bearing on the *interpretation* of his text. But in this case it helps us to notice a difficulty which might otherwise have been overlooked.

INDEX

232

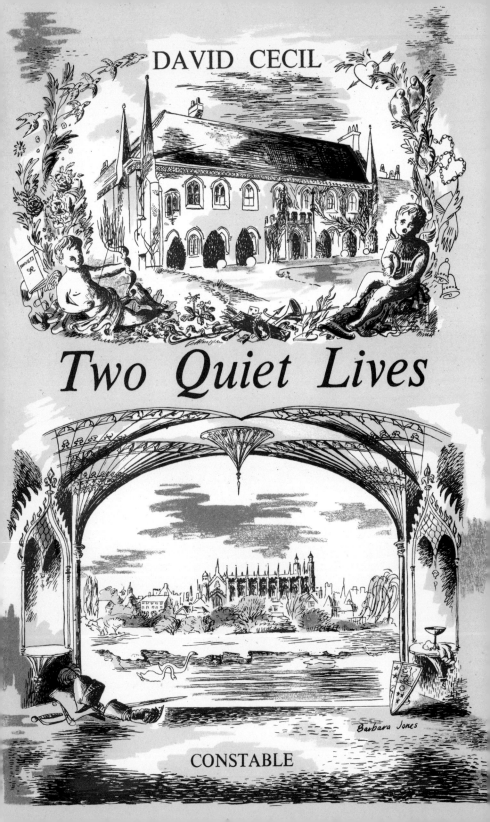

DAVID CECIL

Two Quiet Lives

Barbara Jones

CONSTABLE

To
The Lady Desborough
"La Reine des Reines"

LONDON
PUBLISHED BY
Constable and Company Ltd.
10–12 ORANGE STREET, W.C.2

·

INDIA
Longmans, Green and Company Ltd.
BOMBAY CALCUTTA MADRAS

·

CANADA
Longmans, Green and Company Ltd.
TORONTO

First published . . . 1948

PRINTED IN GREAT BRITAIN BY THE CHISWICK PRESS
NEW SOUTHGATE, LONDON, N.11

TWO QUIET LIVES

Dorothy Osborne
Thomas Gray

PREFATORY NOTE

THESE studies are not a work of research. All the information in them is already in print. But the two characters, who are their subject, seem to me curious and complex enough to deserve a closer analysis and a more extended interpretation than they have up to now received. Further, they illustrate with unusual clearness a peculiar and interesting variety of the human temperament. For, widely as their characters differed in many important respects, temperamentally they were akin. Both were shy, anxious, pensive personalities, with a rich inner life and few but intense affections, who, inspired by an ineradicable distrust of the world, strove, with varying success, to retire from it to a life exclusively personal, private, contemplative. The character that such a life assumed for each of them was not quite the same; for it was modified by the fact that they lived in different ages and different societies. In fact, it is not possible to understand Gray or Dorothy without having first learnt to understand the worlds in which their lives were set. My book, then, aspires to be at once an account of two remarkable persons, a study of a certain phase of human nature and, finally, a picture of private life as lived in two contrasting periods.

My thanks are due to the Viscountess Mountbatten, to the Lord Walpole and to the Trustees of the National Portrait Gallery and of the Fitzwilliam Museum, Cambridge, for their great kindness in allowing me to reproduce portraits in their possession.

DAVID CECIL

vii

CONTENTS

A*   ix

ILLUSTRATIONS

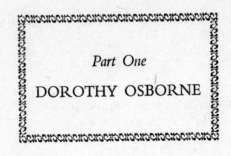

Part One

DOROTHY OSBORNE

"When I am gone, dreame me some happinesse
Nor let thy looks our long hid love confesse."

JOHN DONNE

DOROTHY OSBORNE

ANTHEA, Lucasta, Castara, Sacharissa—the lady loves of the cavalier poets certainly have romantic names: and they look romantic too, gazing down at us in pearly satin and pensive grace from the canvases of Lely and Vandyck. But were they in reality romantic persons? Ah! that is hard to say: indeed it is hard to imagine them as human beings at all. The art that has made them celebrated has also concealed their humanity. After all, they cannot always have worn satin. Nor in fact were they known to their friends by these fanciful names. They were called Margaret or Mary, or Jane. But of Margaret and Mary and Jane, of these ladies in their everyday flesh and blood reality, we know little. We have no idea how they would have struck us, if we had found ourselves next to them at the dinner table. Always a curtain of splendid ceremony hangs between them and us; their voices are always drowned by a concert of elaborate lyrical music. Always—but for one exception: in the letters of Dorothy Osborne, the music is hushed, the curtain drawn aside. We hear Anthea's voice in ordinary conversation, we get a glimpse of Lucasta's real face.

It is only a glimpse. The correspondence covers no more than a few months of its author's life. Moreover, it is a narrow glimpse. Since Dorothy's letters are the only full record we have of her circle, she is the only figure in it that is steadily illuminated. Its other members remain shadowy and indistinct, save when they emerge for a moment into the clear candlelight of her vision. But her own personality is revealed

3

in intimate detail, and during the course of the supreme crisis of her life. So that the correspondence does not give us a feeling of incompleteness. By a freak of fortune this slender chance-kept bundle of letters has composed itself into a brief drama that has the unity and concentration and harmony of a conscious work of art.

Its setting is the world of aristocratic country life during the first years of the Commonwealth. In some ways English high life does not seem to have altered much since then. Here we are in a country house. The gentlemen, just in from hunting, are starting to argue about politics; the ladies, bent over their needlework, gossip about the shocking conduct of Lady Mary Sandys in appearing publicly with her lover Colonel Paunton at Winchester Races. On the other hand we notice with surprise that they take it as quite natural that the gentlemen of their acquaintance should have been fighting a duel, and that they have all, so they say, been drinking beer at breakfast. Their dresses are not very clean; when a visitor comes in they sink to the ground in a magnificent curtsy; while in the corner of the room, a girl is writing to her lover in words of accomplished poetical eloquence. All this is not very like the high life we know.

Indeed, this society presents such a bewildering blend of the familiar and the unexpected that it is hard at first to get one's bearings in it. Its conditions of living were primitive and home-made. People remained for years together buried in the country, subsisting on food grown on their own land, and dwelling in houses built by their own workmen. Countesses superintended jam-making and counted the holes in their husbands stockings; if the house was full of visitors, the hostess thought nothing of packing three ladies of title into one bed; the arrival of a new book was a rare event, only one uncertain post came and went in the week. People, most of them, were of a piece with the way they lived, normal, ingenuous, un-

4

inhibited, their interests revolving round the elemental facts of birth and death and marriage. Their feelings were ardent and unsophisticated, their speculations full of wonder and ignorance. Even sceptical Sir Thomas Browne believed in witches. Educated people would recommend each other to take powdered mummy by moonlight as the cure for an ailment. Nobody was afraid of uttering a platitude. "Youth is the time for love", they told one another, "death comes equally to all". Indeed, death did loom insistently before them. Medical science was as primitive as household management; and, though couples often had thirteen children, it was seldom that more than a few of them lived to grow up. Their parents lamented their loss with biblical extravagance, but took it very much as a matter of course. For their life was too close to the earth for them to be unrealistic about it. The cavalier gentry accepted the plain facts of existence without questioning. Money for instance, and all the solid security that money implied, mattered to them a great deal. They never married without it; they generally married to get it. And, though they felt the family bond very strongly, the closest relations would squabble for years about the terms of a dowry or an inheritance.

Yet they were not materialists. Their outlook was made spiritual by the sublime background of religious belief, against which they envisaged it. Man was an immortal soul; and his sojourn on this planet was but the brief prelude to an eternity of earthly bliss, or torment, to which he was destined according as to how far he had attained to true virtue. Their idea of virtue, too, was exalted and spacious, appreciative of every nicety of conscience, every impulse of magnanimity. Their hearts glowed for honour, for chivalry, for the excellent passion of friendship, the divine flame of love, the high mystery of virginity. With moral sensibility went sensibility of the imagination. They delighted in beauty. Did they not adorn themselves with velvet and lace and lovelocks perfumed

5

with orange flower? Their walls were rich with carving and pictures; they wrote verses and sang them to the lute; they planted gardens to refresh the troubled spirit; their religion expressed itself in the jewelled and courtly mode of George Herbert. This idealism and this artistic sense combined to incarnate themselves in their way of living. Life they felt should have a noble and rhetorical form. Manners were ceremonious. The lover fell on his knees; the mourner draped his room with black cloth; boys and girls alike were taught to move with courtly dignity. Conduct too was regulated by a strict code of convention. Everybody had their place in the hierarchy of society and was expected to behave in a manner befitting it. Children must not marry without their parents' consent, women must obey their husbands; a duke was a duke, a commoner was a commoner, and must conduct themselves as such. Nor did people resent these rules as imposing a check on their lawful freedom. For they did not believe in convention—as later ages did—because they thought it helped life to function smoothly. Their faith was sacramental; convention was the outward and visible sign of their inward and spiritual sense of values. A man owed it to himself as much as to society to keep to it. Openly to flout convention, to imperil public reputation, was to him almost as heinous a crime as it is to the Japanese; it was an offence against his personal ideal of what he ought to be.

This mixture of primitive simplicity and formalized behaviour made their life lacking in variety. Surely it must have been monotonous to live in a world where so much was taken for granted, and where there were so few things to think about. On the other hand their existence was far more integrated than ours. They felt no awkward dissonance between the ideal and the real, the poetic and the prosaic. They did not distinguish between a man's public and his private personality. Accepting equally the earthly and the spiritual, their vision

6

embraced all experience in one harmony. They wrote a lyric, and called on the name of God, and went to law about a will with the same unembarrassed wholeheartedness. Further, the fact that they were undisturbed by complex and heterogeneous issues enabled them to cultivate to the finest perfection those qualities they did value. Their poetry had a narrow range of theme, but it was the poetry of Lovelace and Vaughan; their music, confined within a few rigid forms, was yet the subtle polyphony of Orlando Gibbons. Naïve intellectually, they achieved an exquisite civilization of the heart. The naïveté enhanced the exquisiteness. It was their child-like lack of self-consciousness that allowed them to pray and converse and make love with so richly decorated a beauty. And they had the peculiar charm which comes from a refinement so natural as to be unaware of itself. How it speaks from the portraits of the age with their shy distinction, their silvery candour of glance! More profoundly aristocratic than their descendants of the eighteenth century, their good breeding seemed so fundamental as to be a quality of the soul. Yet there was always something homely and countrified about them. Through the mullioned casement open to the air, a whiff of cowslip breathes in to linger freshly amid the tapestry and the panelling.

This society reached its most delicate flowering in the early years of Charles I's reign. The blaze of the Elizabethan noonday had faded to a cooler gleam. Some of the old magnificent exuberance was gone; but its loss was balanced by an increased fastidiousness of sensibility. Instead of Marlowe there was Marvell; instead of the flamboyance of the Jacobean mansion, the classic grace of Inigo Jones; and among the more sensitive spirits of the time, we can discern, beneath their ceremoniousness of demeanour, hints of a new feeling for the pleasures of intimacy, of retirement, of introspection. Alas, it was not to be satisfied. The crash of violent political conflict broke in

7

upon their world. The victory of the Parliamentary forces undermined that aristocratic supremacy which was necessary for the security of their existence. Sons and brothers fell in battle; fortunes were lost or confiscated; the country houses, in which their ideal of private life found its shrine, were sequestrated from their owners. Even if a man managed to shelter himself from the full shock of the storm, its rumour reverberated always in the distance, its shadow brooded darkly over the landscape. An uneasy sadness pervaded the spirit.

II

The Osborne family felt it. The war had found them in a position which, if not splendid, was solidly prosperous and dignified. Peter Osborne, head of an old-established Bedfordshire family had, like his father and grandfather before him, devoted his life to the public service; with such effect that at the age of fifty-eight he was a Knight, Governor of the Island of Guernsey, the husband of a Baronet's daughter, and the possessor of an income of £4,000 a year. Three of his children, it is true, had died; but since five survived, their loss did not, by the standards of the day, constitute much of a blot on his good fortune. Nor did the variety of his activities interfere with the amenity of his existence. Serving the State then was a much more easy-going affair than it is now; and, after doing his work in Guernsey and London, Sir Peter still had plenty of time left to spend at his family home of Chicksands, near Bedford.

But the moment the war broke out, his luck began to turn. A fine old cavalier gentleman, all sturdy loyalty and high-spirited honour, he did not hesitate which side to take. No more Chicksands for him, for the time being; he was off to Guernsey, prepared to hold it for his King till the last breath was out of his body. He very nearly had to. Guernsey rose in support of the Parliament; and the King's garrison was driven into the rocky citadel of Castle Cornet, where they remained in a state of siege for the rest of the war. The long lonely defence of this outpost of the Crown was a heroic exploit. It was also a thankless one. For Sir Peter, like so many supporters of the Stuart family, got worse than no help from his own side. Colonel Carteret, Governor of Jersey, intrigued incessantly against him; while Charles I's failure to send assistance of any kind, in spite of piteous demands for it, was made particularly irritating by his characteristic habit of writing frequently to say he was sending some at once. Sir Peter did his best to get supplies locally, only to have them confiscated on the way for his own use by Colonel Carteret. However Sir Peter's spirit was not quelled. He pawned his own clothes to get other provisions; and though the leader of the Parliamentary forces often proposed generous terms of surrender, he repudiated his offers in terms of resounding defiance. "God, I hope" he proclaimed, "whose great name I have sworn by, will never so much forsake me, but that I shall keep that resolution—by yourself misnamed obstinacy—to maintain unto my Sovereign that faith inviolate to the last."

Inspired by his fortitude, for four years in the wild sea-girt fortress, exposed alike to the onslaught of their enemies and the gales and breaking seas of the channel, the little garrison hung on, though they were forced to break up the doors for firewood and their bread ration was sometimes reduced to four biscuits a week. And then, after all, Colonel Carteret's intrigues succeeded. Sir Peter got word giving him gracefully to understand that the King would be glad if he resigned. "I pray you" he replied with courteous bitterness "to grant my direct going to St. Malo, where I may for a while quietly recollect myself and recover some patience for what I suffer and foresee I am still like to do."

9

The news from home was not such as to revive his spirits. His third surviving son had been killed early in the war; he had spent a large part of his fortune in the defence of Castle Cornet; his house was taken over by the Parliament and his family turned homeless into the world. Poor Lady Osborne had toiled with her children over to St. Malo, the nearest she could get to Guernsey, where she had thrown herself manfully into the task of selling the family plate to get supplies for Sir Peter, and writing letters to influential persons in England complaining about Colonel Carteret. Her health, however, had given way under the strain, and after a year or two she had returned to her own country, where she eked out a dreary life trailing about from relation to relation and often compelled to seek refuge in the uncomfortable atmosphere of a Roundhead brother's house in Chelsea. By the time Sir Peter was ejected from Guernsey, it was not safe for him to go back to an England now mainly under Parliamentary control. He remained at St. Malo for three years in extreme poverty, gloomily watching from across the Channel the final defeat of his party. The execution of Charles I brought his situation to a crisis; he learnt that if he did not make terms with his enemies, Chicksands would be confiscated for ever. Very reluctantly he sat down and wrote a dignified letter to Charles II, explaining that, in spite of the fact that his loyalty was still unshaken, he saw no way but to submit. He paid a large portion of the remains of his fortune in return for the right to live retired in his country home, and sailed for England. As a crowning misfortune, his wife died within a year of his returning. By 1652, however, all this was a thing of the past. The clash of battle had died away, and the life of the Osborne family was settled into a muted melancholy. Sir Peter was still alive; but he was now a very old man, his health and spirits alike broken by all he had gone through, his friends exiled and impoverished, and himself reduced to an income of £400 a year,

lingering out his last days down at Chicksands in an England, over which Cromwell and his Major Generals seemed to have established a permanent dictatorship. Now and again a relation came to visit him; but most of the time he lived alone there with his youngest child, the twenty-two year old Dorothy.

Chicksands was a fitting setting for such an existence. The grey rambling low-storied old house, with its mediaeval stonework and dusky Jacobean parlours—it had been an ancient Gilbertine monastery, secularized and altered after the Reformation—lay near the gently sloping banks of a river, amid the sleepy rural green of the Bedfordshire landscape, like a fragment of the past survived by chance into a later age. Day followed day there in eventless monotony, heavy with the memories of vanished days. Young though she was, Dorothy did not repine in such an atmosphere. It chimed with her prevailing mood. From her pale, well-bred countenance, framed by the dark ringlets and pearl eardrops of a Caroline lady, her heavy-lidded eyes looked out at the world—as they look out at us from her portrait still—with an expression of profound unostentatious sadness. Her eyes could not have looked sadder, so her mother used to tell her, if every friend she had in the world had died. And her demeanour was in keeping with her appearance. Strangers often found her formidable. Her manner was so reticent and "stately". She sat generally silent and abstracted in company, laughed very seldom, however uproarious the mirth around her, welcomed the departure of a visitor with hardly-concealed relief. This aloof gravity, however, was a deceptive mask. Beneath it quivered the flame of an exquisite responsiveness to life. In Dorothy Osborne, the society, of which she was a child, put forth its last fine flower. To something of her father's gallant nobility of temper, she joined a delicate Herrick-like sensibility. How she delighted to roam solitary by stream and pasture: she would sit absorbed for hours in a romance or a book of verses: her piety found its true echo in the melodious flowered pages of Jeremy Taylor. Above all her heart was imaginative; appreciative of every shade of intimacy and affection, and identifying itself so sensitively with other people's feelings that it was almost impossible for her to resist an appeal from anyone she loved. Yet there was nothing extravagant about her. Her taste was chastened by a vigilant sense of the value of dignity and restraint. Nothing disgusted her more for instance than to see a married couple too demonstrative to one another in public. Nor was she sentimental. Romantic though her feelings might be, they were checked at every turn by the judgments of her commonsense and her humour. For she had humour. The sad eyes could observe the world with a sharp-eyed amusement, that in the company of a sympathetic spirit, quickened to the bewitching mischief of a Rosalind. Indeed there is a lot of Rosalind about her—or is it Viola? Women like that actually did exist in that golden age: Shakespeare is a less unrealistic author than one might be inclined at times to suppose. Moreover, Dorothy had the Shakespearian natural-ness. Though she hated to give pain, it was impossible for her to say what she did not think. Even her shrewdness and her distinction had a naïve untaught freshness about them. The soft glow of poetry which trembles round her every move-ment exhales from her personality involuntarily, as the scent from a rose.

Alas, it was not time for roses to bloom. They shivered, they wilted in the wintry hurricane that was sweeping Eng-land. So sensitive a nature as Dorothy's was especially sus-ceptible to the shock of the contemporary catastrophe; and it attacked her at her most impressionable age. The break-up of her old home, the long miserable, poverty-stricken months of suspense at St. Malo, made still darker by the news of her brother's death, came on her during those early years before

the spirit has had time to grow a shell of philosophy or indifference, with which to withstand the blows of harsh
experience. She lost all her youthful spirits. "I was thought"
she says "as well-humoured an young person as most in
England; nothing dispirited, nothing troubled me. When I
came out of France nobody knew me again; I was so altered.
From a cheerful humour that was always alike, never over
merry, but always pleased, I was grown heavy and sullen,
froward and discomposed: and that country which usually gives
people a jollyness and gaiety that is natural to the climate, had
wraught in me so contrary effects, that I was as new a thing to
them as my clothes." Subsequent events had not been of a
kind to cheer her; the dismal years spent as a homeless refugee
in other people's houses, in an atmosphere loud with rumour
of battle and execution, and with the foundations of the world,
in which she had been brought up, crumbling around her;
then the return to a Chicksands, shorn of its former glory,
her father's decline, her mother's death. Not indeed that Lady
Osborne, embittered by years of misfortune, had been a
companion likely to brighten her daughter's view of life. By
nature Dorothy hated to think ill of people; but Lady Osborne
used to say to her "I have lived to see that it is almost
impossible to believe people worse than they are; and so
will you". Reluctantly, Dorothy began to fear she might be
right.

In fact, however, she had too generous a spirit to become a
misanthrope. All the same, experience had left an indelible
mark on her. Her gaiety had never come back. The brave
Elizabethan music was transposed into a minor key; Rosalind,
driven from Arden into a region of grim reality, had lost for
ever her sunshiny high-heartedness. And her adventurousness:
more tenaciously even than most of her contemporaries,
Dorothy clung to the security of established rule. Conventions
were an anchor of stability in an unstable universe. Besides,

those who broke them were objects of contempt and pity.
Dorothy was obsessed by a nervous horror of being pitied: it
was another effect of her misfortunes to intensify her sensitiveness to a morbid degree. This was why strangers found her
manner so unforthcoming. The strain of her first encounter
with the rough world had made her shrink from its contact:
so that now she instinctively hid her true self behind the
shield of an aloof formality. Her charm, her wit, became a
secret treasure locked up in the cabinet of her reserve. But all
this was symptomatic of a deeper injury. Calamity had undermined her fundamental confidence in life. Nothing was safe
in the world she felt, man was not meant to be happy there.
If he let himself believe he could be, so much the more dreadful would be his disappointment. This feeling was reinforced
by the sterner elements in her creed. Did not Scripture teach
her that the glories of this world were a snare and a delusion?
Better then surely to withdraw from it; and, alone with her
books and the meadows, in the twilight shelter of her old
home, to dream away the days.

Dorothy might have resigned herself completely to such an
existence but for one thing. So ardent and tender a temperament as hers was made for love: and already she had found it.
In 1648 she and her youngest brother Robin, on their way to
pay a visit to their father at St. Malo, found themselves delayed for a night or two, along with some other travellers,
near Carisbrooke in the Isle of Wight, where Charles I was at
that time lying imprisoned under the harsh guardianship of
the Governor, Colonel Hammond. Robin Osborne's youthful cavalier blood boiled with indignation when he learned
how his Royal Master was being treated. And, when the
time came for them to continue their journey, he slipped away
to scrawl a parting insult on a window-pane of the Inn.
"Haman" it ran "was hanged on the gallows he had prepared
for Mordecai." This was soon discovered: before they had

gone far, messengers arrived to haul the impudent young
malignant back to receive punishment. But when the party
was led into the presence of Colonel Hammond, Dorothy
sprang forward and said that it was she who had done it. On
hearing this, Colonel Hammond allowed them to proceed.
In those days even conscientious revolutionaries could be
chivalrous. Still, it had been a brave act of Dorothy's: and it
made a deep impression on one of her fellow travellers, a
young man called Temple, who was journeying abroad in
order to finish his education on the Continent. Already he
had made her acquaintance: now, stirred by the romantic
light in which she had shewn herself, he hastened to improve
it. It cannot have been difficult for him. Lean and shapely,
with beautiful curling hair falling on his shoulders, and a vivid,
dark-eyed positive face agleam with intelligence, Temple's
appearance was extremely prepossessing. And he had only
to open his mouth to reveal himself as a fascinating talker,
bubbling over with wit and fancy and bold entertaining
opinions. Sea voyages are notoriously encouraging to intimacy. As the two young people sat talking on the deck of
the little sailing ship, watching the changing spectacle of wave
and cloud and fleeting glimpses of land, acquaintanceship
warmed into friendship, friendship into something more.
Love himself rose, like his mother, from the fresh sea foam,
and, on footfall so soft that she was scarcely aware of it, stole
into Dorothy's virgin heart. Temple's glowed with an
answering fire. They arrived at St. Malo deeply committed to
one another.

It was not to be wondered at. What man of taste could resist
Dorothy if she allowed her charm to disclose its full sweetness?
And Temple also, quite apart from his good looks, was exactly
the type to attract her. William Temple had been born in
1628, the son and heir of Sir John Temple, Master of the Irish
Rolls. In spite of the disturbances of the time, his education

had managed to follow the course thought suitable for a gentleman. At school, Temple learnt to be an accomplished classic; at Cambridge he explored the pleasures of social life and played a lot of tennis. This versatility was typical of him. His vivacious mind responded to almost every kind of stimulus. Politics interested him intensely; so did Science, History, the Arts, human nature in general. Interest stirred him to thought. Incessantly he questioned, reflected, drew conclusions. These were sometimes surprising. Temple had all the clever young man's pleasure in opinions likely to shock the conventional. Aristotle, in his view, had prostituted Philosophy; and Queen Elizabeth, or "Bess Tidder" as he preferred irreverently to call her, was a ridiculously over-rated monarch, not to be mentioned in the same breath as Boadicea! Indeed, young Temple was not a solid thinker. But he was an enlivening one, sparkling with whim and spirit and personal idiosyncracy. "I never saw any sight, heard any sound . . . but I could say I would rather have it continue or rather have it cease" he notes. This fact about himself interested him. Montaigne was one of his favourite authors; and he took a Montaigne-like pleasure in examining his own mental processes. Why should he feel such a repulsion to tobacco, he wondered, or to people with a stooping gait? Why should he take for granted that any one woman called Arabella was likely to be beautiful? Absorbed in such speculations, he would sit for hours oblivious of the outside world following his train of thought wherever it might lead him. "I know not what 'tis" he lamented ruefully, "that makes me so prone to the posture of musing . . . what the French call reverie, a crowd of restless capering antique fancies, bounding here and there, fixing nowhere, building in one half hour castles in Ireland, monasteries in France, palaces in Virginia, dancing at a wedding, weeping at a burial, enthroned like a king, enragged like a beggar, a lover, a friend, an indifferent person, and sometimes things of as little relation one with another as the Great Turk and a red-herring."

He was equally responsive to other kinds of pleasure—gambling, music, good wine, the charm of nature. "A fine day is a kind of sensual pleasure" he once said. Yet, there was nothing unbridled about his enjoyment. Always he was restrained by a natural moral fastidiousness, an innate temperance of taste. Indeed, though none of his talents were of the first order, he had the judgment and the sense of style to make the very most of them. Already, at twenty-one, he was a brilliant example of the Caroline ideal of a gentleman, in whom every element of the good life, moral, intellectual, and physical, were blended together in a cool harmony.

He had the weaknesses of his type though. Pride for instance: Temple could not endure taking orders from anyone, and so disliked being under an obligation that, if he was given a present, he was uneasy till he had sent back a better one. His sensitiveness too, could be altogether too much of a good thing. In later life he refused to spend even a night in London, he thought it smelt so disagreeable; damp weather produced in him a fit of nervous depression. He could not stand being kept waiting, loathed the sound of church bells, lost his temper in an argument, had no patience with a fool. When a young man told him that he thought Montaigne like St. Augustine—it certainly was a silly remark—Temple simply turned his back on him. Even with those he loved he could be extremely difficult; sometimes sunk in a black gloom in which he would scarcely speak, at other moments protesting violently that they did not respond to him with the ardour that such an affection as his deserved.

Indeed he had something of the egotism and all of the arrogance of the brilliant young man he was. In consequence, more commonplace people did not take to him. They thought his manners conceited, and suspected the mocking tone of his

17

conversation. Most likely he was at heart a rebel and an atheist. These last two accusations were unjustified. His aristocratic tastes and temperament combined to make Temple a steady supporter of Church and King. But it is true that he was in strong reaction against the fanatical partisanship which had animated the previous generation. He had seen too much of its unpleasant fruits at home. Sir John Temple— a less heroic spirit than Sir Peter Osborne—had striven to drive a middle course in the political and religious struggle; with the result that he had quarrelled first with the Court and then with Cromwell, who in 1648 had dismissed him from his offices. His son had grown up disgusted with extremism in any form, sceptical of any kind of enthusiasm, in favour of any policy which seemed likely to make things work smoothly and tranquilly, and with a premature realization of the stable concrete satisfactions of existence. "What do you wish for most in the world?" a friend once asked him. "Health, peace, and fair weather" replied the youthful Temple. Now and again, if his mind chanced on some scheme which he thought might solve a political problem, he felt an impulse to fling himself into the mêlée. But most of the time he yearned for a life of civilized retirement in which he could cultivate the pleasures of mind, and senses, and observe with smiling detachment the humours of mankind.

He had Dorothy with him here. He had Dorothy with him everywhere. It was not only that he must have been far more attractive and intelligent than the other young men she had met. At last amid the thronging hordes of a humanity immersed in practical business and political conflict, her eyes had met those of a kindred spirit; someone who set the same supreme value, as she did, on reading and the country and intimacy and contemplation. More important, he fortified her where she was weakest. For it was not in Temple to be pessimistic— at least not for long. He refused to believe that man was intended to be unhappy. If circumstances were untoward, circumstances could and must be altered. In the presence of his sanguine vitality, Dorothy felt her old lost confidence in living, stealing deliciously back. There is no affinity more perfect than that founded on similar tastes and complimentary temperaments. Even Temple's weaknesses appealed to her, his intolerance, his wilfulness. She recognized them as wrong, but she liked him all the better for being wrong in that sort of way. The very fact that Dorothy's feelings, naturally so ardent, had for so long been frustrated by her fear of life, made her yield herself all the more completely once her defences were broken down. Her heart was Temple's for ever, even if fate should decide they were never to be united.

By 1652 it looked sadly probable that this was fate's decision. It was a difficult time to get married in any circumstances, with the order of life uprooted and everyone scattered and impoverished. In wistful day-dream Dorothy pictured herself and Temple stealing away to some remote place, perhaps the little island of Herm which they had passed, lying serene and forgotten in the ocean, on their voyage out; there to dwell safe from the injuries of the world. "Do you remember Herm and the little house there?" she was to write to him later; "Shall we go thither? that is next to being out of the world: there we might live like Baucis and Philemon and grow old together, and for our charity to some shipwrackt stranger, obtain the blessing of both dying at the same time. How idly I talk! 'tis because the story please me, none in Ovid so much. I remember I cried when I read it. Methought they were the perfectest character of a contented marriage, where piety and love were all their world." It was not only the world that stood between Dorothy and a contented marriage. In those days marriage was looked on as a social arrangement, in which the approval of the family counted for far more than the inclinations of the parties. Both families were against this match. Why they were so strongly against it is a little obscure: as usual in those days, money seems to have been the trouble. The Osbornes thought that Dorothy would be throwing herself away on a suitor with no better financial prospects than Temple; while Sir John Temple considered that an accomplished young man like his son had a right to expect a more splendid fortune than Dorothy could offer. It was he who first put his foot down. After arriving at St. Malo, Temple had lingered on there for a month or two to enjoy Dorothy's society. Suddenly he got a message from his father, who had somehow got news of his entanglement, peremptorily commanding him to leave at once for Paris in order to pursue the education for which he had been sent abroad. Reluctantly the lovers said farewell; it was two years before they saw each other again.

Themselves they did not look on this farewell as final. There was no question indeed—even in their own minds—of defying the family ban. But they still hoped that, if they waited, fortune might change. Meanwhile, the separation was pretty complete. Dorothy was soon settled at Chicksands, while Temple roamed about France and the low countries. Owing to distance and to family disapproval they could only manage to write very rarely. Temple almost wished it was never, so exasperating did he find the suspense when he did expect a letter from Dorothy and it failed to come. To his high-strung, uncontrolled temperament the whole situation was a dreadful strain. He found it equally hard to sleep at night or to get up in the morning; and lay abed for hours railing at fortune, and analyzing his state of mind. To distract himself, he started adapting into English some French love stories. The task occupied his sleepless hours, and the translation of his heroes' amorous speeches provided an outlet for his pent-up emotions. "I send you these stories" he writes in a dedication to Dorothy, "whose rememberance indited whatever is

passionately said in any line of them." As an additional relief
to his feelings, he interspersed the narrative with cutting comments on the crass stupidity of parents who pretend to understand their children's dispositions.

In 1651 he returned to his country, but not to peace of mind.
Impossible as it was for him to visit Chicksands, he was almost
as cut off from Dorothy as he had been on the Continent: and
the strain on his nerves was aggravated by the fact that his
father was always worrying him with proposals to marry him
to other ladies. William passed his time as best he could,
talking and writing in London, or staying at his friend
Richard Franklyn's place at Moor Park, whose stately garden,
with its grottoes and plashing fountains, and leafy balustrated
vistas, did something to soothe his unquiet spirit. One day
there, looking out of the window, his eye was caught by a
statue of Leda, gazing in classic and eternal repose across the
terraced sward. Moved by a fanciful impulse, he wrote with a
diamond on the pane:

> "Tell me Leda which is best
> Ne'er to move or ne'er to rest.
> Speak that I may know thereby
> Who is happier thou or I."

Towards the end of the summer, Dorothy contrived some
pretext to come to London; and at last they met. But again
Sir John Temple got wind of it. Summoning William to
York, where he was then living, he ordered him to go on his
travels once more.

Our information about William during the period that
followed this second disappointment is tantalizingly scanty.
But it looks as if, under its shock, his hopes had begun to flag;
and with them, his determination. The very impulsiveness of
his temperament made him ill-equipped to stand the ordeal of

an indefinitely long frustration. He still wrote for his pleasure; but instead of love romances, his literary efforts now consist of reflections on topics suggested by his life abroad; the character of the Archduke Leopold, the influence of chance on politics, the languages of Flanders and Germany. These last did not please him. "The Almane" he says "is a language I should never learn unless 'twas to fright children when they cried; yet methinks it should be good to clear a man's throat that was hoarse with a cold. I have heard some speak it so as they have made me expect the words should break down their teeth as they rushed out of their mouth. . . . Flemish is a lower, yet to my mind a worse sound. I could never esteem a lady handsome whilst she spoke it; and I believe the ladies are generally conscious of it, for in company none of them will ever speak it. The tone is the more displeasing because it sounds as if those who spoke it were displeased and seeming arrogant withal. They talk as if a man owed them money and would not pay them." In spite of their unmelodious tongue, however, he liked the Flemish well enough to contemplate settling in their country permanently. Meanwhile, he only wrote to Dorothy once in a year: and, when in the Autumn of 1652, he paid another visit to England, he took no step to get into touch with her.

She for her part had also begun to relinquish hope. Though she was more patient by nature than Temple, she was also far more easily disheartened. Moreover, it was harder for her to put up a fight. Even more than men, women were expected then to bow to the will of their relations in affairs of the heart: they were hardly supposed to admit to themselves that they felt an affection unless they knew it would be approved. After Dorothy got back to England, suitors began to appear: and her family, taking for granted that all was over between her and Temple, opened negotiations with them. Luckily these fell through. But, while they were on, Dorothy, though she raised every objection she could, had to behave as though she were perfectly ready to entertain any really eligible offer. Indeed, she was far too sensible not to realize that whatever her feelings for Temple, she might in the end have to resign herself to marrying someone else. Such marriages, were, after all, the common way of the world. The difficulty of her situation began to tell on her nerves. Temple's second departure plunged her into a morbid melancholy. She was consumed by a superstitious fear that she was destined never to see him again. His subsequent silence intensified this fear. The long, empty days at Chicksands spent brooding on the unpromising future reduced her to such a state of nervous depression that her family noticed it and took her for a cure to the waters of Epsom. By the winter she was calm again, but not more hopeful. After three years waiting, her union with Temple seemed further off than ever. Family opposition had not grown less; and now perhaps Temple himself was sheering off. Dorothy was the more disposed to be impressed by these facts because they chimed with her temperamental despondency. The course of her love story had only served to confirm her conviction that it was no use her looking to this life for happiness. "I do not know" she wrote "that I ever desired anything earnestly in my life but 'twas denied me; I am many times afraid to wish a thing, merely lest that my fortune should take that occasion to use me ill." She could not help still cherishing Temple's image in her heart; but she had made up her mind that she had better give up thinking that she was ever likely to marry him.

Then, in December, he wrote her a letter. It had not turned out so easily for a discriminating young man to forget Dorothy Osborne; now that he was within reach of her, the dwindling flame of his passion had begun to burn up afresh. She wrote back at once. In this reply Dorothy makes her first personal appearance on the stage of recorded history; for the first time we hear her voice.

23

Its accents are not those of a lover. Till she knew what he really felt, pride forbade her to commit herself. Besides, she was too tactful. What could be more foolish than to adopt a tone that would be embarrassing to both of them if, as was only too likely, the relationship between them was destined to grow no closer. Temple's letter, we gather, was a light tentative affair, designed to discover whether she was willing to reopen the relationship. Long ago he had laughingly bet her ten pounds that she would be married before they met again. Now he asked her if he owed her the money. Her reply is a little masterpiece in the art of handling a delicate situation. No, she says in the easy tones of old friendship, he did not owe her the ten pounds: yes, she was extremely glad to hear from him. And then at the end, consciously or not, she allows just a hint of her warmer interest to betray itself.

"To find that you have overcome your long journey, that you are well, and in a place where it is possible for me to see you, is such a satisfaction as I, who have not been used to many, may be allowed to doubt of. Yet I will hope my eyes do not deceive me and that I have not forgot to read. But if you please to confirm it to me by another, you know how to direct it; for I am where I was, still the same, and always

yours humble servant,
Dorothy Osborne."

This gave him an opening; but not too obviously. If he should not choose to follow it up no harm was done. However he did. By return of post came a request to know what had happened to her. And soon they were exchanging long letters into which they poured all the chronicle of their life and feelings during the period of separation. Dorothy's tone, however, though intimate and evidently out to please, was still carefully not serious. If she says an affectionate thing, it is half flippantly. Temple's inflammable spirit began to chafe at this: he was also disturbed by her references to other suitors. What did she mean by them? He demanded that she should declare her feelings to him more ardently, or, as he put it "more kindly". At this, Dorothy, gaily, but firmly, pulled him up. What reason had he to distrust the sincerity of an old friend like herself? It was he who was unkind to complain. And a little later, she lets fall a remark reminding him demurely that he had given her reason to be cautious. "I have foresworn being deceived twice by the same person" said she. No—till Dorothy was quite sure of her position she was not going to be drawn, protest Temple as loudly as he liked. He did not have to protest long. Early in February Dorothy went to London for ten days, and Temple got a note from her: "This is to tell you that you will be expected about nine o'clock at a lodging over against the place where Charing Cross stood, and two doors above the Goat Tavern. If with this direction you can find it out, you will find one that is very much your servant." Beyond the fact that they enjoyed a good laugh together listening to the agitated prophesyings of an Anabaptist preacher, there is no record of what passed between them during Dorothy's sojourn in the capital. But her letters, after she got home, reveal that the meeting had been enough to set her doubts at rest. Once in each other's presence it had been clear that the years of separation had made no difference to their sentiment for one another. No longer does Dorothy make any secret of her feelings; and, though she still talks airily of her suitors, and even proposes herself to find a wife for Temple, there is now no doubt that this is all a joke. The practical obstacles to their marriage might seem as insurmountable as ever. But each was sure of the other; and this made all the difference. Once more they settled down hopefully to wait. Meanwhile they alleviated the pains of absence by means of a regular correspondence.

It was conducted under certain difficulties. On Monday Dorothy's letter left for London by carrier; and, perhaps because she did not wish her family to know how often she wrote to Temple, Dorothy directed it under cover to a Mrs. Painter in Covent Garden, whence the carrier fetched Temple's answer early on Thursday. Much too early, grumbled Temple, who, if he had not managed to get his letter off in good time, had to get up at four o'clock in the morning in order to catch the post. Dorothy teased him about the dreadful way she interfered with his most cherished habits. Still, we need not pity him too much; the effort must have been worth it. For it is now that Dorothy's talent as a letter writer gets into its stride. The window which she opens for us into seventeenth century England swings wide; and for a year we watch, week by week and at the closest quarters, the movement of her thought and mood, and the manner of her life.

It was a confined sort of life. In those days it was considered impossible for an unmarried girl of good family to travel alone. Before she could move, therefore, Dorothy had to wait till she could find someone, preferably a relation, who happened to be travelling and could act as chaperone. The gentry of England were for the most part living in such a quiet way that Dorothy's relations seldom found occasion to travel. Soon an event took place which further limited her opportunities for moving. Sir Peter Osborne, attending service at his private chapel on Easter Sunday, was suddenly taken very ill. After a week or two spent hanging between life and death, he recovered from this particular attack. But under its shock, his already weakened health finally gave way. From this time on he was an invalid and never left his room. Somebody had to look after him: and since none of his other children lived at home regularly, this somebody was inevitably Dorothy. For eight months she never left Chicksands. She was not without companions, however. A gentleman's

household in the seventeenth century was still feudal enough
to be a community of which master and servant alike felt
themselves a living member. Although Dorothy's servants
regarded her no doubt as a being of a superior order, she was
on personal terms with them. And the simplicity of living,
which mingled so strangely with the formality of that world,
made these terms easy and intimate. At the crisis of her father's
illness she sat up night after night watching by his bedside,
with his manservant—"a poor moping creature" said Dorothy
—who she had to keep on talking to in order to stop him
dropping off to sleep. To refresh them a maid would bring
up a bottle of ale. And then, by the light of a candle shaded
from where, in the dim recesses of the sick-chamber, the old
Knight dozed in his curtained four-poster, all three would
drink together. The Chicksands household had also its
superior dependents—the clergyman, the bailiff, and their
families—who formed, as it were, a little court round the
monarchs of the great house which was the centre of their
existence. The daughter of Sir Peter Osborne's old bailiff, a
Miss Jane Wright, actually lived at Chicksands for a time;
where she acted as a sort of lady-in-waiting, Nerissa to
Dorothy's Portia. She talked to guests if Dorothy felt disinclined; she helped to preserve the proprieties by staying in a
room when a gentleman called; she helped Dorothy to get
exercise in wet weather by playing battledore and shuttlecock
with her. Above all, she was valuable as a confidant. Jane
Wright seems to have been the only person in the secret of
Dorothy's romance. Temple got to know her; and when she
left to go to London she brought him the latest news of his
love.

   Dorothy's solitude was also qualified by an occasional
visitor. These were always relations; her brothers, her
brother-in-law Sir Thomas Peyton and his daughter, her
cousins Mrs. Thorold and Mr. Molle. Dorothy did not enjoy

having these last two to stay. Cousin Molle was a pompous fussy, Cambridge don, preposterously proud of his pedantic style of letter-writing, and so exercised about his health that Dorothy came to the conclusion he preferred being ill, since only then had he the excuse to cosset himself as much as he wanted. This hypochondria, however, was sometimes a godsend. Once, seized by a fancy that he had got dropsy, cousin Molle cut his visit short in the middle in order to hurry off panic-stricken to Cambridge to see his doctor. The widow Thorold was equally trying. Two days of her incessant conversation was enough to leave Dorothy prostrate with boredom; even though she had played cards with her by the hour, regardless of how much money she herself might lose, in order to check its flow. Compared with the widow, her niece Miss Peyton—"a girl sent into the world" says her aunt "in order to show that 'tis possible for a woman to be silent"— must have been a relief. Dorothy found her a sympathetic spirit in other ways. Shy and pensive, Miss Peyton appreciated the melancholy charm of Chicksands, where she liked to wander in the woods for hours, collecting mosses. She was also agreeably pretty. "If I had any desire to gain a servant" remarked Dorothy archly—"I should not like her company."

As it happened, Dorothy—apart from the fact that she was by nature singularly free from feminine jealousy—was, in her present circumstances, anxious to check, rather than to encourage male attentions. Her suitors, or "servants" as she called them, were the chief bane of her existence. For two years now hardly a month had passed without a new one appearing: and there seemed no reason to suppose that the unwelcome procession would ever stop. They were very varied. The greatest catch among them was Henry Cromwell, second son of the Protector. It is a measure of the relative mildness of temper in which the Civil War was conducted that neither Cromwells nor Osbornes seemed to have objected to such an alliance.

Henry Cromwell indeed was very different from his formidable father; shockingly different, strict puritans lamented. A cheerful, convivial, sporting young gentleman, he wooed Dorothy with presents of greyhounds. Though she liked greyhounds, Dorothy found nothing in him to incline her to weaken. Nor in her cousin Thomas Osborne, afterwards the famous Lord Danby. Other people might think him handsome, she did not: besides, he told lies, and had an interfering mother. If these suitors failed to move her, she was not likely to yield to a dumb young man with whom she had to converse by signs and grimaces. "I wonder people live, who have to do so" she exclaimed.

Young gentlemen, however, whether dumb or talkative, were exceptional among Dorothy's wooers. Her dignified demeanour and reputation for discretion made her an especial magnet for middle-aged men anxious to get married, but nervous lest too youthfully exuberant a bride might disturb the staid harmony of their existence. There was Mr. Bennett, the High Sheriff of Cambridgeshire, there was Mr. Wingfield—"a modest, melancholy, reserved man" observed Dorothy "whose heart is so taken up with little philosophical studies that I wonder how I found a room there". Above all, there was Sir Justinian Isham. Sir Justinian was the most importunate of her suitors. Rich, learned, reputed to be a pattern of wisdom, and highly respected in Northamptonshire, he had entered on to the scene two years before with such a conquering flourish of trumpets that Dorothy wondered what possible excuse she should ever find for rejecting him. To her mingled amusement and relief, however, Sir Justinian, or "the Emperor" as she irreverently called him, turned out to be not up to his reputation. "'Twas the vainest impertinent, self-conceited, learned cockscomb that ever I saw", said she. An elderly widower with four depressed grown-up daughters, whom he kept immured in his gloomy house in Nottinghamshire, he expressed himself in a jargon of fantastic pomposity, and was so vain that he warned Dorothy that he had been forced to keep his attentions to her a secret, lest they should arouse the jealousy of the magnificent Lady Sunderland. Dorothy managed to put him off the first time he proposed: but, after fruitlessly trying the effect of his charms on six other ladies, he returned to the attack; explaining, surprisingly, that he was sure there was a peculiar affinity between himself and Dorothy, because, shortly after hearing that she was suffering from an ague, he had contracted one himself.

Altogether, Dorothy's opinion of mankind was not raised by her suitors. If they had done nothing else for her, they had taught her what she did not want in a husband. As a relief to her feelings she expatiated on this topic to Temple.

"He should not be so much a country gentleman as to understand nothing but hawks and dogs, and to be fonder of either than of his wife; nor of the next sort of them, whose aim reaches no further than to be Justice of Peace, and once in his life High Sheriff, who read no book but Statutes and studies nothing but how to make a speech inter-larded with Latin, that may amaze his disagreeing poor neighbours, and fright them rather than persuade them into quietness. He must not be a thing that began the world in a free school, was sent from thence to the University, and is at his farthest when he reaches the Inns of Court; has no acquaintance but those of his form in these places, speaks the French he has picked out of old laws, and admires nothing but the stories he has heard of the revels that were kept there before his time. He must not be a Town-gallant neither, that lives in a tavern and an ordinary, that cannot imagine how an hour should be spent without company, unless it be in sleeping, that makes court to all the women he sees, thinks they believe him, and is laughed at equally. Nor a travelled monsieur whose head is all feather inside and outside; that can talk of nothing but dances and duels, and has courage enough to wear slashes when everybody else dies with cold to see him. He must not be a fool of no sort, nor peevish ill-natured, nor proud nor covetous, and to all this must be added 'he must love me'."

These spirited portraits were drawn from her neighbours as well as her suitors. Dorothy saw a certain amount of the neighbours: for, though the disturbances of the time had diminished the social life of the country gentry, it had not upset the structure of society so much as to stop it altogether. On occasions of official festivity, like Christmas, people still climbed into their coaches to jolt over the cart-tracks they called roads, in order to consume a heavy dinner together. Married couples and recent arrivals to the district still paid and received visits of ceremony. County society was no more brilliant then than it is now; certainly not so brilliant as to lure Dorothy from her shell. For the most part she found these entertainments a burden. Still, they had their compensations. It was delightful to get the chance to look at beautiful Lady Grey de Ruthin for example; or to talk over the news with charming, intelligent Lady Diana Rich. Though Dorothy preferred living out of the great world, she was always interested to hear about it. Now, especially, when she was buried down at Chicksands, she drank up every item of information. Sometimes the news was political. With ironical amusement Dorothy heard of the difficulties overtaking the revolutionary government. Cromwell's expulsion of the Parliament, for example; what would Mr. Pym have said, she wondered, had he lived to see this consequence of the victory of the so-called party of freedom. No doubt such speculations were treasonable, she commented sarcastically; she had better check them. She was also entertained that people should be so shocked at General Monk marrying a seamstress. Surely she was no more unsuitable to her position than the rest of the Parliamentary ladies. For the most part, however, Dorothy kept off politics. They reminded her too painfully of what she longed to forget. For the dark cloud of death and defeat still brooded, ominous and unbroken over the landscape of the private scene. If one raised one's eyes there it was, casting a shadow over the spirit. Nearly every family of her acquaintance had its tragedy. Lady Diana Rich's father had been executed; so had Lady Ann Wentworth's. Dorothy heard that Mr. Waller, the poet, was writing a romance about the recent war. "If he does not mingle it with a great deal of pleasing fiction, it cannot be very diverting, sure" she said "the subject is so sad."

There was nothing sad about social news, however. Dorothy enjoyed this thoroughly. The scandals and the vagaries of the Caroline aristocracy dance their way through her pages, blending strangely with the melancholy of her reflections on life and the sweetness of her words of love. Fancy Lady Isabella Thynne marrying a man "no better than a beast, only because he had a great estate"; or Miss de Mayerne falling in love with "a buffle-headed French Marquis" and kissing him publicly in the Park too; or Lord Leicester quarrelling with his wife after forty years of tranquil marriage, and dismissing all the servants just to spite her; or the fantastic Lady Newcastle publishing a book of verses! "They say 'tis ten times more extravagant than her dress", said Dorothy; and, when she had read it, "I am satisfied there are many soberer people in Bedlam".

News and visitors, however, were only an occasional interruption in her sequestered existence. Indeed, though they might entertain her for a moment, they only ruffled the surface of her attention. During the long hours she spent alone she thought little about them; and these were the hours she valued most. Throughout the cold spring months, she escaped from company whenever she could to muse with a book over the fire; or, when the days warmed and lengthened, to wander in the countryside. Summer weather quickened her feelings to a peculiar intensity. Living as they did far closer to the primitive earth than we do, the Carolines were far more affected by its moods. How untiringly and with what an unfailingly responsive zest do their poets harp on the changes of the seasons; green Spring, Summer with its July flowers, the rich fecundity of Autumn. The cold dark Winter months, spent in those unheated houses, chilled and darkened the hearts of their inhabitants. At the turn of the year, when the buds broke and the birds began to sing and build, their spirits too bloomed and carolled in sympathy. Dorothy has left us a record of a typical summer day at Chick-sands. She rose early, and after seeing to the household, stepped out into the garden to taste the morning freshness. When it grew too hot—they seem to have been strangely sensitive to heat in those days—she went in to pay a visit to Sir Peter lying always immobile in his bedroom before settling down to array herself in all the elaboration of Caroline full dress. Next came dinner, conducted—even if she were alone or with a single guest—with formal ceremony in the great dining-room. The afternoon was spent in retirement reading or sewing. Then, when the fierceness of the day's heat had begun to abate, she went out once more. "About six or seven o'clock I walk out into a common that lies hard by the house, where a great many young wenches keep sheep and cows and sit in the shade singing ballads. I go to them and compare their voices and beauties to some ancient shepherdesses that I have read of, and find a vast difference there. But, trust me, I think these are as innocent as those could be. I talk to them and find they want nothing to make them the happiest people in the world but the knowledge that they are so. Most commonly, when we are in the midst of our discourse, one looks about her and spies a cow going into the corn, and away they all run as if they had wings at their heels. I that am not so nimble stay behind, and, when I see them driving home their cattle, I think 'tis time for me to retire too." Supper followed; and after supper back into the open air where, amid the fading twilight, sweet with the vagrant scents of a country evening, she would stroll in the garden or sit by the banks of the stream, dreaming—of Temple and love undying and hope deferred—while time slipped by unnoticed, till suddenly she looked up and it was night and she must steal back into the silence of the sleeping house, and, candle in hand, climb the shadowy staircase to bed.

The current of her meditations was coloured by her reading. Dorothy read enormously, anything she could lay hands on, poetry, travels, devotional works, romances. Romances were what she liked best. It seems odd that it should have been so; for the romances of that age are, to our eyes, very tedious affairs; incredible, interminable tales, couched in a style of stilted rhetoric about Amestris and Aglatides, Artibis and Cleobuline, kings and princesses of preposterous beauty and virtue, who strut their way, volume after volume, through a monotonous labyrinth of improbable intrigue, conventional sentiment, and far-fetched punctilios of honour. Dorothy, however, discussed their characters as seriously as we should discuss that of Anna Karenina, cried over their troubles, and was so enthralled by their adventures that she would sit up reading, night after night, long after she should have been in bed. Like the rest of her contemporaries, she was accustomed to rhetoric, and found no difficulty in believing the improbable. Besides, the subject of these romances was love. And love was to Dorothy the most interesting subject in the world.

How should it have been otherwise! In the radiant warmth of her re-union with Temple, the flower of her passion had opened wide, so that it now diffused its invisible perfume over her every mood and thought. "My very dreams are yours", she cries to him. Wherever she was and whatever she was doing—gazing at the shepherdesses, topicing with cousin Molle, drowsily watching by her father's bedside in the silence of the night—the figure of Temple floated before her mental eye, obscuring the outside world. She grew more abstracted than ever. One evening, seated by the fire in company with her brother and a friend of his, lost in her own thoughts, she found her attention suddenly seized by their conversation. They were talking about flying. Ah! If she could cover the distance between herself and Temple with such an airy swift-ness! To their amused surprise Dorothy suddenly broke silence, demanding excitedly if flying was really going to be possible. Nor did love only increase her absent-mindedness. The arrival of the post, for instance, agitated her so violently as to make her for the time being quite unlike her usual con-trolled self. She would shout to the maid, calling her in the dim dawn, to tear open the curtains in order that she might see if any of the letters, that had come to her, were from Temple; she would drop her hand in the middle of a game of cards because she heard a courier from London riding by; and she would stand in the mud and straw of the stable exasper-atedly upbraiding the groom for daring to unharness his horse before opening the letter bag. When they did come, Temple's letters never seemed long enough for her. "If you do not send me long letters, then you are the cruellest person that can be. If you love me you will, and, if you do not, I shall never love myself."

Interest in her own love-story led her to speculate on the subject of love in general. In this she was the child of her age. It is hardly to be supposed that the Carolines felt the passion of love more intensely than we do; but certainly they thought about it much more. Four-fifths of their poetry is love-poetry; and their prose too is largely devoted to celebrating its glories, analysing its nature and cataloguing its varieties. The fact that they were an aristocratic society accounts partly for this preoccupation. Alas, it is only people, untroubled by the necessity of making a living, who have the leisure and energy to study their sentiments with this elaborate refinement. But in the Carolines, natural tendency was encouraged by their ideal mode of thought. If love was a worthy passion, then it had to be fitted into their general philosophical scheme, and its relation to the principle of virtue must be discovered and defined. Further, believing in form as they did, they were interested to decide the correct mode for love's expression. How should a lover speak and dress and behave himself in the presence of his mistress, they asked themselves. With what appropriate graces should he adorn the utterance of his heart? At once a faith and a fine art, love was to them a necessary element of the good life, and as such required intensive study.

Yet their view of it was not the same as that of latter-day amorists. Nowhere does their peculiar blend of realism and romance appear more conspicuously. In some ways it was a highly romantic view. Did they not see in the affinity of two noble spirits a symbol and revelation of the divine harmony of the universe, and in the lover's desire for the beloved an expression of the desire of the soul for perfection? But they did not think, in the Byronic fashion, that love had a right to override every other consideration in order to achieve its fulfilment. On the contrary, the very fact that they considered it a necessary element of the good life meant that it must not be permitted to clash with its other elements. At every turn passion must take account of the obligations of religion, of man's duty to society and his family. Dorothy's conviction of the value of convention made her especially conscious of these obligations. For although love meant so much to her, she thought it should be kept on a tight rein. Unbridled passion was always wrong, above all, in women. A woman must be sure her love was requited before she yielded to it, much less confess it to the man of her choice. Even then she should make sure that it was a rational passion, founded on esteem for his character. Apart from anything else, what she had seen of the world had taught Dorothy that unless it was so founded, it would soon evaporate. "When there is no reason to uphold a passion", she notes, "it will sink of itself."

"But", she goes on "when there is, it may last eternally." If all the conditions were satisfied, if it was grounded on regard and ruled by principle, then Dorothy conceived of love with all the enthusiastic elevation of her age. True love was the expression of a complete and unique harmony between two minds and hearts. An equal harmony too; for, though for form's sake, lovers might speak of one another as mistress and servant, in relation to their love they were free and equal partners. How contemptibly mistaken a view of the subject did it reveal in Lady Sunderland, that she should say that she had given her heart to Mr. Smith only out of pity for his passion for her. Then, true love implied complete confidence. If each lover was genuinely the other's affinity, there could be no reason for tactful concealments, let alone for jealousy. The franker lovers were, the more fully would the harmony between them appear, and both must realize that no one else could ever supply the other's place. Indeed, this realization was a primary condition of true love. Dorothy could never, she said, believe in the homage of a heart that had been offered to another. So monogamous a conception of love could only find its true fulfilment in marriage. As a matter of fact, Dorothy's religious principles were far too strict for her to try and imagine it on any other terms.

On the other hand, she was forced only too often to imagine marriage without love. Like everyone else in the seventeenth century, Dorothy accepted the view that marriage was a social institution not necessarily entered upon for sentimental reasons. This meant that it had its own problems unconnected with those of the heart. These also Dorothy found extremely interesting. Next to love, marriage—its demands and duties and difficulties—was the main subject of her hours of reflection. Here once more her moral principles combined with commonsense to decide her notions. Rank and money were solid goods—Dorothy was far too clear-sighted not to recognize this—but they were insufficient in themselves to make a good marriage. A woman was not justified in marrying a man she did not respect unless divine authority, in the shape of her parents, absolutely ordered her to do so. But if they did so order, or if she found she had been deceived as to her husband's character—what then? Then, said Dorothy, she must patiently make the best of it. She thought it dreadful for a woman to bully her husband: and, with a slightly bitter smile she praises the discretion of a lady she knew, who, married to a man whose disturbing habit it was suddenly to get up in the middle of the night and beat a table with a stick, made no protest; but took care to put a cushion on the table before she went to bed. It was the woman's rôle to submit to the man: and generally her fault, so Dorothy had noted, if a marriage failed to go smoothly. All the same, Dorothy could not approve of La Reine Margot being so easy-going about her husband's infidelities. A woman must keep her dignity. This concern for dignity made Dorothy oddly severe on anyone who married a second time. They could only do it for worldly advantages, or out of uncontrolled physical passion. Both motives were ignoble. She also thought it ignoble for a woman to try and rule her husband by wheedling and flattery. She herself could never stoop to do it. But indeed, when she came to consider her own case, she did not see how she could make a success of marriage to anyone she cared for less than she cared for Temple. It was nothing to be proud of. Simply she found it too difficult to subdue her will and hide her true feelings. Still, perhaps she was not alone in this. For as far as she could see most marriages were unhappy; and most couples if they had been able to live together for a year before marrying, would have broken off their engagement. In marriage, as in every other human institution—so ran Dorothy's characteristic conclusion—things seemed likely to turn out badly.

Such was the scene, such the preoccupations mirrored in the pages that, traceried over in Dorothy's delicate, precise hand, found their way each Thursday morning on to Temple's writing table. Her handwriting was a work of art: so were her letters. In addition to their historical and personal interest, they were exquisite pieces of literature. Not that they give the effect of conscious art. Indeed, half the charm of Dorothy's letters comes from the fact that she seems to be just writing whatever comes into her head, without any eye to the impression she is making; mingling grave and gay, turning from a declaration of love to Lady Newcastle's oddities, from Lady Newcastle's oddities to a practical request—will Temple go to the Royal Exchange and order some orange flower water for her, or can he get her one of the new fashionable engraved seals—and then from a practical request to a reflection on the vanity of human wishes. Her style seems as unstudied as her matter. Dorothy was strongly of the opinion that any other sort of style was unsuitable for letters. "All letters methinks should be free and easy as one's discourse, not studied as an oration, nor made up of hard words like a charm. 'Tis an admirable thing to see how some people will labour to find out terms that may obscure a plain sense; like a gentleman, I knew, who would never say 'the weather grew cold', but that 'winter began to salute us'. I have no patience for such coxcombs."

Her practice followed her precept. The language of her letters is colloquial; the tone intimate and easy. She exclaims, interrupts herself, breaks off—just as if she were talking. We seem less to read her letters than to overhear them. Here it is, though, that her art lies. It is not easy to get the sound of the voice into the written word. Spontaneous though she wanted her letters to appear, in fact Dorothy selected and arranged her matter; so that her every sentence contributed to bring her personality breathing and alive on to the page. Further, she had a natural artist's sense of style, which led her always to try and present her thoughts in a delightful form. The simple word is the right word; and the movement of her sentences, whether lightly dancing or slowing down to a grave andante, or swelling out in the lingering interweaving cadences of seventeenth-century eloquence, is always the clear echo to the movement of her mood and thought. Nor, for all her intimacy, is she ever vulgarly informal. That curious blend of naïveté and ceremoniousness, which characterized her period, was so bred in her bone that even at her most natural, she instinctively preserves a charming courtliness. Her exclamations and interruptions are never abrupt. She always remembers to end her briefest note with a turn of finished grace:

"Chide me when I do anything that is not well; but then make haste to tell me that you forgive me, and that you are, as I shall ever be,

A faithful friend

Dorothy Osborne."

Indeed, Dorothy was too unself-conscious to be shy of saying something pretty, if it was needed to convey her meaning. This was a great help to her when it came to writing love-letters. The love-letters of more self-conscious ages make depressing reading. Their shame-faced slangy endearments sound both flat and embarrassing. Passion needs the restraint of a formalized mode of utterance, to give it shape and to crystallize its intensity. No one ever wrote better love-letters than stately Dorothy. There are few endearments in them, and no rhapsodies. But even when she is telling the news, or asking Temple to do some commission for her, the emotion that filled her heart vibrates through every modulation of her voice; and now it gleams out in an enchanting playfulness; and now, as a wave of passionate longing for Temple floods over her, it flows forth in a strain of tenderness, all the more poignant for the delicate reticence with which it is expressed. "You are as much pleased, you say, in writing to me, as I can be to receive your letters. Why should not you think the same of me? In earnest you may; and if you love me, you will. But then, how much more satisfied should I be if there were no need of these; and we might talk all that we write and more. Shall we ever be so happy? Last night I was in the garden until 11 o'clock. It was the sweetest night that e'er I saw, the garden looked so well, and the jessamine smelt beyond all perfume: and yet I was not pleased. The place had all the charms it used to have when I was most satisfied with it; and, had you been there, I should have liked it much more than ever I did. But that not being, it was no more to me than the next field."

Temple, it must be admitted found her at times a trifle too restrained—at any rate during the first month of their correspondence. Need she end her letters to him "your humble servant" he asked; and could she not call their sentiment for one another love, instead of friendship? His ardour could not fail to thaw her a little. She stopped saying "your humble servant". The word "love" however, still stuck in her throat. This shrinking was due less to personal disinclination—did he not in fact entirely possess her heart—than to an uncertainty as to the prospects of their marrying, which made her hesitate to let herself go completely. These prospects were, if possible, more uncertain than ever. Dorothy had declared to Temple earlier in their correspondence that her principles forbade her

41

to consider marrying him without her family's consent. As the months passed, the Osbornes began to get wind of her renewed intimacy with Temple, and their opposition increased. Sir Peter himself did not take much part in it, he was too old and too ill. But his place was filled, more than adequately, by her relations. Her two brothers, her aunt Lady Gargrave, cousin Thorold, and cousin Molle were at Dorothy so continuously about it, that she scarcely knew which way to turn. Uneventful as life at Chicksands might seem to the casual observer, it was, throughout the summer of 1653, the scene of an ever-intensifying struggle. It was not an open struggle. Dorothy took care not to enlighten her family fully about her situation, for fear of provoking them to a definite prohibition: while the Osbornes, ignorant precisely how far she was committed to Temple, shrank from assuming too much, for fear of antagonizing her irretrievably. It seems likely that they, like other people, were a little frightened of Dorothy. Accordingly, the campaign was conducted by hints, speaking silences and awkward questions. The Osbornes' proposed suitors talked a great deal of the importance of marrying prudently, and regretted loudly that so agreeable a man as Temple was not eligible. On her side, Dorothy, while making no objection to marriage in theory, found good reasons for refusing each particular match. To their hints about Temple, she presented a front of demure impassivity. Besides resisting the attacks of her family in force, she had to be on her guard against individual onslaughts on her firmness of mind. Lady Gargrave bombarded her with invitations to London in order to meet new suitors; her elder brother would suddenly ask her with a teasing, meaning smile, if she had heard that Temple was going to be married. These last attacks did not worry Dorothy very much. She could always tell Lady Gargrave that Sir Peter was too ill for her to leave Chicksands. And her elder brother—genial easy-going John

Osborne—was, she knew, too like herself in his hatred of a row, ever to push things disagreeably far.

It was very different with her brother Henry. Colonel Henry Osborne was the most formidable of all Temple's opponents. From the fitful glimpses of his figure that flit across the pages of Dorothy's correspondence, and which are all we know of him, he emerges as an extremely difficult character; unbalanced, ungoverned, and egotistic, an uneasy mixture of worldly cunning and uncontrolled impulses of passion. Moreover, his opposition was actuated by a different and more compelling motive than that of her other relatives. He was possessed by a strange and obsessing love for Dorothy—a stranger, she said, would take his letters to her for love letters written to a mistress—which made him violently jealous lest she should care deeply for anyone else. That she would have to marry, he recognized as inevitable; but at all costs let it not be for love. With the sharp eye of jealousy he divined her feeling for Temple: and, since he was a bachelor without a profession, and could, therefore, spend a great deal of time at Chicksands, he put all his energies into the task of preventing its fulfilment. He produced suitor after unattractive suitor, he spied on her during her visits to London, he questioned the servants as to what she did when alone, he searched her drawers for letters, he tried to intercept the post from London. Above all, he argued with her. Sometimes assuming a false air of judicial calm, he urged the paramount importance of wealth and rank in a husband: at others, more ardently, he expatiated on the transience of passion and the disastrous consequences of yielding to it. Then again, he would try by a thousand devices to get her to betray herself about Temple, or he would paint a pathetic picture of his own sufferings, should she ever make a breach between him and her; or, his voice rising in anger, he would threaten to pursue her with unrelenting hostility should she marry without his approval. Dorothy was far

43

from being unmoved by his pleadings. She hated distressing anyone; and, besides, she seems to have felt a deep, though painful, affection for him. However, there was no question of her giving in. Night after night the contest would go on, often with both of them in tears, till the candles were guttering in their sockets and twelve, one, and two o'clock had, in turn, reverberated through the midnight quiet of the house. Feeling had sometimes grown so high that for a time they were hardly on speaking terms. Then Henry, in a revulsion of feeling would apologize, and the quarrel would be made up, only to break out with renewed violence a day or two later. "We have had such a skirmish and on so foolish an occasion", so runs a typical account of one of these scenes. "The Emperor and his proposals began it. I talked merrily on, until I saw my brother put on his sober face; and could hardly then believe he was in earnest. It seems he was; for, when I had spoke my meaning, it wrought so with him as to fetch up all that lay upon his stomach. All the people that I had ever in my life refused were brought again upon the stage, like Richard III's ghosts, to reproach me with. . . . Well, 'twas a pretty lecture and I grew warm with it after a while; and, in short, we came so near an absolute falling out, that it was time to give over; and we said so much then, that we have hardly spoken a word together since. But 'tis wonderful to see what courtesies and legs pass between us; and, as before we were thought the kindest brother and sister, we are certainly now the most complimentary couple in England. 'Tis a strange chance and I am sorry for it; but I will swear I know not how to help it. I look upon it as one of my great misfortunates, and I must bear it, as that which is not my first, nor likely to be my last."

Henry Osborne became so obsessed about Dorothy and Temple, that, besides tormenting her about the subject, he held forth on it to everyone he met; with the result that it became the talk of the county. This was peculiarly upsetting to

Dorothy, with her horror of publicity. Altogether the situation was a great and growing strain on her nerves; a strain which began to betray itself in her letters. Temple remarked it. Early in the summer, in order to ease the tension, he wrote offering to release her from any formal engagement. When everything was so uncertain, would she not be happier if she felt herself absolutely free? Such a thought had never entered Dorothy's head. "Alas," she cried, "alas, if I could purchase the Empire of the world at that rate, I should think it much too dear!" His chivalry in making such a proposal bound her all the closer to him. But it could not remove the causes of her uneasiness; and, do what she would, the tone of her letters continued gloomy. She could promise him confidently not to marry anyone else—except under duress—but, she said, had not they better face the fact that the prospects of their being able to marry each other were almost nil. Temple exclaimed against such pessimism. She replied to his exclamations with the tartness of a spirit thoroughly on edge. "You must pardon me if I cannot agree to give you false hopes," she said. "I must be deceived myself before I can deceive you; and I have so accustomed myself to tell you what I think, that I must either say nothing or that which I believe to be true." Such a retort was not of a kind to tranquillize Temple. The situation was beginning to tell on his nerves too. His active masculine spirit chafed at delay. If Dorothy did not want to break the engagement off, why was he not able to marry her at once? Moreover, as we have seen, indefinite frustration had a peculiarly exacerbating effect on his highly-geared nervous organization. His feelings of exasperation began to break out in sudden impulses of irritation and suspicion. He accused Dorothy of being severe, unjust, unmerciful, unkind; she wrote too seldom or too shortly; once more he would harp on her lack of demonstrativeness; he was seized with a jealous fear lest her suitors might in the end prevail. After all, they were on the spot and he was not. Could he not come down to Chicksands, he asked? No, said Dorothy, Henry might be there, and would think that she had asked Temple in order to annoy him. If, on the other hand, he came when Henry was away, she would appear to be acting in an underhand fashion. For fear of this she even refused to suggest going to Epsom Wells for her health again, lest Henry should suspect she went in order to meet Temple. It was so much against Dorothy's most sacred and traditional instincts to oppose the lawful authority of her family, that she could only bring herself to do so as long as she was absolutely sure that she was taking no action that might give them a legitimate grievance against her. All she could do was to tell Temple again and again, how much she longed to see him; and, for the time being, to try and soothe him, now by gently laughing at his violence, now by earnestly protesting her love. Her own mood was too anxious for her to be able to do either with the right kind of conviction. There was little heart in her jokes; and her protestations were backed by no confident hope in the future.

Prospects were no brighter during the months that followed. In one respect Dorothy might have been expected to feel easier. What with her own obduracy and the rumours about Temple, her suitors one by one had begun to drop away. By the autumn almost all were married, even Sir Justinian. "The spiteful man, merely to vex me, has gone and married", commented Dorothy. "What a multitude of willow-garlands shall I wear before I die! I think I had best to make some into faggots this cold weather; the flame they would make in the chimney would be of more use to me than that which was in the hearts of all those that gave them me, and would last as long." This defection of her lovers, however, so far from tranquillizing Dorothy's situation only intensified her family's anxiety that she should marry soon, before all her chances were gone. New suitors were produced, new arguments put forward; Henry Osborne showed himself as temperamental as ever.

Certainly country life at Chicksands that autumn was not cheerful. In September the atmosphere was further darkened by the news that Dorothy's brother Robin had suddenly died. Dorothy herself was less distressed by this than one might have expected, considering how fond she was of her family. She hardly mentioned her loss to Temple except to say what a good thing it was that so few people saw her nowadays—she looked such a fright in mourning—and was surprised that her oldest brother should not be in better spirits seeing that he had inherited Robin's fortune. The truth was that her love for Temple now filled her heart so completely as to render all other ties unimportant to her. "Sure", she says, "I am not insensible only from ill-nature; and yet I will swear I think I do not afflict myself half so much as another would do, that had my losses. I pay nothing of sadness to the memory of my poor brother, but I presently disperse it with thinking what I owe in thankfulness that 'tis not you I mourn for." Still, Robin Osborne's death added to her general feeling of melancholy. Once more she wondered if, born to misfortune, she was fated to lose everyone dear to her.

Temple's letters did nothing to reassure her. Now that his sense of frustration had been roused, it had made its usual violent effect on his moody temperament. Dorothy was horrified to hear how changed he appeared. No longer sanguine and social, he spent his days alone and plunged in depression. At the same time, inconsistently, he scolded her for what he considered the shocking pessimism of her outlook. How mistaken too it was of her to suggest that unhappiness might be good for the character! More insistently than ever he besought her to come to London. Once Dorothy explained that this was her first wish, but at the moment it was

impossible for her to find anyone to take her. Temple does not
seem to have been convinced. At any rate, he only increased
his urgings. Gradually his unresponsiveness began to react on
Dorothy. Her letters still strove to pursue the old tone. She
laughed, she coaxed, she sent him her portrait by Lely, she
gossiped about Lady Carlyle, but, beneath the polished surface, we can detect a steadily dwindling confidence, an ever-
sharpening sense of tension.

At last, towards the end of October, she did contrive to get
to London. This second visit, however, though it lasted a
month, did not succeed in dissipating the cloud that overhung
her spirit. Circumstances were more disagreeable for one
thing. Henry Osborne came too, and Dorothy still had to sit
up till two in the morning disputing with him. Nor were her
interviews with Temple much more peaceful. The friction
implicit in their recent letters now showed itself openly.
Temple's pent up feelings burst out in passionate pleading. If
Dorothy persisted in pointing out the difficulties of the
position, he turned on her with accusations of inconstancy
and hard-heartedness. She parted from him only to lie awake
in anguish; and then, when dawn broke, to rush to her
writing-table to scribble a note of explanation and apology.

"I have slept as little as you and may be allowed to talk as
unreasonably. Yet I find I am not quite senseless; I have a
heart still that cannot resolve to refuse you anything within
its power to grant . . . I do but ask though, do what you
please, only believe you do a great injustice if you think me
false. I never resolve to give you a final farewell, but I
resolve at the same time to part with all the comfort of my
life; and, whether I told you or not, I shall die
Yours,
Dorothy.
Tell me what you will have me do."

48

No—the longed-for, waited-for, hardly-achieved meeting had proved no solution of her difficulties. And, when back at Chicksands, alone but for the old knight dying upstairs, and amid the echoing faded walls of the great house, standing solitary in the damp, low-lying countryside under the sad November sky, she began to review her situation, a perturbation such as she had not known before, began to invade her spirit. People who had not seen her since she went to London thought she must have been very ill there; she looked so ghastly. Well she might! She had come to the crisis of her history. Two impulses dominated in Dorothy. She was a born lover, one of those natures which can only find its fulfilment in the art and ecstasy of love. But almost equally strong in her was that fundamental distrust of life implanted in her by the misfortunes of her early years. These two impulses were not compatible. To satisfy her gift for love, she must accept experience with all the risks attendant on it. Her distrust of life, on the other hand, inclined her to shrink from experience as bound to bring her to disaster. From the time she had first met Temple, the two had been at war within her heart. It was a hard struggle for her distrust had powerful allies—absence, uncertainty, family influence, regard for established authority and, simply, the loss of heart induced by long delay. All the same, for eight years her love had proved strong enough to keep the ascendant. But now a new force arose to enlist itself in the armies of opposition. The irritation produced by the strain of the situation had begun to make itself felt in the relation between her and Temple, with the result that her very tenderness for him began to sap the force of her resistance. If her engagement was to involve quarrelling not only with her relations, but with Temple himself, then Dorothy—exhausted with four years' struggle—felt she could hardly bring herself to face the ordeal of going on with it. Perhaps she had better give him up. After all, her instinct had always told her that passion was a dangerous thing. And her creed too: her fear of life now began to rationalize itself as a conviction that her love was, in itself, sinful. Was it not idolatry to offer to a mortal that adoration which was due to God alone? A superstitious sense of guilt began to obsess her. She felt that God had raised up so many obstacles against her reunion with Temple because he disapproved of it; that her sufferings were a punishment rightly inflicted on her for loving man more than God; and that now as a final penalty, love itself was to be poisoned. What then ought to be done? How was God's wrath to be allayed. There was only one way surely, the way of sacrifice. If the lovers voluntarily were to give each other up, then punishment for sin might be averted, and peace descend upon the soul once more.

Thus, during the long lonely hours with autumn darkening to winter round her, Dorothy endlessly and tormentedly brooded. Thus steadily the force of her love gave ground to the forces of her fear. At last, in December, she hesitated no longer; and sitting down, in as controlled a tone as she could command, she wrote to Temple breaking it off.

"I have seriously considered all our misfortunes, and can see no end to them but by submitting to that which we cannot avoid, and, by yielding to it, break the force of a blow which, if resisted, brings a certain ruin. I think I need not tell you how dear you have been to me, nor that in your kindness I placed all the satisfaction of my life; 'twas the only happiness I proposed to myself, and had set my heart so much upon it that it was therefore made my punishment, to let me see that, how innocent soever I thought my affection, it was guilty in being greater than is allowable for things of this world. 'Tis not a melancholy humour gives me these apprehensions and inclinations, nor the persuasions of others; 'tis the result of a long strife with myself, before my reason could overcome my passion, or bring me to a perfect resignation to whatever is allotted for me. . . .

We have lived hitherto upon hopes so airy that I have often wondered how they could support the weight of our misfortunes; but passion gives a strength above nature, we see it in most people; and not to flatter ourselves, ours is but a refined degree of madness. What can it be, to be lost to all things in the world but the single object that takes up one's fancy, to lose all the quiet and repose of one's life in hunting after it, when there is so little likelihood of ever gaining it, and so many more probable accidents that will infallibly make us miss on't. And which is more than all, 'tis being mastered by that which reason and religion teaches us to govern, and in that only gives us a pre-eminence over beasts . . . as we have not differed in anything else, we could agree in this too, and resolve upon a friendship that will be much the perfecter for having nothing of passion in it. How happy might we be without so much as a fear of the change that any accident could bring! We might defy all that fortune could do, and putting off all disguise and constraint, with that which only made it necessary, make our lives as easy to us as the condition of this world will permit. I may own you as a person that I extremely value and esteem, and for whom I have a particular friendship, and you may consider me as one that will always be

Yours faithful
Dorothy Osborne."

Temple was not prepared to consider anything of the kind. In spite of his own offer to release her from the embarrassments of a formal engagement, in spite of his recent fits of despondency, he had not, since their reunion, ever conceived of giving Dorothy up. He answered her letter at once and in a

fury. Far from accepting the view that it was his duty to break
with her, he refused to believe that she thought it their duty
either. All this pious talk of hers was just a hypocritical mask
for weakness, perhaps for ambition. It was likely enough, as
far as he could see, that she was breaking with him in order to
marry Henry Cromwell. For the rest, he announced his intention of coming down to Chicksands immediately, in order
to have it out with her.

Dorothy's first reaction to this onslaught was anger. Temple
thought only of himself; he did not make the slightest effort
to understand her; he positively wanted to make her miserable. For what else could he mean by insisting on coming to
Chicksands. She was not going to change her mind. The only
purpose his visit could serve was to render her situation in the
world even more intolerable than before. Already, as an
earnest of the finality of her decision, she had formally announced to her brother Henry that all was over between her
and Temple. What was he likely to think of her if she now
received on familiar terms a man she did not intend to marry?
Her good name was the only thing of value left her; now
Temple seemed to want to deprive her of that. Anyway, she
simply must insist on his not coming till after Christmas.
Christmas she intended to dedicate to her devotions and for
her devotions she must try and preserve some tranquillity of
spirit. As a symbol of her considered change of heart, she
signed this second letter in the earlier colder form "your
humble servant". Dorothy allowed herself to write all the
more strongly because her genuine anger was reinforced by
her desire to sacrifice herself. To arouse Temple's hostility
was possibly the only way to make him agree to the breach.
If so, it was her duty to make their quarrel as bitter as possible.

Dorothy's conception of her duty seemed to be growing
more and more painful. Indeed, her decision had done nothing
as yet to bring her that peace of soul she longed for. The

agonies of irresolution had left her only to be succeeded by a numb lassitude of despair. Temporarily, her capacity for emotion was exhausted. She wished for nothing, she longed for nothing. Even those relatives she was fondest of no longer stirred in her the slightest feeling of affection. Her heart, she said, with a sad topical irony, was like a country after a civil war, so ravaged as to be of no use to anyone. The truth was that love had grown to be the necessary element of Dorothy's existence. Deprived of it, life in this world was literally not worth living to her; and, in fact, now that she surveyed it in the bleak light of her renunciation, there welled up in her spirit a wave of disgust at the whole miserable ignoble spectacle. How bitterly justified her distrust of the world had proved! Death was preferable to life. There were moments when Dorothy longed for death. "May I enjoy", she said, "an early and a quiet grave, free from the trouble of this busy world, where all with passion pursue their own interests at their neighbours' charges; where nobody is pleased, but somebody complains on't; and where it is impossible to be, without giving and receiving injuries." What must have made Dorothy's desolation worse was that she had to keep it a secret. Christmas was upon her; and she must needs take part in the heavy elaborate junketings with which the seventeenth century thought fit to celebrate that festival, was forced to smile and converse, dine out, and entertain parties at Chicksands, all without betraying a sign of her inner suffering.

However, her ordeal was nearly at its period. Dorothy's obstinacy had not succeeded in persuading Temple to resignation. On the contrary, it had made him realize, as never before, how acute was the danger of losing her; with the result that all the force of his vehement and wilful temperament rose up in frantic resistance. He became so beside himself that Sir John Temple, who was staying in London at the time, did not like to let him out of his sight; he was afraid his son might

C   53

do himself an injury. And indeed Temple did write a wild letter to Dorothy threatening apparently to kill himself if she persisted.

Thunderstruck with horror Dorothy read his words. Here was a development she had not reckoned with. Her anger, her insensibility, even her deep concern for the honour of her name were instantly forgotten in the flood of terrified tenderness that swept over her at the thought of his condition. Almost distraught at what he must be going through, she dashed off to him first one letter, then another, conjuring him, by any love he had ever felt for her, to moderate the extravagance of his emotion.

"Sir, if you ever loved me do not refuse the last request I shall ever make; 'tis to preserve yourself from the violence of your passion. Vent it all upon me; call me and think me what you please; make me, if it be possible, more wretched than I am. I will bear it all without the least murmur. Nay, I deserve it all. And had you never seen me you would certainly be happy. 'Tis my misfortunes that have this infectious quality as to strike me, and all that is dear to me . . . . If I ever forget what I owe you or ever entertain a thought of kindness for any person in the world besides, may I live a long and miserable life. 'Tis the greatest curse I can invent: if there be a greater may I feel it. This is all I can say. Tell me if it be possible I can do anything for you, and tell me how I may deserve your pardon for all the trouble I have given you. I would not die without it."

And again, an hour or two later:

"If I loved you less I would allow you to be the same person to me, and I would be the same to you as heretofore. But to deal freely with you, that were to betray myself, and I find that my passion would quickly be my master again if I gave it any liberty. I am not secure that it would not make me do the most extravagant things in the world, and I shall be forced to keep a continual war alive with it as long as there are any remainders of it left;—I think I might as well have said as long as I lived. Why should you give yourself over so unreasonably to it? Good God! no woman breathing can deserve half the trouble you give yourself. If I were yours from this minute I could not recompense what you have suffered from the violence of your passion, though I were all that you can imagine me, when, God knows, I am an inconsiderable person, born to a thousand misfortunes, which have taken away all sense of anything else from me, and left me a walking misery only. I do from my soul forgive you all the injuries your passion has done me, though, let me tell you, I was much more at my ease whilst I was angry. Scorn and despite would have cured me in some reasonable time, which I despair of now. However, I am not displeased with it, and if it may be of any advantage to you, I shall not consider myself in it; but let me beg, then, that you will leave off these dismal thoughts. I tremble at the desperate things you say in your letter; for the love of God, consider seriously with yourself what can enter into comparison with the safety of your soul. Are a thousand women, or ten thousand worlds, worth it? No, you cannot have so little reason left as you pretend, nor so little religion. For God's sake let us not neglect what can only make us happy, for trifles."

Dorothy may reiterate her religious scruples. But the pleading uncertain tone of these last letters is very different from that of her former communications. Temple noticed it at once: he also noticed that in the tumult of her anxiety, she admitted the ardour of her love more freely than ever before. He redoubled his efforts to persuade her to weaken. Dorothy's resolution had been the result of too long and too painful a process for her to yield at once. But, in fact, the tide of her feeling had turned. For that factor, which had just swayed the scale in her original decision, had now lost its force. She had managed to screw herself up to breaking with Temple only because she thought that the engagement was making him miserable; and that, in the end, he might be happier if he were free. Now she saw that the only result of her action had been to render him more unhappy than before. She found that she was driving the man whose happiness was the object of her every thought and feeling, into frenzied despair. This was more than she could face. It was not that she felt any more hopeful about the future. Her reason still told her there was little chance their engagement would end in marriage; but no longer did she feel that she could herself take the responsibility of putting an end to it. For a week she hesitated. Then she wrote giving in completely. Since Temple's love seemed to be incurable, she might as well own to him that hers was too. Of course she would marry him, even if it meant waiting indefinitely. Only they simply must try not to make the strain worse than it need be, by quarrelling with each other: no more doubts, no more jealousies.

The most dangerous crisis in their relationship had passed: and a major crisis in Dorothy's inner life. Renunciation would have meant her spiritual ruin. For love was her vocation: her distrust of life, whether justified or not by the facts of human history, was a negative force, an alien destructive importation that could only thwart the fruitful fulfilment of her nature. That it was defeated was due to Temple: and ironically enough, to his faults as much as to his virtues. His sanguine fire, it is true, had, as always, revived her fainting spirit. But his egotism had helped too. He had simply refused to enter into

her feelings in so far as they were opposed to his desires; so that her instinct for self-sacrifice, perverted temporarily to support the dictates of her fear, was now forcibly recalled to the service of her love. If Temple would not look at things from her point of view, she had no choice but to look at them from his. Luckily, on this occasion his happened to be the right one. Selfishness is sometimes necessary to salvation.

Their reconciliation was sealed by a meeting. Temple paid a flying visit to Chicksands. It was a little awkward, for Henry Osborne was still there, and Dorothy did not dare tell him that the engagement was on again. However, she got out of the difficulty by explaining, truthfully as it happened, that Temple was about to go and stay with his father, who had just left London to settle in Ireland, and that he had only come to say goodbye. Fortunately, when the time came for Temple to depart, the lovers appeared so depressed that Henry thought they must be taking a final farewell of one another. Indeed, during their brief snatched tantalizing time together, the excitement of seeing Temple and reaction after the blank despair of the previous weeks, did combine to throw Dorothy into a strange turmoil of conflicting emotions—gaiety and sadness, anxiety and relief. The day sped by in a dazed dream; after Temple had gone, she remembered a hundred things she had meant to say to him, and forgotten in her confusion of mind. However, she had said the only things that mattered. In the sunlight of each other's presence, the last thin shadow of misunderstanding had vanished. They parted more closely bound to one another than ever before. A week or two later, as a pledge of their bond, Temple sent her a ring—gold, with a tortoishell guard. Inside it was engraved a couplet expressive of their sworn and secret faith—

"The love I owe
I cannot showe."

57

They also exchanged locks of hair. Alone in her room for hours together Dorothy would gaze at Temple's curling handsome tress, and kiss it, and comb it, and go to bed to dream of it, in a trance of happy love.

Meanwhile, to outward appearance, the course of her life had slipped back into its old grooves. Her letters, save that they are suffused ever so delicately with a brighter glow of sentiment, are written in the same tone and about the same topics as those of the previous summer. Once more the picture of those quiet days recomposes itself for us. Now Dorothy is wandering into the garden in her nightgown very early on a fine morning, now whiling away an evening drawing Valentines with Jane Wright, now asking Temple to get her some tweezers, now gossiping. "What did Temple think of Lady Ruthven marrying a man who clacked like a mill?" she asked; "what a number of marriages seemed to be breaking up! How surprisingly loose the manners of young people had grown!" Dorothy put this last phenomenon down to the absence of a Court. There was no longer any accepted social authority, she said, to set a standard, and maintain convention; and few people were strong enough morally not to be better for submitting their wills to authority. This last reflection struck Temple as savouring dangerously of her old defeatist habit of mind. He protested. Dorothy replied teasingly that she found support for her view in the works of no less a person that Bishop Jeremy Taylor. She read as much as ever—she would rather read than talk, she said, unless it was to Temple—Taylor's *Holy Living,* Don Fernando Pinto's *Travels in China,* the romance of Parthenissa. And as much as ever she complained about her suitors. For they had begun again. Her elder brother proposed another well-to-do widower for her; and there was a pushing little neighbour called Beverley, who so persecuted her with his attentions that at last, in order to make her feelings quite clear to him, she threw his letters unopened into the fire before his very eyes. Temple remembered Beverley at College; he called him "the whelp". On his side, Beverley thought Temple "the proudest, imperious, insulting, ill-natured man that ever was". It was the impression that Temple usually produced on inferior persons.

Beverley's was not the only abuse of her lover to which Dorothy was forced to listen. Henry Osborne had begun to suspect the engagement was not so much at an end as he had been led to believe. And one night he began violently attacking Temple on the ground that he was a man of no honour and no religion. This last was to Dorothy the most unforgivable accusation that could be brought against anyone. She flared up once more:

"I forgot all my disguise, and we talked ourselves weary; he renounced me and I defied him, but both in as civil language as it would permit and parted with great anger with the usual ceremony of a leg and a courtesy, that you would have died with laughing to have seen us.

The next day I, not being at dinner, saw him not till night; then he came into my chamber, where I supped but he did not. Afterwards Mr. Gibson and he and I talked of indifferent things till all but we two went to bed. Then he sat half an hour and said not one word, nor I to him. At last, in a pitiful tone, 'Sister', says he, 'I have heard you say that when anything troubles you, of all things you apprehend going to bed, because there it increases upon you, and you lie at the mercy of all your sad thought, which the silence and darkness of the night adds a horror to; I am at that pass now. I vow to God I would not endure another night like the last to gain a crown.' I, who resolved to take no notice what ailed him, said 'twas a knowledge I had raised from my spleen only, and so fell into a discourse of

melancholy and the causes, and from that (I know not how)
into religion; and we talked so long of it, and so devoutly,
that it laid all our anger. We grew to a calm and peace with
all the world. Two hermits conversing in a cell they
equally inhabit, ner'er expressed more humble, charitable
kindness, one towards another, than we. He asked my
pardon and I his, and he has promised me never to speak
of it to me whilst he lives, but leave the event to God
Almighty."

When he was in this softened, pathetic mood, Dorothy still
found it painful to resist Henry. Indeed, settling down to her
old life did entail, in some degree, settling down to her old
worries. The practical obstacle confronting the lovers remained. What prospect was there that the Osbornes would
ever be brought to approve the marriage? Or Sir John Temple
either. For he too was still hostile: he told Temple Dorothy
was not worthy of him, that she was behaving very badly,
shilly-shallying like this; he made no offer to increase his
allowance to Temple. And Temple's lack of money was,
officially at any rate, the main obstacle to him in the Osbornes'
eyes. Temple, encouraged by his recent victory over her
religious scruples, urged Dorothy to pay no attention to this,
and marry him all the same. Here, however, she was adamant.
It was not only that it was against her principles to disobey her
parents. She was also possessed by an extraordinary horror
of the scorn and disapproval she would expose herself to
from the world at large, if she made what it would consider
an imprudent marriage. Again and again, with hysterical
emphasis she refers to this feeling.

"Possibly it is a weakness in me to aim at the world's
esteem, as if I could not be happy without it. But there
are certainly things that custom has made almost of absolute

necessity; and reputation I take to be one of those. If one could be invisible, I should choose that; but since all people are seen and known and shall be talked of in spite of their teeth, who is it that does not desire at least that nothing of ill may be said of them whether justly or otherwise? I never knew any so satisfied with their own innocence as to be content the world should think them guilty. Some out of pride have seemed to condemn ill-reports, when they have found they could not avoid them; but none out of strength of reason, though many have pretended to it."

This nervous regard for public opinion is at first glance extremely mysterious to a modern reader. It seems inconsistent alike with Dorothy's passion, her unworldliness and her independence of mind. Was it vanity? Temple suggested so, in a spasm of irritation. But, replied Dorothy truthfully, no one ever cared less for admiration than she did; her most cherished wish was to pass through life unnoticed. Nor was she conventional in the sense that she accepted standards without question just because they were held by the majority. Yet it is true that the ideas of her rank and her period do partly account for her attitude. To the Caroline gentry public reputation was inextricably bound up with private honour: it was part of a man's duty to himself not to drag his good name in the mud. And, since the order of society was thought to have a divine sanction, the Carolines thought it a very serious act to incur the considered disapproval of its most respect-worthy members. Nor was there any doubt that to marry imprudently did mean incurring such disapproval. Marriage to them, as to the French still, was not the culmination of a love affair, but an essential part of the social system, whose function it was to maintain the institution of the family. As such it must rest on a sound financial basis. To marry in disregard of this, and from purely sentimental reasons, was a feckless act which no conscientious person would have felt justified in committing. Dorothy was far too conscientious not to agree with this view.

She embraced it so desperately, however, from deeper and less rational motives. Dorothy could feel neither the confidence in her own judgment to challenge public opinion, nor the strength of spirit to endure its disapproval. Her bruised nerves flinched uncontrollably at the prospect of publicity and obloquy and misunderstanding. Better to avoid them by conforming to established custom. Even if she suffered all the same, it would be custom's responsibility, not her's; and as such easier to bear. Moreover, to engage in a fight one must, like Temple, be encouraged by the faith one will win. In her darker moods Dorothy was without such a faith. Do what she would, she could not rid herself of the feeling that she was peculiarly doomed to disappointment. It was the old trouble. Deep psychological wounds are not so easily healed. After the first exhilaration of her reconciliation with Temple had worn off, Dorothy's morbid distrust of life raised its head once more. Her deference to convention, like her sense of sin, was only an attempt to find some rational justification for it. And though she strove to argue the case for prudence in cool and reasonable tones, after a paragraph or two she falters, to let the inexplicable foreboding that haunted her heart tremble forth in a sigh of hopeless yearning.

"Dear, shall we ever be so happy, think you? Ah I dare not hope it; yet 'tis not want of love that gives me these fears. No, in earnest I think—nay I am sure—I love you more than ever, and 'tis that only gives me these despairing thoughts. When I consider how small a proportion of happiness is allowed in this world, and how great mine would be in a person for whom I have a passionate kindness, and who has the same for me; as it is infinitely above what I can deserve and more than God Almighty usually allots to the best people, I can find nothing in reason but seems to be against me; and methinks 'tis as vain in me to expect it, as t'would be to hope I might be a Queen."

"Shall we ever be so happy?"—it is not the first time she has said it. The wistful little phrase echoes like a refrain through all her correspondence.

Nevertheless, in spite of occasional fits of melancholy, Dorothy was in better spirits than ever before. The fact that the forces of her distrust had been defeated in the decisive battle of December had permanently weakened their hold over her. There was no more any question, even when she was feeling most despondent, of her voluntarily giving up Temple. Her confidence was gradually growing. By the beginning of March it was strong enough to make her, for the first time, take the offensive in her conflict with her family. She announced to Henry that she was engaged to Temple. Two days later fate, whom she had so long and so justifiably counted her enemy, came to her aid. Sir Peter Osborne died. In the first shock of bereavement a wave of depression swept over Dorothy. Not only had she loved him with peculiar tenderness—he had been peculiarly affectionate to her—but she felt very lonely. Her home was taken from her; and, since in those days it was not thought possible for a young lady to set up house on her own, Dorothy, shy, proud and twenty-six years old, was faced with the prospect of making her life as a dependant in the home of whatever member of her family would have her. Considering how strained her relations with them had lately been, she did not expect to find them sympathetic companions. "Kindred, not friends," she called them; and she complained to Temple that, though she was to pay them as much for her keep as though she were a stranger, they still thought they were doing her a kindness. All the same, as regards the crucial issue of her life, she was better off. Brothers and aunts had not the legal authority over her that a parent had; and she did not feel the same moral obligation to respect their wishes. It was much easier for her to marry whom she liked. All the more so that Henry in particular now began to put himself even more in the wrong than before. Utterly insensitive to any sorrow she might be feeling, he began arguing with her about Temple within twenty-four hours of her father's death; and, when he found her firm, relieved his feelings by lamenting to all and sundry that his sister had gone and engaged herself to an arrogant and impecunious atheist. Dorothy's fighting spirit rose. She had tied up her hands, she told Henry, so that she could not marry anyone but Temple. Moreover, if everyone was to know about her engagement, let them know it officially. No longer did she wish to keep it a secret. This was a great step forward. With Dorothy committed in the eyes of the world, it was much harder for the Osbornes to make her withdraw. Anyway, in the tenacious mood she now showed herself, they began to despair of ever making her give way. Things were growing easier on the Temple side too. Under the continual and tempestuous pressure of his son, Sir John had begun to waver in his opposition, and, apparently, offered to give him some more money. In face of this the Osbornes could resist no longer. Even Henry resigned himself, and for the time being spoke kindly to Dorothy about it. By the beginning of the summer both sides had, in principle at any rate, agreed to the match.

All anxiety was not over though. Getting married in those circles was like making an international treaty. Indeed it was a sort of treaty—a financial treaty, in which preliminaries must be laid down, representatives appointed, negotiations conducted according to carefully prescribed forms, before the final settlement was arrived at. And at each step a fatal hitch might occur. Throughout the summer months the stately interminable business proceeded, impeded at every turn by objections and qualifications: and, until the last document was signed, no one could be quite sure that the marriage would come off. Certainly, Dorothy could not be. Do what she would Dorothy could not acquire the habit of hope: and the hint of a set-back sent a chill of discouragement coursing through her. Luckily however, her love had now established a permanent ascendancy over her despondency. Against her strongest instincts, and simply because she knew Temple wanted her to, she did her best to combat despair. "I hope merely because you bid me" she said sadly, "and lose that hope as often as I consider anything but yours. Would I were easy of belief! They say one is so to all that one desires. I do not find it." No amount of good fortune could completely cure Dorothy of her temperamental weakness.

Nor could it cure Temple of his. Early in May, while he was still in Ireland, he did not hear from her for several weeks. It was the fault of the postal service; Temple might have been expected to guess this, after all that had happened. Instead, however, he was at once in a fever of nervous suspicion and anxiety, scarcely allayed when her letter did arrive.

"Well now in very great earnest," he wrote, "do you think 'tis time for me to come or no? Would you be very glad to see me there? And could you do it in less disorder and with less surprise than you did at Chicksands? . . . I know you love me still, you promised it me, and that is all the security I can have for all the good I am ever like to have in this world. 'Tis that which makes all things else seem nothing to it, so high it sets me; and so high indeed that should I ever fall, t'would dash me all to pieces. Methinks your very charity should make you love me more now than ever, by seeing me so much more unhappy than I used, by being so much further from you. . . . Justice I am sure will oblige you to it, since you have no other means left in the world of rewarding such a passion as mine, which, sure, is of a much richer value than anything in the world besides. Should you save my life again, should you make me absolute master of your fortune and your person too, yet, if you love me not, I should accept none of all this in any part of payment, and look upon you as one behind hand with me still. 'Tis not vanity this, but a true sense of how pure and how refined a nature my passion is, which none can ever know besides my own heart, unless you find it out by being there. . . .

How hard it is to think of ending when I am writing to you. But it must be so, and I must ever be subject to other people's occasions and so never, I think, master of my own."

Up to the very altar, Temple was to remain the most agitated and Dorothy the most pessimistic of lovers.

This particular letter of Temple's reached her in London. Since Sir Peter's death her mode of life had undergone a swift and sensational change. After six years seclusion in the shadowed backwater of Chicksands, she found herself swept into the glaring rushing midstream of the world. No longer had she a regular home; for the time being her life passed in a succession of country visits followed by a month or two in London. Even there she changed her lodgings every few weeks, according as it was convenient for her friends to take her in. With none of them did she find a tranquil existence. London social life under the Commonwealth was less sober than might have been expected. The playhouses were, it is true, closed, and at any moment political events might rudely interrupt the course of private existence. Dorothy was stopped going on a visit to the country because a plot had been

discovered against Cromwell's life; and till all the conspirators
had been rounded up, no one was allowed to leave London.
Still, people bred of a life of pleasure generally can contrive to
keep it going in some degree, however unpropitious their
circumstances. The aristocracy dined with each other every
night; such places of public amusement, as were still open, were
crammed; from her window in the Strand, Dorothy watched
the sporting set of the Beau Monde driving off to the races.
She took part in fashionable life, as well as observing it. New
faces, new places crowded in on her. Now she is off to dine
at the Swan Tavern; now going masked with a party to walk
in Spring Gardens: now visiting the celebrated Samuel
Cooper to commission him to paint her miniature; now
having her fortune told by the famous astrologer, Lilly.
Dorothy was not impressed by his powers. "No old woman,
who passes for a witch, could have been more puzzled
what to say to reasonable people than he was. He asked us
more questions than we did him."

Indeed, she was not dazzled by the whirling glitter of the
new world into which she had entered. Now and again it
afforded agreeable material for her satiric sense; she found
it entertaining to meet Lady Tollemache for example.

"'Tis not unpleasant methinks to hear her talk, how at
such a time she was sick and the physicians told her she
would have the small-pox, and showed her where they
were coming out upon her; but she bethought herself that
it was not at all convenient to have them at that time.
Some business she had, that required her going abroad, and
so she resolved she would not be sick; nor was not. Twenty
such stories as this she told us; and then falls into discoveries
of the strength of reason and the power of philosophy till
she confounds herself and all that hear her."

On the whole, however, the chief consequence of Dorothy's

encounter with the great world was to confirm her in the conviction that she was unfitted for it. She was too shy for one thing; do what she would, she could not help blushing when she heard Temple's name mentioned. For another, she was incapable of concealing her true opinions. If she thought a party boring—and she was easily bored—she could not help saying so. This did not tend to make her popular with her companions and, as she admitted apologetically to Temple, she knew herself that it did no good. It was a pity to be thought a spoil-sport and a wet blanket even by people who bored one.

In July she left London to spend the rest of the summer with her brother-in-law, Sir Thomas Peyton, at Knowlton, his house in Kent. This was no improvement on London as far as quiet went. "I can only be allowed time to tell you," she writes shortly after her arrival, "that I am in Kent and in a house so strangely crowded with company that I am weary as a dog already." Indeed, staying at Knowlton does sound a great strain. Lady Peyton was a very sociable woman, and life in her house was a continual party, where guests seldom could get to bed till daylight, where they were compelled to take part in private theatricals—Dorothy found herself cast rather ominously for the rôle of the Lost Lady—and so crammed full that she had sometimes to share her bed with two other ladies, and was forced to write to Temple in a room thronged with chattering people. Nor, for the most part, were they sympathetic people. On one night two Colonels arrived to dinner, both revoltingly drunk, and another time when Dorothy said that she wanted to marry a man who would continue to be in love with her all their lives, the young gallants of the party burst into fits of derisive laughter. In addition to this Sir Thomas Peyton, exhausted perhaps by the continual social effort which his wife's tastes compelled him to make, wrangled with her in public all day

long. The only people in the house with whom Dorothy
felt easy were a lady, grown misanthropic as the result of a
quarrel with her husband, and a gentleman whose heart had
been broken early in life by the death of his bride to be. These
two at least were quiet. But they were not enough to reconcile
Dorothy to life at Knowlton. "I would not live thus a twelve
month," she writes to Temple in comic desperation, "to gain
all that the King has lost, unless it were to give it him again."

Fortunately there was no question of her staying there a
twelvemonth. By August events were hurrying to their
conclusion. Temple was back from Ireland, and the negotiations for the marriage settlement were fully under way.
Before all was over, Dorothy had still to undergo a few
painful moments. Her experience of the summer made her
recoil with horror from the thought of a public wedding
with all its attendant celebrations. Ah! if she could just steal
out secretly and marry Temple and drive off! In September
too, Sir John Temple suddenly objected to Henry Osborne
appearing as a representative of Dorothy's family in the
settlement negotiations: he thought he had been too openly
hostile to William to deserve such an honour. At this unexpected hitch so near the end of her troubles, Dorothy's
strained nerves snapped. After all, Henry was her brother;
and, however difficult he may have been in the past, lately he
had been making a creditable effort to behave amiably.
Besides, she did not think that Sir John had the right to cast a
stone; though she had been too considerate of William's
feelings to say so at the time, she had in fact been wounded by
Sir John thinking her so unworthy a bride for his son. If he
persisted in insulting the Osbornes in this way, she burst out,
they had better drop the whole thing. It was only a momen-
tary spasm of exasperation. Never was Dorothy less likely to
give up Temple than at this juncture. Sir John gave in about
Henry and all was soon smoothed over. As a matter of fact,

Henry's subsequent conduct was not to prove such as would have warranted his sister making any sacrifice for his sake. Not only did he begin quarrelling with her again about the marriage at the very last minute, but it was afterwards discovered that he had persuaded her to sign a paper without reading it—on the ground that it was a pure formality—in which she resigned her right to part of her dowry to Henry himself. By the time she found it out, Dorothy now married to Temple, was in no mood to take Henry's side about anything. Feeling grew so high that the families were nearly involved in a law-suit. It is not surprising that during her subsequent life, Dorothy seems never to have had anything more to do with Henry.

But this is to anticipate. By October, at least all was settled. Dorothy came to London for her wedding. We have two little notes she wrote to Temple there; in them her love ripples out, for the first time unqualified by a shadow of anxiety, and sparkling with a sunshiny gaiety, which, coming as it does from one so long forced by hard experience to believe such a mood unattainable, touches us to the heart. "You are like to have an excellent housewife of me. I am abed still and slept so soundly nothing but your letter could have waked me. You shall hear from me as soon as we have done. Farewell! Can you endure that word? No, out upon it, I will see you anon."

And then it turned out that in fact she had been cheerful too soon. Unkindly fate had still a dart in store for Dorothy. A week before her wedding she fell ill with small-pox. It was so bad an attack that the doctors feared for her life. Oblivious of the risk, Temple stayed with her constantly. By December she was out of danger. But small-pox is a cruel disease: Dorothy rose from her bed with her beauty gone. And though Temple married her the moment she was well enough, yet it is related that he found the change in her appearance too great to leave him wholly insensible. It would be unbearably sad to think that his feelings for her were seriously impaired. Nor need we think it. His love, like hers, was grounded on a securer foundation than the perishing red and white of mortal loveliness; on community of tastes, of views, of jokes, on an affinity of the soul. Further, some letters of Dorothy's written two years later breathe a spirit of glad, easy tenderness that could only spring from a union as perfect as any the lovers could have hoped for during the long years of their frustration. She is in the country with her baby Jack: Temple is away on business:

"Can you tell me when you intend to come home. Would you would; I should take it mighty kindly. Good dear make haste. I am as weary as a dog without you. Poor Jack is all the entertainment I have. He remembers his little duty and grows and thrives every day . . . indeed my heart 'tis the quietest best little boy that ever was borne. I am afraid he'll make me grow fond of him, do what I can. The only way to keep me from it is for you to keep at home, for then I am less with him. Now he is all my entertainment, besides what I find in thinking of my dearest and wishing him with his

Dorothy Temple."

The spectre of Dorothy's fears seems laid at last: the distance in her spirit resolved in a final harmonious chord. As in a fairy-tale, the lovers, after trials and troubles innumerable, have settled down to live happily ever after.

* * * *

But had they? Alas, true stories go on after fairy-tales stop; Dorothy lived for forty years more. They were full years too. Men of Temple's energy and talent are not destined to pass their existence in tranquil obscurity, however much they may fancy they would like to. Half unwillingly he found himself drawn for a large part of his life on to the bustling, brightly lit stage of great affairs; where, amid the respectful applause of his contemporaries, he moved through embassies and council chambers and gatherings dedicated to Science and Letters, to end his days, wiser than in his youth, but perhaps a trifle too consciously admirable, living in illustrious retirement amid the apricots and parterres of his delightful house at Moor Park, the trusted counsellor of princes, the stately patron of the youthful Swift. Dorothy supported him in his labours and shared his honours. The records of the day praise her as wife, as ambassadress, as patroness. "Mild Dorothea, peaceful, wise and great"—so Swift extols her. Yet what did she really think of it all? We can only guess; there are no letters left to tell us. But certainly it was a very different sort of existence to that of which she had dreamed in the old days at Chicksands; and there was little time in it for that private life of intimacy and contemplation, in which her heart had laid up its treasure. Moreover, such private life as the Temples did manage to snatch from the pressure of public business, was darkened by catastrophe. Of the six children Dorothy bore to Temple, only one lived to grow up; and he—the little Jack of whom she speaks so lovingly in her last letters—drowned himself in a fit of madness when he was twenty-one. On the occasion of his death we are permitted, after forty years silence, once more to hear Dorothy's voice. She is answering a letter of condolence from a nephew:

"Dear Nephew—I give you many thanks for your kind letter and the sense you have of my affliction, which truly is very great. But since it is laid upon me by the hand of an Almighty and Gracious God, that always proportions His

punishments to the support He gives with them, I may hope to bear it as a Christian ought to do, and more especially one that is conscious to herself of having many ways deserved it. The strange revolutions we have seen might well have taught me what this world is, yet it seems it was necessary that I should have a near example of the uncertainty of all human blessings, that so having no tie to the world, I may the better prepare myself to leave it; and that this correction may suffice to teach me my duty must be the prayer of your affectionate aunt and humble servant,
D. Temple."

These are the last words she speaks to us. They make a sad, ironical epilogue to her love-story. For here, though expressed with an austere impersonal formality of phrase strangely unlike the Dorothy of earlier days, is the old sense of guilt, the old disillusioned despondency. Fraught with more tragic overtones, her ancient cry echoes again through our memory. "Shall we ever be so happy?" After all, and in spite of love requited and fulfilled, she had been right to doubt it.

Part Two

THOMAS GRAY

"Voluntary solitude is that which is familiar with melancholy; and gently brings on, like a siren or shoeing-horn or some sphinx, to that irrevocable gulf."

ROBERT BURTON.

THOMAS GRAY

THERE is no doubt England's ancient seats of learning present an extremely poetical spectacle. The belfrys of Oxford, the pinnacled vistas of Cambridge, the groves and pensive cloisters of Eton and Winchester, made spiritual by the veil of dewy mist that lingers perpetually over the damp river valleys in which their pious founders have seen fit to place them, induce irresistibly in the visitor a mood of exalted, romantic reverie. It might be thought that their regular inhabitants, exposed at every hour of the day to these dreamy influences, would be among the most poetically-minded of mankind. In fact, however, this is not so. Academic persons are often intellectual and sometimes witty: but seldom indeed are they conspicuous for the poetic qualities, for imagination or aesthetic sensibility. Their very intellectuality has something to do with this. Minds accustomed to concentrate habitually on abstractions tend not to notice their physical environment. On the other hand, however much they may admire academic buildings, people with an artistic temperament seldom take to the academic mode of life. They feel it too bloodless, too conventional, too sheltered from the direct violence of experience to satisfy the passionate intensity of their natures; and fly to uglier but more stimulating surroundings. However, there are exceptions. Now and again an artist is born with enough of the academic in him to make it possible for him to settle in school or college. The diverse strains in him blend to produce a personality of curious and complex fascination to the student of human nature. Walter Pater was such a personality; A. E. Housman was another. But the most elegant example of the type is Gray.

He is also the hardest to understand. This is not for want of information about him. Things had changed since Dorothy Osborne's time. In the fifty odd years that had elapsed between her death and Gray's maturity, England had settled down to an epoch of prosperous stability in which, undisturbed alike by bloodshed or by spiritual yearnings, those, who liked, had been able to concentrate on the development of the private life and the cultivation of its modes of expression. Through the course of their long leisurely lifetimes, some people did little else but talk, write letters, pay visits, and keep journals. They learnt to do it with a fullness and elaborate perfection unsurpassed in history. The private papers of Gray and his friends compose a small library in themselves. All are accomplished, and some—Gray's own letters and those written to him by Horace Walpole—are glittering masterpieces in the art of social intercourse; easy as a casual conversation with an old friend, but made exquisite by every grace of style, every refinement of wit and civility.

All the same, they do not completely reveal their authors. We listen, charmed, to the well-bred voices flowing on in never-ending delightful discourse, now serious, now sparkling, glancing from gossip to antiquities, from literature to the political news; but never stiff, never at a loss, never boring. And then, when we shut the book, it strikes us that there is a great deal about these people we have not been allowed to know. They are acquaintances rather than friends. This reserve is outstandingly characteristic of Gray's circle. The very conscious perfection of their agreeability is partly responsible for it. To them, social intercourse was an art whose aim was to give pleasure. They, therefore, kept it clear of anything they thought unlikely to please. Among these things were personal revelations. They did not even think them interesting. Walpole says openly he disliked letters without news but full of "sentiment". Gray, to judge by his correspondence, shared this opinion. For all their refinement, they, like other people in the eighteenth century, took an extroverted common sense view of life. Objective topics—politics, books, works of art—seemed to them far better worth talking about than the fluctuations of the individual mood, the condition of the individual soul. It was not that they were ashamed of expressing emotion, like a modern public-school boy. If they felt unhappy or affectionate or out of temper, they said so and as eloquently as they could. But they were not interested to analyse these feelings; and they expressed them with a formality of phrase that somehow makes them unintimate.

For—and this is the final cause of their reserve—they believed deeply in form. The spontaneous, the unbuttoned, had no charms for them. They had never doubted that it was a purpose of civilization to impose discipline and polish on the crude natural man. As they wore powdered wigs to cover their naked heads of hair, so they put on a cover of good manners over their naked thoughts and feelings. Their manners were not so ceremonious as those of Dorothy Osborne's day: their tone of voice was more colloquial, their ideal of form less stately. But it affected them more profoundly. For their whole being was saturated with it, it modified their every impulse of thought and feeling. Civilization had moved on since the seventeenth century; and, for Gray and his friends at any rate, it had succeeded in expelling every trace of that naïveté which mingled so strangely with the dignity of Dorothy Osborne's world. Their reactions come to us carefully filtered through the fine firm mesh woven by their standards of good sense and good taste.

No wonder Gray is mysterious to us. Yet he is not un-

fathomable. Now and again, the man himself breaks through
the web: and his personality is present by implication in the
ordinary run of his discourse. If we learn to read between the
lines, to interpret hint, emphasis, omission, even to guess a
little—always remembering that we are guessing—gradually
his character and the course of his life begin to take shape
before us.

II

From the first we see him in an academic setting. Gray
makes his entry on the stage of recorded history as an Eton
boy. Not a typical Eton boy, especially of that period.
England in the eighteenth century was a robust, red-blooded,
uproarious place. The England of Fielding and Hogarth
and Parson Woodforde—certainly there was no lack of
earthiness there. How people ate and drank! Mountains of
beef—hogsheads of port or beer, as the case may be. With
what unflagging virile relish they swore, and begat bastards,
and gambled and attended executions and proclaimed their
belief in liberty and their contempt for the wretched frog-
eaters on the other side of the Channel! Eton reproduced in
miniature the characteristics of the nation. To a generation
bred in the disciplined totalitarianism of the reformed public
school, accounts of life there have their charm. There were
only four hours of lessons and no compulsory games. There
was not much order either; sometimes none. Once or twice
in the century open rebellion broke out on a formidable scale.
Then authority violently asserted itself, flogging and expelling
right and left. But within a short time Eton had relapsed into
its customary condition of easy-going anarchy. It was true
that if a boy wrote a bad copy of Latin verses, he was sum-
marily and severely birched. But since classes often numbered
100 boys, discipline in school cannot have been very strict.

Out of school they went to bed any hour, they ran off to the races, they gave large parties at the Inn at Windsor, they drank themselves sick with brandy and stuffed themselves with pies at the pastrycook's, they pummelled and beat each other unmercifully. They also enjoyed beating the local rustics. The rustics—for this was still the age of aristocratic ascendancy—were glad enough to let themselves be beaten, if the young gentlemen would throw them a couple of guineas after the operation was over. For the rest, amid the green fields beside the shining Thames with the battlements of Windsor Castle rising in the wooded distance, the boys entertained themselves by staging full-dress fights with bare fists, playing a rough amateurish cricket, or with gleaming bodies bared, diving in the willow-shadowed water. Meanwhile the younger boys—they came as young as nine sometimes—bowled hoops, played leap-frog, or, with long hair flying in the breeze and shrill cries echoing through the air, fled to escape the sudden onslaught of some bullying senior.

Bullying, however, was as unorganized as everything else. The boys of eighteenth century Eton enjoyed the advantages as well as the dangers of freedom. No pressure, moral or physical, was exerted to force those of them who did not wish it, to cultivate the team spirit. And about 1730 a quartet of boys in their teens were to be observed there, who followed a course of life sedulously aloof from that of the mob of high-born ragamuffins by whom they were surrounded. They seldom came into the playing fields at all. If they did, they stood and watched their rampaging schoolfellows from a prudent distance. More often they were to be seen roaming singly by the river, book in hand, or sitting together in the library, absorbed in animated conversation. They gave a general impression of thinness, pallor and graceful preciosity. Their names were Horace Walpole, Richard West, Thomas Ashton and Thomas Gray.

Common tastes and a common unlikeness to other boys had brought them together; for their origins were widely different. Walpole sprang from the resplendent centre of that Whig aristocracy which governed the country; was not his father the great Sir Robert Walpole himself, for over fifteen years all-powerful First Minister of England? West was the son of a lawyer, Ashton of a schoolmaster. Gray came from a less intellectual sphere. His father was a scrivener, and his mother, together with her sister, ran a warehouse in Cornhill. His childhood, it seems, had not been a happy one. Apart from anything else, his background did not suit him. With his intellectual brow, fastidious mouth and elegant little figure, Gray did not look like a product of a Cornhill warehouse. Nor did his appearance belie him. It would be untrue to say that the world he was born in left no mark on Gray: there was always to be a prudent, solid, middle-class streak in him. But blended with it was a scholarly intelligence, an aristocratic pride and, above all, an extraordinary feeling for the charm of the exquisite and the ancestral. This was an imaginative, not a worldly feeling. Within Gray's precise little frame quivered the flame of a passionate sensibility to any manifestation of beauty and romance. Such a disposition was not likely to feel at home in the Hogarthian homeliness of eighteenth century commercial London. The circumstances of his family life did nothing to reconcile him to his family environment. His mother, indeed, was amiable and intelligent. But his father, though reported to be musical, was in other respects a most disagreeable character; morose, brutal and capricious. He spent his wife's money in building a house he did not want, only, it appeared, in order to annoy her, and from the time he married was liable, if irritated, to revile her obscenely and to pummel her in a painful and alarming fashion. So alarming, that later she was driven to ask a lawyer if she had grounds for a legal separation. In those days, how-

THOMAS GRAY AS A BOY

ever, the laws of England looked unfavourably on women who rose in open rebellion against their husband's authority; and Mrs. Gray was told that she had better try and put up with her sufferings for fear of losing her income. Nor, poor lady, was her unpleasing spouse her only source of sorrow. Of the twelve children she bore to him only Thomas survived childhood; and he was not at all strong.

Such a childhood could not fail to have its effect on him. The fact that he identified himself with his mother in her quarrel with his father encouraged the development of a delicate feminine strain in his temperament and intensified a natural distaste for rough masculinity; while the insecurity of the home, where he got his first impressions of the world, implanted in him an ineradicable sense of insecurity about human existence in general. Precociously aware, as he was, of the possibilities of disaster, his free response to experience was chilled and checked. Even as a boy Gray was not spontaneous. There was a touch of doubtful melancholy in the gaze he turned on the world. Already shrinking uncontrollably from the hurly-burly of active life, he sought stability, safety, peace.

However he was not so abnormal as to be incapable of enjoying himself; and his fortunes early took a turn that put enjoyment in his way. In 1725, when he was nine years old, his mother's brother, Roger Antrobus, who was a master at Eton, by way of assisting his struggling sister arranged for Thomas to enter the school, himself paying some of the fees. There Gray remained for the next nine years. These years were crucial in his development. They shaped his taste and coloured his imagination for life. School was likely to influence him powerfully in any case, seeing how early he was transplanted there, and from a home like his. Though he loved his mother, he turned his back on the world she lived in as soon as he could. It was not long before his holidays, spent wretchedly in Cornhill or in forlorn visits to relations, had become nothing but a disagreeable, insignificant interruption to the course of a life whose centre was Eton. It, not Cornhill, became his native country. By the time he was in his teens, all that he enjoyed and valued most was bound up with his existence there.

It was not to be expected that he should enter into the male boisterousness which displayed itself so flamboyantly in the life of the average Etonian. But this does not seem to have worried him. The boys, we are told, thought he was delicate and let him alone. Anyway Eton had other and more congenial satisfactions to offer. There was the beauty of the landscape; the lush sweetness of the Thames valley country, its pastoral charm, as yet unspoilt by urbanization, stretching level into the soft distance, shadowed by the full-foliaged trees, watered by slow sky-reflecting streams, their banks muffled in meadowgrass thick with wild flowers. Gray loved flowers. His Uncle Roger, a keen botanist, noticed this and introduced him to the study. It appealed alike to the student and the artist in him. He spent happy hours collecting and cataloguing butterfly-orchis and bog asphodel.

The works of man at Eton are beautiful too; the time-tinted brick-work of the School Yard, the traceried pile of Chapel, grey between the boles of the lime trees. It is an ancient beauty: Gothic chapel, Tudor clock-tower, Caroline pilastered Upper School, the oak benches of Lower School carved with generation after generation of names—every place in Eton is haunted by ghosts of the past. The youthful Gray responded to its imaginative appeal. The sense of history woke in him to mingle inextricably with his aesthetic sense. For ever after he was to be moved most profoundly by the beauty that is enriched by association with the mystery and romance of a vanished age.

Then there were his lessons; Gray did well at these. He was

a clever boy with a turn for refined exact scholarship. Reading Horace and Virgil was to him a pleasant occupation. As he grew older it became something else—a profound and rapturous experience. Virgil, in particular, with his delicate finish of style, his sad civilized nobility of temper, set vibrating a sympathetic chord in the depths of Gray's spirit. The joy inspired by reading such poetry—what could be compared with it? Nor was it a passive joy. Obscure and unrecognized, in answer to Virgil's silver call, something creative began to stir to life within him. Here, little though he might know it, was to be the mould in which his own personality was to find its supreme expression and fulfilment. "What first gave you a taste for poetry?" someone asked him in later life. "Reading Virgil at Eton as a boy of eleven," said Gray.

Equally important, at Eton he made his first friends. He was not one to be satisfied by solitary pleasures. His lively mind craved someone to talk to; his sensitive heart thirsted for someone to love. Unluckily it was not easy to find either. Fastidiousness and nervousness between them had iced him over with a stiff reserve only to be thawed by someone with whom he felt a genuine affinity of spirit. Gray was not a common type; such people were few. Certainly they were not to be met with in his home circle, nor among the ordinary run of his schoolfellows. However, in so huge and so free a community as that of Eton, even the oddest boy can hope to find a kindred spirit somewhere. Gray found two, Horace Walpole and Richard West. The three had a good deal in common with one another, clever, fragile, unboyish boys who bore all the signs of having been brought up exclusively by doting mothers. Here, however, the likeness between them ends. West shrank from the world even more than Gray; so much so that to strangers he appeared only sickly and insignificant. Shy, fanciful and unworldly, he was at his happiest day-dreaming in the fields or reading and writing verses. His talents bloomed earlier than those of his friends, who thought him a youthful genius. He was far from insignificant to them. Round his meagre figure hovered a lyrical charm in which a pervading minor-key melancholy was occasionally lit up by a flicker of whimsical humour. The deeper strains in Gray found their perfect affinity in West. Here was someone who cared for Virgil and musing just in the same way as he did; here was someone who, like him, felt alone in an alien universe. An intense and intimate affection sprang up between the two, which was to last till death. Hand in hand "like the two children in the wood" they would be seen wandering away to roam the countryside together.

Walpole never penetrated Gray's heart as West did. But he made an even more sensational impression on him. It was no wonder. To a boy brought up like Gray, the youthful Horace Walpole must have been a dazzling apparition indeed. The mere setting of his existence dazzled. It is difficult for us to realize what a huge gulf separated the life of aristocrats in the eighteenth century from that of other people. Fabulously rich, politically omnipotent, and with their superb self-assurance untroubled by the slightest doubt as to their right to a position of unique privilege, they seemed, like the olympian deities in the painted Baroque ceilings which adorned their great houses, to recline, jewelled and garlanded on an aureate cloud, floating far above the drab earth where common mortals trudged through their humdrum existence. From as early as he could remember, whether in his family's Arlington Street mansion, or amid the Palladian architecture of the country seats where he was taken on visits, Horace Walpole had lived in a whirl of high fashion and high politics peopled by the bright figures of courtiers, cabinet ministers, and reigning beauties: and of them he knew his father was the ruling centre. At Eton, on one occasion, he found him-

self bursting into a torrent of tears at the thought of George I's
death, largely, so he tells us, because he thought the son of the
Prime Minister ought to be especially moved by such an
event. Not that his family life was without its problems.
Like Gray's, Walpole's parents did not hit it off. But how
differently did they conduct themselves! Good sense, good
temper and a large income enabled them to go their own
ways satisfactorily while preserving appearances to the world.
Easy-going, extravagant Lady Walpole pursued a sociable
life in London attended by a succession of lovers; Sir Robert,
whose taste was for robuster pleasures, spent the intervals of
his political activities at his half-finished palace of Houghton
in the jovial company of his mistress, Miss Moll Skerret,
keeping open house to a crowd of hard riding, hard drinking
hangers-on with whom he exchanged doubtful stories and
drank bottle after bottle of port wine. Horace stayed with his
mother. As the youngest, cleverest and sickliest of her children
he was recklessly indulged and petted. Once, when he was
ten, he expressed a desire to see the King: a few days later he
was taken off to Kensington Palace for a private audience
specially arranged for him after dark, lest the news of it might
awake the envy of less privileged persons. Haloed by the
glory of such a background, he might well have impressed his
schoolfellows, even if he had not been personally remarkable.
This, however, was far from being the case. Indeed, for his
precocity was freakish, this skinny, vivacious child, with the
sharp black eyes and tiptoe walk—"Ariel in slit shoes", as he
afterwards described himself—was the same brilliant figure
as was to decorate London society for the next sixty years.
His schoolboy letters were as accomplished and sophisticated
as those of his prime. They are also as inscrutable. Walpole
is an even more enigmatic character than Gray. Not only
was the delicate, gleaming enamel of his high-bred reserve of
a yet more impenetrable quality, but the nature beneath it

was inherently more puzzling. There is something paradoxical in the very essence of Horace Walpole. Countless
writers have discussed him, but at the end all have confessed
themselves baffled. At moments, with his gush, his bric-a-
brac and his touchiness, one is tempted to dismiss him as an
affected petit-maître who happened to be gifted with a talent
for letter writing. One would be wrong, however, to yield
to the temptation. Beneath his affectations lay a shrewd
knowledge of the world and a steely patrician toughness.
He bore agonies of gout without a word of complaint and
made it a matter of principle never to wear an overcoat or to
change his shoes when he got wet. Again, what are we to
make of his taste? His own letters, it is true, are exquisite
pieces of art. But in them he admits to thinking nothing of
Richardson because his tone was middle-class, or of Johnson
because his manners were bearish. This was superficial of him.
In a sense he was both superficial and conventional. Ultimate
problems bored him: he was satisfied to accept the standards,
social and moral, of the world into which he had been born.
Yet his superficiality was too deliberate to be completely
genuine. Because he preferred it, he chose to remain on life's
surface, beautifully polishing it. As for conventions, they
never prevented him doing anything he really felt inclined
to. If he wanted to decorate his drawing-room like a Gothic
Chapel, he did so regardless of what anyone might
think.

Even his health was paradoxical. Ailing and feeble from
birth, there yet throbbed within him a quenchless vitality
that made him able at seventy to dance a quadrille with the
zest of an eighteen-year-old. Had he, finally, a heart? Certainly he loved his friends with a fiery affection full of ardours
and jealousies, and generous impulses of sympathy. How
then was he a born celibate, hating ties, and who, when poor
blind old Mme. du Deffand declared her love for him with a

frankness which he feared might make him look ridiculous, checked her with a cold ruthlessness that makes one wonder for a moment if he was human at all. Ariel—the name suits more than his appearance; only it is the modish Ariel of the *Rape of the Lock*, not Shakespeare's wild wind-elf. Ageless, sexless, tireless, with his diamond glitter, his waspish irritations, his airy dragon-fly elegance, Horace Walpole was more like a sprite than a man. And how can poor flesh and blood mortals be expected wholly to understand a sprite?

Perhaps it is impossible to love one either. Horace Walpole is not exactly lovable. But he is wonderful. Never was anyone born with a greater talent for living. For he combined, in a most unusual way, the gusto and curiosity needed to enjoy life with the judgment and self-discipline required to regulate it: so that—and this is the secret of successful living—he never wasted a moment doing anything for which he was unfitted. Perceiving precisely where his taste and capacities lay, he constructed his scheme of existence rigidly within the limits revealed by this perception. Like his letters, his life was a conscious work of art. And since it was executed with an unflagging spirit and an incomparable sense of style, it was, of its kind, a masterpiece. Even now, a hundred and sixty years after his death, and when his personality can only communicate itself to us through the cold medium of print, we enjoy the spectacle of Horace Walpole, as we enjoy a perfect performance of some Mozartian aria. "Que voulez-vous?" says the wise Lemaître. "La perfection absolue fait toujours plaisir."

It pleased Gray all right. Walpole's easy good breeding, his charming rococo airs were just the things to fascinate him, especially since he can never have come across them before. On his side Gray had something to offer Walpole. Aristocratic circles, however polished, tend to be philistine. Walpole was unlikely to have met anyone at home to whom the life

of art and imagination was the precious thing it was to Gray.
He was also far too clever to be put off by Gray's superficial
awkwardness of manner. Never indeed was Walpole's easy
mastery of the art of living more evident than in the independent track he cut calmly for himself through the rough and
tumble of Eton life. That rough and tumble appealed to
him as little as it did to Gray. He was too grown-up, as well
as too unathletic. "I can reflect with great joy," he wrote to a
friend during the holidays when he was fourteen years old,
"on the moments we passed together at Eton; and long to
talk 'em over, as I think we could recollect a dozen passages
which were something above the common run of schoolboys'
diversions. I can remember with no small satisfaction we
did not pass our time in gloriously beating great clowns. . . .
We had other amusements."

Neither did Walpole work very hard at his lessons. Culture
in his view was meant to be a pleasure, not a form of hard
labour. If his tutor set him any task extra to the regular
requirements of the curriculum, he would make a point of
not getting it done. "What, learn more than I am absolutely
forced to learn!" he exclaimed in comic horror. These dusty
pedagogues must, he felt, be made to realize that Sir Robert
Walpole's son was not to be bullied. Instead he spent his time
reading poems and romances, and still more in talking to his
friends. He made a great many of these, more than Gray was
able to do. Gay, gossipy, and not at all shy, he loved company:
and the fact that, unlike Gray, he came from the same patrician
background as the majority of his schoolfellows gave him
more in common with them. With those of them who
seemed to be sufficiently civilized to be possible companions,
he was amused to discuss the events of the world, of politics
and fashion, from which they all sprang. Still, these friends
had nothing to offer to the artist in Walpole. To satisfy this
he struck up with Gray and West. The more they saw of

each other, the more they proved to have in common. Soon they were inseparable.

To the trio a fourth attached himself, Thomas Ashton. He was not much of an addition; a smug-faced ungainly boy, clever enough at his books but with none of the others' genuine sensibility. Moreover he was intriguing and pushing, rather too well aware of the future advantages to be gathered by making friends with the Prime Minister's son. He took pains to acquire the conversational tone of the group. He did not do it very well, but well enough to succeed in his aim. Boys— even boys like Gray and Walpole—seldom pause to examine the motives of those who take pains to make themselves pleasant to them. The trio became a quartet. Children are ritualists delighting in formal ranks and titles. As less sophisticated boys enjoy belonging to gangs and secret societies with names like the "Hidden Hand", so these christened their association "the Quadruple Alliance". Each member had a nickname taken from the stories they read, and the plays they acted together. Gray was Orozamades, Ashton, Almanzor, West, Zephyrus and Walpole, Celadon.

The names are romantic. Indeed the spirit that animated the Quadruple Alliance was extremely romantic, in the mild and artificial sense in which the eighteenth century understood the word.

"Were not the playing fields of Eton food for all manner of flights?" wrote Walpole some years later. "No old maid's gown, though it had been tormented into all the fashions from King James to King George ever underwent so many transformations as those poor plains have in my idea. At first I was contented with tending a visionary flock, and sighing some pastoral name to the echo of the cascade under the bridge. How happy should I have been to have had a kingdom only for the pleasure of being driven from it, and living disguised in an humble vale! As I got further into Virgil and Clelia, I found myself transported from Arcadia to the garden of Italy; and saw Windsor Castle in no other view than the *Capitoli immobile saxum.* I wish a committee of the House of Commons may ever seem to be the senate; or a bill appear half so agreeable as a billet-doux. You see how deep you have carried me into old stories; I write of them with pleasure, but shall talk of them with more to you. I can't say I am sorry I was never quite a school-boy: an expedition against barge-men, or a match at cricket, may be very pretty things to recollect; but, thank my stars, I can remember things that are very near as pretty."

They all indulged in similar fancies. Shepherds, knights errant, disguised princesses filled their thoughts. They read Spenser, Milton, Shakespeare, with passionate enthusiasm. From each book new figures arose to throng their day-dreams.

Their affection for each other was romantic, too. School-boys' affections tend to be. In them the capacity for love awakens, and, as it were, tries out its paces. Nor in the eighteenth century were such feelings inhibited by the fear of being thought silly or unmanly. Even to one of his less poetic friends Walpole could write: "My dearest Charles, I find we not only sympathise in the tenderest friendship for one another, but also in the result of that which is the jealousy you mention."

In the atmosphere of the Quadruple Alliance, the emotional temperature was, as it might be expected, yet higher. Walpole and West, Gray and Ashton saw themselves as Damon and Pythias, Orestes and Pylades, inheritors of the glorious tradition of antique comradeship, united to one another by a refined affinity of soul beyond the reach of commonplace persons. Carefully tended, as on some classical altar, the flame of sentimental friendship gave light and warmth to their fastidious existences. They yielded themselves with rapture to its ardours and tendernesses: and they expressed them with a stilted elaboration which is a trifle absurd. Indeed there is something absurd about the Quadruple Alliance, with its pretences of maturity, its mincing graces. But it was also charming. The spectacle of children playing at being grown up always has charm. Moreover, these particular children did it so prettily. The exaggerations of their youthful affectations did not conceal the fact that they were possessed of an unusual sensibility and feeling for style. These demure boys performing their florid minuet of fancy and sentiment, amid the lawns and moss-grown cloisters of the ancient school present a picture of Watteaulike delicacy, all the more piquant for the contrast between the artificial formality of the dance, and the youthful freshness of the dancers.

Nor did they take themselves so seriously as to be over-solemn. In Gray and Walpole at any rate, the sense of comedy was quite as acute as the poetic sense. They enjoyed reading about Lady Wishfort and Falstaff as much as about Hamlet and Dido: and themselves they exercised their growing wits in mocking, not without pride in their own intellectual superiority, at the dolts and fools around them. Moreover, unboyish though they might be in many respects, they had a boyish love of pure fun. They delighted in comic nicknames, innocent coarsenesses, private jokes endlessly repeated, but always with renewed pleasure: their gravest talks were liable to be suddenly interrupted by flights of exuberant nonsense, fits of delicious uncontrollable giggles.

They were happy. To Gray indeed, looking back in later years, these days seemed the happiest of his life. Men are apt to think this, when reflecting sentimentally on their school days. In his case, however, it seems likely to have been true.

At Eton he had discovered for the first time, and glowing all the brighter by contrast with his unhappy home, an existence centred on those pleasures of literature and friendship for which his nature instinctively craved. Its monastic seclusion protected him from the rough world, and he was still too young to worry about the future. Moreover, his actual capacity for enjoying himself was greater than it was ever to be again. For he was of that sensitive, un-vital type, in whom high spirits evaporate with boyhood.

Certainly it was a delightful existence. But it was not to last. By 1735 Gray had grown into a man, and must enter the world. Superficially at any rate, he was ready for it. People grew up much earlier in those days. Gray and his friends were precocious even for the period. By eighteen, the Quadruple Alliance—to judge by the letters they wrote to one another— were as advanced as young men of twenty-three are to-day. Not only did they express themselves with a self-assured ease, unmarked by a trace of clumsiness or naïveté, but they had matured into a coherent social group, with its own characteristic manner, its own characteristic outlook. The manner was formal and Frenchified, full of gesture and compliment, graceful gush, and ornate flourishes of wit and fancy. The outlook was aesthetic. The Quadruple Alliance loved to cultivate the finer pleasures of taste and sentiment. If they were in a serious mood they talked of literature and the opera: if frivolous, they gossiped about personalities and fashions. Even when they turned their attention for a moment to history or natural science, the motive was aesthetic. These things appealed in some way to their imagination or sense of beauty. Strenuous intellectual questionings attracted them as little as sport or practical business. There is no arguing in the letters. The Quadruple Alliance was dedicated to the service of the Muses and the Graces.

So far its members were like aesthetic young men in any

period: but the fact that they were children of the eighteenth century, the rational, worldly-wise eighteenth century, made them strikingly different from the Paterian aesthete of a later age. They did not go in for eccentricity or ecstasy; their manners, though flowery, were not unconventional; and their culture was no soul adventure into regions of strange beauty, but a lucid, sensible affair of good taste and good scholarship. "What was the correct diction for an epic?" they asked each other. "How should one interpret some difficult passage of Ovid or Tibullus?" Nor did art inspire them with mystical feelings. "Poetry is the most enchanting thing in the world," said West. His friends would have agreed with him: but they meant that it was the most exquisite of pleasures, not the revelation of a spiritual mystery. As for rhapsodizing about it after the fashion of the Paterian aesthete, the Quadruple Alliance would have thought such a thing ridiculous. Their sense of comedy was far too strong. Even when they were talking about the subjects they loved best, their characteristic tone was a light, urbane, irony. This lightness was encouraged by the fact that there was a strain of the man-of-the-world in the ideal they set up for themselves. Provinciality and rusticity disgusted them: they admired sophistication and elegance. And sophistication and elegance implied a certain airy flippancy of tone that excluded the possibility of rapture. Here we may detect the influence of Walpole on the group. Its mental atmosphere was a blend of the spirit of Gray on the one hand, and of Walpole on the other. The interests that bound them together were Gray's: but the tone in which they discussed them was Walpole's. Walpole, with his dazzling aura of fashion inevitably set the standard of style for his humbler friends. He affected them all the more because concern for style was the outstanding characteristic of the group. Orthodox enough in their opinions, the members of the Quadruple Alliance differed from the average in the elaborate refinement with which they sought to present them to the world.

They succeeded in their aim. No young men can ever have been more exquisitely civilized. Perhaps too civilized. The Quadruple Alliance, it must be owned, were mannered, finnicky, hard to please, and unspontaneous. Deliberate stylishness inhibits spontaneity. Even with each other they could not relax in a homely friendliness. However, they did not want to. Homely friendliness was not at all the sort of thing that appealed to their taste. Besides, they enjoyed showing off to each other; and being shown off to, as well. They were enthusiastic about each other's talents, and like other coteries of clever young men they took pleasure in thinking that they formed a front; that they stood for civilization against the hordes of barbarians and philistines, of uncouth pedants, and hard-drinking hallooing hunting men, of which the world seemed so largely and so regrettably composed; and in whose company they felt as comfortable as four cats among a pack of dogs. Not that they wanted to enter into combat with them. Cats do not attack dogs. With a shudder of delicate ironic horror, the Quadruple Alliance preferred to turn their backs on the displeasing spectacle of average mankind, and to seek solace in the delights of each other's society.

Unfortunately Fate did not permit them to do this for very long. In October, 1734, West left Eton for Oxford, and Ashton and Gray for Cambridge; Walpole followed them there six months later. His life, however, soon began to develop on lines which made the close, continuous association of Eton days impossible. Aristocratic young men in the eighteenth century took their University careers very lightly. They came and went as they felt inclined; though they sometimes did a little leisurely reading in some author who took their fancy, they seldom embarked on a regular course of study: and hardly ever bothered to take a degree. Walpole, launched for the first time as a grown-up young man into the intoxicating world of London social life, appeared at Cambridge only occasionally. Gray missed him very much. His first years at the University were not happy. It was not only that he felt cut off from his former friends. He was also very poor. £20 a year in scholarships, and with the little his mother could save from the depredations of her husband, was all he had to live on. Though he practised a rigid economy, it was enough. Unluckily, too, he was the type of character who minds poverty particularly acutely. It intensified his nervous anxiety about the future, and it made him feel dependent on circumstances in a way that outraged his pride. Moreover his temperament desired those graces and elegancies of living which, alas, are not to be had without money. These four years left him for the rest of his life possessed by a sense of the necessity of financial independence.

Further, he did not at first take to Cambridge. This is hardly to be wondered at. An English University of the time was no place for the civilized spirit, as Gibbon was to find forty years later. Cambridge, when Gray went there, was a stagnant backwater, cut off from the flowing mainstream of contemporary culture, a sort of stuffy, unspiritual monastery, ruled over by an inert mass of stodgy celibates—how smugly their bewigged countenances still stare down at us from the panelled walls of combination rooms—who, having risen from narrow circumstances to achieve their Fellowships, had relaxed for the rest of their lives into a monotonous existence of over-eating, over-drinking, and petty College business. Now and again a distinguished scholar appeared among them. But for the most part, their intellectual standards were low. Promotion went by patronage; so that a man might be made a Professor in a subject he knew nothing about, just because he had known how to flatter and pull strings in the right quarter. As for the ordinary College tutor, he was often an idle, ignorant man, who scarcely bothered to see his pupils more than twice in the term. Fancy, thought Gray, being put under the direction of a drunken illiterate like Mr. Birkett! As a matter of fact, even if he had approved of Mr. Birkett, Gray would not have much enjoyed working under him. For he found the curriculum uninspiring; a dry old-fashioned logic-chopping affair, involving a good deal of mathematics and metaphysics, and with nothing in it to appeal to the poetic spirit. "Must I plunge into metaphysics?" he complained to West. "Alas, I cannot see in the dark: nature has not furnished me with the optics of a cat. Must I pore upon mathematics? Alas, I cannot see in too much light: I am no eagle. It is very possible that two and two make four, but I would not give four farthings to demonstrate this ever so clearly: and if these be the profits of life, give me the amusements of it."

Nor did the company of his fellow students offer much compensation for the deficiencies of the dons and the curriculum. Undergraduates were divided mainly into two classes. Of these, the scions of the aristocracy occupied such time as they spent at Cambridge in racing by day, and by night revelling round the streets, breaking the heads of unoffending townsmen: while the rest—dons and country parsons in embryo—sat about in an atmosphere of beer and tobacco smoke, exchanging trivial gossip, and ponderous jokes. Gray was too poor to associate with the aristocrats, even had he wanted to. Now and again, however, he was drawn into the company of the others. In a letter to Walpole he expatiates on his sufferings there.

"Do but imagine me pent up in a room hired for the purpose, and none of the largest, from 7 o'clock at night, till 4 in the morning! 'midst hogheads of liquor and quantities of tobacco, surrounded by 30 of these creatures, infinitely below the meanest people you could ever form an idea of; toasting bawdy healths and deafened with their unmeaning roar; Jesus! but I must tell you of a fat mortal who stuck close to me. . . . Well! he was so maudlin and so loving, and told me long stories interrupted by the sourest inter- jections, with moral discourses upon God knows what; I was almost drunk too. . . . You will think it a strange compliment when I tell you how often I thought of you, all the while: but will forgive me when you recollect that it was a great piece of philosophy in me to be able, in the midst of noise and disturbance, to call to mind the most agreeable thing in the world."

As was to be expected in these circumstances, Gray spent most of his time by himself; musing his way through the streets to lectures under the low-lying Cambridge sky, or in the ancient quiet of his College rooms, reading, learning Italian, and playing toccatas and sarabands on the pianoforte.

It does not sound such an unsuitable life for him in its minor-key way. After all, his occupations were congenial; he liked learning Italian and playing the pianoforte. Indeed, these particular years, too, turned out profitable to his mental development. Their very emptiness gave him room to cultivate those aesthetic and literary interests in which his creative impulse was to find fulfilment: their very silence enabled him to listen more attentively to the immaterial voices of the mighty dead, of Milton and Tasso, Horace and Racine, Spenser and Mme de Sevigné. For he soaked him- self in the literature of many ages and nations. Under their enriching influence his taste refined itself, his imaginative life acquired shape, strength, amplitude.

Nor was it as if he felt more at home in other places; amid the sordid quarrellings of his Mother's house in Cornhill, or staying with his sporting Uncle at Burnham Beeches—an object of contempt, because he read and walked when he could have been out with the hounds, and where he was forced to write his letters standing up, because all the chairs were occupied by his Uncle's stinking, barking dogs. Cambridge, with all its defects, was better than this. As the years passed, though he hardly liked to admit it, the place began to get a hold on him. When he got an invitation to go away, he found himself disinclined to accept it. "I don't know how it is, I have a sort of reluctance to leave this place, unamiable as it may seem. It is true Cambridge is very ugly, the Town is very dirty, and very dull, but I am like a cabbage; where I am stuck, I love to grow."

Moreover with the years some of the chief ills which at first he complained of at Cambridge began to disappear. He had contrived, with the help of the despised Mr. Birkett, to persuade the authorities to allow him to give up taking a degree, in spite of the fact that he was receiving a scholarship from them; so that he could now devote himself undisturbed to the studies he liked. And he began to find a few kindred spirits in the place, notably a comfortable, kindly scholarly man called Wharton, and a pleasant, vigorous little scholar named Brown. He managed, too, to keep up his connection with the Quadruple Alliance. Ashton was at Cambridge. And though he seems to have grown steadily less attractive with the years—sedulously planning his career, pompously fussing lest he had unconsciously offended someone who could obstruct his advancement—yet Ashton was an original member of the group with whom one could recall time past, and laugh at the old jokes. With Walpole and West, Gray maintained his connection mainly by letters. Not entirely though; now and again the door of his rooms would open and in flashed Walpole, voluble and intimate as ever, and bubbling over with fascinating news about the newest Italian castrato

singer, or the latest scandal in high society. Gray loved
hearing about high society, or indeed, about any society.
One of his chief pleasures in talking to Walpole arose from
the fact that Walpole acted as a link between his friend's
solitude and the world, that with Walpole Gray could share
vicariously in that easy intercourse with his fellow man
which in reality he found so difficult. He enjoyed this the
more because it was intercourse in surroundings so agreeable
to his imagination. Beauty did not have to be solemn to
please Gray. He was very susceptible to the decorative
quality in fashionable life, its frills and pretty fopperies, and
he had an eye for their details. With what delighted precision
does he observe Queen Caroline's costume, watching the
opera "in a green velvet sac, embroidered on the facings and
sleeves with silver, and a little French cap, and big black hood,
and her hair in curls round her face." He was full of the blue
and gold feux d'artifices that adorned the new production of
Handel's "Atlanta". Walpole was the only one of his friends
equally interested in these frivolities. Walpole, too, was the
only one who could tell him about them. Routs, balls,
masquerades—Gray wanted to hear about everything.

"Thou dear envious Imp," he exclaimed to him, "to set
me a longing with accounts of plays and operas, and masquerades, after hearing of which, I can no more think of
Logick and stuff, than you could of Divinity at a ball, or of
Caudle and Carraway-Comfits after having been stuffed at
a Christening: heaven knows! we have nobody in our
College that has seen London, but one; and he, I believe,
comes out of Vinegar-yard, and looks like toasted Cheshire
cheese, strewed with brown Sugar. I beg you, give me the
minutest Circumstances of your Diversions and your
Indiversions; tho' if it is as great a trouble to you to write,
as it is a pleasure to me to get 'em my heart, I fear I shan't

hear from you once in a twelvemonth, and dear, now be very punctual and very long."

Indeed absence only served to increase the unique glamour with which, in Gray's eyes, Walpole's figure was irradiated. How wonderful it was to find a friend as fastidious and fussy as himself—Walpole rushes to him for sympathy when he is forced to spend a dreadful week in the sporting atmosphere of his Father's country house—who was yet somehow possessed of the savoir faire and zest for living which he, Gray, longed for and lacked.

"I am sufficiently awake to answer your letter," he told him, "though likely to be more dull than you write in sleep: and indeed I do not believe that you ever are so much asleep, but you can write to a relation, play a sober game of piquet, keep to a tête-à-tête conversation, seal a bargain, or perform any of the little offices of life with tolerable spirit: certain I am there are many people in the world who in their deep spirits are no better awake than you are at four in the morning, reclined upon your pillow."

Of course the very fact that his friend was such a brilliant figure imposed a certain strain in Gray's relations with him. It is to be noted in the foregoing quotation that Gray apologizes for being dull. At all costs he felt he must avoid dullness, if he was to be worthy of Walpole's interest in him. His letters to him now cast in the form of a mock oriental tale, now in that of an epistle from a god-daughter, now interspersed with verses, now expressed in a comic parody of Shakespearean English—are elaborate essays in the art of entertainment; frothy, sparkling confections, in which he has exercised himself to put all his powers of wit and fancy, and from which anything which might be thought boring is carefully excluded. Walpole, not unnaturally, accepted the version of Gray's character thus carefully presented to him. Humour he took to be Gray's natural mood. His gravity he dismissed as a mere trick of manner, and his occasional sighs of melancholy as pardonable affectations.

West was in no danger of falling into this error. For, if Walpole provided a link between Gray and the outer world, West was the companion of his inner life. Not that their relations were without rubs. They met very seldom, not more than twice in three years. And on one of these occasions at least, they were too shy to feel completely easy with one another. "West sup'd with me the night before I came out of town," Gray related; "we both fancied at first we had a great many things to say to one another; but when it came to the push, I found, I had forgot all I intended to say, and he stood upon Punctilios and would not speak first, and so we parted." There is a caustic truthfulness about this account which is a little formidable. It was characteristic of Gray though. Critical and insecure, he was always, as it were, taking the temperature of his friendships to see if they were providing the requisite warmth and light. If they were not, he was not the man to try and hide it from himself. However, the affection between him and West was too deep to be impaired by one awkward interview. Within a month he is writing to him as affectionately as ever. Though Gray always tries to be agreeable, his letters to West were both franker and graver than those to Walpole. He writes a great deal about scholarship and literature, sends verses for West's criticism, or comments on verses West has sent to him. Together they lamented the aridness of intellectual life at their respective Universities. "Sure it was of this place now Cambridge," exclaimed Gray, "but formerly known as Babylon, that the prophet spoke when he said 'that the wild beasts of the forests shall dwell there, and their houses shall be full of doleful creatures'." To West Gray allowed himself to betray his troubled mind, as he could not do to Walpole: and now and again the emotional tone deepened as with a charming, shy smile, Gray revealed that he was writing to one of the very few human beings he loved. "As the most undeserving people in the world most often have the vanity to wish somebody had a regard for them, so I need not wonder at my own in being pleased that you care about me. You need not doubt, therefore, of having a first row in the front box of my little heart, and I believe that you are in no danger of being crowded there."

West responded ardently to these declarations. Unlike his friends, he was unreserved: and he was touchingly pleased to find that anyone cared for him. Since leaving Eton, his life had been even drearier than Gray's. He had no old friends at all at Oxford, and he shrank too much from the novelty of making new ones. Besides, he was a tenderer plant than Gray. There was nothing in him of that fundamental self-discipline and solidity of mind that enabled Gray to construct a life of fruitful study out of the loneliness of Cambridge. Wretched health—West was a victim of acute attacks of headache, which, while they lasted, prostrated him completely—had increased the natural weakness of a disposition high strung, unconcentrated and the prey to waves of black despair, in which joy, youth, life itself, seemed to be slipping through his nerveless fingers, gleaming and insubstantial as the waters of a stream. He could not bring himself to get down to any regular work. Only as he wandered forlornly by the willows and fritillaries of Addison's Walk, brooding endlessly over those Eton days when alone he had been happy, while Magdalen Tower chimed out the melancholy hours overhead, his over-burdened heart sighed itself forth in a strain of elegiac sadness.

Saint of this learned awful grove,
While slow along thy walks I rove,
The pleasing scene, which all that see
   Admire, is lost to me.

The thought, which still my breast invades,
Nigh yonder springs, nigh yonder shades,
Still, as I pass, the memory brings
   Of sweeter shades and springs.

Lost and inwrapt in thought profound,
Absent I tread Etonian ground;
Then starting from the dear mistake,
   As disenchanted, wake.

What though from sorrow free, at best
I'm thus but negatively blest:
Yet still, I find, true joy I miss:
   True joy's a social bliss.

Oh! How I long again with those,
Whom first my boyish heart had chose,
Together through the friendly shade
   To stray, as once I stray'd!

Their presence would the scene endear,
Like paradise would all appear,
More sweet around the flowers would blow,
   More soft the waters flow.

No wonder he was grateful to Gray, when he said he loved
him. "I singled you out for a friend," West cried passionately,
"and I would have you know me to be yours, if you deem me

worthy—alas Gray, you cannot imagine how miserably my time passes away; my health and nerves and spirits are, I thank my stars, the very worst in Oxford . . . give me leave to say I find no physic comparable to your letters."

Gray could sympathize with West's lamentations. His own feelings were, at times, all too similar. Since leaving school his own prevailing mood had been a melancholy one. It was nothing like so acute as West's. Ennui, a sense of emptiness, apathy, a sort of greyness of the spirit which prevented him enjoying anything completely, were its characteristics. "When you have seen one of my days," he writes, "you have seen a whole year of my life. They go round and round like a blind horse in the mill, only he has the satisfaction of fancying he makes progress, and gets some ground: my eyes are open enough to see the same dull prospect, and having made four and twenty steps more, I shall now be just where I was." And again, "low spirits are my true and faithful companions. They get up with me, go to bed with me, make journeys and returns as I do; nay, and pay visits, and will even affect to be jocose, and share a feeble laugh with me, but most commonly we are alone together, and are the prettiest, insipid company in the world."

The origin of this melancholy of Gray's is to be found partly in a constitutional languor of temperament, partly in that fundamental suspicion of life engendered in him by too early an acquaintance with its power to hurt. Latent during his school days, it was bound to make itself felt when he was first as a man compelled to confront the world. The world—it loomed up before his troubled, adolescent gaze, a bewildering, dangerous place, in which his shrinking spirit felt incurably alien. His mode of life did nothing to reconcile him to it. Poverty and solitude encourage despondency: the monastic seclusion in which he lived made him shyer than ever. Why did he feel disinclined to leave Cambridge, since he found it so dull? Because leaving it meant venturing into a hostile region, where nothing was to be had which he felt worth winning. Instead he devoted himself to study. This, as we have seen, was good for him: in it, the intellectual half of his nature found fulfilment; this was why he was not as unhappy as West. But he was not sufficiently impersonal to be completely satisfied by intellectual activity. He needed the sweetness of human contact, he needed love. If he had been a normal young man he would, at this stage in his development, have fallen in love. But Gray was very far from being a normal young man. Stiff and academic, he was embarrassed in the company of young women, checked by what he felt to be his lack of worldly polish. He could not bear to imagine himself taking part in any love affair, unless it was conducted with elegant ease. And how in the world was he, of all people, to acquire elegant ease? When Walpole wrote to tell him about an amorous intrigue in which he was engaged, Gray replied, with a forced jauntiness of tone, which ill concealed his painful sense of inferiority, that he had sometimes considered embarking on a similar adventure himself, but that he had, in the end, come to the conclusion that he was not equipped for it.

"Would you believe it, 'tis the very thing I would wish to apply to myself. Ay! as simply as I stand here. But then the apparatus necessary to it calls for so much; nay, a part of it is wholly out of one's power to procure. Then who should pare one, and burnish one? For they would have more trouble and fuss with me than Cinderaxa's sisters had with their feet to make 'em fit for the little glass slipper. Oh yes! to be sure, one must be licked; now to lick oneself I take altogether impracticable, and to ask another to lick one, would not be quite so civil. Bear I was born, and bear I believe I am likely to remain."

Gray was further inhibited in these matters by the fact that relations with a woman meant adventure, meant plunging into that risky, earthy world of adult manhood, where he felt so out of place. Nor was it natural for him to take the masculine and dominant rôle expected in such a relationship. Native temperament and childish experience had combined to make him neither dominant nor masculine where his personal emotions were concerned. In consequence of all this, his capacity for romantic sentiment tended to be diverted into his feeling for his old friends, for West and Walpole. These feelings, though deep and productive at moments of an exquisite happiness, could not fully satisfy the needs of his heart. The relationships involved in them were careful, delicate, precarious affairs of rarefied sentiment and subtle intellectual sympathies, liable to be disturbed by the slightest breath of discord, and quite unable either to bring him down to earth, or to dispel his sense of insecurity. His suspicion of life remained, and with it his lack of spirits.

It was in no sanguine mood, therefore, that in September, 1738, Gray packed his boxes to leave Cambridge. He had to go; if he was ever to mend his wordly fortunes, he must take up a profession. But what profession? Unenthusiastically he considered the Bar. West was thinking of this too. Perhaps they might make a start together. Even so Gray did not find the prospect exhilarating. However, before anything was fixed, something happened which changed his plans entirely. Sir Robert Walpole, in accordance with Whig tradition, was sending Walpole abroad to finish his education by a protracted grand tour of the Continent. Now Walpole wrote and asked Gray to come with him as his guest. There could be no question of a refusal. To see with his own eyes all the historical places and famous works of art, which for so many years had filled his imagination; to see them in the company of dearest Celadon, and on a journey where he would travel in the greatest possible comfort—this was a chance not to be missed. At the end of March, 1739, the two young men were across the Channel. They were not back again till 1741.

This two years' sojourn abroad was a unique adventure in Gray's retired life. It was also decisive in shaping his subsequent character and career. All this makes it the more irritating that, as usual with Gray, we do not know enough about it. Not that he is silent on the subject. Page after page scored over with his scholarly handwriting arrived regularly in England by every postbag. But, as always, there is a great deal that these pages do not tell us. Gray's barrier of gentlemanly reserve interposes itself between us and intimate confession: and it is rendered more tantalizingly effective by the fact that he was so interested in the sights he saw, that he devotes a large part of his space to describing them in detail, instead of telling us about himself. Like many cultured travellers, Gray tended to confuse a good letter with a good guide-book. The result is that the journey passes before our mental eye rather like a cinema film of which we do not catch all the words. Vividly we see the contrasting figures of the two young men—Gray's short, neat, and prim, Walpole's slim, vivacious and modish—as they stepped their delicate way through an ever-changing succession of varied, multi-coloured scenes, Louis XV's Paris, Alpine crags and torrents, the masques and torch-light of the Florentine carnival, the crumbling magnificence of baroque Rome, the ruins and sunset distances of the Campagna. But we have to guess at the ebb and flow of feelings which animated them during their progress; mainly by hints do we follow the course of the drama of which this picturesque background was the setting. For it was a drama: an entertaining, distressing little tragi-comedy of old friendship exposed to new strains, wearing thinner and thinner under their pressure, till, with a painful, resounding snap, it breaks.

The strains were inevitable. Travelling abroad is notoriously a hard test for any friendship. At home friends meet when they feel inclined, and on common ground, where only those sides in them which are sympathetic are apparent. Abroad they are together all the time, whether they feel like it or not. Worst still, they are forced to know each other completely; each is brought face to face with those aspects of his friend's character with which he has no particular affinity. More often than not he finds them intolerably jarring. So it was with Gray and Walpole. Their friendship had grown up at Eton and Cambridge, where they were drawn together by the fact that they both liked art and literature, and both disliked athletics and rough boys. In some other respects not so apparent at school, they were very different. Walpole was a born gay citizen of the world, to whom the things of the mind and imagination, keenly as he enjoyed them, came second to the pleasures of social life. Gray, on the other hand, was a pensive recluse, with neither taste nor talent for social pleasures, to whom the things of the mind and imagination were the centre of existence, the source of all his most precious and memorable experiences. Up to now these differences, in so far as they were aware of them, only added to the charm each found in the other. Gray, as we have seen, was exhilarated by the whiff of fashion that blew from Walpole: Walpole enjoyed savouring the atmosphere of cloistered contemplation which floated round Gray. When they were living together, however, and had, in practice, to adjust their lives to one another, these differences were bound to cause trouble. All the more when they were accentuated by the differences in their social positions. Here was another source of friction discovered by their journey. In the democracy of school and college, Gray and Walpole had been on equal terms. Out in the world, and more especially in that world of cosmopolitan high society into which Walpole inevitably went, a gulf

disclosed itself. Walpole was the son of the rich Prime
Minister of England; Gray was the insignificant child of a
warehouse keeper, only admitted into these exalted circles
because he was Walpole's friend. To anyone nervously
proud as he was, this must produce a painful sense of inferiority.
It was not diminished by the fact that he knew, and Walpole
knew, that Walpole was paying for him.

Of course, if they had been outstandingly easy-going, or
outstandingly insensitive, they might have got on in spite of
these causes of ill feeling. But Gray and Walpole were neither
of them easy-going or insensitive. It was not in either to let
things slide, or to take the rough with the smooth. On the
contrary, they were a touchy, huffy, critical pair, quickly
irritated, quickly bored, agonizingly conscious of every shade
in each other's moods, and sharp to detect any failings in
another person, however fond they might be of him. In
addition, Walpole had much of the easy inconsiderateness
and unconscious arrogance of the young patrician that he
was; while Gray suffered from a middle-class readiness to
suspect slights and then take solemn offence at them. Altogether it would have been a miracle if they had managed to
get through their journey without serious trouble.

It took some time in coming, however. They started off
under a cloudless sky. Indeed, on the eve of departure,
Walpole was seized with such an ardent impulse of affection
for his dear Orozmades, that he made a will bequeathing to
him everything of which he might die possessed. And for the
next nine months, in spite of an occasional rub, they seemed
to have got on pretty well. Gray, it is true, so Walpole recalled
later, had shown he could be tiresome as early as their arrival
at Calais. He had persisted in feeling sick on a calm sea.
This was soon forgotten, however, in the intoxicating excitement both felt at being abroad for the first time. Bowling
along in their post-chaise, they gazed out of the windows,

delightedly noting each detail in which the French scene differed from the English. The methodical Gray began keeping a journal in which he carefully described any object which struck him as of particular interest. Characteristically these objects were nearly always inanimate; landscape and historical monuments, not people. They made their first protracted stay in Paris. There their zest for sight-seeing remained undiminished. They visited Versailles—very disappointing they thought it, with its pompous, trivial façade and childish waterworks—Trianon, Nôtre Dame, the theatre, the opera. They also bought some new clothes. Gray, who was interested in his own clothes, as well as those of other people, had himself got up in the height of French fashion, tight silk breeches, a muff, and hair powdered and curled "en Bequille". He enjoyed his new appearance; he enjoyed Paris altogether. There was so much to see, he said, that he was quite happy walking about the streets. However, his enjoyment of Paris was qualified by a faint shadow of storms to come. Paris with Walpole meant social life. They were invited to parties. It is possible that Gray fancied he might enjoy them. What with his silk breeches and his muff, perhaps he might not feel himself "a bear" any longer. If he did cherish any such idea, he seems to have been soon disappointed. We remark that he often remains at home in the evening when Walpole is out, also that Walpole, if he does stay in, complains of finding the evening a little flat. Not indeed that he enjoyed going out very much either. French society turned out to take little interest in young foreigners, unless it could gain some practical profit from them, by winning their money at cards. Walpole did not care for cards; he was therefore driven for company to the English Colony. It hardly seemed worth coming abroad for this. Perhaps, after all, it was better to stay at home with Gray. Certainly it was, when their party was enlarged by the arrival of Walpole's charming young cousin, Henry Conway, who had been sent to France to learn the language. The three young men got on extremely well; so well that Walpole and Gray were persuaded by Conway to change their plans and accompany him to Rheims, where he was to spend the summer. Rheims, a quiet provincial town, whose social life was ruled over by a stiff little group of local nobility and garrison officers, was not the place to seduce Walpole from Gray's side. One evening, indeed, it did brighten up. Some ladies and gentlemen had met together to walk in someone's garden; inspired by Walpole's indefatigable party spirit, the sober gathering suddenly blossomed into a graceful Lancret-like fête champêtre. Supper was called for and spread in the open air by a murmuring fountain; after supper came songs; after songs, dancing. With their silks and satins gleaming shadowy in the July moonlight, the company swam and tripped through minuet and country dance, till at five in the morning, the violins still playing before them, they capered their way through the sleeping streets, to bed. Encouraged by the success of this impromptu festivity, Walpole proposed giving a ball. But Rheims society, after this unprecedented outburst, had sunk back into its customary languor, and the scheme fell through. For the rest of their stay, the young men had to entertain themselves by reading and talking to each other. Gray found nothing to complain of in such a mode of life.

He had still less to complain of in the next phase of his travel. Starting in September, for two months he and Walpole wended their way through Burgundy, Savoy and Switzerland, to Italy; a leisurely, discursive, enchanting journey, made romantic by a thousand glimpses of vineyard and mountain gorge, abbey and ruined castle, the tombs of the Burgundian kings near Dijon, the shining levels of the Lake of Leman, sublime Alpine vistas, culminating in the wild St. Gothard Pass—masked and muffled in fur, they were carried across it in the snow by sturdy mountaineers—and then the gradual descent into the olives and autumnal sunshine of the Italian plain. The peaks and passes of the high Alps were a trifle too alarming for the cautious Gray to take much pleasure in them—"They carried the permission mountains have of being frightful, rather too far", he said—but otherwise he found himself deeply stirred by mountain scenery. Here he was a pioneer in taste. Only a few years before travellers turned from such "horrid" sights in disgust. But by 1739, imaginative spirits were beginning to find the order and rationality which eighteenth-century civilization imposed on the world, disagreeably cramping and prosaic; and they turned in reaction to seek nourishment for their day-dreams in the savage and the "Gothick". None more than Gray. Even at Eton he had delighted in romance and fairy tale. Since then, in his Cambridge solitude he had fed his fancy on Spenser and mediaeval history. And now here in the flesh were the scenes exactly like those he had dwelt on so often in imagination. It was too good to be true. The precipitous scenery around the Grande Chartreuse impressed him especially; so it did Walpole. They responded to it, however, differently. Walpole enjoyed it simply as a spectacle, the natural counterpart, as it were, to the finest stage scenery imaginable.

"But the road, West, the road! winding round a prodigious mountain and surrounded with others, all shagged with hanging woods, obscured with pines or lost in clouds! Below a torrent breaking through cliffs, and tumbling through fragments of rocks! Sheets of cascades forcing their silver speed down channelled precipices, and hasting into the roughened river at the bottom! Now and then an old foot-bridge, with a broken rail, a leaning cross, a cottage, or the ruin of an hermitage! This sounds too bombast and too romantic to one that has not seen it, too cold for one that has."

Gray, less observant of the picturesque surface, was far more profoundly moved. To him the sight was a landmark in his life, a momentous experience, revealing, as in an awe-inspiring flash, the spiritual nature of the universe.

"In our little journey up to the Grande Chartreuse, I do not remember to have gone ten paces without an exclamation that there was no restraining: not a precipice, not a torrent, not a cliff, but is pregnant with religion and poetry. There are certain scenes that would awe an atheist into belief, without the help of other argument. One need not have a very fantastic imagination to see spirits there at noon-day: you have Death perpetually before your eyes, only so far removed, as to compose the mind without frighting it. I am well persuaded St. Bruno was a man of no common genius, to choose such a situation for retirement; and perhaps should have been a disciple of his, had I been born in his time."

A life of seclusion spent in surroundings as spirit-stirring as these—that would have been delightful indeed.

Nothing in Italy roused this sort of emotion in him. But he got a great deal out of Italy, too. If the Chartreuse had made him realize, for the first time, the full power of nature to move the soul, Italy made him realize the full power of art. Genoa with its marble palaces, gleaming white against the sapphire of the Mediterranean, the Correggios at Palma, the colonnaded streets of Bologna, his first sight of the towers of Florence rising pearly through the mists of an October evening—each had its contribution to make to his growing store of exquisite and fertilizing impressions.

At Florence they were welcomed by the Minister, Sir Horace Mann. He turned out to be a very sympathetic personality: a fastidious, invalidish bachelor of thirty-eight, extremely intelligent, and with an affected manner. Delighted to find such kindred spirits after the dreary horde of loutish English youths, bear-led by pedantic parsons, who made up the greater part of English visitors to Florence, and pleased also that one of these kindred spirits should be the son of the Prime Minister, Mann pressed them to make a long stay. They were quite willing. Walpole was tired of bad inns and jolting journeys, and Gray wanted time thoroughly to study the antiquities of the place. For the next few months they were settled at Florence. With their establishment there, a new phase opened in their journey. Walpole was responsible for it. By this time he had begun to discover that he could have a great deal too much of sightseeing.

"A force d'en avoir vu, I have left off screaming, Lord! this! and Lord! that! To speak sincerely, Calais surprised me more than anything I have seen since. I recollect the joy I used to propose if I could but once see the Great Duke's gallery; I walk into it now with as little emotion as I should into St. Paul's. The statues are a congregation of good sort of people, that I have a great deal of unruffled regard for. The farther I travel, the less I wonder at anything."

His appetite for social life, on the other hand, was still far from satisfied. From this point of view Paris and Rheims had proved disappointing. His first impressions of Florence were hardly more promising. It seemed just another provincial capital, and the society there, though more pleasure-loving and informal than that of Rheims, was equally monotonous.

"Men are so much the same everywhere," he told West,
with all the blaséness of his twenty years, "that one scarce
perceives any change of situation. The same weaknesses,
the same passions, that in England plunge men into elec-
tions, drinking, whoring, exist here, and show themselves
in the shapes of Jesuits, Cicisbeos, and Corydon ardebat
Alexins. . . . Thus child, 'tis dull dealing here!"

However, as time passed, Walpole began to find himself
liking Florence better. The people might not be so varied as
those in London, but their manners were better, and their
mode of living more agreeable. If you felt a desire for culture,
why, there were the most famous museums in Europe at your
door: otherwise you could relax at pleasant little parties in
palaces, or saunters in the Boboli gardens, or in delightful
hours spent with Mann over a cup of coffee—admirable
Mann disliked strong drink as much as Walpole did—talking
about the latest social and political news. Walpole was
sufficiently the son of the Prime Minister to enjoy a chance to
be in touch with active politics again. The fact that he was
the son of the Prime Minister was an advantage to him in
Florentine society. Everyone was out to please him, never
had he been so appreciated. This naturally made him like
Florence better and better.

With the coming of Carnival in 1741, liking warmed to
enthusiasm. His youthful capacity for gaiety had not had
much opportunity to gratify itself since he came abroad.
Dammed up for so long, it now poured itself forth with a
foaming irresistible rush into the festivities of the Carnival.

"Well, West," he chatters, "I have found a little unmasked
moment to write to you; but for this week past, I have been
so muffled up in my domino that I have not had the command of my elbows. But what have you been doing all

the morning? Could you not write then? Then I was masked too; I have done nothing but hop out of my domino into bed, and out of bed into my domino. The end of the Carnival is frantic and bacchanalian; all the morn one makes parties in masks to the shops and coffee houses, and all the evening to the operas and balls. Then I have danced, *good gods*, how have I danced! . . . there are but three days more. The two last are to have balls all the morning at the fine, unfinished palace of the Strozzi; and on Tuesday night, a masquerade after supper."

Days and nights like this—ah, surely they were worth a hundred spent staring at mouldering abbeys, and broken-nosed statues!

Gray did not think so. Carnivals were not for him. He was born a trifle middle-aged, and he felt as embarrassed as ever in the company of strangers. Closer acquaintance with society had only served to prove to him that he was unfitted for it. The paths of the two young men began to diverge. While Walpole dined and danced, Gray walked round the galleries, listened to concerts, or made careful records of his learned observations. Walpole, casting a casual glance over his shoulder at these activities, felt a spasm of irritation. "By a considerable volume of charts and pyramids, which I saw at Florence, I thought it threatened a publication," he told Ashton tartly.

In the Spring they proceeded to Rome. The old Pope had just died, and both young men were excited to have the chance of being there when a new one was elected. Change of scene did nothing to bring them closer together. Walpole was bored by Rome. The historical sights were no doubt extraordinary enough to revive a little his waning interest in sight-seeing; and he enjoyed bargaining for objets d'art, with a view to setting up as a collector. On the other hand, society

HORACE WALPOLE IN MASQUERADING DRESS
DURING HIS ITALIAN TOUR
From a portrait by Rosalba Carriera in the possession of the Lord Walpole

was stuffy and dull, the Pope did not get elected, there was no Carnival, and no Mann. Taking it all in all, Florence was much more agreeable. He solaced himself by writing frequent letters to Mann about the goings-on of the Old Pretender, who was now visiting Rome.

Gray, too, was interested to see so celebrated a personage.

"I have more time than I thought, and I will employ it in telling you about a Ball that we were at the other evening. Figure to yourself a Roman villa; all its little apartments thrown open, and lighted up to the best advantage. At the upper end of the gallery, a fine concert, in which La Diamantina, a famous virtuosa, played on the violin divinely, and sung angelically; Giovannino and Pasqualini (great names in musical story) also performed miraculously. On each side were ranged all the secular grand monde of Rome, the Ambassadors, Princesses, and all that. Among the rest Il Serenissimo Pretendente (as the Mantove Gazette calls him) displayed his rueful length of person, with his two young ones, and all his ministry around him. 'Poi nacque un grazioso ballo', where the world danced, and I sat in a corner regaling myself with iced fruits, and other rinfrescatives."

This letter tells us something about Gray, as well as about the Old Pretender. Even when he was persuaded to go to a ball, he did not dance, but sat in a corner. There is an acid undertone to the urbane sentences in which he relates these facts. Indeed, he was beginning to feel the limitations of his position unpleasantly; and in more ways than one. Why was he too poor to be able to buy antiques easily? He knew he appreciated them more than many who could. All the same, unlike Walpole, Gray was not disappointed in Rome. Not a step he took, but he set his foot upon some reverent history.

There was the Colosseum, there was the Forum, there was
Frascati to visit, Palestrina, the myriad rainbow-tinted
cascades of Tivoli, Alba with its memories of Pompey's
villa; there were the tombs and broken aqueducts of the
Appian Way. No doubt, as Walpole told him, these places,
apart from their historic associations, were no better worth
seeing than Richmond or Windsor. But such associations
were to one with Gray's intensity of historical imagination,
the source of half his pleasures in seeing anything.

"I am now at home," he breaks out to West, "and going
to the window to tell you it is the most beautiful of Italian
nights, which, in truth, are but just begun. . . . There is a
moon! there are stars for you! Do not you hear the fountain? Do not you smell the orange flowers? That building
yonder is the Convent of S. Isidore; and that eminence,
with the cypress trees and pines upon it, the top of M.
Quirinal. This is all true, and yet my prospect is not 200
yards in length."

For two months, broken by an excursion to Naples, they
lingered on in Rome, waiting in vain for the Cardinals to
come to a decision about the election. At last, Walpole's
impatience got the better of him. He decided to go back to
Florence. Gray could willingly have stayed for months more,
happily spelling out time-blurred inscriptions, and conjuring
up gorgeous visions of imperial Rome from crumbling arch
and grass-grown foundation. But since Walpole paid the
piper, he must call the tune. Protestingly, Gray submitted.

Back at Florence, their life took up its old course. But the
divergence between the friends was now more open. It is to
be noted that they no longer lived under the same roof:
Walpole stayed with Mann, Gray had rooms in a neighbouring
house. In spirit, they were yet more widely separated. Wal-

pole enjoyed Florence more than ever. He loved the lounging, festive way of life; getting up at twelve, dining at three, and then a succession of strolls and little parties, that ended with a late supper of iced fruit out of doors on the marble bridge, with the violins discoursing delicate music to the stars. Florentine society, too, now struck him as the most agreeable in the world, as it loitered through the radiant summer days, gaily gossiping, lightly making love. For no longer did Walpole look with contempt on the ceremonious philanderings of lady and Cicisbeo. On the contrary, he aspired to be a Cicisbeo himself; embarked on a cool elegant amour with the beautiful Countess Grifone. Mann, too, was as good company as ever, and Walpole met with a new friend in the person of a Mr. Chute, who, with his cousin, Whithed, was travelling in Italy. Cultured and entertaining, Chute would lean back at the supper table, gesturing extravagantly with a fan, to the disgust of more conventional Englishmen. Here was another kindred spirit. Altogether, Walpole had never felt happier.

Not so Gray. He did, it is true, very much like Chute, who in addition to his other charms, turned out to be very musical, and so concerned about his health that he lived almost entirely on milk and turnips. Gray also appreciated the sensuous pleasures of life in Florence, the beauty of the town, the fruit and ices, and above all, the wonderful Italian weather, so warm that he could sit on his balcony late into the night, clad only in his dressing gown, watching the waters of the Arno, as they lapsed by, gleaming inky in the brilliant moonlight. But he was not happy. "Florence," he said, "is an excellent place to employ all one's animal senses in, but utterly contrary to one's rational powers." Something fundamental in his nature, something bourgeois, English, Protestant, rose up in outraged affront, against the glittering conscienceless hedonism of the South. He sought to occupy himself by making a collection of music, and by writing a long Latin poem about the philosophy of Locke. Even this desperate remedy, however, did not stop him from feeling that he was wasting his time.

Dissatisfaction with his mode of life was sharpened by a growing exasperation with Walpole, an exasperation in which personal resentment was swelled by moral disapproval. Surely it was shocking that a man of Walpole's intelligence should throw away his opportunities for improving the mind for the sake of such vapid frivolities. One instance of this seems particularly to have rankled with Gray. There were several places of interest in the neighbourhood that they had missed seeing on their first visit. Gray wanted to visit them now. Walpole, however, after Rome and Naples, was finally sick of sightseeing. He said he would not go, though he offered to send Gray without him. At this, to him, insulting proposal, Gray's temper began to give way. He told Walpole what he thought of his selfishness and triviality. Peppery Walpole was not the man to stand this; and from Gray, of all people. Who was he to lecture him? Sharply he would remind Gray of his dependent position. Gray, deeply hurt, rushed off to Mann, to whom he poured out in floods of tears his despair at Walpole's apparent change of feeling towards him. With Mann's tactful help, the quarrel would be smoothed over; but only temporarily. Another rub brought another row. Clearly things could not go on like this. Indeed the crisis in their relationship was approaching. It is now that we feel most acutely our want of sufficient information about the story. There is not a word in the letters left to us to trace exactly the steps that lead to the final breach. All we know is that the storm finally broke in August at the little town of Reggio, where they had gone to see the Fair. Its immediate occasion seems to have been some trouble about a letter written by Gray to Ashton. Perhaps Walpole opened it, and

found some disagreeable remarks about himself. Perhaps—
and this is more likely—Ashton, thinking he could ingratiate
himself with Walpole by a little discreet mischief-making,
repeated Gray's words in a letter to Walpole. Anyway
Walpole taxed Gray with treachery, and a furious quarrel
blazed up, which ended with Gray leaving immediately and
dramatically for Venice. A few days later, Walpole, seized
with a fit of remorse, asked Gray to come back for a reconciliation. Gray came, but only to declare himself adamant.
It was six years before they spoke to one another again.

Such was the celebrated quarrel between Gray and Walpole. Many years later Walpole wrote an account of it, in
which he took most of the blame for it on himself.

"I am conscious that in the beginning of the differences
between Gray and me, the fault was mine. I was too young,
too fond of my own diversions, nay I do not doubt, too
much intoxicated by indulgence, vanity, and the insolence
of my situation as a Prime Minister's son, not to have been
inattentive and insensible to the feelings of one I thought
below me; of one whom presumption and folly perhaps
made me deem not my superior *then* in parts, though I
have since felt my infinite inferiority to him. I treated him
insolently: he loved me and I did not think he did."

This is very handsome of him: it seems hard that most
subsequent writers on the subject have taken him at his word,
and speak as though Gray was the injured party. As a matter
of fact, from the scanty information we have, he seems to
have behaved the more unreasonably of the two. After all,
it was natural for a young man of twenty-one like Walpole
to want to dance and flirt: Gray was the odd one to prefer
inspecting ancient monuments. Moreover, Walpole could
not be expected to plan his tour just to suit Gray's tastes. Nor,

though he sometimes felt irritated with him, did he try and divert Gray from them. He was perfectly willing to live and let live. Besides he showed the more generous feelings on the matter. Did not he in the end apologize and try to make it up? But, if Gray were the more difficult, he was also far the most to be pitied. For he was the one who suffered: he it was who felt lonely and left out and awkward and poor. Above all, he was the one who cared the most. There is a crucial, revealing sentence in Walpole's statement. "He loved me, and I did not think he did." No doubt Walpole did not think so, because Gray had grown so disagreeable. In situations of this kind, the one who feels least is likely to make this mistake. Temperate affections are sufficiently under their owner's control for him to remember to try always be pleasant. Walpole's affection, for all its demonstrativeness, was of the temperate kind. He had too much to make him enjoy life to be dependent for his happiness on his relationship with any one person. This was not true of Gray. His disagreeableness was a proof of the peculiar and painful intensity of his attachment. He had very few friends; and his relationship to them was one of the few things that made life bright to him. Walpole was one of them. Gray had thought that his love for him was returned with equal strength. Gradually, inexorably, painfully, his experiences abroad had forced him to recognize that this was not so. This was why he could not resign himself to neglect; this was why it was unbearable for him to watch Walpole gossiping and flirting with Madame Grifone, when he could have gone away alone with him; this was why, finally, he could not bring himself to forgive him. Their situation in regard to one another was so delicate that they were bound to quarrel some time or other during the journey. But it was the fact that Gray was bitterly disillusioned in the tenderest depths of his heart that made the breach, when it did come, so catastrophic.

He lingered for a time at Venice, wretchedly depressed, and so hard up that he did not know how he could manage to pay for the journey home. Walpole, arriving at Venice a little later with Chute, was horrified to hear of his financial embarrassment. He did not dare, for fear of offending him, to offer him money directly, but contrived to get some to him disguised as a loan from Chute. In July Gray started to wend his sad way homewards. By September, 1741, he was in England.

Two days after his arrival he wrote to Chute.

"If this be London, Lord send me to Constantinople. Either I, or it, are extremely odd. The boys laugh at the depth of my ruffles, the immensity of my bagg, and the length of my sword. I am as an alien in my native land. Yea! I am as an owl among the small birds. It rains; everybody is discontented, and so am I. You cannot imagine how mortifying it is to fall into the hands of an English barber. . . . The natives are alive and flourishing. The fashion is a grey frock with round sleeves, bob-wig, or a spencer, plain hat with enormous brims and shallow crown, cock'd as bluff as possible; muslin neckcloth twisted round, rumpled, and tuck'd into the breast; all this with a certain seafaring air, as if they were just come back from Cartagena. If their pockets had anything in them, I should be afraid of everybody I met. Look in their face, they knock you down; speak to them, they bite off your nose. I am no longer ashamed in publick, but extremely afraid. If ever they catch me among 'em, I give them leave to eat me."

Indeed he had every reason to feel strange. It was not only his clothes that made him different from the unsettled in-experienced youth who had quitted England two years before. He had come back a man; the same man, broadly speaking, as he was to remain for the rest of his life. Let us take a look at him. He is not so handsome as most famous poets. A short plumpish figure with a tottery walk is surmounted by a head in which the noble impression made by a lofty forehead and large dark eyes, eloquent beneath their sharply pencilled angular brows, is contradicted by the tight mouth and long prim chin. It is a sensitive, intellectual face; it is also a stiff suspicious shut face. His demeanour was in keeping with it. Shyness and awkwardness had taught themselves to hide behind an assumed air of disdain and an effeminate affectedness of manner, which increased in proportion as he felt that the people he was with did not like him. As for the man beneath the manner, let Gray speak for himself. There is a letter written to West during his last days at Florence, in which he gives an account of the changes he had observed in his own character since he left England.

"As I am recommending myself to your love, methinks I ought to send you my picture (for I am no more what I was, some circumstances excepted, which I hope I need not particularize to you); you must add then, to your former ideas, two years of age, reasonable quantity of dullness, a great deal of silence, and something that rather resembles, than is, thinking; a confused notion of many strange and fine things, that have swum before my eyes for some time, a want of love for general society, indeed an inability to it. On the good side you may add a sensibility for what others feel, and indulgence for their faults or weaknesses, a love of truth, and disdain of everything else. Then you are to deduct a little impertinence, a little laughter, a good deal of pride, and some spirits. These are all the alterations I know of, you perhaps may find more. Think not that I have been obliged for this reformation of manners to

reason or reflection, but to a severer schoolmistress, Experience. One has little merit in learning her lessons, for one
cannot well help it; but they are more useful than others,
and imprint themselves in the very heart."

Gray was comically wrong in thinking that he was indulgent to the weaknesses of others. Walpole would have had
something to tell West about this. But otherwise the account
is fair enough. Gray's maturity appears in the detached clear-
sightedness with which he could observe his own character.
It was true that he was a sadder man; at least more consistently
sad. Such remnants of boyish high spirits as had remained
with him up to his departure, were now completely vanished.
Experience had finally convinced him that his early suspicions
of the world were justified. It was a hard disillusioning
place, where happiness was transient, and sorrow sure;
where few people shared his tastes or understood his feelings;
and where no-one's affection seemed wholly to be trusted.
"I am a fool to be surprised at meeting with brutishness or
want of thought among mankind," he exclaimed bitterly.
Moreover, he realized that he was peculiarly unfitted to
battle with such a world. As he saw it, humanity was divided
on the one hand into public sociable characters, whose nature
and function it was to keep the world going, and on the other
into private contemplative persons who must, if their natures
were to find fulfilment, retire into their own inner life. He
faced the fact that he belonged, for good or ill, irretrievably
to the second category. He was at once too jealous of his own
independence, and too bad at mixing with his fellows to hope
for success in the mêlée. But even as a private person, he
doubted if he was likely to be happy. Human life, of its nature,
involved more pain than pleasure.

Yet he was not a pessimist in the full sense of the word.
For one thing, the whole tradition of thought in which he

had been brought up, would not let him be. Theoretically he believed in free will, in man's power to control his circumstances. "Our inclinations," he said, "are more than we imagine in our power; reason and resolution can direct them, and support us under many difficulties." Reason and resolution taught him that he must strive not to despair. Profoundly moral in his outlook he thought that man lived to be virtuous. And he did not doubt that suffering, if taken in the right spirit, so far from being an unmixed evil, was an aid to virtue. Did it not discipline the character and soften the heart to sympathize with the sufferings of others?

Gray was the more disposed to think this because he was a religious man. It was a sober straightforward Anglican sort of religion. He did not have mystical visions; and his mind was too unmetaphysical to appreciate the significance of dogmatic theology. But his poetical temperament, responsive as it was to the appeal of the ancient and the mysterious, made him unsympathetic to purely rationalist interpretations of the universe, and also susceptible to the religious sentiment. He readily accepted the creed in which he was brought up; and his faith in it was confirmed by that awe-inspiring sense of divinity that came to him at such times as his journey up to the Grande Chartreuse. Nor was his belief shaken by his melancholy. On the contrary, melancholy made him cling to it. Was not religion the only sure gleam of hope in a dark and disillusioning universe? Thinkers like Shaftesbury and Voltaire, who sought to undermine their fellow men's belief in it, were behaving to them with heartless and irresponsible cruelty. And Gray hated them for it.

The pleadings of piety and principle were further reinforced by those of good sense. Since life had to be lived, it was surely foolish not to make the best of it, rather than to waste one's time in unavailing lamentations against the Universal Plan. Besides, he must remember that he was not worse off than

many other people, nor so admirable as to be justified in
thinking he deserved to be specially saved from trouble.
For all his pride, Gray was not self-pitying, nor unreasonably
self-admiring. Even when, with an ironical eye, he watched
his fellows absorbed in the world of business and pleasure
without, apparently, a thought of the brevity and insigni-
ficance of their lives, he would remind himself that his own
mode of living was not much superior—especially as he,
unlike them, was not enjoying himself:

> "Methinks I hear in accents low," he sang,
> "The sportive kind reply:
> Poor moralist! And what art thou?
> A solitary fly!
> Thy joys no glittering female meets,
> No hive hast thou and hoarded sweets,
> No painted plumage to display:
> On hasty wings, thy youth is flown;
> Thy sun is set, thy Spring is gone—
> We frolic, while 'tis May."

He was the more easily able to take a balanced view of his
lot, because there were things about it that he did enjoy. Its
comic side for example; the spectacle of the world was
entertaining as well as saddening. He could not look at it for
long without finding something that forced him to smile.
His cool, sharp-eyed sense of comedy was always glinting
out to maintain his sense of proportion and impose a check
upon his impulses of gloom. More important, the outer world
was far from being the only world for Gray. Equally vivid
was the world of his solitary imaginative life. And this had
been enriched a thousand-fold by his years abroad. When
he was by himself—reading, listening to music, gazing at
mountains or ruined abbeys—his spirit suffered no
sense of frustration; but expanded in a delight, which if not

exactly ecstatic, was, within its sphere, endlessly satisfying. Nor was it merely a passive delight. What he read, what he heard, what he saw, stimulated him to think and analyse, dream and compose. This solitary Gray was very unlike the Gray whom the world knew. Gone were the nervous inhibitions, the prim regard for decorum. Instead, absorbed in an inner dream and for once utterly careless of outward appearances, he would loiter along, smiling, frowning, murmuring aloud to himself, and then suddenly flinging down, to lie for hours beneath the shadow of oak or beech tree. He was able to be so unselfconscious because he was at last on ground where he was confident. In the world of the imagination he knew he was not an alien. Spenser and Virgil would not let him down as his flesh and blood friends did. He did not feel out of it in ancient Rome as he did in modern Florence.

Thus, what with one thing and another, Gray strove to keep his tendency to melancholy within bounds. And for much of the time he succeeded in doing so.

"Mine, you are to know," he told West, "is a white melancholy, or rather Leucocholy for the most part; which though it seldom laughs or dances, nor even means what one calls Joy or Cheer, yet is a good easy sort of state, ça ne laisse que de s'amuser. The only fault of it is insipidity; which is apt now and then to give a sort of ennui, which makes one form certain little wishes that signify nothing. But there is another sorrow, black indeed, which I have now and then felt, that has somewhat in it like Tertullian's rule of faith, credo quia impossibile est; for it believes, nay, is sure of everything that is unlikely, so it be but frightful; and, on the other hand, excludes and shuts its eyes to the most possible hopes, and everything that is pleasurable; from this the Lord deliver us! For none but He and sunshiny weather can do it."

In this passage Gray was making things out a little better than they really were. In reality he did suffer from the black sort of melancholy more often than he wanted his correspondent to think. He admitted ruefully he found it easier to preach his gospel of good sense than to practise it. Indeed, he had special reason to be depressed at this time. Two things made life worth living to him, the life of contemplation and the love of his two intimate friends. He had quarrelled with one of these two; and was not able to feel any certainty of achieving the contemplative life. Practical and financial circumstances seemed likely to make it impossible. Nor was he the sort of man to alter such circumstances in the face of difficulty. Like many intellectual persons, Gray had remained immature in practical affairs, in proportion as he had matured mentally. Man has only a certain capacity for growth within him. All Gray's had gone into the development of his mind and heart: when it came to action he was still an inexperienced boy.

"Is it not odd," he writes to West; "to consider one's contemporaries in the grave light of husband and father? There is my Lords Sandwich and Halifax, they are statesmen: do not you remember them, dirty boys playing at cricket? As for me, I am never a bit the older, the bigger, nor the wiser than I was then." No—the problem of coping with the future was too difficult. Instead, turning his back on the world, he buried himself in reading or writing long letters on literary subjects to West. "You see by what I send you," he told him, "that I converse as usual with none but the dead: they are my old friends and almost make me long to be with them."

West responded to Gray as eagerly as ever. For, as much as ever, he needed him. During the two years his friends had been away, his life had grown steadily more unhappy. He had tried the Bar: but he disliked it so much that he had given it up. This brought him up against the same problem as

Gray. What was he to do instead? Vaguely and desperately he canvassed the various professions. First he thought of being a clergyman, then a soldier. This last was a preposterous idea: no one was less military. But the romantic-minded West was without much sense of reality. In the Army, he suddenly fancied, he might find means to cut the knot that held his life frustrated: either he would win glorious distinction or meet heroic death. Attracted by these alluring alternatives, he wrote off to Walpole, begging him to use his influence to get him a commission. Luckily Walpole, or the army authorities, showed a stronger grasp of fact than West: the letter produced no result. Anyway, by the time Gray got back to England any such active profession would have been out of the question for West. His always delicate health was breaking up. Moments of febrile agitation alternated with fits of lassitude in which he felt he could take no interest in anything: he was afflicted with a hacking cough which grew ominously worse with every month that passed. Whether West realized it or not, here were the dreadful symtoms of consumption. And now, if rumour is to be believed, mental anguish added itself to physical, to increase the strain on his already wasted frame. Dark hints reach us of a sinister drama of crime and guilty passion in which he was involved. He discovered unexpectedly, so it is said, that his mother, whom he loved and revered, was engaged in a sordid amour with an old friend of his own. It was even suggested that the two had conspired together to murder West's father in order that they might be able to marry each other. Whatever the truth of this lurid Hamlet-like tale, it is certain that in the Spring of 1742 West's condition took a quick turn for the worse. On 17th June Gray opened the newspaper and read some commemorative verses revealing the fact that West was dead.

The immediate shock was great; he had not realized how

ill his friend had been. The fundamental shock was greater. Even twenty years later, it was noticed that he could not mention West's death without nearly breaking down. Indeed it had produced the central crisis of his life. For, coming as the culmination of a sombre year of calamity, it broke his last link with the steady solid happiness of Eton days. Experience had not hardened Gray's heart. On the contrary, disillusionment with mankind in general had made him cling all the more desperately to those few individuals with whom he could feel in sympathy. After the quarrel with Walpole, West was the only one of those left. On to him had flowed forth all the force of Gray's thwarted, powerful capacity for affection: on to West who was as shy and sensitive and poor as himself, who cared for books and meditation as much as he did, and whom, he knew, would never be seduced away from him by the tawdry glitter of the world. Now West was gone. How right he had been—more cruelly, horribly right even than he had imagined—in thinking life a cheat! Even if for once one did find a friend who could be trusted to be faithful, yet it was impossible to be sure of keeping him. The ruthless impersonal forces of disaster and death might wrest him away just when one needed him most. There was no end to life's capacity to wound poor helpless humanity.

The structure of philosophy and piety that he had carefully erected to shield him from the blows of fate, was exposed to the full blast of misfortune. It stood the strain. That it did so is evidence of the strength of mind that lurked within his frail, fussy body. Gray did not allow himself to fall into despair. What is more remarkable, he did not grow apathetic. On the contrary, the unprecedented turmoil of emotion which swelled up in his heart at this culminating disaster quickened his spirit to an unprecedented activity. Gray was born a creative artist: deep within him glinted a spark of the true divine fire. But it was not a strong spark: and somehow he had never yet managed to heat it up to an active flame. Constitutional languor had something to do with this. He was further inhibited by too highly developed a critical faculty. If he did screw himself up to begin writing something, he soon grew disgusted with the result, and dropped it. Now at last the pressure of anguish broke down his inhibitions. His heart was so full that he felt compelled to unburden it—and never mind if the result was not all he wished! For once his temperament was warmed to an intensity that had to find release in creation. It is not the first time that the suffering of the man has been the salvation of the artist.

As usually happens, his creative mood came upon him a little time after the experience which engendered it, when he was able to recollect his emotion in sufficient tranquillity to turn it into poetry. In August Gray went to Stoke Poges, near Eton, to stay with an aunt. There, as he roamed about the Buckinghamshire countryside lying placid in the summery stillness, all the confused surging flood of thought and feeling which had agitated him during the last few months began unbidden to settle and crystallize and take shape in phrase and stanza. Poem after poem streamed from his pen. They formed a considered comment on his whole previous history. In them appear all the dominating and characteristic phases of his sentiment: his passionate love for his friends, his responsiveness to the beauties of art and nature, his feeling for the ancient past, his sadness, his acute awareness of the vanity of human wishes. And along with them the forces, which he invoked to govern his emotions, also found expression; his stoicism, his piety, his irony. So that the sentiments that inspired them come to us subdued into a measured elegiac sadness, lit once or twice by a bitter-sweet smile. Now he asserts his determination to profit by the hard lessons of adversity: "Teach me to love and to forgive!" he cries—was he thinking of Walpole? Now gazing across the fields to where the russet towers of Eton loomed faintly through the hazy August distance, like the visible ghosts of his happy irretrievable past, he moralizes on the contrast between his present mood and that of the care-free days of boyhood.

> "Ah happy hills! Ah pleasing shade!
> Ah fields beloved in vain!
> Where once my careless childhood strayed
> A stranger yet to pain.
> I feel the gales that from ye blow
> A momentary bliss bestow,
> As waving fresh their gladsome wing,
> My weary soul they seem to soothe
> And, redolent of joy and youth,
> To breathe a second spring."

Now as the beloved figure of West rose before his mental eye, his grief sighed itself forth in quiet, beautiful, hopeless lamentation.

> "In vain to me the smileing Morning's shine,
> And redning Phoebus lifts his golden Fire;
> The Birds in vain their amorous Descant joyn;
> Or chearful Fields resume their green Attire;
> These Ears, alas! for other Notes repine,
> A different Object do these Eyes require:
> My lonely Anguish melts no Heart but mine;
> And in my Breast the imperfect Joys expire.
> Yet morning smiles the busy Race to chear,
> And new-born Pleasure brings to happier Men:
> The Fields to all their wonted Tribute bear;
> To warm their little Loves the Birds complain:
> I fruitless mourn to him that cannot hear,
> And weep the more because I weep in vain."

One evening wandering in the rural churchyard of Stoke Poges, scattered with mossy time-blurred gravestones, hints of a grander conception began to shadow themselves forth in his imagination; it's theme, human life looked at in the light of its inevitable end. How transient it was! How insignificant its greatest men and most famous achievements! And for that matter, its most dreadful woes. To let oneself be overwhelmed by them was as futile as to be dazzled by its achievements.

"The thoughtless World to Majesty may bow,
  Exalt the brave and idolize Success;
But more to Innocence their Safety owe
  Than Power and Genius e'er conspir'd to bless.

And thou, who mindful of th'unhonour'd Dead,
  Dost in these Notes their artless Tale relate,
By Night and lonely Contemplation led
  To linger in the gloomy Walks of Fate:

Hark! how the sacred Calm, that broods around,
  Bids ev'ry fierce tumultuous Passion cease;
In still small Accents whisp'ring from the Ground,
  A grateful Earnest of eternal Peace.

No more, with Reason and thyself at Strife,
  Give anxious Cares and endless Wishes room;
But thro' the cool sequester'd Vale of Life
  Pursue the silent Tenour of thy Doom."

Thus, in sculptured phrase, and grave tolling music, spoke themselves forth the deepest conclusions borne in on Gray from twenty-six years of troubled life. But before he had time to organize them into a complete work, the wave of emotion which had borne him up since June began to ebb: and with it the creative energy which was its expression. Languor and self-criticism once more began to assert their inhibiting hand. His aesthetic impulse spent itself, never to return with the same strength. But it had lasted long enough to place him among the great English poets. The most miserable year of his life turned out also to be the most fruitful.

It also decided him finally to take up a life of retirement. Bruised by grief, his spirit now shrank uncontrollably from the hurly-burly of the rough world. His one sortie into it had turned out too painful for him to consider risking another. He did not like to declare this openly, for his mother, ambitious for his future, still wanted him to go to the Bar. But he got round this difficulty by telling her that he could read Law just as well at Cambridge. For it was Cambridge Gray now chose as his refuge. Not that his feeling had changed about the place. He still thought it odiously uncouth and provincial. But practical reasons made it the only choice. By the easy-going University regulations of those days he could go on residing in the college free, for as long as he wanted. Accordingly in October, 1742, we find him unpacking his boxes in Peterhouse once more. In accents of half-bitter, half-humorous resignation, he greeted his unrevered Alma Mater.

"Hail, horrors, hail! ye ever gloomy bowers,
　Ye gothic fanes, and antiquated towers,
　Where rushy Camus' slowly-winding flood
　Perpetual draws his humid train of mud:
　Glad I revisit thy neglected reign,
　Oh take me to thy peaceful shade again."

III

We know nothing about Gray for the next two years. Presumably, shut away from the world in the brown and healing silence of library and college room, he set to work to mend his heart and re-establish his equilibrium. If so, he was successful. When he re-emerges, he is his urbane composed self once more. His spirits have stabilized: so has his mode of life. Human beings can be divided into those who allow themselves to be the sport of circumstances, those who try and force circumstances to their will, and those who, while accepting circumstances in the main, in detail seek to manipulate them to suit their desires. Of this last category, Gray is an outstanding example. All he had gone through during his first twenty-six years had left him with a clear idea of what he wanted to have in life, and also of what he was likely to get. For he was far too sensible to fancy he could get all he wanted. Accordingly, cautious and unhurried, he proceeded to devise a plan of living, the best for his taste and temperament possible in the conditions in which fate had seen fit to place him. Having established it, he stuck to it. Though in later years he sometimes got a chance of making a change, he always refused it at once. No doubt his plan of life had its disadvantages. But so, also, as far as he could see, had every other plan. Why then change? Further, he had matured so early that his inner self was no longer susceptible of much development. He and his form of life are alike fixed. The consequence is that after his return to Cambridge his story, as a story, almost comes to an end. Reading it is less like following a stream than contemplating a pool.

It is, however, a pool well worth contemplating; as it lies secluded in its green shade and with a whole soft landscape of lawn and sky and antique spire reflected in its calm surface. Its setting was Cambridge. Gray desired a life of retirement and study in which he would not have to suffer the humiliation of being dependent on anyone else. At Cambridge, he had all the books and quiet he wanted: and he could live there in independence. Not an easy independence. Gray was still very poor: this was one of the inevitable disadvantages forced on him by circumstances. Sometimes he found himself compelled to borrow forty guineas from a friend in order to keep going. He could imagine too vividly the pleasures of affluence—going where he felt inclined, buying all the pretty things he wanted, and seeing as much as he liked of those few persons with whom he did feel an affinity—not to mind poverty. "It is a foolish thing," he sighed, "that one can't, not only not live as one pleases, but where and with whom one pleases, without money. Swift somewhere says that money is liberty: and I fear money is friendship too, and society, and almost every external blessing. It is a great, though ill-natured comfort to see most of those who have it in plenty, without pleasure, without liberty, and without friends."

It was no use repining though. He had better make up his mind that his Peterhouse rooms were his permanent home: and to make them as agreeable as conditions permitted. This cannot have been difficult. The low-ceilinged, sash-windowed set of apartments, set high in the fourth floor above the peaceful small-town busyness of King's Parade, made a pleasant place of retirement. Gray saw that the college servant kept them meticulously clean and tidy: and gradually accumulated in them such amenities as his exiguous purse could command. There were his books and prints and collection of music, there was his little pianoforte, there were a handsome pair of blue and white Japanese vases—these were a great feature of his domestic interior—above all there were flowers. Mignonette bloomed in the windows, bright nosegays were placed about the room: so that with the smell of leather and old woodwork, was blended ever a fresh waft of garden sweetness.

So much for the physical framework of his days. The mental was provided by his scheme of work. "Employment is happiness" was one of his favourite maxims: and he was always occupied in a definite course of study. From time to time the subject of this altered. During the first years his main interests seem to have been classical; Plato, the Greek Anthology, Strabo. He meditated an edition of Strabo at one time. Later his curiosity turned to English poetry, more especially its obscure origins in Provençal song, Anglo-Saxon epic and the Norse sagas. How interesting to write a history of it! He got as far as making a rough plan for such a work. Before he had got far with it, however, he became interested in Gothic architecture, then almost virgin soil in England. In the last years of his life Gothic in its turn was supplanted by natural science, above all that branch of natural science, botany, which he had loved ever since he went gathering bog asphodel in the fields round Eton. Gray's curiosity was boundless, and his standard of knowledge rigidly high. Here was where his academic training had left its mark on him. He did not feel justified in coming to any conclusion till he had taken trouble to learn everything that could possibly be thought relevant to the subject. Each successive interest involved him in exploring fields far outside his original intention. Thus English poetry led him to learn Icelandic; Gothic architecture proved unintelligible without a thorough knowledge of heraldry and mediaeval history. Archaeology, zoology, philology—he had gone into them all before he had finished. It is not surprising to learn that he ended up as one of the most learned men in Europe. Nor, though his knowledge was so diverse, was it disordered. In the library at Cambridge one can still see the notebooks in which, logically

ordered and neatly written, lie the lucid record of his researches. He also found time to keep a naturalist's calendar
in which each day he noted down such things as the temperature, the prevailing wind, what flowers were coming into
bud, what birds were singing. For example:

> 1760. April 20.
> Therm. at 60. Wind S.W. Chaffinch, lark, thrush,
> wren and robin singing. Horse chestnut, wild briar,
> Bramble, and Sallow had spread their leaves. Haw-
> thorn and Lilac had formed their blossoms. Black-
> thorn, double Peach, Peas in full bloom. Double
> Jonquils, Hyacinths, Anemones, single Wallflowers,
> and Auriculas in flower. In the fields Dog violets,
> Daisies, Dandelion, Buttercups, Red-Archangel and
> Shepherd's purse.

Such an entry, where a poet's sensibility glints involuntarily
through the sober factual botanist's phrasing is curiously
characteristic of Gray's tone of mind.

Serious study did not occupy all his time. Gray had not the
vitality for continuous work: and much of his day was given
up to rest and pleasure. His pleasures were as deliberately
pursued as his work. They were mainly aesthetic. Music
was a chief one. The silence of his room was often broken
by the frail sound of the pianoforte, as he sat playing Scarlatti
and Vivaldi: Italian music was his favourite. Gray could sing
too; without much voice, but—so the few friends, whom he
allowed to hear him, said—with a sensitive understanding of
the music. He also sketched, walked, took an interest in
landscape gardening, interior decoration, dress and cookery.
Into these activities he carried the methodical habits of his
serious studies. There is indeed something slightly comic in
his passion for making lists and classifications. It seemed as

if he was ready to catalogue anything. Even the blank pages of his cookery book are filled with lists of pots and pans and ingredients, receipts, arranged "in a scientific order", and accurately indexed to their respective pages. If a friend asked his advice about decorating his house, back would come a lengthy disquisition on wallpaper and window glass, complete with sizes of patterns and lists of prices. "I much doubt of the effect colours—any others than the tints of stucco—would have on a Gothic design on paper. Those I saw at Ely were green and pale blue with the raised work white, if you care to hazard it. One of threepence a yard in small compartments thus might perhaps do for the stairs."

He did not stay at Cambridge all the time. Once or twice a year, after diligent consideration, he would go off for a change. Sometimes it was a brief change, just a day or two in London to listen to a concert or an opera. In Summer his excursions were more extended. For some years he spent August and September at Stoke Poges. His father had died soon after Gray got back to England: and his mother had retired to settle with her sister at Stoke. Gray's affection for her would have made him feel he ought to spend part of the year with her in any circumstances. It cannot have been a disagreeable obligation though: he was the sort of man who feels easy in the society of old ladies, and he loved the country. In 1753, however, his mother died, her sister four years later. Gray took to spending his summer holidays in stately solitary little pilgrimages to some place famous for natural beauty or artistic and historical interest—cathedrals, ruined castles, Elizabethan mansions, the coast of Sussex, the Lake country. He got as far as Scotland once. Each journey led to a new spate of closely-packed, neatly-written notebooks.

In the intervals of sight-seeing, he also visited his friends; Wharton in Durham, Chute in Hampshire, Walpole at Strawberry Hill. For in the end he had made it up with

Walpole—or rather Walpole had made it up with him. Walpole had never wanted to go on with the quarrel. And when, in the Autumn of 1745, he heard from a mutual friend that Gray was in a more approachable frame of mind, he wrote off asking him to come and see him. Gray felt dubious. Such an interview seemed likely to be very embarrassing: and besides he was not at all sure he wanted a reconciliation. He was not one who forgot a quarrel easily, especially when he felt he had been wholly in the right about it. However, good sense and curiosity between them triumphed over his hesitations: so one evening in November he paid a call on Walpole at his house in Arlington Street. The meeting did not go off very well, at least as far as Gray was concerned. Once more the differences between the two men entertainingly reveal themselves. Gray's moralistic outlook and his romantic conception of the higher friendship alike led him to think that personal relations should be conducted on a basis of absolute frankness and sincerity. Unless he could be given a thorough and satisfying explanation of Walpole's behaviour to him in Italy, he did not feel justified in forgiving and forgetting. It is doubtful whether he was right about this. Thorough explanations generally involve home truths: and home truths seldom produce good will. Anyway, Walpole had no intention of embarking on anything of the kind. He always hated going into things. Besides, accustomed as he was to the thousand ephemeral insignificant tiffs of the fashionable world, and skilled in all its graceful white lies and easy breezy evasions, he saw no necessity for explanations. Far better to behave as if nothing had happened. Accordingly when Gray, stiff with shyness and suspicion, entered the room, Walpole rushed towards him, kissed him warmly on both cheeks—"with all the ease of one who receives an acquaintance just out of the country"—and, pressing him into a fauteuil, poured out for three hours an uninterrupted torrent of Beau Monde gossip. "I took my leave very indifferently pleased, but treated with wondrous good-breeding," said Gray sarcastically. However he was not so put off as to refuse Walpole's invitation to dine the next day. This went better: a third interview on the following morning, in which Gray did manage to extract some sort of explanation of his previous conduct from Walpole—as much, he thought, as he was ever likely to get—confirmed his favourable impression.

He was the more willing to receive it because, during his stay in London, he had become convinced that the person most to blame in his quarrel with Walpole had been Ashton. Ashton had been dining with Walpole the same night as Gray. Taking the line that he had more reason to complain of Gray than Gray of him, he had insisted on coming to see him the next morning to explain his part in the whole affair. The interview should have made Gray realize the dangers attendant on frank explanations. The more Ashton explained, the worse did his conduct appear. There was no question that here was the end of this friendship. In his subsequent correspondence, Gray only refers to Ashton once at any length: and that is as a character in a nightmare.

Meanwhile, during the next months, Walpole continued his advances. Gray was still a trifle suspicious. "There has been *in appearance*," he said, "the same kindness and confidence almost as of old: what is the motive I cannot yet guess." Gradually, however, he began to thaw. By the time two years had passed, a relationship had re-established itself between them that was to endure for life.

It was not the same sort of relationship that it once had been. Each knew too much about the other for that to be possible: Gray in particular was never going to forget how badly, in his opinion, Walpole was capable of behaving. And both, if irritated, could say very acid things about each other. The romantic friendship of youth, founded on a rapturous sense of soul affinity, was over for good and all. In its place was a middle-aged friendship based on a rational community of tastes. It was a more stable basis, especially since Walpole, with the advancing years, became less predominantly interested in social life as compared with art and letters. More and more he grew to value someone with whom he could talk of book-bindings and painted glass, of Anne Boleyn's ruff and the Duke of Bedford's genealogy. For this purpose who so good as Gray? Walpole had only to hazard a query on one of those topics, and back would come six pages of minute, reliable information, complete, of course, with references. It was better still when Gray came to Strawberry Hill, and they could talk. Gray was very much at home at Strawberry Hill. He liked the company, he liked the stylishness, he liked the fantasy. Every time he came, there was something new to admire: a ceiling powdered with papier maché stars, a chimney piece inspired by the High Altar of Rouen Cathedral, a bed hung with purple cut velvet on a ground of stone-coloured satin. A decorous Georgian gentleman, Gray wandered through the "long-drawn aisles and fretted vaults" of the queer miniature mock-Gothic dream palace, with feelings of great satisfaction. Nor, though he might shrink from himself taking part in the life of the great world, was he so changed as no longer to like hearing about it at secondhand. The whiff of high fashion and high politics he got from Walpole's conversation still had power mildly to intoxicate him. And he still laughed at Walpole's jokes. So did Walpole at his. Perhaps this was the strongest bond between them. A common taste in humour, the inclination to find the same things comically incongruous, reveals the deepest kind of affinity of spirit: deeper far than that implied by a common creed or cause. Once, by way of cheering up the grief-stricken Lady Waldegrave, the two read aloud to her the autobiography of the seventeenth century Lord Herbert of Cherbury. "We could not get on for laughing and screaming," says Walpole. No wonder he found Gray such a kindred spirit. There can have been few people in England who found Lord Herbert a side-splitting author.

Unexpectedly Walpole turned out to be practically useful to Gray: and in a very important way. Once relations were resumed between them, Gray fell back into his old habit of sending Walpole anything he had written, for criticism. He showed him the group of poems he had composed after West's death: and also newer efforts, including, bit by bit as it slowly grew to completion, the Elegy in the Country Churchyard. Walpole—it was one of his attractive qualities—could admire passionately, especially the work of a friend. Gray's poems gave him something worth admiring. He bubbled over with excitement. Here surely was true genius! He showed the poems round in manuscript; and later persuaded Gray to let him get them published—all the more ardently because he fancied himself as an impresario and much enjoyed busily supervising the details of printing and publication. It was lucky he did; for Gray turned out to be extremely difficult in these matters. Not only was he endlessly fussy about the form in which his work appeared, but he was so suspicious that he was liable to fancy that Walpole and the publisher were deliberately conspiring together to defeat his wishes. The most trivial points—the size in which his name was printed on the title-page, a proposal that his portrait should be used as a frontispiece—was enough to produce a violent explosion of prima donna temperament. To meet it Walpole brought all his diplomatic talents into play. He wrote back at once in answer to Gray's hysterical expostulations, sympathizing, explaining, cajoling, soothing. But it generally took two or three letters to get the agitated poet back into anything like a reasonable frame of mind.

It was ungrateful of Gray to be so difficult. For Walpole

was, in fact, making him famous. It was a slack time in English poetry. Nothing of the first interest by a new writer had appeared for several years. As the result the impression made by Gray's poems, and in particular by the Elegy, was tremendous. Statesmen and generals quoted it: Stoke Poges Churchyard became a celebrated place. Within a few years and on the strength of half a dozen shortish poems, Gray was acknowledged by almost everybody as the first of ving English poets.

Walpole was far from being his only great friend. Gray had always prized the pleasures of friendship as much as those of learning and art. And he made it part of his plan of life to cultivate them. If he chanced to come across a kindred spirit—it was not often—he set aside time to establish and maintain a relation with him. Every few years, a new name appears among his correspondents: gradually he accumulated a circle. Old friends formed its nucleus; Walpole, Chute, Brown, Wharton. Later, and more especially after Gray became famous, it was enlarged by the addition of some younger men who were drawn to him by his distinction and looked upon him as their master. These youthful friendships meant a great deal to Gray. They did something to fill the gap made in his emotional life by his celibacy. Gray had enough in common with young men, given they were of a sympathetic type, not to feel awkward with them, as he did with young women: nor was he bothered by the fear lest friendship with them might rouse sentimental expectations that he could not fulfil. Yet their ardour and high spirits and fresh young faces gave their company some of the gay exhilarating sweetness that less inhibited men find in that of girls. Through them also he was enabled to experience at second hand as it were and belatedly, a little of the youth he had never had. The young men with their boyish gusto and confidence and irresponsibility let in an invigorating breath of morning to the cloistered twilight of his prematurely middle-aged existence. In a discreet sort of way Gray unbent with his young disciples, liked teasing them, scolding them, talking nonsense with them. And instructing them: where we come to the third source of the peculiar charm he found in their society. He was a born don: the relation of master to pupil suited him. Having the advantage in age made him less shy, especially since—combined with his position—it interposed a respectful barrier between him and the risk of any impertinence on the pupil's part. With enthusiasm he threw himself into the task of opening a young man's mind, refining his taste, directing his studies, sympathizing with him in his difficulties, warning, advising. If one of his young friends sent him a poem he had written, Gray would put all his own work aside, to go through it line by line and send back an elaborate criticism. Indeed, Gray was master of the art of friendship between older and younger man. His disciples got all the benefit of his learning and stimulating intelligence, made soft and light by the glow of his affection. But he did not spoil and he did not flatter: while his rational sense of his position stopped him from ever letting the relationship become undignified and over-familiar.

Whether the young men were always worth the attention he lavished on them is another matter. The only two whose figures are at all clear to us, William Mason and Norton Nicholls, are of the type that had always attracted him: clever, precocious, vivacious youths, gossipy with an edge of malice to their gossip, and much given to sentiment and culture. Mason was in addition a poet. His letters are an odd mixture of spicy anecdotes about high life, and lengthy disquisitions on a ponderous tragedy he had written on the formidable subject of Caractacus. Gray smiled at the anecdotes and— strange to relate of one so critical—was much impressed by Caractacus. He was very fond of Mason, called him "Scroddles", and twitted him playfully about his long nose. Norton Nicholls he teased too—about his curious Christian name. "How can people subscribe such a devil of a name—I warrant you call it a Christian name—to their letters, as you do. I always thought I had a small matter of aversion for you mechanically rising in me, and doubtless this was the reason. Fie, fie! put on a white satin mantle and be carried to church again."

Otherwise—though Gray was careful to tell Nicholls how little he thought intellectual accomplishments should be valued in comparison with moral virtue—his discourse to him was mainly about learned topics. These had brought them together. They had met in 1761 drinking tea at another don's rooms. Gray had quoted a line of Milton: Norton had suggested that it was an echo of Dante. "Sir, do you read Dante?" cried Gray, turning to him with excited interest. From that instant they were close friends. Others might find Nicholls an affected coxcomb; Gray saw nothing to complain of in him. While Nicholls constituted himself the champion of Gray against any breath of criticism. Fancy a frivolous dilettante like Mr. Walpole presuming to quarrel with his "dear Mr. Gray!" It only showed how unworthy he was to be his friend. Nicholls' attitude to Gray—and Mason's too— is a trifle irritating; the assiduity with which they play up to him, the proprietary tone they assume when talking of him to those inferior beings who have not been admitted to the privilege of his intimacy. The professional disciple of the great is a tiresome type. One is not surprised to learn that both Mason and Nicholls turned later into successful men-of-the-world clergymen.

Amid the all-male cast of Gray's circle appears one female name. This was yet another result of his literary fame. In the summer of 1750, Walpole had been showing the manuscript of the Elegy round to such of his friends as went in for culture:

among them a certain Lady Cobham who, with her ward, the twenty-one-year-old Miss Henrietta Speed, lived at the Manor House of Stoke Poges. Both professed themselves in ecstasy at the poem. How thrilling to think that the author was sometimes a neighbour! They longed to know him. With Miss Speed to wish was to act. One afternoon, Gray, returning from his daily walk, was surprised to find a mysterious note on his writing table. "Lady Schaub's compliments to Mr. Gray," it ran, "she is sorry not to find him at home, to tell him that Lady Brown is very well." Lady Brown was a distant acquaintance of Gray's: Lady Schaub, a friend of her's, was staying with Lady Cobham. Miss Speed, discovering the tenuous link, had made use of it to scrape acquaintance. Politeness required that Gray should make a return call. He enjoyed it enormously. The old Elizabethan mansion, with its mullions and panelling and dark discursive passages and picturesque associations with Sir Christopher Hatton, was just the place to appeal to his imagination. Nor were its inhabitants less agreeable than their dwelling. Lady Cobham was pleasant: Miss Speed was more. Plump, dark and prepossessing-looking, she united the finished agreeability of a woman of fashion to a quick satirical intelligence and an irrepressible vitality that made her enjoy everything. Though not intellectual herself, she liked the society of intellectual men, and knew just how to make them like her. Now she devoted herself to drawing Gray out. It is unlikely that it had ever happened to him before. He succumbed at once. So inspired indeed was he by her company, that, on getting home, he sat down and wrote off a comic poem for her about the unusual circumstances of their meeting. Miss Speed replied enthusiastically appreciative, and with another invitation. Gray accepted. It led to other meetings. Soon his friends were amused to hear that Gray was spending his summer rattling about in a butcher's cart, driven by the spirited hands of Miss Speed.

This, as might be expected, was followed by a rumour that he was in love with her. Everything we know about Gray goes to make this unlikely. But, as much as most artists, he responded to the pleasure of being lionized by a lady of fashion, more especially as this particular lady, with her Walpole-like mixture of spirits, wit and modishness, was just the type to please him. Nor was he averse to a pretence of flirtation. Though he denied to his friends that he was in love, it was in a tone of gratified coyness, that indicated that he rather liked them to think he was. After all it was a new thing for him to be suspected of an entanglement with a fine lady. He even tried in a mild way to play up to his rôle in it. When Miss Speed told him she would like to hear his muse sing of love, he answered with a correct little copy of eighteenth century amorous verse addressed to her under the name of Delia.

"Sighs sudden and frequent, looks ever dejected,
  Sounds that steal from my tongue, by no meaning connected:
  Ah say, Fellow Swains, how these symptoms befell me?
  They smile, but reply not. Sure Delia will tell me."

Altogether the swooping down of this bright humming-bird into his quiet garden was pleasant enough for him to want to have it repeated. For the next few years it became a settled thing that during his stay at Stoke Poges, he should spend a good deal of time at the Manor House.

In addition to extending his inner circle, his renown brought him some pleasant acquaintances. Distinguished scholars and antiquarians entered into correspondence with him. Or a young nobleman would call at his rooms with a letter of introduction; Lord John Cavendish it might be, "a sensible boy, but awkward and bashful beyond belief and eats a buttock of beef at a meal"; or the magnificent Lord Nuneham. "You would delight in Lord Nuneham," Mason had written

to him: "He's so peevish and hates things so much and has so
much sense." Gray was certainly amused by him. Reeking of
jessamine powder and arrayed in all the elaboration of great
sleeves and a bouquet of jonquils—"a little too fine even for
me, who love a little finery," said Gray—Lord Nuneham
arrived in Cambridge at the time of the Newmarket races,
only, it seemed, to advertise the fact that he did not think
them worth attending. If it did not happen too often, Gray
enjoyed a visit from a young nobleman. Talking to strangers
was always an ordeal. But, if he had to entertain one, he
preferred him to be polished, or at any rate, haloed by the
romantic interest of a historic name.

Acquaintances, however, took up little of his time. It was
not that he had lost interest in observing the world. He never
tired of Walpole's social news; and his political too. A staunch
Whig and a thorough-going patriot—what a wretched pack
of fribbles the French were—Gray was all agog to hear the
latest about the foundation of Pitt's government, or the progress of the Seven Years War. After the '45 rebellion he leapt
at the chance of attending the trial of the Jacobite lords:
observing, with sharp interested eye, how the tough old
Balmerino casually fingered the edge of the axe that was to
cut his head off. Equally he enjoyed the events of the Cambridge scene: Poor Smart the crazy poet has been arrested
for debt, he gossips gaily to a correspondent; young Mr.
Delaval has been sent down for having his mistress up to
stay with him in College, disguised as an Army Captain; that
old nuisance, Dr. Chapman of Magdalen has died from eating
a whole turbot at one meal—"they say he made a very good
end" commented Gray demurely. As from a box in a theatre,
he sat gazing from the window of his rooms, at the comedy
of University life.

But he did not go down on to the stage. There was little
temptation. The dons were as stodgy as ever: and as for such

female society as the place provided—"the women here," said he, "are few, squeezy and formal, and little skilled in amusing themselves or anyone else". Though, as a matter of fact, even if Cambridge society had been very agreeable, Gray would have shrunk from taking part in it. For him, relations with his fellows should always be private individual affairs, conducted, as it were, in a series of tête-à-tête interviews. Even if his friends knew each other, he preferred himself to see them separately. Mankind, in any corporate manifestation, was something to be avoided.

Such then was Gray's life: a deliberately worked-out plan, in which the different elements that pleased him in existence— study and idleness, solitude and friendship, nature and art— were blended together in balanced and temperate proportion. He put all his delicate sense of style into its execution. Artists' lives are often disillusioning to read about: for they are so surprisingly unaesthetic, so lacking in unity of design and harmony of tone, such a muddle of loose ends and false starts and jarring notes. Verlaine's life. Dostoieffsky's life, D. H. Lawrence's life—how could people so sensitive endure to live so tastelessly, one asks oneself. Perhaps the question is silly, perhaps the very explosive fire of their genius set them inevitably at odds with order and tame seemliness. All the same, Gray's life makes a pleasant contrast to theirs. Here all is in order, all is of a piece. In its own way it is as consummate a work of art as Horace Walpole's own.

Nor was it merely urbane and graceful. It was given depth and spirituality by the rich inner life of its creator. For this still went on. Behind the mask of the gentleman and the scholar, the poet dreamed and brooded. Though it was less disciplined and self-conscious than the life his fellows saw, Gray's inner life was in tune with it. There was nothing wild or unaccountable about it; and nothing visionary. The region of his dreams was a minor-key silver-tinted place, of reverie and pensive reflection and delicate half-smiling fancy. Nor did the contemplation of it ever carry him away to such an extent as to make him forget the existence of the external prosaic world. He knew his dreams were dreams: he did not take them so solemnly as to be unable lightly to make fun of them. His emotions about them never got out of the control of his reason. Indeed emotion and intellect played an equal part in his meditations. It was half of his satisfaction in them to analyse and discriminate the flights of his imagination, the impulses of his sensibility.

For, as always, his inner life was primarily concerned with his response to the beautiful. And, as always, this response was stimulated by two things, his feeling for nature, and sense of the historic past. Generally the two were blended together.

"In the bosom of the woods," he writes, "concealed from profane eyes—lie the ruins of Netley Abbey. There may be richer and greater houses of religion, but the abbot is content with his station. See there at the top of that hanging meadow, under the shade of those old trees that bend into a half-circle about it, he is walking slowly—good man! —and bidding his beads for the souls of his benefactors, interred on that venerable pile that lies beneath him. Beyond it—the meadow still descending—note a thicket of oaks, that mask the building and have excluded a view too garish and too luxuriant for a holy eye, only on either hand they leave an opening to the blue glittering sea. Did you not observe how, as that white sail shot by and was lost, he turned and crossed himself, to drive the Tempter from him, that had thrown that distraction in his way. I should tell you that the ferryman who rowed me, a lusty young fellow, told me that he would not for all the world pass a night at the Abbey—there were such things seen near it was thought there was a power of money hid there."

Was it the radiant landscape or its picturesque historical associations, that inspired this passage? The two are inextricably mixed: we cannot say. Similarly as he stood on the willowy banks of Cam in the first pale glow of a summer dawn, or, by night, paced the college cloisters where the tracery cast its intricate shadow, black on the moonlit pavement, his imagination was stirred half by the actual beauty of the scene and half by its power to conjure up before his mental eye the spectres of the illustrious dead who had walked there before him—monarchs, bishops, students, poets, stern Edward I, forlorn Henry VI, straddling Henry VIII, Newton and Milton absorbed in the ardent contemplations of their mighty youth.

> "High potentates, and dames of regal birth
> And mitred fathers in long order go:
> Great Edward, with the lilies on his brow
> From haughty Gallia torn,
> And sad Chatillon, on her bridal morn
> That wept her bleeding love, and princely Clare,
> And Angou's heroine, and the paler rose,
> True rival of her crown, and of her woes,
> And either Henry there.
> The murdered saint, and the majestic Lord
> That broke the bonds of Rome."

To Gray no place existed only in the present. Behind the England of his own day, he discerned as in a vision the long perspective of its past, peopled with figures of bygone generations, stretching away to the dim horizons of antiquity. As he wandered through the stone-paved great gallery of Hardwick Hall with its dim tapestries and sculptured chimney-pieces, and beruffed inscrutable Tudor portraits, he could hardly believe that Mary, Queen of Scots, had not left it the moment before he entered: in the avenues of Warwick

Castle "the elms", he said, "seem to remember Sir Philip
Sidney, who often walked there—and talk of him to this
day." Music too was powerful to evoke Gray's sense of the
past. He was spellbound when the old Welsh harper Parry
sang the wild traditional ballads of his native land. The unintelligible words and irregular rhythms seemed to be the
very voice of the long-dead world of the Druids, echoing
strangely down the ages.

Natural sounds were not less active to stir his feelings and
his imagination. The singing of the young birds as he walked
with Nicholls one sunny spring day in the fields near Cambridge, caused his heart to rise involuntarily to carol with
them.

"There pipes the woodlark", so he improvised "and the
song thrush there,
Scatters her loose notes in the waste of air."

And the wail of the winter wind too, lamenting round the
chimneys on a winter night—"Did you never observe," he
cries, "that pause, as the gust is recollecting itself and rising up
on the ear in a shrill and plaintive note, like the swell of an
Aeolian harp? I do assure you there is nothing in the world so
like the voice of a spirit."

In this passage he speaks with a more impassioned accent
than when he is talking about Netley Abbey or the avenues
of Warwick. And, in fact, for all that his sense of history was
so strong, scenes of pure nature were the source of his intensest
and most profound spiritual experiences. All the more as he
grew older: it was as if, with the gradual failing of youthful
hope, and youthful energy, his spirit more and more sought
sustenance from the earth of which it was made and to which
it must decline. Not for nothing was botany the favourite
study of his later years. Descriptions of natural scenery take an
increasing space in the journals of his summer tours. With a

tireless concentration, an extraordinary loving particularity, he lingers over their typical details: the shining reaches of Ullswater "just ruffled by the breeze enough to show it is alive"; a walk by the river Kent made memorable by the strange contrast of the bright calm evening weather with the roar of a cataract and the thumping from the hammer of an iron forge, hidden in the trees near by: Derwentwater at twilight, with the shadows of the mountains lengthening across the glassy water and the air so still that he could hear the murmur of a waterfall far away in the distance; the pastoral charm of Grasmere, its banks broken into little bays, their outlines half hiding, half revealing the gleaming lake, and with a promontory jutting out into it, where a village and church clustered together, white against the emerald turf. "Not a single red tile," he mused, "no flaring gentleman's house or garden walls break in on the repose of this unsuspected little paradise, but all is peace, rusticity, and happy poverty in its neatest most becoming attire."

Sometimes nature disturbed a deeper chord in him. Never as long as he lived would he forget, so he said, the shuddering awe that possessed him, as he stood, one chill and gloomy afternoon, in the savage gorge of Gordale Scar, his cheek wet with the spray from a torrent that thundered foaming down from a rocky precipice frowning six hundred feet above his head: what a sense of glory and wonder flooded his heart when he chanced to witness the sun rise over the sea one summer morning on the Hampshire coast.

"I must not close my letter without giving you one principal event of my history; which was, that—in the course of my late tour—I set out one morning before 5 o'clock, the moon shining through a dark and misty autumnal air, and got to the sea-coast time enough to be at the sun's levee. I saw the clouds and dark vapours open gradually to

right and left, rolling over one another in great smoky
wreaths; and the tide—as it flowed in gently upon the
sands—first whitening, then gently tinged with gold and
blue: and all at once a little line of insufferable brightness
that, before I can write these fine words, was grown to half
an orb, and now to a whole one, too glorious to be distinctly seen. It is very odd, it makes no figure upon paper:
yet I shall remember it as long as the sun, or at least as long
as I endure. I wonder whether anybody ever saw it before?
I can hardly believe it."

This description illustrates perfectly the individual distinguishing quality of Gray's imaginative life. Precisely he dis-
cerns the features in the scene that give it its character:
exquisitely he responds to its sentiment. Yet it never sweeps
him right away in a Ruskinian rhapsody of lyrical ecstasy.
His tone of voice remains a conversational *prose* tone: and the
little quip that closes the passage expresses, as it were, the
smiling shrug with which, after his brief flight into the em-
pyraean, he brings himself down to firm earth once more.
Thus Gray's instinct for harmony extended to the relation
between his inner and outer life. They were not inconsistent.
All the same they were different. The solitary Gray is a more
impressive personality than the sociable. Gone are the timidity
and suspiciousness that hamper and deform his relations with
his fellows. Instead his sensibility, his imagination, his deep
capacity for feeling, soar up, unalloyed and unimpeded, to
their fulfilment. So that narrow and artificial as his mode of
living might seem, the impression it leaves on us is not one of
artificiality and narrowness. For he himself was too continually in touch with the majestic processes of the elemental
earth, too profoundly aware of the transience and insigni-
ficance of the individual life in comparison with the huge
dimension of past time. As in a canvas of Gainsborough, the

silken formal figure stands out before us shaded by the trees of the woodland and against a dreamy illimitable distance.

Once or twice he allowed his inner life to disclose itself to the world in a poem. In veiled fashion though; never again was he to open his heart, as in the months after West's death. The two great odes—The Bard and The Progress of Poesy—which are the chief poetic achievement of these later years are ceremonious, impersonal productions in which he hardly mentions himself or his own feelings. But they are inspired by matter drawn from his lonely contemplations and vivified by the spirit that infused them. Intensely enough to awake a response in his readers; they confirmed and increased his fame. In 1757 Gray was offered the Poet Laureateship. This however he at once and emphatically refused. His life was to be a private life: writing was no more than one of his diversions: he was not going to set up as a professional author. As a matter of fact it would have been difficult for him to, considering how little he produced. Only seven or eight not very long poems in thirty years: and some of these he never finished. As for bringing any prose work to a conclusion, he found that impossible. The Edition of Strabo, the History of English poetry, all those projects, so carefully meditated, so sedulously prepared for—none of them got further than his note-books.

From time to time Gray lamented this inability to finish: but without much hope of curing it. Indeed its causes were beyond his control. They were partly physical. Gray had never been strong: in middle life he became sickly. A gouty tendency, inherited from his father—his father seems to have been a disaster to him in every way—began to manifest itself, now in headaches, now in constipations, now in violent fits of dizziness. These afflictions were not very serious. But while they lasted, they prostrated him. And even when he was free from them, he felt lethargic. All this sapped his energy for concentrated work. Nine days out of ten he simply did not feel up to it. It was not only bad health, however, that inhibited him. Psychological causes also played their part. He was morbidly nervous of failure, morbidly sensitive to criticism. This last he would have denied. He was always protesting and declaring that he did not mind what other people thought of his work. But the very unnecessary emphasis with which he insists on his indifference suggests that it was, in part at least, assumed. Moreover, as we have seen, he liked sending his poems, while they were still in process of composition, round to his friends, that he might have a chance of remedying any defect they might complain of in them, before they were irretrievably launched on the world. Not that he would have altered anything in them against his own better judgment, just because someone else did not like it: he was too disinterestedly an artist for that. But the meticulous attention he paid to his friends' suggestions shows that he was not at all the sort of man who is completely satisfied so long as he has pleased himself. Here was something to inhibit still further his creative impulse. The standard of perfection he set himself was so high, and involved such a labour of polishing and re-writing that it was very seldom he felt strong enough to make the effort necessary for it. No—creative work was not for him. With relief, with despondency, with a tired, obstinate defiance he relaxed back to his routine of reading and note-taking and idle, aimless meditation.

"It is indeed for want of spirits, as you suspect," he told Wharton, "that my studies lie among the cathedrals and the tombs and the ruins. To think, though to little purpose, has been the chief amusement of my days: and when I would not, or cannot think, I dream. At present I find myself able to write a catalogue, or read the Peerage book, or Miller's *Gardening Dictionary*; and am thankful that there are such employments and such authors in the world. Some people who hold me cheap for this are doing perhaps what is not half so well worth while. As to posterity, I may ask—with somebody who I have forgot—what has it ever done to oblige me?"

This incapacity to work was the sign of a deeper and more general malady of spirit. It was the old trouble. He still suffered from the fear of l fe. It showed itself every day of his existence. He was haunted by morbid unreasonable apprehensions. Heights frightened him; so did dogs, so did horses. In that age of horsemen, he never brought himself to learn to ride. If he had to cross the water, he at once fancied he was going to be drowned. After a rough crossing over the Firth of Forth, he went thirty-five miles round on the return journey rather than risk such an ordeal again. Fire was worse than water. In 1758 he became filled with terror lest a fire should break out in College; and that, living, as he did, four storeys up, he should be trapped by it. Immediately he took elaborate precautions for his safety: had a horizontal iron bar fixed outside his window with a rope-ladder, specially procured from London, attached to it. Away from Cambridge, the same fear possessed him. "'Tis strange," he wrote from London once, "that all of us here in town lay ourselves down every night on our funeral pile and compose ourselves to rest: while every drunken footman and drowsy old woman has a candle ready to light it before morning." Thieves were another source of anxiety. He could not get off a parcel without fearing it might get stolen before it reached its destination. When he had to send luggage ahead, he marked every item in it according to an elaborate system of crosses and letters, so that he should at once be able to recognize if everything had arrived safely. Things might also get broken: here was another anxiety. To assuage it, he insisted on his possessions being carefully packed in straw and paper. But this precaution, in its turn, revived an old terror. Paper and straw were inflammable. Supposing a careless servant left a lighted candle about in the room in which he had been unpacking! It seemed impossible to be safe from one danger without involving oneself in another.

Such a temperament was not likely to take ill-health placidly. And indeed from middle life Gray was a confirmed hypochondriac; watching every slight up-and-down of his health with the microscopic concentration of a scientist conducting an important experiment. Here was occasion for a new set of notebooks and classified lists. Daily Gray set down the mournful catalogue of his aches and eye-troubles and digestive disturbances, together with that of the remedies he took to alleviate them. He dieted, he gave up wine, he never went for a walk in the wind without wrapping up his face in a shawl. Even if for once he was not feeling ill, he continued to worry. Was he not, he asked himself, feeling like someone who is shortly going to feel ill? Suffering from a definite ailment was in some ways a relief: then at least he was free from the pains of suspense.

Mental dangers troubled as much as physical. Seeing his lawyer, doing his accounts, going on a journey—all these were liable to set him worrying. Going on a journey was particularly agitating: it often is to neurotic persons. For days before he started, Gray was in a state of anxiety. Would he be ready in time? Would he remember to leave his address behind? Getting off did not always calm him. Once when he was travelling, he got news that an important-looking letter had arrived for him, at Cambridge. At once he began to rack his brains as to what might be in it. There was no peace of mind for him till it was safely in his hands.

But it was in his relations with other people that his nervousness showed itself most forcibly. The seclusion in which he now lived made him more painfully shy than ever, if he did find himself forced by unlucky chance into company. During a visit to a sociable hotel at Malvern during the Season he did not speak for a week: Lady Ailesbury told Walpole that once when she had managed to persuade him to come on a day's picnic party, he only opened his mouth once. "Yes, My Lady, I think so," he murmured, and then relapsed into an unbroken silence. No wonder the voluble Walpole got irritated with him. How could such a master of words as he knew Gray to be, endure to be such a wet blanket! Gray could not help it: society merely made him feel inadequate and depressed. And the merrier it was, the gloomier he became. "People in high spirits and gaiety overpower me," he said to Wharton, "and entirely take away mine. I can yet be diverted with their sallies, but if they take notice of my dullness, it sinks me to nothing." In the effort to cover up his shyness, he involuntarily exaggerated his supercilious artificiality of manner. The consequence was that he did not make a good impression on strangers. Obscurely he felt this; and became stiffer than ever. But things were hardly better at Cambridge, where he was not among strangers. The average don found him very uncomfortable company: while the undergraduates could not conceal their laughter at the finicky figure with its tottery walk and wrapped-up face and ridiculous fears and fads. At one time poor Gray even became a recognized object of undergraduate jokes. He was not the man to take this in good part, especially as undergraduate jokes in the eighteenth century were on the crude side. Indeed they were the cause of an event that, in a life so preternaturally quiet as Gray's, can only be called sensational. It occurred in 1759. Some rooms on his staircase were occupied by two horsey young men of fashion, Mr. Williams and Mr. Forrester. When they were feeling particularly high-spirited, they worked it off by playing pranks on Gray, and waking him up in the middle of the night by the noise they made. Gray complained to the authorities; but the authorities did not receive his complaints with much sympathy. Gray grew very annoyed. The climax was reached very early one March morning when Mr. Williams and Mr. Forrester in company with a friend of their's, young Lord Percival, were starting off for a day's hunting. Passing below Gray's rooms, they noticed the iron bar he had erected against fire. It was, we must admit, a considerable temptation to anyone with a taste for practical joking. "Let's make Gray bolt!" they said: and accordingly they sent Lord Percival's servant to go upstairs and bellow "Fire!" outside Gray's door as loud as he could, in the hope of luring Gray down the ladder so that they could, as they put it, "whip the butterfly up again". The plot seemed as if it were going to succeed: in due course a pale face surmounted by a silken nightcap was seen, in the grey dimness of dawn, peering agitatedly out of the window. Suddenly, however, it was withdrawn. Gray had caught sight of the upturned faces of his tormentors in time to avoid delivering himself into their hands.

He cannot be said to have suffered any very dreadful experience, by ordinary standards. But to a man with his tendency to persecution mania, it was the last straw. He tore off to the Master of Peterhouse clamouring for vengeance on the perpetrators of so shocking an insult to his dignity. What was his sense of outrage when the Master pooh-poohed the whole affair as "a young man's frolic"? Not for a day longer was Gray going to demean himself by remaining in such a bear garden. He resigned his fellowship. How far he thought this involved the drastic step of leaving Cambridge altogether we do not know. Anyway there was no question of this. For Pembroke just over the way, where his friend Brown was a Fellow, offered to take him in. A month later we find him writing from there to his friends telling them that, for reasons too tedious to go into, he had left Peterhouse. When they discovered the truth, these friends praised his magnanimity in not mentioning the real cause of his departure. Perhaps, though, his silence was due to another reason; perhaps he was afraid that if he did mention it, he would look a little silly.

After this his troubles seem to have stopped. There is no record of any unseemly practical jokes being played on him at Pembroke. But he did not become more sociable. On the contrary, during his last years he lived more retired a life than ever. He was by now one of the most famous of living writers. Yet when he took his daily walk to the Botanical gardens, hardly anyone recognized him.

There was nothing very new in all this however. Gray never had got on with strangers. But now even his relations with his small cluster of close friends had become a touch inhibited. It came partly from an inevitable clash between his temperament and his mode of living. Instinctively he still craved an intense relationship; by nature he longed to be first in another's affections. But this could not be done without entangling his life with theirs. And the whole aim of his scheme of existence was to be free of entanglement. Entanglement would upset the regular order of his days: worse, it was a threat to the security of such peace of mind as he had managed to achieve. Never again did he wish to suffer as he had over West and Walpole. Anyway he was, for the time being at any rate, incapable of the self-surrender required for that kind of friendship: he had not the confidence in other human beings that it implied. Here was where his fear of life showed itself. His reserve now spread itself over the whole surface of his personality. He lived within the system of solitary habit he had erected for himself, as in a locked citadel. At regular intervals, it pleased him to sally forth and enjoy the delights of an hour's conversation with a sympathetic spirit. But when it was over, he went back: nor did he ever take anyone in with him. To none of his friends did he write as openly and intimately as he had to West. And though he was too sensible to quarrel, he was if anything more critical than before. With detached clarity, he noticed his friends' faults; so that his affections though genuine and constant, were not glowingly warm. The full free current of his impulse to love was checked.

Sometimes it pretty well dried up. This was what happened with Miss Speed. She can never have understood him very well: for on one occasion we find her reproaching him, on the extraordinary ground that he paid insufficient attention to his health. Most likely she was under the not uncommon delusion that poets are impractical, up-in-the-clouds creatures, incapable of running their own lives: and only too grateful that an efficient female friend, like herself for instance, should take on the job for them. This was the last sort of thing Gray wanted. However Miss Speed did not get much chance to try it: and for some years their relationship jogged along comfortably enough. Then in 1760 Lady Cobham died, leaving her the heiress to thirty thousand pounds, a house in London, and a great deal of china. Rendered confident by these advantages, she began to display her dominating bent more clearly. At once and with displeasure, Gray noticed it. She asked him to stay with her, but then changed the date of his visit several times to suit her whim, a most disturbing thing to a man who liked to know his exact plans months beforehand. And then when he did arrive, she plunged him into a vortex of social activity. "I am come to my resting-place," he wrote tartly once he was safe back at Cambridge, "and find it very necessary after living for a month in a house with three women, that laughed from morning to night and would allow nothing to the sulkiness of my disposition. Company and cards at home, parties by land and water; and what they call *doing something*, that is racketting about from morning to night, are occupations, I find, that wear out my spirits: especially in a situation where one might sit and be alone, with pleasure." It is not surprising that, as far as we know, he did not visit her again.

How Miss Speed took his defection we are not told. It was rumoured that she had hoped to marry him. This seems unlikely seeing that she was, by all accounts, of a shrewd cool temperament, and as such, not at all the woman to fix her affections on someone so unlikely to return them. In any case, she soon cut her losses. In 1761 she married the Baron de la Perrière, a Sardinian nobleman, six years younger than herself, and left England to settle in Switzerland. Considering that this must have seemed likely to mean permanent separation from her, Gray heard it very philosophically. "My old friend Miss Speed has done what the world calls a very foolish thing," he said, " . . . what she has done with her money I know not: but—I suspect—kept it to herself." When however four years later she came back to England on a visit, he called on her. "She has grown a prodigious fine lady," he told Wharton, "and a Catholic—though she did not expressly own it to me: not fatter than she was. She had a cage of foreign birds and a piping bullfinch at her elbow, two little dogs on a cushion in her lap, a cockatoo on her shoulder and a slight suspicion of rouge on her cheeks." Though he professed himself to have been very pleased to see her, this description is more satirical than affectionate. Gray was not going to forget that Miss Speed could be very tiresome.

Chute, too, seems in the end to have lost Gray's friendship. For some years Gray often stayed with him enjoying pleasant talks about music and invalid symptoms. But, after 1760, Chute's name disappears from the list of Gray's correspondents. Presumably he had said or done something—we do not know what—which had made Gray strike him off the

carefully selected list. Even of Walpole—as we have seen—
he could at times be very critical. The only people with whom
his relations were calm and stable were his young disciples
and solid old friends like Brown and Wharton. But Brown
and Wharton had never been the object of his intenser romantic sentiment: while the difference of age and position between
himself and his disciples kept them always at a cool respectful
distance from him. Never, once he had settled into maturity,
did he achieve a friendship that fully satisfied the demands of
his nature. Always there was something strained, or something lacking.

No—in spite of all his care and judgment and self-discipline, Gray failed to find that solid tranquillity of spirit
which above all things he longed for. It was impossible he
should. To avoid the suffering which had blighted his youth,
he had taken refuge in a universe of his own, constructed to
exclude the occasion of anything that might give him pain.
But pain, alas, is an ineradicable constituent of human existence. It comes primarily from within: and is at least as much
due to character as to circumstance. Certainly this was true
of Gray. He was constitutionally languid, temperamentally
melancholy; and early education had left him incurably the
prey to a neurotic fear of life. These weaknesses were bound
to affect him whatever his mode of living. If his neurosis
did not find a big thing to nourish itself on, it fed upon a small
one: if he had nothing else to worry about, he worried about
losing his luggage. He had erected elaborate defences against
the assault of outside events, only to discover that, like Sir
Thomas Browne, he had Lucifer and all his angels within
him. Nor, as a matter of fact, did his defences turn out to be
impervious against external enemies. Gray was, he could not
help being, an artist with all the artist's lightning responsiveness to the mental atmosphere of the world around him. It
was no use his saying that he thought so poorly of mankind

that he despised its opinion. The fact remained that, as we have seen, when the undergraduates laughed at him, he felt outraged: and that when Walpole proposed using his portrait as the frontispiece to his poems, he was in a fever lest it should make him appear a fool in the eyes of his readers. He even refused to take a degree, for fear he should be confused with another Dr. Gray, who had made himself ridiculous by publishing a worthless edition of Hudibras. The proud contempt for mankind and its ignoble preoccupations which he professed to be his motive for retiring from the arena of active life, was not serene and self-sufficient, but a strained, nervous, vulnerable affair, and in part at least, a cover to hide his shrinking from the pain and mortification in which he feared that a struggle might involve him.

> "Too poor for a bribe," so he wrote of himself,
>   "and too proud to importune,
> He had not the method of making a fortune."

He had not the nerve either.

Moreover, Gray's mode of living did lay him open to some peculiar dangers. It tended to weaken such little energy as he possessed. To work, if you do not have to, is always hard and needs a more forceful character than Gray's. He only embarked on any creative work if the mood took him. And, since he did nothing to induce such a mood, it took him less and less often. The eventless regular round of his days, as they ticked slowly away amid the sequestered college courts, was profoundly unstimulating. He was, as it were, becalmed. Further, so much of his vitality was occupied in warding off disaster, that there was little left for anything else. With the harsh invigorating gale of the world excluded carefully from every cranny, the mental atmosphere in which he lived grew airless and exhausted; his spirit began to flag even from those activities which he enjoyed. He felt no heart for writing: his talent for friendship was checked of fulfilment. If a man rejects life, life soon begins to reject him.

All the same Gray did not make a mistake in living as he did. He was faced with a choice of evils. And he chose the lesser. He simply could not have stood the strain of an active life: it would have entailed his acting perpetually against the whole bias of his nature. The consequence could only have been collapse. The life he did choose, on the other hand, was in accordance with this bias. And, when all is said and done, he got more pleasure than pain out of it. Moreover the pain was moderated by the exercise of those qualities that had served him so well in previous crises: his fortitude, his irony, his unegotistic good sense. Though he could not overcome his weaknesses, he recognized them as such, and made no attempt to excuse them. Neither did he yield to the temptation to indulge in self-pity. Except in moments of extreme agitation, he speaks of his own fears and fusses with something of the same amusement as he would speak of other people's follies. And he took care always to remind himself that his troubles were most likely no worse than those the rest of the world had to put up with: and, as such, could and should be endured without complaint. "A life," he told Mason in one of his letters of paternal advice, "spent out of the world has its hours of despondence, its inconveniences, its sufferings as numerous and as real—though not quite of the same sort— as a life spent in the midst of it. The power we have, when we will exert it, over our own minds, joined to a little strength and consolation, nay a little pride, caught from those that seem to love us, is our only support in either of those conditions. . . . I can only tell you that one that has far more reason than you, I hope, will ever have, to look on life with something worse than indifference, is yet no enemy to it; and can look back on many bitter moments partly with satisfaction and partly with patience; and forward too, on a scene not very promising, with some hope and some expectations of a better day." Sometimes he even wondered if a certain amount of suffering was not necessary to joy. Perhaps pleasure was only acute when it came as a contrast to preceding pain.

"The hues of bliss more brightly glow
   Chastised by sabler tints of woe," he sang,
"And, blended, form with artful strife
   The strength and harmony of life.

See the wretch that long has tost
   On the thorny bed of pain,
At length repair his vigour lost
   And breathe and walk again:

The meanest flowret of the vale,
The simplest note that swells the gale,
The common sun, the air, the skies,
To him are opening Paradise."

Indeed Gray's life, as it rises before us from letter and poem, was nothing to be ashamed of. It is highly creditable surely for a man to make his existence into a finished work of art in which, to outward appearance at any rate, all is dignity and order, harmony and grace, and whose every manifestation bears the signature of an exquisite and individual taste. That it should not always have succeeded in making its creator perfectly happy is a pity; and stirs melancholy reflections on the incorrigibly unsatisfactory nature of the human lot. But it should not lead us to condemn Gray. Rather must he be praised for producing something so admirable in face of such difficulties. Moreover his creative impulse was not completely frustrated. Unintentionally it found

expression in the carefully composed letters which he des-
patched with regularity to his friends. Not that those letters
were unaffected by his inhibitions. That they were reserved
was to be expected; but they were also unspontaneous and a
little impersonal. One misses the sound of the speaking voice,
the ardent unselfconscious intimacy of tone which marks
Dorothy's letters, even at their most ceremonious. Still,
Gray's are classics of their kind, as perfect examples of English
eighteenth century taste as a Chippendale cabinet, and with
the same mixture of elegance and substance. For even at
their lightest, there is usually a firm centre of intelligence and
information to them, some penetrating literary judgment,
some shrewd comment on character or affairs. Yet all is
charming, all is easy; and ever and again the page glitters with
a stylish caustic stroke of wit or glows to beauty as in musical
cadence and precise delicate phrase, he discloses some picturesque vista or indulges in a flight of airy fancy. The author
of such letters cannot be said to have wholly failed to fulfil
his talents. And he must have known the happiness that comes
from such fulfilment.

On the whole too, he grew happier as time passed. The
hope of better days he expressed to Mason was not unfounded.
In spite of recurrent intervals of depression, the middle-aged
Gray was more serene than he had been since boyhood. Circumstances had something to do with this. The death of his
aunt in 1758 made him both richer and freer. Not only could
he spend his summers wandering about to see as many abbeys
and beauty spots as he felt inclined instead of stagnating at
Stoke Poges, but he was able to engage a manservant of his
own to help him in the arduous task of looking after the
luggage and the medicines. So inspirited did he begin to
feel that in the summer of 1759, when he was toying with the
idea of writing his *History of English Poetry*, he took the unprecedented step of setting up his headquarters in London for

three years, in order to research in the British Museum. Not that his mode of living there was very different from what it had been at Cambridge. He found some quiet comfortable rooms in Jermyn Street, filled them with such flowers as were in season—we get a glimpse of his sitting-room one July, all gay with scarlet Martagon lilies and flowering marjoram—and settled down to a life of retirement and study. All day he worked at the British Museum; and in the afternoon dined off a choice little meal, sent in from a neighbouring tavern, alone or in the company of a chosen friend, with whom he sipped a glass or two of sweet wine and, "as he sipped, talked of great people". His circle of friends was growing at this time—this was another reason that he was happier. It was round about now that he collected most of his young disciples. In the sunshine of their admiration, his spirits softened and brightened. His prevailing mood became mellower; the tone of his letters is more playful: now and again he even broke out in one of those flights of exuberant fantastic humour which had characterized him in the first carefree days of the Quadruple Alliance. Once—this was after he had returned to Cambridge—he was persuaded to write an ode on the Installation of the Duke of Grafton as Chancellor of the University. Nicholls called on him while it was in process of composition. What was his astonishment when Gray flung open the door exclaiming in loud and hollow tones "Hence avaunt! 'tis holy ground!" For a moment Nicholls felt a spasm of alarm. He knew Gray well enough to realize his nervous instability. How dreadful if he had suddenly gone off his head! It was a relief to find he was only reciting the first lines of the ode he was writing.

Finally, to his growing private happiness was added the gratification of public recognition. In 1768 Gray was made Regius Professor of History at Cambridge. This was a most agreeable job; £400 a year with only nominal duties attached to it. Gray had long hankered after the Professorship; so much so that in 1762 he had broken his rule of life, and applied for it. He was refused. When in 1768 it had again become vacant, he did not risk the humiliation of a second refusal. This made it all the more delightful to get a letter offering it to him; and in the most flattering terms. He accepted at once. There was one more hurdle to be negotiated before he could relax to enjoy the sweets of the position undisturbed. He had to pay a ceremonial visit of acknowledgment at Court. He made as heavy weather of this as might have been expected. His manner, it was noted, exhibited more than ever his usual mixture of shyness and superciliousness: himself, he felt so overcome that he did not know who was talking to him or what they said. Conscious that he had not cut an impressive figure in the presence of his Sovereign, Gray became noticeably ill-humoured whenever the subject was mentioned to him. However, this was a very small spot on a brilliant sun. Gray wrote round to tell his friends the news together with the compliments he had received about it, in an airy off-hand manner which did not conceal the exhilaration with which it filled him. Was he still so certain after all, the reader wonders, that the applause of mankind was not worth having?

Gray only lived for three more years after this. It would be pleasant to relate that his spirits maintained their improvement to the end of his life. Alas, Fate proved too ruthlessly conscientious an artist to finish a tale so melancholy on an incongruously cheerful note. Nothing very catastrophic happened: catastrophe also would have been incongruous with Gray. But clouds arose to hide the temperate gleam of sunshine, which had for a short time irradiated him, and the evening of his days was grey and troubled. Ironically the first cloud was caused by the event which, when it came, had promised to bring him such unalloyed pleasure, his appointment to the Professorship. One of its chief attractions had been that it appeared to involve no work: his predecessors, most of them, had gone through their term of office without lecturing to anyone. Unluckily, however, the autumn of 1768 saw the outbreak of one of those regrettable and ineffective impulses to self-improvement which arise from time to time to disturb the serenity of University life. It happened at Oxford. People there began saying that the Professor of History really did not do enough to earn his salary; some revolutionary spirits went so far as to demand that he should be required to give fifty lectures a year. The noise of the agitation penetrated to London: government circles became interested and began to make formal inquiries as to what should be done. Gray was asked, in his new official capacity, to give his opinion. Reluctantly he found himself forced by his conscience to say that a professor ought to do something: perhaps he should lecture, if not fifty, at any rate three times a year. After this the agitation seems to have died down: for the Oxford professor went on for the rest of his life happily giving no lectures at all. But the fact that the question had arisen had been enough to destroy Gray's precarious peace of mind. Not only did he suspect—groundlessly as it happened—that everyone was criticizing him for idleness behind his back, but he became a prey to the pangs of his fretting, scrupulous conscience. Even if no-one minded, was he justified in receiving £400 on what, if he had been offered it two years later, might possibly have been considered false pretences? Painfully and without enthusiasm he began preparing an inaugural lecture. It was conceived on a formidable scale; embracing as it did one section on the study of history, another on the study of the sources of history and a third on the study of those subjects necessary to prepare oneself for studying the sources of history. Clearly all his notebooks should be called into use to provide information for such a task. Gray rendered his task even more laborious by deciding that he ought to write it in Latin, a language in the composition of which he had lately grown rather rusty. It was not to be expected that he, who for twenty years had found it difficult to complete a short poem, should accomplish a labour of this kind. Alike his inhibitions and his standard of perfection made it impossible: months passed without the lecture getting further than the first sketch. Nobody at Cambridge seemed to notice. But Gray did. He could not get it out of his head. To his other neuroses was added a gnawing sense of guilt.

He was in no state of mind to stand an emotional crisis. And now suddenly, after nearly thirty years, he was required to face one, as violent, in its own way, as that which succeeded West's death. In the November of 1769, Nicholls, who was staying at Bath, went to a ball at the Assembly Rooms. In order to get a better view of the dancers he climbed on to a table. In doing so, he knocked against a young man who, with the same purpose in view, was climbing on to it from the other side. The contretemps led to apologies, apologies to acquaintance. The stranger turned out to be a foreigner, a twenty-one-year-old Swiss called Bonstetten, who was paying a visit to England. Nicholls took to him at once. Small and handsome with delicate colouring, expressive mouth, and bright eyes "full of a smiling sweetness", he combined the ease and polish of one accustomed to the best society with an electric foreign vitality, all aquiver with sensibility. In a flood of attractively broken English, he poured out about the enthusiastic feelings stirred in him by the Alpine scenery of his native land, with its towering sombre pine glades, to whose atmosphere the cry of a distant eagle added a pleasing horror. All this was thoroughly in the taste of the Gray circle. Nicholls wrote off at once to Gray saying he simply must get to know him. A month later, Gray, while staying for a day or two in London, took the opportunity to follow his advice. He was even more struck than Nicholls had been. So much so that forgetting his usual diffidence, he persuaded Bonstetten to come down to Cambridge on a visit. Closer acquaintance did not prove disappointing. Indeed his new friend, if a trifle absurd sometimes, was a genuinely engaging and original personality. Charles Victor de Bonstetten was the son of an ancient aristocratic family residing in the Canton of Berne. From his earliest years he had shown himself clever, vital and mercurial—too much so to feel at home in the prim and prosaic atmosphere of Berne society. However at the age of fifteen he was sent to finish his education in Geneva, then a minor centre of European social and intellectual life. Here he blossomed. He entered with delight into society, the civilized little evening parties where he quickly learnt to sparkle, flirt and pay compliments: still more he took to the new Romantic fashion in thought and feeling—all mountains and ruins and tender sentiments and rebellious noble aspirations—which, under the influence of Rousseau, was now sweeping Europe. He dreamed of a life which—while retaining the gaiety and elegance of a high civilization—was yet dedicated to the worship of Virtue, Liberty and the Ideal. These words, indeed, were seldom off his lips. After the delights of Geneva, Berne, where he returned in 1767 to start on a professional career, seemed to him more intolerably philistine than ever. In fact he became so depressed by it that, in approved Romantic fashion, he threatened suicide. His parents, alarmed at the new vagary on the part of their brilliant and unaccountable offspring, were only too willing to accept an alternative suggestion, that he should complete his education by a little foreign travel. Accordingly, after a short stay in Holland—he disliked the Dutch who seemed to him as uninspiring as the Bernese themselves—he found himself in England. Here his spirits soared up as high as they had sunk in Berne. The English were extremely friendly: they were also extra-ordinary—extraordinary in Bath, extraordinary in London, extraordinary above all at Cambridge. To his up-to-date continental eye, it seemed as if he had been wafted back three centuries into some monastery of the Middle Ages. He could not get over the strangeness of the cavernous Gothic halls and shadowy echoing stone cloisters through which young gentlemen, disguised as monks in long dark gowns, flitted, quite content apparently to live for weeks deprived of those pleasures of the Beau Monde, to which their birth gave them the entrée. And such social life as the place did provide, was even odder: slow ceremonious morning calls where dowdy ladies and solemn begowned dons sat in a circle, sometimes silent for a quarter of an hour at a time and then—this struck Bonstetten as peculiarly astonishing—only speaking when they had something to say. He thought of trying to brighten the party by making himself agreeable in the Geneva style—returning a handkerchief she had dropped to a lady with a graceful compliment, or saying something civil to a gentleman: but he refrained. He saw he would only embarrass.

However if Cambridge social life was stiff, it was, unlike that of Berne, eccentrically, fascinatingly stiff. Besides, the place had other things to offer to a man with Bonstetten's intellectual aspirations. He threw himself into making the most of them, took lessons in every sort of subject from botany to Italian, and cultivated the society of Gray. He went in for intellectual hero-worship—it was part of his "Romantic" rôle —and already in Switzerland he had sat at the feet of M. Haller the philosopher. Never would he forget how inspiring it had been to sit in M. Haller's library watching him write his letters, read the English newspaper and conduct a valuable discussion on the nature of free-will, all at the same moment. When he learnt that Gray was generally regarded as the greatest living English poet, Bonstetten determined to fling himself at his feet too.

Gray was only too willing that he should. He had always

liked enthusiastic pupils: but never had he met a pupil, never since he grew up, had he met anyone who had attracted him so immediately. Bonstetten was all that Gray liked most. For to that blend of gay aristocratic stylishness with sensibility and love of learning which had originally enchanted him in Walpole, he added a faculty of poetic enthusiasm and a warm foreign demonstrativeness, of which the satirical and worldly-wise Walpole was quite incapable; and which, like a burst of sunshine melted the film of ice which for so long had enclosed Gray's shivering heart. On to Bonstetten flowed out all the dammed-up unused emotion of years. It was the stronger and sweeter because it was so long since Gray had permitted him-self anything of the kind. And it had a peculiar poignancy because, unlike his sentiment for the friends of his youth, there was a streak of the paternal in it. The frustrated father in Gray went out to Bonstetten, making him yearn to guide his steps, to protect his fresh innocence against the corruptions of the wicked world. Within a few weeks his liking for Bon-stetten had swelled into an obsessing affection. He could not think or talk of anything else. He was intoxicated. And transfigured: his fear of letting himself go, his anxiety lest the order of his life should be upset, vanished almost in a night. Bonstetten, it is interesting to note, alone of his friends, seems to have been unaware that Gray could appear stiff or for-bidding. For with him Gray never did. On the contrary he pressed him to come and see him every hour of the day. At first Bonstetten had not liked to call before five in the evening. But soon the two were together from breakfast on. They walked together, read together—if Bonstetten had some work of his own to do, he came and did it in Gray's room—had their meals together, made music together, even wrote letters together. "I am in a hurry from morning till evening," so Bonstetten will write off to Nicholls, "at 8 o'clock I am roused by a young square-cap with whom I follow Satan through chaos and night. He explained me in Greek and Latin the *sweet reluctant amorous delays* of our grandmother Eve. We finish our travels in a copious breakfast of muffins and tea. Then appears Shakespair and old Lineus struggling together as two ghosts would do for a damned soul. Sometimes the one gets the better, sometimes the other. Mr. Gray, whose acquaintance is my greatest debt to you, is so good as to show me Macbeth and all witches, beldams, ghost and spirits, whose language I should never have understood without his interpretation. I am now endeavouring to dress all those people in a french dress which is a very hard labour. I am afraid to take a room, which Mr. Gray shall keep still better. So I stop hier my everrambling pen." As he put down his ever-rambling pen, Gray took it up. "I never saw such a boy: our breed is not made on this model. He is busy from morning to night, has no other amusement than that of changing one study for another, likes nobody he sees here, and yet wishes to stay longer, though he has passed a whole fortnight with us already. His letter has no corrections whatever, and is prettier by half than English."

It is indeed a change to find Gray so uncritically delighted by anyone. It is also a change to find him so bewildered. Bonstetten's displays of temperament, the way he yielded himself completely to every passing mood, struck the inhibited Gray as so extraordinary that sometimes he wondered if his young friend was quite sane. But this suspicion of exotic lunacy only added an exhilarating strangeness to his charm. Nor was this charm always so volatile. Bonstetten could be beautifully quiet. Of an evening especially: delicious unforgettable evenings when, with the chill January night shut out by curtains and the wail of the wind, as it blew over the surrounding fen country, only serving to emphasize by contrast the warm security of the candlelit room, Gray dreamed by the fire while Bonstetten's fingers strayed softly over the keys of the pianoforte; or Bonstetten lay stretched on the sofa pouring forth into Gray's sympathetic ear all the secrets and troubles and aspirations of his youthful heart, or listened with eyes aglow as, in measured tones and picked felicitous phrase, Gray discoursed of Shakespeare and Milton and the classical languages and the course of English history and the folly of atheism. Of everything but himself: Bonstetten noticed that if he asked Gray anything about his own life and past history, he became at once, and strangely, silent. He also remarked that through the surface sparkle of Gray's talk was discernible a profound melancholy of spirit. Clearly there was some mystery about him; it piqued Bonstetten's lively inquisitiveness. His romantic spirit found a romantic explanation for it. "Gray n'avait jamais aimé," he said— Gray had never loved.

It is a cruelly ironical sentence, considering who uttered it. For, though Gray may well have been inhibited from loving in the conventional and physical sense of the word, his heart was very far from invulnerable. And who should have known it better than Bonstetten? The god of love is a vindictive deity: and seldom allows those who seek to evade his influence to go for ever unpunished. For twenty-eight years Gray had contrived by viligant care to keep his deeper emotions unstirred. And now at fifty-two he was the helpless victim of an infatuation as vain as it was irresistible. For what satisfaction could he hope for from a romantic attachment to a youth of twenty-two, restless, sociable, and whose home was in Switzerland? He could not even expect to see him often. Indeed within five weeks of his arrival in Cambridge, Bonstetten got a letter from his parents pressing him to come home. He had to obey them: and all the sooner because he wanted to see a little more of the world on his way back. Sorry as he was to leave his cher M. Gray, it seemed a pity to lose a chance of sampling the pleasures of Paris. For Bonstetten, once more like Walpole, liked parties and pretty women and being at the glittering centre of things. At the end of March, 1770, Gray accompanied him to London, in order to be with him up to the last possible moment. Two days later, in the mirk of a spring dawn, Bonstetten climbed into the Dover coach and said good-bye. Gray never saw him again.

He arrived back in Cambridge in a state of black depression such as he had not known for years. Everything in his life seemed suddenly to have lost its savour. He got no pleasure from reading or listening to music, or looking at flowers. The charming room, in which he had lived so long and on which he had lavished so much care, now served only to remind him at every turn, and agonisingly, of the happy hours he had spent there with Bonstetten. Bereft of that vivid life-enhancing figure, what was it but a place of dull lonely horror? It is extraordinary that eight short weeks should have effected such a revolution in his feelings. But those eight weeks had been the first for years in which Gray had lived with the full intensity of which his nature was capable. And, by contrast, all the long-established, carefully built-up structure of his existence, with its rigid habits and delicate, deliberate pleasures, now showed up as repulsively bloodless and empty. He cursed Cambridge—"Never has the place appeared so horrible to me as it does now!" he cried—cursed the selfish possessive love of parents, cursed himself. So miserable was he that for once his reserve showed signs of breaking. It was more that flesh and blood could bear to be silent. Seated at his writing table, he poured out to Bonstetten, in accents of trembling emotion quite unlike anything else in his correspondence, the utter desolation that filled his heart.

"Never did I feel, my dear Bonstetten, to what a tedious length the few short moments of our life may be extended by impatience and expectation, till you had left me: nor ever knew before with so strong a conviction how much this frail body sympathizes with the inquietude of the mind. I am grown old in a compass of less than three weeks, like the Sultan in the Turkish tale, that did but plunge his head into a vessel of water and take it out again—as the standers-by affirmed, at the command of a Dervish, and found he had passed many years in captivity and begot a large family of children. The strength and spirits, that now enable me to write to you are only owing to your last letter—a temporary gleam of sunshine. Heaven knows when it may shine again! I did not conceive till now, I own, what it was to lose you, nor felt the solitude and in-sipidity of my own condition, before I possessed the happi-ness of your friendship."

And then a week later:

"Alas! how do I every moment feel the truth of what I have somewhere read: *Ce n'est pas le voir que de s'en souvenir.* And yet that remembrance is the only satisfaction I have left. My life now is but a perpetual conversation with your shadow—the known sound of your voice still rings in my ears—there on the corner of the fender you are standing or tinkling on the pianoforte or stretched at length on the sofa. Do you reflect my dearest friend, that it is a week or eight days before I can receive a letter from you, and as much more before you can have my answer, that all the time, with more than Herculean toil, I am employed in pushing the tedious hours along and wishing to annihilate them: the more I strive, the heavier they move and the longer they grow. I cannot bear this place, where I have spent many tedious years, within less than a month since you left me. . . . You do me the credit—and, false or true,

it goes to my heart—of ascribing to me your love for many
virtues of the highest rank. Would to heaven it were so!
but they are indeed the fruits of your own noble and generous understanding, that has hitherto struggled against the
stream of custom, passion and ill company, even when you
were but a child. And will you now give way to that
stream, when your strength is increased? Shall the jargon
of French sophists, the allurements of painted women
comme il faut, or the vulgar caresses of prostitute beauty,
the property of all that can afford to purchase it, induce you
to give up a mind and a body, by nature distinguished from
all others, to folly, idleness, disease and vain remorse?
Have a care, my ever amiable friend, of loving what you
do not approve."

There is something comic in the agitated concern for Bonstetten's moral welfare, which Gray evinces in these last
sentences. But it is highly illuminating in revealing the
processes of his heart and feeling at this time. It was not just
Bonstetten's physical absence that he minded: he also feared
he might be going to lose him in a more permanent and
spiritual sense. The Bonstetten he loved, the Bonstetten to
whom alone he felt his friendship could be important, was the
ingenuous boy on fire for education and enlightenment, who
needed an older friend to whom he might unburden his soul
and who asked no stronger pleasure than that provided by the
innocent hours of talk and music by Gray's fireside. But
now he was going out into the world, that world Gray had
always shunned and feared. Worse still to Gray's sturdy
British virtue, it was the world of eighteenth-century Paris,
notorious, meretricious home-town of vice and Voltaire.
Just because Bonstetten was so unusually attractive, it would
do its best to corrupt him; just because he was so responsive,
he would easily be tempted to yield to its seductions. The

ingenuous boy would disappear, to be replaced by a man, cynical, superficial, godless, and licentious. It is significant how Gray harps on this last danger. Like so many confirmed celibates, he seems to have recoiled from sex as from something in itself repulsive and frightening, at any rate in its more animal manifestations: so that the mere thought of any connection between it and the beloved object struck him as indescribably revolting. Perhaps too he feared lest the intoxications of love would blunt Bonstetten's taste for the more ethereal pleasures of friendship. After the accomplished embraces of a Parisian woman of fashion, he might well find reading *Paradise Lost* with Gray a trifle insipid. Thus, disguised as moral disapproval, jealousy crept in to increase the dead weight of regret and loneliness and hopeless apathy that lay on Gray's breast.

So oppressive did it become that he found the solitude of his days at Cambridge intolerable. He wrote off to Nicholls imploring him to come down for a few days: "It would be sunshine to me in a dark night," he pleaded. Nicholls asked Gray to stay with him in Suffolk instead. Gray went, but found himself no more cheerful for it. After a fortnight he returned to Cambridge: and once more sat down to write to Bonstetten.

"I am returned, my dear Bonstetten, from the little journey I had made into Suffolk, without answering the end proposed. The thought that you might have been with me there has embittered all my hours. Your letter has made me happy; as happy as so gloomy, so solitary, a being as I am is capable of being. I know and have too often felt the disadvantages I lay myself under, how much I hurt the little interest I have in you, by this air of sadness so contrary to your nature and present engagements: but sure you will forgive me though you cannot sympathize with me. It is impossible with me to dissemble with you. Such as I am, I expose my heart to your view, nor wish to conceal a single thought from your penetrating eyes. All that you say to me, especially on the subject of Switzerland, is infinitely acceptable. It feels too pleasing ever to be fulfilled; and as often as I read over your truly kind letter written long since from London I stop at these words: 'La mort qui peut glacer nos bras avant qu'ils soient entrelacés.' "

The principles and practice of a life-time, however, are not so easily forgotten. Gray had never been one to abandon himself to grief: and, when the first shock occasioned by Bonstetten's departure was over, he did not do so now. Once again, as after West's death, good sense and self-discipline began to re-assert their influence. After all nothing had happened, so far as he could see, to shake his conviction that it was weak to waste one's time in unavailing lament, foolish not to try and distract oneself by occupation and rational pleasure, and shocking bad manners to worry one's friends by tedious complaining about one's own sorrows. How far he also called on his religion to strengthen his resolution we do not know. But it is interesting to find him, during the following months, attacking atheism with especial vehemence. Was not Hume's philosophy merely an excuse for yielding to one's desires, however reprehensible? As for the new French school of thinking—well, he was not feeling sufficiently well-disposed towards the French to regard them with any unnecessary charity! "Atheism is a vile dish," he said to Walpole, "though all the cooks of France combine to make new sauces to it. As to the soul, perhaps they may have none on the Continent; but I do think we have such things in England. Shakespeare, for example, I believe, had several to his share. As to the Jews—though they do not eat pork— I like them, because they are better Christians than Voltaire."

Determination was reinforced by habit. Gray's order of living was, by now, second nature to him: and it was difficult for him to break it. Even during the wretched days after Bonstetten left, he contrived to make himself answer his letters by return of post and keep his calendar of the seasons up to date. After he got back from Suffolk, he took up his old routine to all appearance as if nothing had happened: read, made notes, took his daily walk to the Botanical Gardens, dosed himself with sage tea, made arrangements for his summer holiday—it was to be to the West Country this time—composed letters to his friends in which, as before, disquisitions on subjects of literary and historical interest are relieved by delicately-drawn glimpses of landscape and flashes of urbane humour. Now he is advising Mr. Beattie the poet, on the principles of prosody, now giving Mr. Warton of Oxford, the benefit of his researches into the early English authors, now regaling Mason with tit-bits of Cambridge gossip—"Our friend Foljambe has resided in College and persevered in the ways of godliness till about ten days ago, when he disappeared; and no-one knows whether he is gone a-hunting or a-fornicating"—now welcoming Nicholls and his wife, with a graceful playfulness, to Cambridge: "Venga, venga, si serva! I shall be proud to see you both. The lodgings over the way will be empty, but such an entry, such a staircase! How will Mrs. N. be able to crowd through it? With what grace, when she gets out of her chair, can she conduct her hoop-petticoat through this auger-hole and up the dark windings of the *grand escalier* that leads to her chamber?" Even though his creative impulse might be dead, Gray the artist in living, still managed to put up as technically finished a performance as ever.

The fact that he did so reacted back on him. By behaving as he had always behaved, Gray began to feel a little more as he had been used to feel. If not happier, he grew calmer. And all the more because the Bonstetten episode had been so brief: though the emotions it had roused in him had been uniquely violent, they simply had not had the time to cut so deep into him as those inspired by West and Walpole. After the first few weeks he did not go on missing Bonstetten as he had done, because he had not known him long enough to have acquired the habit of depending on his society. Moreover as the months passed and his usual mental atmosphere re-established itself, Gray's attitude to Bonstetten underwent a slight and subtle change: and all the more swiftly because Bonstetten had been irritatingly casual about answering his letters. He began to speak of him more in the tone in which he spoke of his other friends. This meant that he criticized him. There was no use, for instance, his blinking the fact that Bonstetten had a streak of silliness in him. He sent Gray his portrait—"You will think it was intended for his father," Gray told Nicholls; "doubtless he meant to look like an Englishman or an owl." Nor, now he was no longer under the spell of Bonstetten's actual presence, could Gray enter with full sympathy into the bewildering and melodramatic extravagance of Bonstetten's ever-changing moods. When some months later, Bonstetten, plunged on a sudden once more into temporary despair by the unconquerable philistin-ism of Berne society, wrote talking darkly of "un pistolet et du courage," Gray was more amused than concerned. "He is either disordered in his intellect—which is too possible," so he said—"or has done some strange thing that has exasper-ated his family and friends at home, which I am afraid is at least equally possible." Not that Gray had turned against Bonstetten. He still thought of him with tenderness and yearned to see him: and it is with an indulgent smile that he refers to his weaknesses. But no longer was he obsessed by him. Bonstetten had receded to a position in Gray's thoughts, from which his character could be surveyed with detachment.

Altogether by the autumn of 1770, to outward appearance, Gray was his old self again.

To outward appearance only, however. He was not really the same man as he had been a year before. What he had been through had confirmed and intensified his melancholy. He had received another and painful proof of the precariousness of human joys: he had learnt that no amount of self-protective care can succeed in saving man from pain. The realization of this, coming at a time when he was no longer young, cast a new shadow over his brightest moments. Further, the whole experience had been a shock to his already shaken nervous system, from which he no longer had the strength completely to recover. He became more than ever a prey to hypochondria and nervous fears. In particular his sense of guilt at what he conceived to be his failure to carry out the obligations of his professorship, began to worry him more and more. By now he recognized that he would never be able to get his lecture finished: it would involve too great a strain. But then what should he do? It was sad to give up £400 a year: but it was more tolerable than to suffer perpetually from the pangs of conscience. He told Mason that he intended to resign.

Bonstetten was not solely responsible for his depression. There was also a physical cause for it. In the summer of 1770, the malady to which he had long been intermittently subject— it seems to have been some kind of kidney disease—took a serious turn for the worse. His recurrent fits of headache and dizziness became sharper and more frequent, and left him far more exhausted; with the result that he was permanently in a state of languor and lassitude. For the first time he suffered from what he called "mechanical low spirits", that is, low spirits induced purely by physical causes. Even an improvement in the weather did not make him feel better: this was a new thing in his life. The winter was one long gloom. When the spring did at last come, he felt as bad as ever. Surely, he began to wonder, this must mean that there was something dangerously wrong with him. A chilling premonition of death began to steal into his heart. He spoke of it to no-one. But it added a new and ominous darkness to the cloud that hung over him.

In March 1771 it was momentarily lightened by a flicker of brighter things. He got a letter from Nicholls saying that Bonstetten had written, inviting the two of them to spend part of the summer in Switzerland. Partly because he thought it might cheer Gray up, partly because he himself was delighted at the idea of breaking the monotony of a country clergyman's life by a continental holiday, Nicholls was enraptured with the proposal. "Let us go, my dear Gray, and leave low-thoughted care at the foot of the mountains; for the air above is too pure for it," he exclaimed in an access of refined enthusiasm. Gray was not unresponsive to his appeal. Though by now his feelings for Bonstetten were under control, he was not so detached as to have lost his longing to see him again. To revive the joys of the previous year, and amid that sublime Alpine scenery, through which in the flood of youthful hope he had passed with Walpole so long ago—wistfully he let his fancy play with so enchanting a prospect. For three months he hesitated: then in June, shortly before they were to start, he wrote to Nicholls to say that he had decided, after all, not to go. He felt too ill: and, he added, too sad. With his illness his depression had grown so settled that he no longer hoped it could be removed, even by seeing Bonstetten. More easily, perhaps, could he picture the pain he would feel, when for a second time, he would be forced to part from him. And had he not always made it his principle to avoid unnecessary pain? Better to stay quietly at Cambridge. Yet once again Gray's fear of misfortune had proved stronger than his expectation of happiness.

Nicholls came to see him before he set off. Gray made

him a characteristic request. Would he promise solemnly not to call on Voltaire while in Switzerland? "What could a visit from me signify?" asked Nicholls. "Every tribute to such a man signifies," replied Gray vehemently. Nicholls made, and conscientiously kept, the promise. Otherwise, excited no doubt by those care-dispelling properties in the mountain air on which he had expatiated to Gray, he seems to have let himself go, once he got abroad. He cast off clerical costume in favour of a waistcoat of flame-coloured satin with huge pockets, from which protruded a thermometer and a pair of spectacles. Thus attired, and to the astonishment of the sober Swiss, he paraded the shores of the Lake of Leman, meditating, in sentimental mood, on its association with La Nouvelle Heloise.

Gray would have enjoyed hearing about this: he always enjoyed hearing about the absurdities of his friends. But before any account could reach him, he was beyond earshot of human folly. On 24th July, while dining in College, he was seized with a fit of nausea that forced him to leave the Hall. Next day he was dangerously ill. Doctors were summoned: his friend Brown, now Master of Pembroke, and a young cousin of Gray's, Mary Antrobus, who was living at Cambridge, hastened to his bedside. But within a few days, it became clear to them that nothing could be done. It became clear to Gray too. For some time he had suspected that his end was near: and he had never been one to refuse to face painful facts. Not that it was a particularly painful fact to him. He had lost such will to live as he had ever possessed. All that remained was to try and quit the world with the same regard for order and comeliness as he had sought to live in it. He succeeded. Gray's last days were marked by an extra-ordinary composure. All sign of his fussiness and nervousness disappeared: only his clear sense and self-command remained. Though racked by violent convulsive fits, he managed, in a

191

quiet interval, to give Brown precise instructions as to where to find his will, should it be needed: and one day, turning to his cousin who was sitting by his bed, "Molly, I shall die," he said calmly. On 30th July he breathed his last.

Mason came down from his home in York, to help Brown in settling Gray's affairs. It turned out to be an easy task. Gray's will and the instructions he had left for his funeral were as rationally devised and meticulously worded as his literary compositions has always been. In the middle of August when all was over Brown took a last look round Gray's rooms. Already every trace of his personality was gone from them. Mason had departed to York with the papers: furniture and pianoforte and blue vases had been packed and sent off to the various persons, to whom they were bequeathed. It looked, thought Brown sadly, like a place where no-one had lived for a very long time.

EPILOGUE

*I*T was late on an August afternoon, with the ebbing sunlight still a-glint on the white and gold of the book-cases and the tortoise-shell butterflies still flickering over the aster beds outside the window, that I finished this book. I sat back feeling contented: it is always agreeable to stop working. But I also felt sad. For I had grown to admire the two persons I had been writing about so much and to find the contemplation of their life so delightful that I hated saying good-bye to them. That I should feel like this was strange enough to start me reflecting. Melancholy, monotonous, thwarted, neither life was a delightful spectacle, as the phrase is generally understood. Nor were they themselves free from faults. Even the exquisite Dorothy could be both morbid and unreasonable: while as for Gray, what with his primness, his touchiness and his ludicrous nervous fads, he was in some respects downright tiresome. Moreover both were noticeably deficient in those social virtues by which the world professes to set such store. They found few human beings likeable: corporate activities were all they most abhorred. However none of this made me like or admire them less. Could it be that steady nerves and social usefulness were not in fact the qualities in other people that most make us feel ourselves inferior to them? Was it not rather some unusual fineness of nature; an eye for the truth, depth and delicacy of feeling, the presence to be detected in them of a strong and beautiful inner life? These Dorothy and Gray possessed. It was because their hearts were so civilized that they found the world so barbarous: their melancholy arose in part from the fact that they never committed the blasphemy of thinking human existence adequate to satisfy the aspirations of the soul. Whatever their defects, they were never hard or shallow or godless. Or dull: the clear twilight, in which they lived, gleamed and trembled with the play of their *humour and their imagination: those two qualities, which more than all others, distinguish the man from the animal. And with what enchanting an eloquence did they present them to the world! Their every utterance is as deft and graceful as the flicker of the butterflies over the aster beds.*

After all, I thought, it was no wonder that I sought their company so ardently: and, as the sunlight ebbed ever more palely over the book-cases, that I said good-bye to them with regret.